Hands-On Linux Administration on Azure - Second Edition

Develop, maintain, and automate applications on the Azure cloud platform

Kamesh Ganesan, Rithin Skaria, and Frederik Vos

Hands-On Linux Administration on Azure - Second Edition

Authors: Kamesh Ganesan, Rithin Skaria, and Frederik Vos

Technical Reviewers: Ashvith Bangera, Janaka Channa Bandara Rangama, and Toni Willberg

Managing Editor: Afzal Shaikh

Acquisitions Editors: Alicia Wooding and Clint Rodricks

Production Editor: Deepak Chavan

Editorial Board: Sonali Anubhavne, Vishal Bodwani, Ewan Buckingham, Alex Mazonowicz, and Jonathan Wray

First Published: August 2018

Second Edition: December 2019

Production Reference: 1060120

ISBN: 978-1-83921-552-0

Published by Packt Publishing Ltd.

Livery Place, 35 Livery Street

Birmingham B3 2PB, UK

Table of Contents

Chapter 3: Basic Linux Administration — 49

Chapter 5: Advanced Linux Administration

Preface

About

This section briefly introduces the author, the coverage of this course, the technical skills you'll need to get started, and the hardware and software requirements needed to complete all of the included activities and exercises.

About Hands-On Linux Administration on Azure, Second Edition

Thanks to its flexibility in delivering scalable cloud solutions, Microsoft Azure is a suitable platform for managing all your workloads. You can use it to implement Linux virtual machines and containers, and to create applications in open source languages with open APIs.

This Linux administration book first takes you through the fundamentals of Linux and Azure to prepare you for the more advanced Linux features in later chapters. With the help of real-world examples, you'll learn how to deploy virtual machines (VMs) in Azure, expand their capabilities, and manage them efficiently. You will manage containers and use them to run applications reliably, and in the concluding chapter, you'll explore troubleshooting techniques using a variety of open source tools.

By the end of this book, you'll be proficient in administering Linux on Azure and leveraging the tools required for deployment.

About the Authors

Kamesh Ganesan is a cloud evangelist and a seasoned technology professional with nearly 23 years of IT experience in all major cloud technologies, including Azure, AWS, GCP, and Alibaba Cloud. He has over 45 IT certifications, including 5 AWS, 3 Azure, and 3 GCP certifications. He's played many roles, including certified multi-cloud architect, cloud native application architect, lead database administrator, and programmer analyst. He architected, built, automated, and delivered high- quality, mission-critical, and innovative technology solutions that helped his enterprise, commercial, and government clients to be very successful and significantly improve their business value, using multi-cloud strategy.

Rithin Skaria is an open-source evangelist with over 7 years' experience managing open-source workloads in Azure, AWS, and OpenStack. He is currently working in Microsoft and is a part of several open-source-community activities conducted within Microsoft. He is a certified Microsoft trainer, Linux Foundation engineer and administrator, Kubernetes application developer and administrator, and also a Certified OpenStack Administrator. When it comes to Azure, he has 4 certifications, including solution architecture, Azure administration, DevOps, and security, and he is also certified in Office 365 administration. He has played a vital role in several open-source deployments, and the administration and migration of these workloads to cloud.

Frederik Vos, living in Purmerend (a city near Amsterdam in the Netherlands), works as a senior technical trainer of virtualization technologies, such as Citrix XenServer and VMware vSphere. He specializes in data center infrastructures (hypervisor, network, and storage) and cloud computing (CloudStack, CloudPlatform, OpenStack, and Azure). He is also a Linux trainer and evangelist. He has the knowledge of a teacher and the real-world experience of a system administrator. For the last 3 years, he has been working as a freelance trainer and consultant within the ITGilde Cooperation, delivering a lot of Linux training sessions, such as Linux on Azure training for the Linux Foundation.

Learning Objectives

By the end of this course, you will be able to:

- Grasp the fundamentals of virtualization and cloud computing
- Understand file hierarchy and mount new filesystems
- Maintain the life cycle of your application in Azure Kubernetes Service
- Manage resources with the Azure CLI and PowerShell
- Manage users, groups, and filesystem permissions
- Use Azure Resource Manager to redeploy virtual machines
- Implement configuration management to configure a VM correctly
- Build a container using Docker

Audience

If you are a Linux administrator or a Microsoft professional looking to deploy and manage your workload in Azure, this book is for you. Although not necessary, knowledge of Linux and Azure will assist with understanding core concepts.

Approach

This book provides a combination of practical and theoretical knowledge. It covers engaging real-world scenarios that demonstrate how Linux administrators work on the Azure platform. Each chapter is designed to facilitate the practical application of each new skill.

Hardware Requirements

For the optimal student experience, we recommend the following hardware configuration:

- Processor: Intel Core i5 or equivalent
- Memory: 4 GB RAM (8 GB preferred)
- Storage: 35 GB available space

Software Requirements

We also recommend that you have the following, in advance:

- A computer installed with Linux, Windows 10, or macOS operating system
- An internet connection so you can connect to Azure

Conventions

Code words in the text, database table names, folder names, filenames, file extensions, pathnames, dummy URLs, user input, and Twitter handles are shown as follows:

"The following code snippet creates a resource group with the name **MyResource1** and specifies the SKU as **Standard_LRS** that stands for the redundancy option in this context."

Here's a sample block of code:

```
New-AzStorageAccount -Location westus '
  -ResourceGroupName MyResource1'
  -Name "<NAME>" -SkuName Standard_LRS
```

At many instances we have used the angle brackets, **<>**. You need to replace this with the actual parameter, and not use these brackets within the commands.

Download Resources

The code bundle for this book is also hosted on GitHub at https://github.com/PacktPublishing/Hands-On-Linux-Administration-on-Azure---Second-Edition. You can find the YAML and other files used in this book which are referred at relevant instances.

We also have other code bundles from our rich catalog of books and videos available at https://github.com/PacktPublishing/. Check them out!

Exploring the Microsoft Azure Cloud

People often get confused due to the ambiguity surrounding the term **cloud computing**. Here, we are not referring to cloud storage solutions such as OneDrive, Dropbox, and so on. Instead, we are referring to actual computing solutions that are used by organizations, companies, or even individuals.

Microsoft Azure (previously known as **Windows Azure**) is Microsoft's public cloud computing platform. It offers a wide range of cloud services, including compute, analytics, storage, networking, and more. If you go through the list of services offered by Azure, you'll see that you can work with practically anything—from virtual machines to artificial intelligence and machine learning.

Starting with a brief history of virtualization, we will explain how the transformation of physical hardware into virtualized hardware made it possible to go beyond the borders of classic datacenters in many ways.

After that, we'll explain the different terminology used in cloud technology.

Here is the list of key topics that we'll cover:

- Virtualization of compute, network, and storage
- Cloud services
- Cloud types

Fundamentals of Cloud Computing

When you first start learning a new subject in **Information Technology** (**IT**), you'll usually begin by studying the underlying concepts (that is, the theory). You'll then familiarize yourself with the architecture, and sooner or later you'll start playing around and getting hands-on to see how it works in practice.

However, in cloud computing, it really helps if you not only understand the concepts and the architecture but also where it comes from. We don't want to give you a history lesson, but we want to show you that inventions and ideas from the past are still in use in modern cloud environments. This will give you a better understanding of what the cloud is and how to use it within your organization.

The following are the key fundamentals of cloud computing:

- Virtualization
- **Software-Defined Datacenter** (**SDDC**)
- **Service-Oriented Architecture** (**SOA**)
- Cloud services
- Cloud types

Let's take a look at each of these and understand what these terms refer to.

Virtualization

In computing, virtualization refers to the creation of a virtual form of a device or a resource, such as a server, storage device, network, or even an operating system. The concept of virtualization came into the picture when IBM developed its time-sharing solutions in the late 1960s and early 1970s. **Time-sharing** refers to the sharing of computer resources between a large group of users, increasing the productivity of users and eliminating the need to purchase a computer for each user. This was the beginning of a revolution in computer technology where the cost of purchasing new computers reduced significantly and it became possible for organizations to utilize the under-utilized computer resources they already had.

Nowadays, this type of virtualization has evolved into container-based virtualization. Virtual machines have their own operating system, which is virtualized on top of a physical server; on the other hand, containers on one machine (either physical or virtual) all share the same underlying operating system. We will talk more about containers in *Chapter 9, Container Virtualization in Azure*.

Fast-forward to 2001, when another type of virtualization, called hardware virtualization, was introduced by companies such as VMware. In their product, VMware Workstation, they added a layer on top of an existing operating system that provided a set of standard hardware and built-in software instead of physical elements to run a virtual machine. This layer became known as a **hypervisor**. Later, they built their own operating system, which specialized in running virtual machines: VMware ESXi (formerly known as ESX).

In 2008, Microsoft entered the hardware-virtualization market with the Hyper-V product, as an optional component of Windows Server 2008.

Hardware virtualization is all about separating software from hardware, breaking the traditional boundaries between hardware and software. A hypervisor is responsible for mapping virtual resources on physical resources.

This type of virtualization was the enabler for a revolution in datacenters:

- Because of the standard set of hardware, every virtual machine can run on any physical machine where the hypervisor is installed.

- Since virtual machines are isolated from each other, if a particular virtual machine crashes, it will not affect any other virtual machine running on the same hypervisor.

- Because a virtual machine is just a set of files, you have new possibilities for backup, moving virtual machines, and so on.

- New options became available to improve the availability of workloads, with **high availability** (**HA**), and the possibility to migrate a virtual machine, even if it's still running.

- New deployment options also became available, for example, working with templates.

- There were also new options for central management, orchestration, and automation because it's all software defined.

- Isolation, reservation, and the limiting of resources where needed, sharing resources where possible.

SDDC

Of course, if you can transform hardware into software for compute, it's only a matter of time before someone realizes you can do the same for network and storage.

For networking, it all started with the concept of virtual switches. Like every other form of hardware virtualization, it is nothing more than building a network switch in software instead of hardware.

The **Internet Engineering Task Force** (**IETF**) started working on a project called **Forwarding and Control Element Separation**, which was a proposed standard interface to decouple the control plane and the data plane. In 2008, the first real switch implementation that achieved this goal took place using the OpenFlow protocol at Stanford University. **Software-Defined Networking** (**SDN**) was commonly associated with the OpenFlow protocol.

Using SDN, you have similar advantages as in compute virtualization:

- Central management, automation, and orchestration

- More granular security through traffic isolation and providing firewall and security policies

- Shaping and controlling data traffic

- New options available for HA and scalability

In 2009, **Software-Defined Storage** (**SDS**) development started at several companies, such as Scality and Cleversafe. Again, it's about abstraction: decoupling services (logical volumes and so on) from physical storage elements.

If you have a look into the concepts of SDS, some vendors added a new feature to the already existing advantages of virtualization. You can add a policy to a virtual machine, defining the options you want: for instance, replication of data or a limit on the number of **Input/Output Operations per Second** (**IOPS**). This is transparent for the administrator; there is communication between the hypervisor and the storage layer to provide the functionality. Later on, this concept was also adopted by some SDN vendors.

You can actually see that virtualization slowly changed the management of different datacenter layers into a more service-oriented approach.

If you can virtualize every component of a physical datacenter, you have an SDDC. The virtualization of networking, storage, and compute functions made it possible to go further than the limits of one piece of hardware. SDDC makes it possible, by abstracting the software from the hardware, to go beyond the borders of a physical datacenter.

In an SDDC environment, everything is virtualized and often fully automated by the software. It totally changes the traditional concept of datacenters. It doesn't really matter where the service is hosted or how long it's available (24-7 or on demand). Also, there are possibilities to monitor the service, perhaps even adding options such as automatic reporting and billing, which all make the end user happy.

SDDC is not the same as the cloud, not even a private cloud running in your datacenter, but you could argue that, for instance, Microsoft Azure is a full-scale implementation of SDDC–Azure is, by definition, software-defined.

SOA

In the same period that hardware virtualization became mainstream in datacenters and the development of SDN and SDS started, something new appeared in the world of software development for web-based applications: SOA, which offers several benefits. Here are some of the key points:

- Minimal services that can talk to each other, using a protocol such as **Simple Object Access Protocol (SOAP)**. Together, they deliver a complete web-based application.

- The location of the service doesn't matter; the service must be aware of the presence of the other service, and that's about it.

- A service is a sort of black box; the end user doesn't need to know what's inside the box.

- Every service can be replaced by another service.

For the end user, it doesn't matter where the application lives or that it consists of several smaller services. In a way, it's like virtualization: what seems to be one physical resource, for instance, a storage **LUN (Logical Unit Number)** could actually include several physical resources (storage devices) in multiple locations. As mentioned earlier, if one service is aware of the presence of another service (it could be in another location), they'll act together and deliver the application. Many websites that we interact with daily are based on SOA.

The power of virtualization combined with SOA gives you even more options in terms of scalability, reliability, and availability.

There are many similarities between the SOA model and SDDC, but there is a difference: SOA is about the interaction between different services; SDDC is more about the delivery of services to the end user.

The modern implementation of SOA is microservices, provided by cloud environments such as Azure, running standalone or running in virtualization containers such as Docker.

Cloud Services

Here's that magic word: *cloud*. A **cloud service** is any service available to organizations, companies, or users provided by a cloud solution or computing provider such as Microsoft Azure. Cloud services are appropriate if you want to provide a service that:

- Is highly available and always on demand.

- Can be managed via self-service.

- Has scalability, which enables a user to scale up (making the hardware stronger) or scale out (adding additional nodes).

- Has elasticity – the ability to dynamically expand or shrink the number of resources based on business requirements.

- Offers rapid deployment.

- Can be fully automated and orchestrated.

On top of that, there are cloud services for monitoring your resources and new types of billing options: most of the time, you only pay for what you use.

Cloud technology is about the delivery of a service via the internet, in order to give an organization access to resources such as software, storage, network, and other types of IT infrastructure and components.

The cloud can offer you many service types. Here are the most important ones:

- **Infrastructure as a Service** (**IaaS**): A platform to host your virtual machines. Virtual machines deployed in Azure are a good example of this.

- **Platform as a Service** (**PaaS**): A platform to develop, build, and run your applications, without the complexity of building and running your own infrastructure. For example, there is Azure App Service, where you can push your code and Azure will host the infrastructure for you.

- **Software as a Service** (**SaaS**): Ready-to-go applications, running in the cloud, such as Office 365.

Even though the aforementioned are the key pillars of cloud services, you might also hear about **<u>FaaS</u>** (**<u>Function as a Service</u>**), **<u>CaaS</u>** (**<u>Containers as a Service</u>**), **<u>SECaaS</u>** (**<u>Security as a Service</u>**), and the list goes on as the number of service offerings in the cloud increases day by day. Function App in Azure would be an example for FaaS, Azure Container Service for CaaS, and Azure Active Directory for SECaaS.

Cloud Types

Cloud services can be classified based on their location or based on the platform the service is hosted on. As mentioned in the previous section, based on the platform, we can classify cloud offerings as IaaS, PaaS, SaaS, and so on; however, based on location, we can classify cloud as:

- **Public cloud**: All services are hosted by a service provider. Microsoft's Azure is an implementation of this type.

- **Private cloud**: Your own cloud in your datacenter. Microsoft recently developed a special version of Azure for this: Azure Stack.

- **Hybrid cloud**: A combination of a public and private cloud. One example is combining the power of Azure and Azure Stack, but you can also think about new disaster recovery options or moving services from your datacenter to the cloud and back if more resources are temporarily needed.

- **Community cloud**: A community cloud is where multiple organizations work on the same shared platform, provided that they have similar objectives or goals.

Choosing one of these cloud implementations depends on several factors; to name just a few:

- **Costs**: Hosting your services in the cloud can be more expensive than hosting them locally, depending on resource usage. On the other hand, it can be cheaper; for example, you don't need to implement complex and costly availability options.

- **Legal restrictions**: Some organizations would not be able to use the public cloud. For example, the US Government has its own Azure offering called Azure Government. Likewise, Germany and China have their own Azure offerings.

- **Internet connectivity**: There are still countries where the necessary bandwidth or even the stability of the connection is a problem.

- **Complexity**: Hybrid cloud environments, in particular, can be difficult to manage; support for applications and user management can be challenging.

Understanding the Microsoft Azure Cloud

Now that you know more about virtualization and cloud computing, it's time to introduce you to the Microsoft implementation of the cloud: Azure.

Starting again with some history, in this section, you'll find out about the technology behind Azure and that Azure can be a very good solution for your organization.

A Brief History of the Microsoft Azure Cloud

In 2002, Microsoft started a project called Whitehorse to streamline the development, deployment, and implementation of an application within an SOA model. In this project, there was a focus on delivering small, prebuilt web applications and the ability to transform them into services. This project died silently around 2006.

Many of the lessons learned in that project and the appearance of **Amazon Web Services** (**AWS**) were the drivers for Microsoft, in 2006, to start a project called **RedDog**.

After a while, Microsoft added three other development teams to this project:

- **.NET Services**: Services for developers using the SOA model. .NET Services offered Service Bus as a secure, standards-based messaging infrastructure.

- **Live Services and Live Mesh**: A SaaS project to enable PCs and other devices to communicate with each other through the internet.

- **SQL Services**: A SaaS project to deliver Microsoft SQL through the internet.

In 2008, Microsoft announced the start of Azure, and with its public release in 2010, Azure was ready to deliver IaaS and PaaS solutions. The name RedDog survived for a while: the classic portal was also known as **RedDog Front-End** (**RDFE**). The classic portal was based on the **Service Management Model**. On the other hand, the Azure portal is based on **Azure Resource Manager** (**ARM**). These two portals are based on two different APIs.

Nowadays, Azure is one of three Microsoft clouds (the others are Office 365 and Xbox) for delivering different kinds of services, such as virtual machines, web and mobile apps, Active Directory, databases, and so on.

It's still growing in terms of the number of features, customers, and availability. Azure is available in more than 54 regions. This is very important for scalability, performance, and redundancy.

Having these many regions also helps compliance with laws and security/privacy policies. Information and documents regarding security, privacy, and compliance are available via Microsoft's Trust Center: https://www.microsoft.com/en-us/TrustCenter.

Azure Architecture

Microsoft Azure runs on a customized, stripped-down, and hardened version of Hyper-V, also known as the **Azure Hypervisor**.

On top of this hypervisor, there is a cloud layer. This layer, or fabric, is a cluster of many hosts hosted in Microsoft's datacenter and is responsible for the deployment, management, and health of the infrastructure.

This cloud layer is managed by the fabric controller, which is responsible for resource management, scalability, reliability, and availability.

This layer also provides the management interface via an API built on REST, HTTP, and XML. Another way to interact with the fabric controller is provided by the Azure portal and software such as the Azure CLI via Azure Resource Manager.

The following is a pictorial representation of the architecture of Azure:

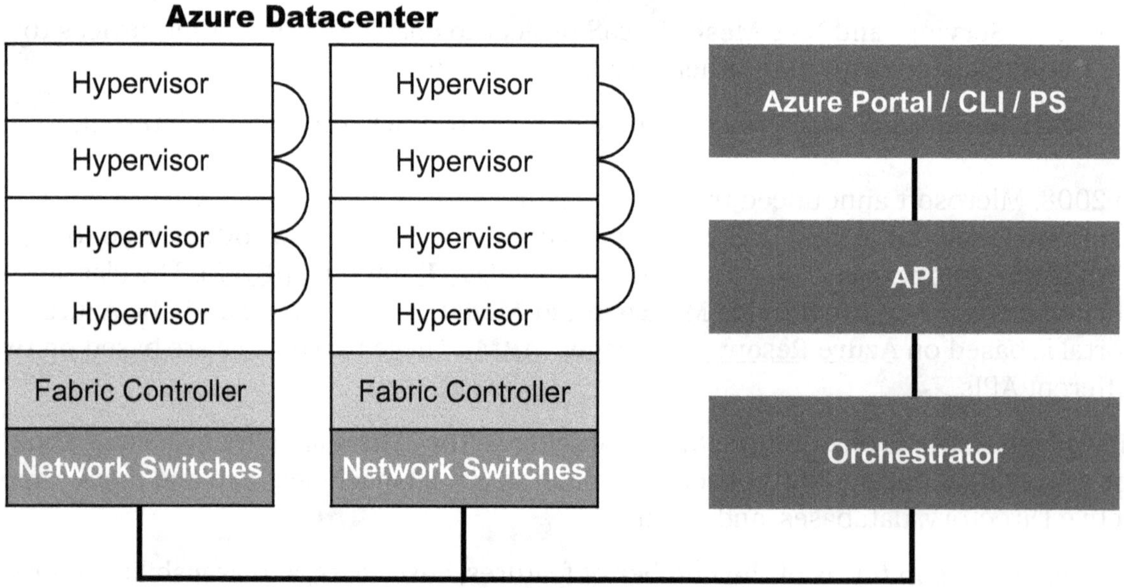

Figure 1.1: Azure architecture

These user-interfacing services (Azure portal, PowerShell, Azure CLI, and API) will communicate with the fabric through resource providers. For example, if you want to create, delete, or update a compute resource, a user will interact with the **Microsoft.Compute** resource provider, which is also known as **Compute Resource Provider** (**CRP**). Likewise, network resources are communicated via **Network Resource Provider** (**NRP**) or the **Microsoft.Network** resource provider, and storage resources are communicated via **Storage Resource Provider** (**SRP**) or the **Microsoft.Storage** resource provider.

These resource providers will create the required services, such as a virtual machine.

Azure in Your Organization

Azure can deliver IaaS: it's easy to deploy virtual machines, manually or automated, and use those virtual machines to develop, test, and host your applications. There are many extra services available to make your life as a system engineer easier, such as backup and restore options, adding storage, and availability options. For web applications, it's even possible to deliver the service without creating a virtual machine!

Of course, Azure can also be used for PaaS solutions; like IaaS, PaaS includes all of the components of your infrastructure but adds support for the complete life cycle of your cloud applications: building, testing, deploying, managing, and updating. There are pre-defined application components available as well; you can save time transforming these components together with your code into the service you want to deliver. Containers can be another part of your PaaS solution. Azure Container Service simplifies deployment, management, and operations on containers using Kubernetes or another orchestrator, such as Mesos.

If you are a company or organization that wants to host a SaaS solution in Azure, this is possible using AppSource. You can even provide integration with other Microsoft products, such as Office 365 and Dynamics.

In 2017, Microsoft announced **Azure Stack**. You can run Azure now in your own datacenter or run it in a datacenter from a service provider of your choice to provide IaaS and PaaS. It gives you the power of Azure in terms of scalability and availability, without worrying about the configuration. You only need to add more physical resources if needed. And if you want, you can use it in a hybrid solution with public Azure for disaster recovery or consistent workloads in both cloud and on-premises deployments.

Azure Stack is not the only thing you can use for hybrid environments. You can, for instance, connect your local Active Directory with Azure Active Directory, or use the Azure Active Directory application to provide **Single Sign-On** (**SSO**) to both local and hosted web applications.

Azure and Open Source

In 2009, even before Azure went public, Microsoft started adding support for open-source frameworks, such as PHP, and in 2012, Microsoft added support for Linux virtual machines, due to requests from many customers.

At that time, Microsoft was not a big friend of the open-source community, and it's fair to say that they really didn't like the Linux operating system. This changed around 2014, when Satya Nadella succeeded Steve Ballmer as CEO of Microsoft. In October of that year, he even announced at a Microsoft conference in San Francisco that *Microsoft loves Linux!*

Since that time, Azure has grown into a very open source–friendly environment:

- It offers a platform for many open-source solutions, such as Linux instances, container technology, and application/development frameworks.

- It offers integration with open-source solutions by providing open and compatible APIs. For instance, the Cosmos DB service offers a MongoDB-compatible API.

- The documentation, **Software Development Kits** (**SDK**), and examples are all open source and available on GitHub: https://github.com/Azure.

- Microsoft is working together with open-source projects and vendors and is also a major contributor of code to many open-source projects.

In 2016, Microsoft entered the Linux Foundation organization as a Platinum member to confirm their steadily increasing interest and engagement in open-source development.

In October 2017, Microsoft said that more than 40% of all virtual machines in Azure are running the Linux operating system and Azure is running many containerized workloads. Looking at the current statistics, the number of workloads has reached more than 60%. Besides that, microservices are all using open-source programming languages and interfaces.

Microsoft is very serious about open-source technology, open-source PowerShell, and many other products. Not every Microsoft product in Azure is open source, but at least you can install and run Microsoft SQL on Linux or you can get a container image for Microsoft SQL.

Summary

In this chapter, we discussed the history of virtualization and the concept of the cloud, and we explained the terminology used in cloud environments.

Some people think that Microsoft was a little bit late entering the cloud world, but actually, they started researching and developing techniques in 2006, and many parts of that work survived in Azure. Some of the projects died, because they were too early, and many people were skeptical about the cloud in those days.

We also covered the architecture of the Azure cloud and the services that Azure can offer your organization.

In the last part of this chapter, we saw that Azure is a very open source–friendly environment and that Microsoft puts in a lot of effort to make Azure an open, standard cloud solution with interoperability in mind.

In the next chapter, we'll start using Azure and learn how to deploy and use Linux in Azure.

Questions

1. What components in your physical datacenter can be transformed into software?

2. What is the difference between container virtualization and hardware virtualization?

3. If you want to host an application in the cloud, which service type is the best solution?

4. Let's say one of your applications needs strict privacy policies. Is it still a good idea to use cloud technology for your organization?

5. Why are there so many regions available in Azure?

6. What is the purpose of Azure Active Directory?

Further Reading

If you want to learn more about Hyper-V and how you can use Azure together with Hyper-V for site recovery and the protection of your workloads, check out *Windows Server 2016 Hyper-V Cookbook, Second Edition* by Packt Publishing.

There are many nice technical articles about the history of virtualization, cloud computing, and their relationship. One we really want to mention is *Formal Discussion on Relationship between Virtualization and Cloud Computing* (ISBN 978-1-4244-9110-0).

Don't forget to visit the Microsoft website and GitHub repository as mentioned in this chapter!

Getting Started with the Azure Cloud

In the first chapter, we covered the history of, and the ideas behind, virtualization and cloud computing. After that, you read about the Microsoft Azure cloud. This chapter will help you take your first steps into the world of Azure, get access to Azure, explore the different Linux offerings, and deploy your first Linux virtual machine.

After deployment, you will need access to your virtual machine using **Secure Shell** (**SSH**) with password authentication or using an SSH key pair.

To take the first steps on your journey into the Azure cloud, it is important to complete all the exercises and examine the outcomes. In this chapter, we will be using PowerShell as well as the Azure CLI. Feel free to follow whichever you're comfortable with; however, learning both won't hurt. The key objectives of this chapter are:

- Setting up your Azure account.

- Logging in to Azure using the Azure CLI and PowerShell.

- Interacting with **Azure Resource Manager** (**ARM**) to create network and storage resources.

- Understanding Linux distributions and Microsoft-endorsed distributions.

- Deploying your first Linux virtual machine.

> **Note**
>
> Everything in this chapter is tested on macOS, Windows Subsystem for Linux, and the latest versions of CentOS and openSUSE LEAP.

Technical Requirements

If you want to try all the examples in this chapter, you'll need a browser at the very least. For stability reasons, it's important to use a very recent version of a browser. Microsoft offers a list of supported browsers in the official Azure documentation:

- Microsoft Edge (latest version)

- Internet Explorer 11

- Safari (latest version, Mac only)

- Chrome (latest version)

- Firefox (latest version)

Based on personal experience, we recommend using Google Chrome or a browser based on a recent version of its engine, such as Vivaldi.

You can do all the exercises in your browser, even the exercises involving the command line. In practice, it's a good idea to use a local installation of the Azure CLI or PowerShell; it's faster, it's easier to copy and paste code, and you can save history and the output from the commands.

Getting Access to Azure

To start with Azure, the first thing you'll need is an account. Go to https://azure.microsoft.com and get yourself a free account to get started, or use the corporate account that is already in use. Another possibility is to use Azure with a Visual Studio Professional or Enterprise subscription, which will give you **Microsoft Developer Network** (**MSDN**) credits for Azure. If your organization already has an Enterprise Agreement with Microsoft, you can use your Enterprise subscription, or you can sign up for a pay-as-you-go subscription (if you have already used your free trial).

If you are using a free account, you'll get some credits to start, some of the popular services for a limited time, and some services that will stay free always, such as the container service. You can find the most recent list of free services at https://azure.microsoft.com/en-us/free. You won't be charged during the trial period, except for virtual machines that need additional licensing, but you do need a credit card to identify yourself.

Logging in Using the Azure portal

Point your browser to https://portal.azure.com and use your credentials to log in. You are ready to start using Azure, or, in other words, to start using your subscription. In Azure, a subscription permits you to create and deploy resources using the Azure portal/the Azure CLI/PowerShell with your account. It is also used for accounting and billing.

The Azure portal takes you to a dashboard that you can modify to meet your monitoring needs. You can now:

- Inspect your resources.
- Create new resources.
- Visit the Marketplace, which is an online store where you can purchase and deploy applications or services that are built for the Azure cloud.
- Get insights into your billing.

You can use the web interface, doing everything graphically, or use Azure Cloud Shell via the web interface, which provides a Bash or PowerShell interface.

Getting Command-line Access to Azure

There are several good reasons to use the command line. That's why, in this book, we'll mostly cover Azure command-line access:

- It can help you to understand the architecture of Azure. In the graphical interface, often you can do many things in one configuration window without understanding the relationships between the different fields and components.

- It is the first step in automation and orchestration.

- The web interface is still in active development; the web interface can, and will, change over time:

  Some features and options are not available yet.

  It is possible that Microsoft will relocate features and options in the web interface.

- The command-line interface, on the other hand, is very stable in syntax and output.

In this book, we will use both the Azure CLI in the Bash shell and PowerShell with the PowerShell Az module. Both are well-suited, platform-agnostic, and there is, besides one or two exceptions, no difference between them in terms of features. Choose your favorite because you're already familiar with it, or give both interfaces a try and choose afterward.

> **Note**
>
> Please note that copying and pasting commands from this book might give you some errors due to spaces and indentations. For better results, always type in commands. Also, this will help you get used to the commands.

Installing the Azure CLI

If you use the Bash interface within Azure Cloud Shell, there is a pretty complete Linux environment Azure command-line interface installing available to play with. It also provides Azure-specific commands, such as the **az** command.

You can also install this utility on Windows, macOS, and Linux. A Docker container is available as well. You can find detailed installation instructions for all these platforms at https://docs.microsoft.com/en-us/cli/azure.

Let's use CentOS/ **Red Hat Enterprise Linux** (**RHEL**) 7 as an example to install the Azure CLI:

1. Import the Microsoft repository's **GNU Privacy Guard** (**GPG**) key:

    ```
    sudo rpm --import \ https://packages.microsoft.com/keys/microsoft.asc
    ```

2. Add the repository:

    ```
    sudo yum-config-manager --add-repo= \
        https://packages.microsoft.com/yumrepos/azure-cli
    ```

3. Install the software:

    ```
    sudo yum install azure-cli
    ```

4. To install the Azure CLI on an Ubuntu- or Debian-based system, use this:

    ```
    curl -sL https://aka.ms/InstallAzureCLIDeb | sudo bash
    ```

    On macOS, you have to install Homebrew first, a free and open-source package management system that simplifies the installation of, mostly, open-source software.

5. Open a Terminal and execute the following:

    ```
    ruby -e "$(curl -fsSL \
        https://raw.githubusercontent.com/Homebrew/install/master/install)"
    ```

6. Update Homebrew and install the Azure CLI:

    ```
    brew update && brew install azure-cli
    ```

7. After installing the Azure CLI, you can verify the version installed using this:

    ```
    az -v
    ```

Logging in with the Azure CLI

The Azure CLI is a command-line tool that's used to access or manage Azure resources, and the good thing is that it's available for macOS, Linux, and Windows platforms. Before you can use the CLI, you have to log in:

```
az login
```

This command will open a browser and requires you to log in with your Microsoft account. If you are getting an error stating that the shell was not able to open the interactive browser, use **az login -use-device-code**. This will generate a code, and you can use it in https://www.microsoft.com/devicelogin to complete the authentication.

If this is successful, it will give you some output in JSON format regarding your subscription, such as your username:

```
[
    {
        "cloudName": "AzureCloud",
            "id": "....",
            "isDefault": true,
            "name": "Pay-As-You-Go",
            "state": "Enabled",
            "tenantId": "....",
            "user": {
                "name": "....",
                "type": "user"
            }
    }
]
```

To get this information again, type the following:

```
az account list
```

You can always format the output in JSON, JSONC, TABLE, or TSV formats by using extra parameters.

JSON (or JSONC, the colored variant) format is easier to parse in programming and scripting languages:

```
~ >>> az group list --output jsonc
[
    {
        "id": "/subscriptions/88525bff-081c-45ad-ba31-
oud-shell-storage-westeurope",
        "location": "westeurope",
        "managedBy": null,
        "name": "cloud-shell-storage-westeurope",
        "properties": {
            "provisioningState": "Succeeded"
        },
        "tags": null
    }
]
```

Figure 2.1: Subscription details in JSONC format

Tab-Separated Values (**TSV**) is a good idea if the output is a single value, if you want to use text-filtering utilities such as AWK, or if you want to export the output to a spreadsheet:

```
~ >>> az group list --output tsv
/subscriptions/88525                          e69/resourceGroups/clo
torage-westeurope          westeurope      None    cloud-shell-storage-we
one
```

Figure 2.2: Tab-separated subscription details

The table output is very human-readable, but is more limited than the default output:

```
~ >>> az group list --output table
Name                                     Location    Status
-----------------------------------      ----------  ---------
cloud-shell-storage-westeurope           westeurope  Succeeded
```

Figure 2.3: Subscription details in tabular format

To get a list of subscriptions that the logged-in account has access to in a table format, execute the following command:

```
az account list -o table
```

To make reading the JSON output easier, you can also query for specific fields:

```
az account list -o table --query '[].[user.name]'
```

If you already have a lot of resources or accounts, going through the entire list will be very hard. Luckily, there is a way to drill down the output and get just the info that you need. Chaining the command with the **--query** parameter will help you do this, using a powerful query language called JMESPATH (http://jmespath.org). Look at the JSON output of the **az account list** command again. This query is searching for the **user** field and the **name** property.

Let's go back to the login procedure. Doing this every time, again and again, may not be the most user-friendly procedure. A better way to do it is by creating a service principal, also known as an app registration, to provide a credential for a specific application:

```
az ad sp create-for-rbac --name <APP_NAME>
```

You can provide a name for your application, but certain special characters are not allowed. The reason is that `APP_NAME` will create a URL, so all the characters that are forbidden in URLs cannot be added to `APP_NAME` (for example, @ and %). The output, again in JSON format, will provide an application ID (the `appID` parameter):

```
{

    "appID": "....",

    "displayName": "APP_NAME",

    "name": "http://APP_NAME",

    "password": "....",

    "tenant": "...."

}
```

Please note down the output on a notepad because we will be using these values for authentication. An application or service principal represents an object in the Azure tenant. A tenant refers to an organization, often denoted as <yourcompany/yourname>.onmicrosoft.com, which manages and owns an instance of Microsoft cloud services. If we look from an Azure perspective, all services deployed will be associated with a subscription, and the subscription will be mapped to a tenant. A tenant can have multiple subscriptions hosting different services.

From the preceding output, we'll get the following values:

- **appID**: The application ID is similar to the username of the application. We will be using this ID as our username when logging in.

- **displayName**: A friendly name given to the application when we created the app. We set the name via the **name** parameter.

- **name**: A URL based on the name we have given.

- **password**: This is the password of the service principal we created. When logging in, we'll use this value in the password field.

- **tenant**: The tenant ID; we discussed tenants in the previous paragraph.

An application that requires access must be represented by a security principal. The security principal defines the access policy and permissions for the user/application in the tenant. This enables the authentication of the user/application during sign-in and role-based authorization during resource access. To summarize, you can use **appID** to sign in.

List the roles that are assigned to the newly created **appID**:

```
az role assignment list --assignee <appID> --o table
```

By default, the contributor role is used. This role has full permissions to read and write to your Azure account.

Now, it's a good idea to test this and log out:

```
az logout
```

Now, log in again using **appID**. You can use the values you copied earlier to complete the authentication:

```
az login --service-principal --username <appID> --tenant <tenant id>
```

Unfortunately, there is no way to store the username, **appID**, or **tenant id** in a configuration file. Optionally, you can add **--password** to the command:

```
az login --service-principal --username <appID> --tenant <tenant id>
--password <app_password>
```

Instead of typing complete commands using the **az** command, you can also open it in interactive shell mode:

```
az interactive
```

One of the greatest features of this shell is that it splits the terminal into two windows. In the upper screen, you can type your commands; in the lower screen, you'll get help while typing commands. There is also auto-complete support for commands, parameters, and often parameter values.

PowerShell

PowerShell is a Microsoft-developed scripting language that is integrated into .NET Framework. It was designed by Jeffrey Snover, Bruce Payette, and James Truher in 2006. PowerShell is not only available for Windows, but also for Linux and macOS. You can find detailed instructions for using PowerShell with these operating systems on the GitHub repository for PowerShell: https://github.com/PowerShell.

For instance, to install it in RHEL or CentOS, follow these steps:

1. Import the Microsoft repository's GPG key if you didn't do so while following the installation procedure for the Azure CLI:

   ```
   sudo rpm -import \  https://packages.microsoft.com/keys/microsoft.asc
   ```

2. Add the repository:

   ```
   sudo yum-config-manager --add-repo= \https://packages.microsoft.com/rhel/7/prod/
   ```

3. Install the software:

   ```
   sudo yum install -y powershell
   ```

4. Use **pwsh -v** to show the installed version.

5. Enter PowerShell:

   ```
   pwsh
   ```

On macOS, you'll need Homebrew and Homebrew Cask. Cask extends Homebrew to install more and bigger applications:

1. Install Homebrew Cask:

   ```
   brew tap caskroom/cask
   ```

2. Install PowerShell:

   ```
   brew cask install powershell
   ```

3. Use **pwsh -v** to show the installed version.

4. To enter PowerShell:

   ```
   pwsh
   ```

After the installation of PowerShell, you're ready to install the Az module. Downloading the module may take some time, depending upon your internet speed. You'll be able to see the progress of the download in the shell:

```
Install-Module -Name Az -AllowClobber -Scope CurrentUser -Force
```

PowerShell uses the **PowerShellGet** cmdlet to download the module and its dependencies from the PowerShell Gallery, an online repository that hosts many modules. Please note that you'll need administrator privileges in Windows and Linux to do this. The PowerShell Gallery isn't configured as a trusted repository:

```
Untrusted repository
You are installing the modules from an untrusted repository. If you trust
this
repository, change its InstallationPolicy value by running the Set-
PSRepository
 cmdlet. Are you sure you want to install the modules from 'PSGallery'?
[Y] Yes  [A] Yes to All  [N] No  [L] No to All  [S] Suspend  [?] Help
(default is "N"): A
```

Answer the question in the listing with **[A] Yes to All**.

It is possible now, due to the **force** parameter, that you have multiple versions of the Az module installed. You can verify the existence of multiple versions with the following command:

```
Get-InstalledModule -Name Az -AllVersions | '        select Name,Version
```

The latest version will be used by default, unless you use the **-RequiredVersion** parameter when importing the module.

Logging in with PowerShell

After the installation is complete, import the module:

```
Import-Module -name Az
```

If you don't create a PowerShell script and only execute commands within the PowerShell environment when playing with Azure, you'll need to execute this command again. But, if you want, you can automatically load the modules.

First, find out where your PowerShell profile is on your filesystem by executing the following:

```
$profile
```

Open or create this file in a text editor and add the following line:

```
Import-Module -name Az
```

> **Note**
>
> It may be necessary to create the directory structure before you can actually create this file.

Now you can execute all the available commands for Azure.

Log in using the following cmdlet:

```
Connect-AzAccount
```

This will open an interactive browser window, where you can use your credentials to authenticate. If the result doesn't show you a tenant ID, execute this:

```
Get-AzContext -ListAvailable | select Tenant
```

And now, log in again using the tenant ID you have found:

```
Connect-AzAccount -Tenant <tenantID>
```

If you have multiple subscriptions, you can add the **-Subscription** parameter and the subscription ID as well. As discussed before, it's maybe a good idea to create a service principal:

```
$newsp = New-AzADServicePrincipal ' -DisplayName "APP_NAME" -Role Contributor
```

If you don't mention **DisplayName**, which is the friendly name for the service principal, Azure will generate a name in the format azure-powershell-MM-dd-yyyy-HH-mm-ss. Next, you need to retrieve the application ID for the newly created service principal:

```
$newsp.ApplicationId
```

And the password can be stored to a variable, which will be encrypted, and we must decrypt it:

```
$BSTR = [System.Runtime.InteropServices.Marshal]::SecureStringToBSTR($newsp.
Secret)

$UnsecureSecret = [System.Runtime.InteropServices.
Marshal]::PtrToStringAuto($BSTR)
```

The **$UnsecureSecret** variable contains the password for your service principal.

To be able to authenticate, we need the credentials of the service principal:

```
$creds = Get-Credential
```

Provide the **ApplicationID** and the password, which are stored in the **$newsp. ApplicationId** and **$UnsecureSecret** variables respectively. Now we have everything we need to connect to Azure using these credentials:

```
Connect-AzAccount -Credential $creds '
    -Tenant <tentant id> '
    -ServicePrincipal
```

Now, save the context:

```
Save-AzContext -Path $HOME/.Azure/AzureContext.json
```

Overwrite the existing content if necessary. Exit the PowerShell environment and execute PowerShell. Make sure that you are logged into Azure and verify the context using the following command:

```
Get-AzContext
```

Azure Resource Manager

Before you can start the deployment of your first Linux virtual machine, it's important to know more about **Azure Resource Manager** (**ARM**).

Basically, ARM enables you to work with resources such as storage and virtual machines. To do so, you have to create one or more resource groups so you can execute life cycle operations, such as deploying, updating, and deleting all the resources in a resource group, in a single operation.

> **Note**
>
> A resource group must be created in a region, also known as a location. Please notice that there may be differences between the services offered in different regions. To find out more about these differences, please visit https://azure. microsoft.com/en-us/global-infrastructure/services/.

Azure has more than 54 regions. If a location is not available, it needs to be whitelisted for your account. For that, you can reach out to Microsoft Support. To get a list of the available locations and supported resource providers for your account, execute the following command in PowerShell:

```
Get-AzLocation | Select-Object Location
```

You can also execute the following in Bash:

```
az account list-locations --query '[].name'
```

Then, create a resource group in one of the regions:

```
New-AzResourceGroup -Location westus2 -Name 'MyResource1'
```

Now, verify the result:

```
Get-AzResourceGroup | Format-Table
```

This is the Bash version of the preceding command:

```
az group create --location westus2 --name MyResource2
```

To verify the result of **Azure Resource Manager (ARM)** this command, execute the following:

```
az group list -o table
```

Besides working with regions and resource groups, you have to understand the concept of storage redundancy. The available replication options are as follows:

- Standard_LRS: Locally redundant storage

  Premium_LRS: Same as LRS, but it supports File Storage as well.

  Standard_GRS: Geo-redundant storage

  Standard_RAGRS: Read-access geo-redundant storage

- Standard_ZRS: Zone-redundant storage; ZRS doesn't support Blob storage

> **Note**
>
> More information is available on the Microsoft website: https://docs.microsoft.com/en-us/azure/storage/common/storage-redundancy.

Understanding this concept is important because, together with your resource group, a storage account is needed in a region. A storage account provides a unique namespace in Azure to store data (such as diagnostics) and the possibility to use services such as Azure Files. To configure redundancy for this data, you have to specify the SKU that stands for the redundancy option in this context:

```
New-AzStorageAccount -Location westus '
  -ResourceGroupName MyResource1'
  -Name "<NAME>" -SkuName Standard_LRS
```

Or you can do it via the Azure CLI:

```
az storage account create --resource-group MyResource2
  --sku Standard_LRS --name <NAME>
```

The storage account name must be unique across Azure, be between 3 and 24 characters in length, and use numbers and lowercase letters only.

Linux and Azure

Linux is almost everywhere, on many different devices, and in many different environments. There are many different flavors, and the choice of what to use is yours. So, what do you choose? There are many questions, and many different answers are possible. But one thing's for sure: in corporate environments, support is important.

Linux distributions

As noted earlier, there are many different Linux distributions around. But there are reasons why there are so many options:

- A Linux distribution is a collection of software. Some collections are there for a specific objective. A good example of such a distribution is Kali Linux, which is an advanced penetration testing Linux distribution.

- Linux is a multi-purpose operating system. Thanks to the large number of customization options we have for Linux, if you don't want a particular package or feature on your operating system, you can remove it and add your own. This is one of the primary reasons why there are so many distributions.

- Open source is Darwinian by nature. Sometimes, a project is forked, for instance, because some other developers don't like the goal of the project or think they can do better and patches of the project are not accepted. Only the strongest projects will survive.

- It is a matter of taste. Different people have different tastes and opinions. Some people like the Debian **apt** package manager; other people may like SUSE's Zypper tool.

- Another big difference is that some distributions are collected and supported by vendors such as Red Hat, SUSE, and Canonical, whereas others, such as Debian, are community-driven.

In production environments, support is important. Before pushing their production workloads to a distribution, organizations will be concerned with certain factors, such as SLA, downtime, and security updates, and the following questions might arise:

- Who is responsible for the updates, and what kind of information comes with the updates?

- Who is responsible for support, and who am I going to call if there is a problem?

- Who is going to advise me if there are legal problems with the software licensing?

Microsoft-endorsed Linux Distributions

In the Azure Marketplace, there are Linux images provided by third parties, also called Microsoft partners. These are Microsoft-endorsed Linux distributions.

Microsoft works Microsoft-endorsed Linux distributions together with these partners and the Linux community to make sure that these Linux distributions work well on Azure.

It is possible to import your own image, or even your own Linux distribution, into Azure. Microsoft contributes directly to the Linux kernel, providing Linux Integration Services for Hyper-V and Azure, and because of this you can run every Linux distribution on Azure as long as support is compiled into the kernel. Also, on every Linux image in the Azure Marketplace, the Azure Linux Agent is installed, and the source code of this agent is available on GitHub as well, so you can install it in your image. Microsoft is even willing to guide you if you have issues with Linux; just buy a support plan!

For some commercial Linux distributions, there are great support options available:

- Red Hat: Microsoft Support will help you to use the Azure platform or services, and will also support issues within Red Hat, but this requires a support plan.

- Oracle Linux: Microsoft offers a support plan; additional commercial support can be bought from Oracle.

- SUSE: There are premium images supported by Microsoft; if needed, they will call SUSE for you. This SUSE premium image includes all software, updates, and patches.

- Other vendors: There are Microsoft support plans to cover other vendors; you don't have to buy a separate plan for this. Microsoft plan details are available at https://azure.microsoft.com/en-us/support/plans/.

> **Note**
>
> Please visit the Microsoft website for a recent list of endorsed distributions and versions, as well as details about the support that is available for a distribution:
>
> https://docs.microsoft.com/en-us/azure/virtual-machines/linux/endorsed-distros

Deploying a Linux Virtual Machine

We've covered the Linux distributions available in Azure and the level of support you can get. In the previous section, we set up the initial environment by creating the resource group and storage; now it's time to deploy our first virtual machine.

Your First Virtual Machine

The resource group has been created, a storage account has been created in this resource group, and now you are ready to create your first Linux virtual machine in Azure.

In PowerShell, use the following command:

```
New-AzVM -Name "UbuntuVM" -Location westus2 '

  -ResourceGroupName MyResource1 '

  -ImageName UbuntuLTS -Size Standard_B1S
```

The cmdlet will prompt you to provide a username and password for your virtual machine:

```
Azure:/
PS Azure:\> New-AzVM -Name "UbuntuVM" -Location westus2 `
>>    -ResourceGroupName MyResource1 `
>>    -ImageName UbuntuLTS -Size Standard_B1S

cmdlet New-AzVM at command pipeline position 1
Supply values for the following parameters:
Credential
User: 
```

Figure 2.4: Providing user credentials for your virtual machine

In Bash, you can use the following command:

```
az vm create --name UbuntuVM --resource-group MyResource2 \
  --image UbuntuLTS --authentication-type password \
  --admin-username student --size Standard_B1S
```

This was very easy, but if you create a virtual machine instance this way, the number of options you can set is very limited. This process will create multiple resources required by the virtual machine, such as the disk, NIC, and public IP, using default settings.

Let's dive a little bit further into the details and get some information about the choices made.

Images

In our example, we deployed a virtual machine with the image name **UbuntuLTS**. You can choose between several Linux images:

- CentOS
- Debian
- RHEL
- UbuntuLTS
- CoreOS
- openSUSE
- SUSE Linux Enterprise

But there are many more images offered by different vendors, called publishers.

Let's get a list of these publishers. In PowerShell, use this command:

```
Get-AzVMImagePublisher -Location <REGION>
```

As you can see in the following screenshot, Azure has a lot of publishers, and we'll pick one of these for the demonstration:

```
Azure:/
PS Azure:\> Get-AzVMImagePublisher -Location eastus

PublisherName                               Location  Id
-------------                               --------  --
128technology                               eastus    /Subscription
1e                                          eastus    /Subscription
2021ai                                      eastus    /Subscription
3cx-pbx                                     eastus    /Subscription
4psa                                        eastus    /Subscription
5nine-software-inc                          eastus    /Subscription
7isolutions                                 eastus    /Subscription
a10networks                                 eastus    /Subscription
abiquo                                      eastus    /Subscription
accedian                                    eastus    /Subscription
accellion                                   eastus    /Subscription
accessdata-group                            eastus    /Subscription
accops                                      eastus    /Subscription
Acronis                                     eastus    /Subscription
Acronis.Backup                              eastus    /Subscription
actian-corp                                 eastus    /Subscription
actian_matrix                               eastus    /Subscription
actifio                                     eastus    /Subscription
activeeon                                   eastus    /Subscription
adastracorporation-4028356                  eastus    /Subscription
```

Figure 2.5: Listing image publishers in PowerShell

In Bash, you can run the following command to get the list of publishers:

```
az vm image list-publishers --location <REGION> --output table
```

The list is the same:

```
rithin@Azure:~$ az vm image list-publishers --location eastus --output table
Location     Name
----------   --------------------------------------------------------------
eastus       128technology
eastus       1e
eastus       2021ai
eastus       3cx-pbx
eastus       4psa
eastus       5nine-software-inc
eastus       7isolutions
eastus       a10networks
eastus       abiquo
eastus       accedian
eastus       accellion
eastus       accessdata-group
eastus       accops
eastus       Acronis
eastus       Acronis.Backup
eastus       actian-corp
eastus       actian_matrix
eastus       actifio
eastus       activeeon
```

Figure 2.6: Listing image publishers in Bash

Now you know the publishers, you can get a list of images provided by
a publisher using:

```
Get-AzVMImageOffer -Location <REGION> '
    -PublisherName <PUBLISHER> | select offer
```

We have selected **Canonical** as the publisher, and now we are trying to get the list of
offers available. **UbuntuServer** is one of the offers, and we will be using this one:

```
Azure:/
PS Azure:\> Get-AzVMImageOffer -Location eastus  -PublisherName Canonical | select offer

Offer
-----
0001-com-ubuntu-server-eoan
0002-com-ubuntu-minimal-bionic-daily
0002-com-ubuntu-minimal-disco-daily
0002-com-ubuntu-minimal-xenial-daily
0003-com-ubuntu-minimal-eoan-daily
Ubuntu15.04Snappy
Ubuntu15.04SnappyDocker
UbuntuServer
Ubuntu_Core
```

Figure 2.7: Listing offers for Canonical publisher

Alternatively, in the Azure CLI, run the following command:

```
az vm image list-offers --location <REGION> '
  --publisher <PUBLISHER> --output table
```

The output is a list of so-called *offers*. An offer is the name of a group of related images created by a publisher.

Now we need to know what SKUs are available for the image. SKU refers to the major release of a distribution. Here is an example using Ubuntu:

```
Get-AzVMImageSku -PublisherName <publisher> -Offer <offer>'
  -Location <location>
```

Now that we have the values for the publisher and offer, let's go ahead and see the major distributions (SKUs) that are available for **UbuntuServer** published by **Canonical**:

```
Azure:/
PS Azure:\> Get-AzVMImageSku -PublisherName Canonical -Offer UbuntuServer `
>> -Location eastus

Skus                    Offer          PublisherName Location Id
----                    -----          ------------- -------- --
12.04.3-LTS             UbuntuServer   Canonical     eastus   /Subscriptions/548
12.04.4-LTS             UbuntuServer   Canonical     eastus   /Subscriptions/548
12.04.5-LTS             UbuntuServer   Canonical     eastus   /Subscriptions/548
14.04.0-LTS             UbuntuServer   Canonical     eastus   /Subscriptions/548
14.04.1-LTS             UbuntuServer   Canonical     eastus   /Subscriptions/548
14.04.2-LTS             UbuntuServer   Canonical     eastus   /Subscriptions/548
14.04.3-LTS             UbuntuServer   Canonical     eastus   /Subscriptions/548
14.04.4-LTS             UbuntuServer   Canonical     eastus   /Subscriptions/548
14.04.5-DAILY-LTS       UbuntuServer   Canonical     eastus   /Subscriptions/548
14.04.5-LTS             UbuntuServer   Canonical     eastus   /Subscriptions/548
16.04-DAILY-LTS         UbuntuServer   Canonical     eastus   /Subscriptions/548
16.04-LTS               UbuntuServer   Canonical     eastus   /Subscriptions/548
16.04.0-LTS             UbuntuServer   Canonical     eastus   /Subscriptions/548
16_04-daily-lts-gen2    UbuntuServer   Canonical     eastus   /Subscriptions/548
18.04-DAILY-LTS         UbuntuServer   Canonical     eastus   /Subscriptions/548
18.04-LTS               UbuntuServer   Canonical     eastus   /Subscriptions/548
18.10                   UbuntuServer   Canonical     eastus   /Subscriptions/548
18.10-DAILY             UbuntuServer   Canonical     eastus   /Subscriptions/548
18_04-daily-lts-gen2    UbuntuServer   Canonical     eastus   /Subscriptions/548
19.04                   UbuntuServer   Canonical     eastus   /Subscriptions/548
19.04-DAILY             UbuntuServer   Canonical     eastus   /Subscriptions/548
19.10-DAILY             UbuntuServer   Canonical     eastus   /Subscriptions/548
19_04-daily-gen2        UbuntuServer   Canonical     eastus   /Subscriptions/548
19_04-gen2              UbuntuServer   Canonical     eastus   /Subscriptions/548
19_10-daily-gen2        UbuntuServer   Canonical     eastus   /Subscriptions/548
```

Figure 2.8: Listing SKUs for UbuntuServer published by Canonical

Alternatively, in the Azure CLI, run the following command:

```
az vm image list-skus --location <LOCATION> \
    --publisher <PUBLISHER> --offer <OFFER> -o table
```

Query for a specific instance within this offer:

```
Get-AzureVMImage -Location <REGION>'
 -PublisherName <PUBLISHER> -Offer <OFFER> '
 -Skus <SKU> | select Version -last 1
```

Let's again go through the values we have. So, using the publisher name, offer, and SKU, we're going to get the version that's available. In the following screenshot, you can see that image version **19.10.201912170** is available. Let's take this image for our virtual machine:

```
PS C:\windows\system32> Get-AzVMImage -PublisherName Canonical -offer UbuntuServer -Skus 19_10-daily-gen2 `
>> -Location eastus | select Version -last 1

Version
-------
19.10.201912170
```

Figure 2.9: Selecting available image version in Azure CLI

This was the latest version available at the time of writing this chapter. If there are any new releases, you might see another version number.

Alternatively, in the Azure CLI, use the following command:

```
az vm image list --location <REGION> --publisher <PUBLISHER> \
    --offer <OFFER> --sku <SKU> --all --query '[].version' \
    --output tsv | tail -1
```

To reduce the output to the latest version, parameters were added to select the last line. The information collected contains parameters for the **Set-AzVMSourceImage** cmdlet; however, before using this command, we need to create a new virtual machine configuration using **New-AzVMConfig**:

```
$vm = New-AzVmConfig -VMName <name> -VMSize "Standard_A1"
Set-AzVMSourceImage -PublisherName <PUBLISHER>'
 -Offer <OFFER> -Skus <SKU> -Version <VERSION>
```

Finally, we are creating a new virtual machine with a size of **Standard_A1**, and we're instructing PowerShell to use image version **19.10.201912170** of the major **19_10-daily-gen2** distribution in the **UbuntuServer** offer published by **Canonical**:

```
PS C:\windows\system32> $vm= New-AzVMConfig -VMName myVm -VMSize "Standard_A1"
PS C:\windows\system32> Set-AzVMSourceImage -PublisherName Canonical -Offer UbuntuServer
>> -Skus 19_10-daily-gen2 -Version 19.10.201912170 -VM $vm


Name            : myVm
HardwareProfile : {VmSize}
StorageProfile  : {ImageReference}
```

Figure 2.10: Creating a virtual machine of Standard_A1 size

In Bash, the collected information contains parameters for the **az vm create** command:

```
az vm create --name UbuntuVM2 --resource-group Packt-Testing-2    --image
canonical:UbuntuServer:19_10-daily-gen2:19.10.201912170 --authentication-
type password    --admin-username pacman --size Standard_B1S
```

> **Note**
>
> In both Bash and PowerShell, it's possible to use the word *latest* instead of a specific version. The collected information is not sufficient to create the virtual machine, though. More parameters are needed.

Virtual Machine Sizing

Another thing you have to take care of is a decision regarding the virtual machine's size based on your needs and costs. More information on the available sizes and the pricing is available at https://azure.microsoft.com/en-us/pricing/details/virtual-machines/linux.

The list on this website, which includes the prices of the instances, changes often! You can get a list (without displaying the costs) on the command line:

```
Get-AzVMSize -Location <REGION> | Format-Table

az vm list-sizes --location <REGION> -o table
```

A small virtual machine is enough to execute the exercises in this book. At the time of writing, **Standard_B1ls** is ideal for the necessary base-level performance. But it's a good idea to recheck the virtual machine sizing/pricing list, as mentioned earlier on.

In PowerShell, the **New-AzVM** cmdlet can take the **-size** parameter, or you can use it in the **New-AzVMConfig** cmdlet:

```
New-AzVMConfig -VMName "<VM NAME>" -VMSize <SIZE>
```

In Bash, add the **--size** parameter of the **az vm create** command.

Virtual Machine Networking

Azure virtual networks allow communication between virtual machines, the internet, and other Azure services over a secure network. When we created the first virtual machine at the beginning of this chapter, several items regarding networking were created automatically:

- Virtual network
- Virtual subnet
- Virtual network interface attached to the virtual machine and plugged into the virtual network
- Private IP address configured on the virtual network interface
- Public IP address

The network resources will be covered in *Chapter 4, Managing Azure*; for now, we're just going to query the private and public IP addresses of the virtual machines. Use this command to get the list of public IP addresses:

```
Get-AzPublicIpAddress -ResourceGroupName <RESOURCE GROUP>'
  | select Name,IpAddress
```

To get the list of private IP addresses of all your virtual machines, use this command:

```
Get-AzNetworkInterface -ResourceGroupName <resource group name> | ForEach
{ $interface = $_.Name; $ip = $_ | Get-AzNetworkInterfaceIpConfig | Select
PrivateIPAddress; Write-Host $interface $ip.PrivateIPAddress }
```

The preceding command may look a little complicated, but it is a handy script for getting the list of private IPs. If you want to get the private IP address of virtual machines in a resource group, you can use this command:

```
Get-AzNetworkInterface -ResourceGroup <resource group name>
```

The output obtained will be in JSON format, and you can see the private IP address under **IpConfigurations**:

```
PS C:\windows\system32> Get-AzNetworkInterface -Name vm-docker-host


Name                            : vm-docker-host944
ResourceGroupName               : about-rithin
Location                        : southeastasia
Id                              : /subscriptions/548f7d26-b5b1-468e-ad4
Etag                            : W/"7c1b4d41-8a46-4e1d-a21c-029f8dee12
ResourceGuid                    : 028a17a8-39ce-42cc-a159-56501401a17d
ProvisioningState               : Succeeded
Tags                            :
VirtualMachine                  : {
                                    "Id": "/subscriptions/548f7d26-b5b1
                                  }

IpConfigurations                : [
                                    {
                                      "Name": "ipconfig1",
                                      "Etag": "W/\"7c1b4d41-8a46-4e1d-a
                                      "Id": "/subscriptions/548f7d26-b5
                                      "PrivateIpAddress": "10.0.0.4",
                                      "PrivateIpAllocationMethod": "Dyn
                                      "Subnet": {
                                        "Delegations": [],
```

Figure 2.11: Private IP address of virtual machines in the resource group

This can be also accomplished using the Azure CLI. To get a list of the private IP addresses of virtual machines, use this:

```
az vm list-ip-addresses --resource <RESOURCE GROUP> --output table
```

The public IP address is the IP address that makes the virtual machine accessible via the internet. The incoming traffic virtual machine networking on this IP address undergoes **network address translation** (**NAT**) to the private IP address configured on the network interface of the Linux virtual machine.

Virtual Machine Information

After the deployment of the virtual machine, all the information attached to the virtual machine is available using PowerShell and Bash, such as the state. Querying the state is important; there are several states:

- Running
- Stopped
- Failed
- Deallocated

If a virtual machine is not deallocated, Microsoft will charge you for it. The **Failed** state means that the virtual machine is not able to boot. To query the state, execute the following command:

```
Get-AzVM -Name <VM NAME> -Status -ResourceGroupName <RESOURCE GROUP>
```

In Bash, it is possible to receive the state of the deployed virtual machines, but if we need to narrow down the output to a single instance, it's not possible without using complex queries:

```
az vm list --output table
```

To deallocate a virtual machine, first stop it:

```
Stop-AzVM -ResourceGroupName <RESOURCE GROUP> -Name <VM NAME>
```

Now you are able to deallocate it:

```
az vm deallocate --name <VM NAME> --resource-group <RESOURCE GROUP>
```

You can get much more information about the deployed virtual machines. In PowerShell, it's quite difficult to receive the properties of the virtual machine. First, create a variable:

```
$MYVM=Get-AzVM -Name <VM NAME> -ResourceGroupName <RESOURCE GROUP>
```

Now ask for the properties and methods of this **MYVM** object:

```
$MYVM | Get-Members
```

View the **HardwareProfile** property to see the size of this instance:

```
$MYVM.HardwareProfile
```

Or, to be more virtual machine information precise, use the following command:

```
$MYVM.HardwareProfile | Select-Object -ExpandProperty VmSize
```

You can also try **NetworkProfile**, **OSProfile**, and **StorageProfile.ImageReference**.

If you want to use the **az** command in Bash, the first command you may want to try is this:

```
az vm list --resource-group <RESOURCE GROUP>
```

The only problem here is that it shows all the information about all the virtual machines at the same time; luckily, there is a **show** command as well, which reduces the output to a single virtual machine:

```
az vm show --name <VM NAME> --resource-group <RESOURCE GROUP>
```

And it's a good idea to limit the output by using queries. For example, if you want to see the storage profile of a particular virtual machine, you can query as follows:

```
az vm show --name <VM NAME> --resource-group <RESOURCE GROUP>\
  --query 'storageProfile'
```

The preceding command should give you the following output:

```
rithin@Azure:~$ az vm show --name suse --resource-group packt --query 'storageProfile'
{
  "dataDisks": [],
  "imageReference": {
    "id": null,
    "offer": "SLES",
    "publisher": "SUSE",
    "sku": "15",
    "version": "latest"
  },
  "osDisk": {
    "caching": "ReadWrite",
    "createOption": "FromImage",
    "diffDiskSettings": null,
    "diskSizeGb": null,
    "encryptionSettings": null,
    "image": null,
```

Figure 2.12: Storage profile of the SUSE virtual machine

Connecting to Linux

The virtual machine is running, ready for you to log in remotely using the credentials (username and password) you provided during the deployment of your first virtual machine. Another, more secure method to connect to your Linux virtual machine is by using SSH key pairs. SSH keys are more secure due to their complexity and length. On top of this, Linux on Azure supports sign-in using **Azure Active Directory** (**Azure AD**), where users will be able to authenticate using their AD credentials.

Logging into Your Linux virtual machine Using Password Authentication

In the *Virtual Machine Networking* section, the public IP address of a virtual machine was queried. We will be using this public IP to connect to the virtual machine via SSH using an SSH client installed locally.

SSH, or **Secure Shell**, is an encrypted network protocol used to manage and communicate with servers. Linux, macOS, **Windows Subsystem for Linux** (**WSL**), and the recent update of Windows 10 come with the command-line-based OpenSSH client, but there are more advanced clients available. Here are a few examples:

- Windows: PuTTY, MobaXterm, and Bitvise Tunnelier

- Linux: PuTTY, Remmina, and Pac Manager

- macOS: PuTTY, Termius, and RBrowser

Using the OpenSSH command-line client, connect to the virtual machine:

```
ssh <username>@<public ip>
```

Logging into your Linux Virtual Machine with an SSH private key

Using a username and password is not the best way to log into a remote machine. It is not a completely insecure operation, but you're still sending your username and password over the connection. It's also difficult to use if you want to execute scripts remotely, perform back-up operations, and so forth.

An alternative and more secure way to log into your system is by using SSH key pairs. This is a pair of two cryptographically secured keys: a private and a public key.

The private key is retained by the client and should not be copied to any other computer. It should be kept absolutely secret. And it is a good idea, during the creation of the key pair, to protect the private key with a passphrase.

The public key, on the other hand, can be copied to all the remote computers you want to administer. This public key is used to encrypt the messages that only the private key can decrypt. When you try to log in, the server verifies that the client owns the private key using this property of working with keys. No password is sent over the connection.

There are multiple ways to create an SSH key pair; for instance, PuTTY and MobaXterm both provide tooling to create them. You have to do this from every workstation that needs access to the remote machine. In this book, we are using **ssh-keygen** because it's available for every operating system:

```
ssh-keygen
```

The output of the preceding command should look like this:

```
~> ssh-keygen
Generating public/private rsa key pair.
Enter file in which to save the key (/Users/frederik/.ssh/id_rsa):
Enter passphrase (empty for no passphrase):
Enter same passphrase again:
Your identification has been saved in /Users/frederik/.ssh/id_rsa.
Your public key has been saved in /Users/frederik/.ssh/id_rsa.pub.
```

Figure 2.13: Using ssh-keygen to create SSH key pair

Don't forget to enter a passphrase!

To understand how to use the SSH key pair to access your virtual machines, let's create a new virtual machine. If you recall, when we created the Linux machine earlier, we used the **az vm create** command and **authentication-type** as password, but in the following command, we are using a **--generate-ssh-keys** parameter. This will generate an SSH key pair and will be added to the **.ssh** directory in your home folder, which can be used to access the virtual machine:

```
az vm create --name UbuntuVM3 --resource-group MyResource2 \
    --admin-username student --generate-ssh-keys --image UbuntuLTS
```

If you want to do it in PowerShell, use the **Add-AzVMSshPublicKey** cmdlet. For more information on the command, refer to https://docs.microsoft.com/en-us/powershell/module/azurerm.compute/add-azurermvmsshpublickey?view=azurermps-6.13.0.

Once the virtual machine has been created, you will be able to access it using this command:

```
ssh student@<IP ADDRESS>
```

Summary

This chapter covered the first steps into Microsoft Azure. The first step always involves creating a new account or using an existing company account. With an account, you're able to log in and start discovering the Azure cloud.

In this chapter, the discovery of the Azure cloud was done using the Azure CLI command **az**, or via PowerShell; example by example, you learned about the following:

- The Azure login process
- Regions
- The storage account
- Images provided by publishers
- The creation of virtual machines
- Querying information attached to a virtual machine
- What Linux is and the support available for Linux virtual machines
- Accessing your Linux virtual machine using SSH and an SSH keypair

The next chapter starts here, with a new journey: the Linux operating system.

Questions

1. What are the advantages of using the command line to access Microsoft Azure?
2. What is the purpose of a storage account?
3. Can you think of a reason why you would get the following error message?

   ```
   Code=StorageAccountAlreadyTaken
   Message=The storage account named mystorage is already taken.
   ```

4. What is the difference between an offer and an image?
5. What is the difference between a stopped and a deallocated virtual machine?
6. What is the advantage of using the private SSH key for authentication to your Linux virtual machine?
7. The **az vm create** command has a **--generate-ssh-keys** parameter. Which keys are created, and where are they stored?

Further Reading

By no means is this chapter a tutorial on using PowerShell. But if you want a better understanding of the examples, or want to learn more about PowerShell, we can recommend you read *Mastering Windows PowerShell Scripting – Second Edition* (ISBN: 9781787126305), by Packt Publishing. We suggest that you start with the second chapter, *Working with PowerShell*, and continue until at least the fourth chapter, *Working with Objects in PowerShell*.

You can find plenty of online documentation about using SSH. A very good place to start is this wikibook: https://en.wikibooks.org/wiki/OpenSSH.

If you wish to explore more about Linux administration, *Linux Administration Cookbook* by Packt Publishing is a good resource, especially for system engineers.

To dive deep into security and admin tasks, this is a good read: *Mastering Linux Security and Hardening*, written by Donald A. Tevault and published by Packt Publishing.

3

Basic Linux Administration

After the deployment of your first Linux **virtual machine** (**VM**), let's log in, discuss some basic Linux commands, and learn how to find our way in the Linux environment. This chapter is about basic Linux administration, starting with the Linux shell, which is used to interact with the Linux system. We'll discuss how to use the shell to accomplish our day-to-day administration tasks, such as accessing the filesystem, managing processes such as starting and killing programs, and many other things.

In the last part of this chapter, we'll discuss the **Discretionary Access Control** (**DAC**) model and how to create, manage, and verify users and groups in Linux and get permissions for files and directories based on the username and group membership. We'll also cover changing file ownership for a user/group and changing and verifying basic permissions and access control lists.

Here are the key topics of this chapter:

- Interacting with the shell and configuring the shell
- Getting help using man pages
- Working with and editing text files via the shell
- Understanding the file hierarchy, managing the filesystem, and mounting new filesystems
- Managing processes
- User and group management

The Linux Shell

In the last chapter, we created the VM and logged in using SSH, but how do we interact with the Linux machine and instruct it to perform tasks? As we mentioned at the beginning of this chapter, we'll use the shell.

We'll be exploring the widely used Bash shell, the configuration of the Bash shell, and how to use it. A shell is a user interface in which you can do the following:

- Interact with the kernel, filesystem, and processes
- Execute programs, aliases, and shell built-ins

A shell provides features such as the following:

- Scripting
- Auto-completion
- History and aliasing

There are many different shells available, such as the KornShell, Bash, and the **Z shell** (**Zsh**). Bash is the default shell on almost every Linux system. Its development started in 1988 as a replacement for one of the oldest shells: the Bourne shell. Bash was based on the Bourne shell and lessons learned from other shells such as the KornShell and the C shell. Bash has become the most popular shell and is available on many different operating systems, including Windows 10, FreeBSD, macOS, and Linux.

These are some of the most important features that were added to Bash version 2.05a (released in 2001) that have made Bash the most prominent shell:

- Command-line editing

- History support

- Autocompletion

- Integer calculations

- Function declaration

- Here documents (a way of getting text input into a separate file)

- New variables, such as **$RANDOM** and **$PPID**

Lately, the Z shell is becoming more popular; the development of this shell started in 1990, and it can be seen as an extension to Bash. There is also a compatibility mode with Bash. It comes with even better auto-complete support, including auto-correction and more advanced pathname expansion. Its functionality can be extended with modules, for example, to get more help with commands. The Oh-My-ZSH (https://github.com/robbyrussell/oh-my-zsh) and Prezto (https://github.com/sorin-ionescu/prezto) projects are worth mentioning: they provide theming, advanced configuration, and plugin management to make the Z shell very user-friendly. All these nice features come with a price: the Z shell is definitely more resource-hungry than Bash.

Executing Commands

One of the most important features of a shell is that you can execute commands. A command can be one of the following:

- Shell built-in (a command that is provided by the shell in question)

- Executable on a filesystem

- Alias

To find out what type of command you're executing, there is the **type** command:

```
type echo
```

Adding the **-a** parameter will show all locations containing an executable named **echo**. In the following screenshot, we can see that when we add the **-a** parameter, the shell gives a reference to the **/usr/bin/echo** directory as well, due to the presence of the executable:

```
[student@localhost ~]$ type echo
echo is a shell builtin
[student@localhost ~]$ type -a echo
echo is a shell builtin
echo is /usr/bin/echo
```

Figure 3.1: Locations containing the executable echo

Let's do the same for **ls**:

```
type ls
```

So, you will get a similar output for **type ls**:

```
root@UbuntuVM:~# type ls
ls is aliased to `ls --color=auto'
root@UbuntuVM:~# type -a ls
ls is aliased to `ls --color=auto'
ls is /bin/ls
```

Figure 3.2: Locations containing the executable ls

Here, we can see that **ls** is an alias for the **ls --color=auto** command with some parameters added. An alias can replace an existing command or create a new one. The **alias** command without parameters will give you aliases that are already configured:

```
alias cp='cp -i'
alias egrep='egrep --color=auto'
alias fgrep='fgrep --color=auto'
alias grep='grep --color=auto'
alias l.='ls -d .* --color=auto'
alias ll='ls -l --color=auto'
alias ls='ls --color=auto'
alias mc='. /usr/libexec/mc/mc-wrapper.sh'
alias mv='mv -i'
alias rm='rm -i'
```

Figure 3.3: Using the alias command

The **ll** alias is an example of a newly created command. The **mv** command is an example of a replacement. Create a new alias with the following:

```
alias <command>='command to execute'
```

For instance, to replace the **grep** command with **search**, execute the following command:

```
alias search=grep
```

The alias you are creating will be added to the **.bashrc** file. If you want to remove an alias you have created, you can use the **unalias** command:

```
unalias <alias name>
```

If you want to remove all defined aliases, you can use **unalias -a**.

The **which** command identifies the location of a program in the **$PATH** variable. This variable contains a list of directories that are? used to find an executable. This way, you don't have to provide the full path:

```
which passwd
```

The output tells you that it's available in the **/usr/bin** directory:

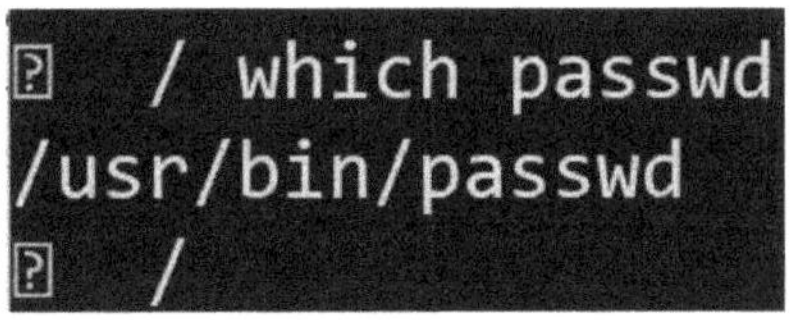

Figure 3.4: Directory location of the program in $PATH variable

Command-line Editing

In many ways, entering commands in the Bash shell is the same as working in a text editor. That is probably the reason why there are shortcuts for actions such as going to the start of a line, and why the shortcuts are the same as in the two most famous, and most commonly used, text editors: Emacs and vi.

By default, Bash is configured to be in Emacs editing mode. If you want to check the current editing mode, run **set -o**. The output will say whether Emacs or vi is set to **on**. The following are a few very important shortcuts:

Shortcut	Use
Ctrl + L	Clear screen
Ctrl + D	Exit
Ctrl + C	Break (interrupt process)
Ctrl + A	Move to the beginning of the line
Ctrl + E	Move to the end of the line
Ctrl + K	Delete until the end of the line
Ctrl + Y	Undo delete
Alt + B	One word backward
Alt + F	One word forward
Ctrl + W	Delete one word backward
Alt + D	Delete one word forward

Figure 3.5: List of Bash shell shortcuts

If you want to use vi mode, execute the following:

```
set -o vi
```

To switch back to Emacs mode, use the following command:

```
set -o emacs
```

> **Note**
>
> The vi editor is covered in a later section of this chapter, *Working with Text Files*. For now, you can use almost every command in command mode, including **navigation**, **yank**, and **put**.

The **set** command is a Bash built-in command that toggles attributes specific to Bash. Without parameters, it dumps environment variables.

Working with history

The Bash shell provides command-line tools that you can use to work with the user's command history. Every command that you execute is registered in a history file in the home directory: `~/.bash_history`. To view the content of this history, execute the following command:

```
history
```

The output shows a numbered list of previously used commands; you can simply redo a command using the following:

- `!<number>`: Execute the command based on the history list number.

- `!<-number>`: For instance, `!-2` executes the command that was executed two commands prior to the last command in the history.

- `!<first characters of the command>`: This will execute the last item that starts with this character.

- `!!`: Redo the last command. You can combine this with other commands. For instance, **sudo !!**.

You can backward-search the history using *Ctrl* + *R* (Emacs mode) or using the forward slash (vi command mode). Browsing is possible using the arrow keys.

The history file is not written directly after the execution of a command, but at the end of a login session. If you are working in multiple sessions, it can be a good idea to write the history directly. To do so, execute the following:

```
history -a
```

To read the just-saved history in another session, execute this:

```
history -r
```

To clear the history of the current session, use this command:

```
history -c
```

If you want to save the history to a file, you can execute this:

```
history -w <filename>
```

So, by saving the cleared history, you emptied the history file.

Another nice feature of working with the history is that you can edit it. Let's say you executed the **ls -alh** command, but you need **ls -ltr**. Just type:

```
^alh^ltr
```

This is actually the same as the following:

```
!!:s/ltr/alh/
```

Of course, you can do this for every entry in the history; for instance, for number **6** in the history list, use:

```
!6:s/string/newstring/
```

Sometimes you need more flexibility, and you want to edit a big line that contains a lot of typos. Enter the **fc** command. Fix the command using the following:

```
fc <history number>
```

This opens a text editor (vi by default) and, after saving the modification, it will execute the modified command.

Autocompletion

Everyone makes typos; no one can remember every parameter. Autocompletion can prevent many errors and helps you in many ways when you enter commands.

Autocompletion works for the following:

- Executables
- Aliases
- Shell built-ins
- Programs on the filesystem
- Filenames
- Parameters, if the utility supports it and the **bash-completion** package is installed
- Variables

If the shell is configured in Emacs mode, use *Ctrl + I* to activate autocomplete; if the shell is configured in vi mode, you can use *Ctrl + P* as well.

> **Note**
>
> If there is more than one possibility, you have to hit *Ctrl + I* or *Ctrl + P* twice.

Globbing

Globbing is expanding a non-specific filename that contains a wildcard into one or more specific filenames in the Linux shell. Another common name for globbing is pathname expansion.

The following wildcards are recognized in the Bash shell:

- ?: One single character.

- *: Multiple characters. Please notice that if you use this wildcard as the first character, filenames starting with a dot won't match. Of course, you can use .*.

- [a-z], [abc]: One character from the range.

- {a,b,c}: a or b or c.

The following are some nice examples of using wildcards:

- **echo *** : This will list the files or directories in the current working directory.

- **cd /usr/share/doc/wget*** : This will change the directory to the directory name starting with **wget** residing in **/usr/share/doc**.

- **ls /etc/*/*conf** : This will list all **.conf** files in all directories under **/etc**. Here's an example of this command:

```
 ~ ls /etc/*/*.conf
/etc/apparmor/parser.conf              /etc/security/namespace.conf
/etc/apparmor/subdomain.conf           /etc/security/pam_env.conf
/etc/apport/crashdb.conf               /etc/security/sepermit.conf
/etc/depmod.d/ubuntu.conf              /etc/security/time.conf
/etc/dhcp/dhclient.conf                /etc/selinux/semanage.conf
/etc/fonts/fonts.conf                  /etc/sysctl.d/10-console-messages.conf
/etc/initramfs-tools/initramfs.conf    /etc/sysctl.d/10-ipv6-privacy.conf
/etc/initramfs-tools/update-initramfs.conf /etc/sysctl.d/10-kernel-hardening.conf
/etc/iscsi/iscsid.conf                 /etc/sysctl.d/10-link-restrictions.conf
/etc/ld.so.conf.d/libc.conf            /etc/sysctl.d/10-lxd-inotify.conf
/etc/ld.so.conf.d/x86_64-linux-gnu.conf /etc/sysctl.d/10-magic-sysrq.conf
/etc/ldap/ldap.conf                    /etc/sysctl.d/10-network-security.conf
/etc/lvm/lvm.conf                      /etc/sysctl.d/10-ptrace.conf
/etc/lvm/lvmlocal.conf                 /etc/sysctl.d/10-zeropage.conf
/etc/mdadm/mdadm.conf                  /etc/sysctl.d/99-cloudimg-ipv6.conf
/etc/modprobe.d/blacklist-ath_pci.conf /etc/sysctl.d/99-sysctl.conf
/etc/modprobe.d/blacklist-firewire.conf /etc/systemd/journald.conf
/etc/modprobe.d/blacklist-framebuffer.conf /etc/systemd/logind.conf
/etc/modprobe.d/blacklist-rare-network.conf /etc/systemd/resolved.conf
/etc/modprobe.d/blacklist.conf         /etc/systemd/system.conf
/etc/modprobe.d/iwlwifi.conf           /etc/systemd/timesyncd.conf
/etc/modprobe.d/mdadm.conf             /etc/systemd/user.conf
/etc/modules-load.d/modules.conf       /etc/tmpfiles.d/screen-cleanup.conf
/etc/rsyslog.d/20-ufw.conf             /etc/udev/udev.conf
/etc/rsyslog.d/21-cloudinit.conf       /etc/ufw/sysctl.conf
/etc/rsyslog.d/50-default.conf         /etc/ufw/ufw.conf
```

Figure 3.6: Listing all the .conf files from all directories

- **mkdir -p /srv/www/{html,cgi-bin,logs}** : This will create **html**, **cgi-bin**, and **log** directories inside **/srv/www** with a single command.

Redirections

In the early days of Unix, one of the developers, Ken Thompson, defined a *Unix philosophy*, an approach based on experience to make everything as modular as possible and to reuse code and programs as much as possible. Particularly in those days, reusability was important for performance reasons and to provide a method that allowed for easy maintenance of the code.

In a version of this *Unix philosophy* modified by Peter H Salus, the objectives of redirection are as follows:

- Write programs that do one thing and do it well.

- Write programs to work together.

- Write programs to handle text streams, because that is a universal interface.

To make this philosophy possible, programs were developed with support for file descriptors, or, in modern parlance, communication channels. Every program has at least three communication channels:

- Standard input (0)

- Standard output (1)

- Standard error (2)

One of the nice features of this implementation is that you can redirect the channels.

To redirect the standard output to a file, use the following:

```
command > filename
```

To redirect the standard output and append to an existing file, use:

```
command >> filename
```

Redirect the standard error and output to a file as follows:

```
command &> filename
```

To redirect standard output first to a file and then redirect the standard error there as well, use:

```
command 2>&1 filename
```

To redirect the standard input, use the following:

```
filename < command
```

Let's do an activity to help us understand the concept of redirection. Please run the command first, verify the output, then redirect to file using the following methods. For example, run **ls** and verify the output, then use **>** to redirect the output to **/tmp/test. list**. You can always check the file using **cat /tmp/test.list**:

```
ls > /tmp/test.list
```

```
echo hello > /tmp/echotest
```

```
echo hallo again >> /tmp/echotest
```

```
ls -R /proc 2> /tmp/proc-error.test
```

```
ls -R /proc &> /tmp/proc-all.test
```

```
sort < /etc/services
```

A special version of input redirection is **heredoc.txt**:

```
cat << EOF >> /tmp/heredoc.txt
  this is a line
  this is another line
EOF
```

The **cat** command concatenates the standard output and appends it to the **/tmp/ heredoc.txt** file. There is no way to interrupt or break the command because the keyboard is not the standard input until it encounters a label, in this example, **EOF**. This method is often used to create configuration files from scripts.

Another possibility is taking the standard output of one command and redirecting it to the standard input of another command using the **|** symbol:

```
command | other command
```

For example:

```
ls | more
```

Using the **tee** command, you can combine the power of redirection and piping. There are times when you want to make sure the output of **command 1** is written to a file for troubleshooting or logging and, at the same time, you pipe it to the standard input of another command:

```
command 1 | tee file.txt | command 2
```

Appending to a file is also possible using the **-a** parameter.

Another use case of **tee** is:

```
<command> | sudo tee <file>
```

This way, it is possible to write into a file without using difficult **su** constructions.

Working with Variables

Every command-line interface, even those without advanced scripting possibilities, has the concept of variables. In Bash, there are two types of variables:

- Built-in or internal variables that affect the behavior of Bash or give information about Bash. Some examples include **BASH_VERSION**, **EDITOR**, and **PATH**.

- Environment variables that are known to one or more applications, including built-in variables and user-defined variables.

To list the environment variables for your current shell, you can use the **env** or **printenv** command. **printenv** is also able to show the content of a specific variable:

```
[linvirt@CentOS-01 ~]$ printenv PATH
/usr/local/bin:/usr/bin:/usr/local/sbin:/usr/sbin:/home/linvirt/.local/bin:/home
/linvirt/bin
```

Figure 3.7: Displaying the content of a specific variable using printenv command

Another way to view the content of a variable is as follows:

```
echo $VARNAME
```

To declare an environment variable, execute **var=value**. For instance:

```
animal=cat
```

```
echo $animal
```

To add more characters to the value, use:

```
animal=$animal,dog
```

```
echo $animal
```

The **animal** variable is only known to your current shell. If you want to export it to child processes, you need to export the variable:

```
export animal
```

Bash is also capable of doing simple calculations:

```
a=$(( 4 + 2 ))
```

Alternatively, you can use this command:

```
let a=4+2
echo $a
```

Another feature is putting the output of a command into a variable—a technique called nesting:

```
MYDATE=$(date +"%F")
echo $MYDATE
```

Of course, this is just a glimpse of what Bash is capable of, but this should be enough for you to learn how to handle Bash configuration files and modify them for the environment you need so that they behave in the way you want.

Bash Configuration Files

There are three important system-wide configuration files for the Bash shell: **/etc/profile**, **/etc/bashrc**, and **/etc/environment**. The purpose of these files is to store information regarding your shell, such as the colors, aliases, and variables. For example, in the previous section, we added a couple of aliases, and they are stored in a file called **bashrc**, which is a configuration file. Each file has its own purpose; we will take a look at each of them now.

/etc/profile is a script that is executed once a user logs in to a system. It is not a good idea to modify this file; instead, use the snap-in **/etc/profile.d** directory. Files in this directory are executed in alphabetical order and must have **.sh** as the file extension. As a side note, **/etc/profile** is not only used by the Bash shell, but by all shells for Linux, except for PowerShell. You can also create a user-specific profile script in the home directory, **~/.bash_profile**, which is also Bash-specific.

Some typical content of a profile script is as follows:

```
set -o vi
alias man="pinfo -m"
alias ll="ls -lv --group-directories-first"
shopt -u mailwarn
unset MAILCHECK
```

> **Note**
>
> If you are using Ubuntu or a similar distribution, **pinfo** is not installed by default. Run **apt install pinfo** to install it.

The **shopt** command changes some default Bash behavior, such as checking for mail or the behavior of globbing. The **unset** command is the opposite of the **set** command. In our example, by default, Bash checks for mail every minute; after executing the **unset MAILCHECK** command, the **MAILCHECK** variable is removed.

The **/etc/bashrc** script is started every time any user invokes a shell or shell script. For performance reasons, keep it as minimal as possible. Instead of the **/etc/bashrc** file, you can use the user-specific **~/.bashrc** file, and the **~/.bash_logout** script is executed if you exit a shell. The **bashrc** configuration files are often used to modify the prompt (the **PS1** variable):

```
DARKGRAY='\e[1;30m'
GREEN='\e[32m'
YELLOW='\e[1;33m'
PS1="\n$GREEN[\w] \n$DARKGRAY(\t$DARKGRAY)-(\u$DARKGRAY)-($YELLOW-> \e[m"
```

Let's look at the parameters for the **PS1** variable:

- Colors (like GREEN, DARKGRAY passed into PS1 variable) are defined in ANSI color code.
- **\e**: Escape character in ANSI.
- **\n**: Newline.
- **\w**: Current working directory.
- **\t**: Current time.
- **\u**: Username.

The **/etc/environment** file (empty by default in Red Hat–based distributions) is the first file that is executed at login. It contains variables for every process, not just the shell. It's not a script, just one variable on each line.

Here is an example of **/etc/environment**:

```
EDITOR=/usr/bin/vim
BROWSER=/usr/bin/elinks
LANG=en_US.utf-8
LC_ALL=en_US.utf-8
LESSCHARSET=utf-8
SYSTEMD_PAGER=/usr/bin/more
```

The **EDITOR** variable is an important one. Many programs can invoke an editor; sometimes it's vi by default, sometimes it's not. Setting a default ensures that you can always use your favorite editor.

> **Note**
>
> If you don't want to log out and log in again, you can use the **source** command, for instance, **source /etc/environment**. This way, the variables will be read into your current shell.

Getting Help

Whether you are new to Linux or a long-time user, from time to time, you'll need help. It's impossible to remember all the commands and their parameters. Almost every command has a **--help** parameter, and there is sometimes documentation installed in the **/usr/share/doc** directory, but the most important sources of information are the information documents and man pages.

Using the man pages

There is a saying, **Read The Fine Manual** (**RTFM**), and sometimes people replace the word *fine* with another, less friendly word. Almost every command has a manual: a man page provides you with all the information you need. And yes, not all man pages are easy to read, especially older ones, but if you use man pages frequently, you'll get used to them, and you'll be able to find the information you need quickly enough. Normally, man pages are installed on your system, and they are available online: http://man7.org/linux/man-pages.

Note that the man pages are removed in the Azure images for openSUSE Leap and SUSE Linux Enterprise Server. You have to reinstall every package to make them available again:

```
sudo zypper refresh

for package in $(rpm -qa);

  do sudo zypper install --force --no-confirm $package;

done
```

Man pages are installed in the **/usr/share/man** directory in GZIP compressed archives. Man pages are specially formatted text files that you can read with the **man** command or **pinfo**. The **pinfo** utility acts as a text browser, very similar to a text-based web browser. It adds hyperlink support and the ability to navigate between different man pages using the arrow keys.

> **Note**
>
> If you want to replace the **man** command with **pinfo**, it is a good idea to create an alias using the **alias man="pinfo -m"** command.

All man pages follow a similar structure, and they are always formatted and divided into sections:

- **Name**: The name of the command and a brief explanation of the command. Usually a one-liner; detailed information can be found in the Description section of the man page.

- **Synopsis**: An overview with all the available parameters.

- **Description**: A (long) description of the command, sometimes including the status of the command. For instance, the man page of the **ifconfig** command explicitly states that this command is obsolete.

- **Options**: All the available parameters of a command, sometimes including examples.

- **Examples**: If the examples are not in the Options section, there may be a separate section.

- **Files**: Files and directories that are important to this command.

- **See also**: Refers to other man pages, info pages, and other sources of documentation. Some man pages contain other sections, such as notes, bugs, history, authors, and licenses.

Man pages are help pages that are divided into several sections; these sections are described in the Description section of the man page. You can use **man man** to understand more about the sections. The following screenshot shows the different sections:

```
DESCRIPTION
        man is the system's manual pager.  Each page argument given to man is normally the name of a p
        each of these arguments is then found and displayed.  A section, if provided, will direc
        action is to search in all of the available sections following a pre-defined order ("1 n 1 8 3
        den by the SECTION directive in /etc/manpath.config), and to show only the first page found, e

        The table below shows the section numbers of the manual followed by the types of pages they co

        1    Executable programs or shell commands
        2    System calls (functions provided by the kernel)
        3    Library calls (functions within program libraries)
        4    Special files (usually found in /dev)
        5    File formats and conventions eg /etc/passwd
        6    Games
        7    Miscellaneous (including macro packages and conventions), e.g. man(7), groff(7)
        8    System administration commands (usually only for root)
        9    Kernel routines [Non standard]

        A manual page consists of several sections.

        Conventional section names include  NAME, SYNOPSIS, CONFIGURATION, DESCRIPTION, OPTIONS, EX
        CONFORMING TO, NOTES, BUGS, EXAMPLE, AUTHORS, and SEE ALSO.
```

Figure 3.8: Different sections of a man page

This sectioning is important to know about, especially if you want to search for documentation. To be able to search for documentation, you'll need to index the man pages:

```
sudo mandb
```

> **Note**
>
> Normally, after installing a package, the index is automatically updated.
> Sometimes, the packager will have failed to add a post-install script to execute the
> **mandb** command. It's a good idea to execute the command manually if you can't
> find the information and you are pretty sure that there should be a man page.

After that, you can use the **apropos** or **man -k** commands to find the information you need. It doesn't matter which one you choose; the syntax is the same:

```
man -k -s 5 "time"
```

In the preceding command, we search for the word **time**, limiting the search to the man page section 5.

Using info Documents

Info documents are another important source of information. The difference between man pages and info pages is that info pages are more freely formatted, whereas man pages are a sort of instruction manual for a certain command. Info documents are, most of the time, complete handbooks.

Info documents are, like man pages, compressed and installed in the **/usr/share/info** directory. To read them, you can use **info** or the more modern **pinfo**. Both commands act as a text-based browser. If you are a big fan of the Emacs editor, you can use InfoMode (https://www.emacswiki.org/emacs/InfoMode) to read the info documents.

One of the nice features is that you can directly jump to one of the hyperlinks in the document using **pinfo** or **info**:

```
pinfo '(pinfo) Keybindings'
```

> **Note**
>
> If you are using Ubuntu or a similar distribution, **pinfo** is not installed by default. Run **apt install pinfo** to install it.

The preceding example opens the man page of **pinfo** and jumps directly to the **Keybindings** section.

The **pinfo** command has a search option, **-a**. If there is a match, it will automatically open the corresponding **info** document or man page. For example, if you would like to know about the **echo** command, use **pinfo -a echo**; it'll take you to the help section of the **echo** command.

The **info** command has a search option as well: **-k**. Using **-k**, the **info** command will look up the keyword in all available manuals. For example, here we've checked for the **paste** keyword, and it returned all possible matches:

```
root@UbuntuVM:~# info -k paste
"(coreutils)paste invocation" -- paste
"(screen)Copy and Paste" -- copy and paste
"(screen)Paste" -- defslowpaste
"(screen)Paste" -- paste
"(screen)Paste" -- pastefont
"(screen)Paste" -- slowpaste
root@UbuntuVM:~#
```

Figure 3.9: Checking for the paste keyword using the info command

Other Documentation

Another source of documentation is the documentation provided by the Linux distribution vendor. The websites of Red Hat, SUSE, Canonical, and Debian host useful handbooks, wikis, and so on. They can be very useful, especially for topics that are distribution-specific, such as software management.

There are two distributions that are not Microsoft-endorsed distributions, Gentoo and Arch Linux, and they have excellent wikis on their websites. And, of course, some of the information in these wikis is specific to these distributions, but many articles are useful and will work on every distribution.

The Linux Foundation hosts a wiki at https://wiki.linuxfoundation.org with documentation regarding topics such as networking, and standards such as the **Linux Standard Base** (**LSB**), which will be covered later in this chapter. Other standards are covered by freedesktop.org (https://www.freedesktop.org). They are also responsible for the Linux `init` system, systemd, and the Linux firewall (firewalld); these topics are discussed in *Chapter 5, Advanced Linux Administration*.

Finally, the Linux Documentation Project can be found at https://www.tldp.org. While many of the documents you can find there are very old, it's still a good starting point.

Working with Text Files

The Unix philosophy started by Ken Thompson aimed to create a capable operating system with a small footprint and a clean user interface. Because part of the Unix philosophy is to *write programs to handle text streams, because that is a universal interface*, communication between programs, configuration files, and many other things is implemented in plain text. This section is all about handling plain text.

Reading Text

On the most fundamental level, reading the content of a file in plain text format means taking the content of this file and redirecting it to the standard output. The **cat** command is one utility that can do that—concatenate the content of one or more files (or another input channel) to the standard output:

```
[linvirt@CentOS-01 ~]$ cat /etc/shells
/bin/sh
/bin/bash
/sbin/nologin
/usr/bin/sh
/usr/bin/bash
/usr/sbin/nologin
/bin/tcsh
/bin/csh
```

Figure 3.10: Using the cat command to generate standard output

Some nice parameters of this utility are:

- **-A**: Show all non-printable characters

- **-b**: Number lines, including empty lines

- **-n**: Number lines, except empty lines

- **-s**: Suppress repeated (**!**) empty blank lines

There is another utility like **cat**, which is the **tac** utility. This will print the file in reverse order:

```
root@UbuntuVM:~# cat file.txt

Hello
World
Welcome
root@UbuntuVM:~# tac file.txt
Welcome
World
Hello

root@UbuntuVM:~#
```

Figure 3.11: Using the tac utility to print files in reverse order

The problem with the **cat** command is that it just dumps the content to the standard output without paginating the content, and the scrollback functionality for the terminals is not very good.

The **more** utility is a filter for paging. It displays the text one screenful at a time and provides a basic search engine that can be activated by using the forward slash. At the end of the file, **more** will exit, with or without the message **Press space to continue**.

The **less** utility is more advanced than the **more** utility. It has the following features:

- Ability to scroll forward, backward, and horizontally
- Advanced navigation
- Advanced search engine
- Multiple file handling
- Ability to display information about the file, such as the filename and length
- Ability to invoke shell commands

In **more** and **less**, the **v** command allows us to switch to an editor, by default the vi editor.

> **Note**
>
> Both **more** and **less** are available on every distribution; however, on some distributions, **more** is an alias for **less**. Use the **type** command to verify!

If you want to see only a specific number of lines at the top of a file, there is a utility called **head**. By default, it shows the first 10 lines of a file. You can modify this behavior using the **-n** parameter for the number of lines and the **-c** parameter for the number of bytes/kilobytes.

The **head** utility is the opposite of `tail`; it shows the first 10 lines by default. For example, we have a file named `states.txt` that contains the names of US states in alphabetical order. If we use the **head** command, it will print the first 10 lines of the file, and if we use the `tail` command it'll print the last 10 lines. Let's have a look at this:

```
root@UbuntuVM:~# head states.txt
Alabama
Alaska
Arizona
Arkansas
California
Colorado
Connecticut
Delaware
Florida
Georgia
root@UbuntuVM:~# tail states.txt
South Dakota
Tennessee
Texas
Utah
Vermont
Virginia
Washington
West Virginia
Wisconsin
Wyoming
root@UbuntuVM:~#
```

Figure 3.12: Using head and tail utilities to list the first and last 10 entries of the file

It recognizes the same parameters as **head** to modify that behavior. But there is an extra parameter that makes this utility extremely useful for logging purposes. **-f** appends the output as the file grows; it's a way of following and monitoring the content of a file. A very well-known example is:

```
sudo tail -f /var/log/messages
```

Searching in Text Files

You might have heard that everything in Linux is a file. Also, many things in Linux are managed by text streams and text files. Sooner or later, you will want to search the text in order to make modifications. This can be done by using regular expressions. A regular expression (regex for short) is a pattern of special characters and text used to match strings when performing a search. Regular expressions are used by many applications with a built-in processor, such as the Emacs and vi text editors, and utilities such as **grep**, **awk**, and **sed**. Many scripting and programming languages have support for regular expressions.

In this book, we'll only cover the basics of this topic—just enough that you can use them in your daily system administration tasks.

Every regular expression is built around an atom. The atom identifies what text is to be matched and where it is to be found when doing a search. It could be a known single-character item (or a dot if you don't know the character), a class, or a range, such as:

[a-z]	From a to z
[abc]	From a, b, or c

Figure 3.13: Examples of atom

A regex can also be expressed in the form of a shorthand class. Here are a few examples of shorthand classes:

[[:alnum:]]	Alphanumeric characters
[[:alpha:]]	Alpha characters
[[:digit:]]	Numbers
[[:upper:]]	Uppercase characters
[[:lower:]]	Lowercase characters
[[:space:]]	White space

Figure3.14: Examples of shorthand classes

We can use position anchors to determine where to find the next character. Some popular ones are:

^	Beginning of the line
$	End of the line
\<	Beginning of the word
\>	End of the word
\A	Start of a file
\Z	End of a file

Figure 3.15: List of position anchors

Using a repetition operator, you can specify how many times a character should appear:

{n}	Exactly n times
{n,}	Minimum of n times
{,n}	Maximum of n times
{n,n}	Minimum and maximum n times
*	Zero or more times
+	One or more times
?	Zero or one time

Figure 3.16: List of repetition operators

A few examples are as follows:

- If you search for the character **b** and the word **boom** is found, it will match the letter **b**. If you search for **bo**, it will match these characters in this order.

- If you search for **bo{,2}m**, the words **bom** and **boom** will match. But if the word **booom** exists, it will not match.

- If you search for **^bo{,2}m**, there will be only a match if the word **boom** is at the beginning of a line.

A reference for regular expressions can be found using:

```
man 7 regex
```

One utility we've already mentioned is the **grep** utility, which is used to search in text files. There are multiple versions of this utility; nowadays, **egrep** is the most commonly used version because it has the most complete regular expression support, including shorthand ranges and the OR alternation operator, **|**.

Common options for **egrep** and **grep** are:

-i	Ignore case
-v	Invert match
-A	Lines after match
-B	Lines before match
-n	Show line number
-o	Match only

Figure 3.17: egrep and grep options

You can also take look at the other options by checking the man page.

Here's a simple example of **grep**:

```
[root@server1 student]# grep -B1 umask /etc/profile

# By default, we want umask to get set. This sets it for login shell
--
if [ $UID -gt 199 ] && [ "`/usr/bin/id -gn`" = "`/usr/bin/id -un`" ]; then
    umask 002
else
    umask 022
```

Figure 3.18: grep example

Another utility that is very useful is **awk**. Now, **awk** is a utility that was created by the developers Alfred Aho, Peter Weinberger, and Brian Kernighan. It is a scripting language used for text files which is used to generate and manipulate log files or reports. **awk** doesn't require any compiling, and you can mention the fields required in the report.

Let's look at an example:

```
awk -F: '/^root/ {print "Homedir of root:", $6}' /etc/passwd
```

It scans the **/etc/passwd** file and splits the content using the field separator, the colon. It searches for the line starting with the **root** string and prints some text (**Homedir of root:**) and the sixth column.

Editing Text Files

Because text files are so important in Linux, a text editor is very important. Every distribution has one or more editors in their repositories for both graphical and non-graphical environments. You can be sure that at least vim, a modern vi implementation, and Emacs are available. There is an ongoing war between vi lovers and Emacs lovers—they have been insulting each other for decades and will do so for many decades to come.

We are not going to make the decision for you; instead, if you are already familiar with one of them, stick with it. If you don't know vi or Emacs, try them both for a while and decide for yourself.

There are also some other editors available:

- **nano**, a free clone of proprietary Pico, the text-editor component of the Pine email client

- **mcedit**, a part of the **Midnight Commander** (**MC**) file manager that can run standalone as well

- **joe**, which can emulate the keybindings of nano, Emacs, and a very old word processor called WordStar (note that, for CentOS, this editor is not available in the standard repository, but is in a third-party repository).

> **Note**
>
> If you want to learn about vi, execute the **vimtutor** command, a tutorial that comes with vim. It's a good starting point for learning all the basics of navigation, the commands, and text editing in vi.
>
> Emacs comes with a very good help function that you can access in Emacs via *Ctrl + H + R*.

Another way to edit text streams and files is by using the non-interactive text editor sed. Instead of text files editing opening a file in a text editor window, it processes a file or stream from the shell. It's a handy utility if you want to do the following:

- Perform edits on file(s) automatically

- On multiple files, make the same edits

- Write a conversion program—for example, to change between lowercase and uppercase, or even more complex conversions

The syntax of the sed editor is very similar to the commands of the vi editor, and can be scripted.

The default behavior for sed is not to edit the file itself, but to dump the changes to the standard output. You can redirect this output to another file or use the **-i** parameter, which stands for **in-place edit**. This mode will change the content of the file. The following command is by far the most well-known **sed** command:

```
sed -i 's/string/newstring/g' filename.txt
```

It will search for a string, replace it, and continue searching and replacing until the end of the file.

Together with a little bit of scripting, you can edit multiple files in the same way:

```
for files in *conf; do sed -i 's/string/newstring/g' $files; done
```

You can limit the search to a single line:

```
sed -i '10 s/string/newstring/g' <filename>
```

The **info** page of **sed** is a great resource for all the commands and, more importantly, it has an example section if you want to know more.

Finding Your Way in the Filesystem

Now that you know how to manipulate and edit text files, it's time to see how these files are stored in the system. As a system administrator, you will have to check, mount, or even unmount the drives. So, now let's take a close look at the filesystem in Linux. The layout of the Linux filesystem is like all other members of the Unix family: very different from Windows. There is no concept of drive letters. Instead, there is a root filesystem (/), and everything else is available on the root filesystem, including other mounted filesystems.

In this section, you'll learn where you can find files, and why they are there.

The Filesystem Hierarchy Standard

In 2001, the Linux Foundation started the **Linux Standard Base Project** (**LSB**). Based on the POSIX specification, the idea behind this process was to have a standardized system so that applications can run on any compatible Linux distribution.

The **Filesystem Hierarchy Standard** (**FHS**) is a part of this project and defines the directory structure and directory contents. Of course, there are still some minor differences between distributions regarding the directory structure, but even on distributions that are not willing to fully support the LSB, such as Debian, the directory structure follows the FHS.

The following screenshots are taken from a CentOS system, using the **tree** utility to show the directory structure. If **tree** is not installed on your system, the shell will prompt you with the command to install. Please do so.

In the root filesystem, the following directories are available:

Figure 3.19: Displaying the directory structure using the tree utility

The **tree** command will layout the filesystem in a tree-like structure. Alternatively, you can use **ls -lah /** to see the structure in a list format.

The following directories are present in the screenshot:

- **/bin**: Contains programs that you need on a minimal system to be executed by an unprivileged user such as a shell. On Red Hat–based systems, this directory is a symbolic link to **/usr/bin**. Commands such as **ps**, **ls**, and **ping** are stored here.

- **/sbin**: Contains programs that you need on a minimal system to be executed by a privileged user (**root**), such as filesystem repair utilities. On Red Hat Enterprise Linux–based systems, this directory is a symbolic link to **/usr/sbin**. Examples include **iptables**, **reboot**, **fdisk**, **ifconfig**, and **swapon**.

- **/dev**: Devices are mounted on a special filesystem called **devfs**. All peripheral devices are here, such as the serial port, disks, and CPUs—except the network interface. Examples: **/dev/null**, **/dev/tty1**.

- **/proc**: Processes are mounted on a special filesystem called **procfs**.

- **/sys**: Hardware information on the **sysfs** filesystem.

- **/etc**: Consists of editable text configuration files required by all programs.

- **/lib**: Library for drivers and non-editable text configuration files. Library filenames are either **ld*** or **lib*.so.***, for example, **libutil-2.27.so**, or **libthread_db-1.0.so**.

- **/lib64**: Libraries for drivers, but no configuration files.

- **/boot**: Kernel and boot-loader. Examples: **initrd.img-2.6.32-24-generic**, **vmlinuz-2.6.32-24-generic**.

- **/root**: User data for the **root** user. Only the **root** user has the right to write to this directory. **/root** is the **root** user's home directory, which is not the same as **/**.

- **/home**: User data for unprivileged users. Similar to the **C:\Users\username** folder in Windows.

- **/media**: Removable media, such as CD-ROM and USB drives, are mounted here. At least read-only for every user. Examples include **/media/cdrom** for CD-ROM, **/media/floppy** for floppy drives, and **/media/cdrecorder** for CD writers.

- **/mnt**: Non-removable media, including remote storage. At least read-only for every user.

- **/run**: Files specific for a user or process, for instance, USB drivers that should be available for a specific user, or runtime information for a daemon.

- **/opt**: Optional software that is not a part of the distribution, such as third-party software.

- **/srv**: Static server data. It can be used for static websites, file servers, and orchestration software such as Salt or Puppet.

- **/var**: Dynamic data. Ranges from print spoolers and logging to dynamic websites.

- **/tmp**: Temporary files, not persistent during reboots. Nowadays, it's often a RAM filesystem (**tmpfs**) that is mounted on this directory. The directory itself is more or less deprecated and from an application perspective, replaced with a directory in **/var** or **/run**.

- **/usr**: It contains all extra software-related binaries, documentation, and source code.

Use the **tree** command again to show the directory structure in **/usr**:

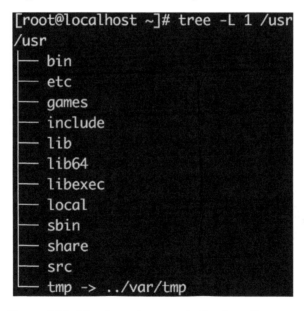

Figure 3.20: Directory structure in the /usr directory

The directory structure of **/usr** is very similar to the structure of **/**. A few extra directories were added:

- **/usr/etc**: If you recompile software that is already a part of the distribution, the configuration files should be in **/usr/etc**, so they can't conflict with files in **/etc**.

- **/usr/games**: Data for old games such as **fortune**, **figlet**, and **cowsay**.

- **/usr/include**: Development headers.

- **/usr/libexec**: Wrapper scripts. Let's say you need multiple versions of Java. They all need different libraries, environment variables, and so on. A wrapper script is there to call a specific version with the correct settings.

- **/usr/share**: Program data such as wallpaper, menu items, icons, and documentation.

- **/usr/src**: Linux kernel sources and sources from software that is included in the distribution.

- **/usr/local**: Software that you install and compile yourself.

The directory structure of **/usr/local** is the same as **/usr**:

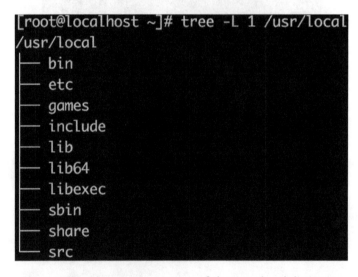

Figure 3.21: Directory structure of the /usr/local directory

This directory is there for software development. There is no need to have this directory in a production environment.

Optional software is placed in **/opt**. The main directory structure is **/opt/<vendor>/<software>/**, for example, **/opt/google/chrome**. A list of the possible vendor/provider names is maintained by the **Linux Assigned Names And Numbers Authority** (**LANANA**) on its website, http://www.lanana.org/lsbreg/providers/. For native Linux software, the structure is the same as **/usr** and **/usr/local**, with one exception: you can choose between **/conf** and **/etc** in the software directory or in the **/etc/opt** directory. Non-native Linux software such as PowerShell can use its own structure within the software directory.

Mounting Filesystems

It may be a good idea to define the root filesystem more precisely. The root filesystem is the filesystem where the root directory, **/**, is located. All other filesystems are mounted on directories created on this root filesystem. To find out what directories are local to the root filesystem and which ones are mount points, execute the **findmnt** command:

```
[student@server1 ~]$ findmnt
TARGET                          SOURCE          FSTYPE    OPTIONS
/                               /dev/mapper/centos-root
                                                xfs       rw,relatime,seclabel,a
├─/sys                          sysfs           sysfs     rw,nosuid,nodev,noexec
│ ├─/sys/kernel/security        securityfs      security  rw,nosuid,nodev,noexec
│ ├─/sys/fs/cgroup              tmpfs           tmpfs     ro,nosuid,nodev,noexec
│ │ ├─/sys/fs/cgroup/systemd    cgroup          cgroup    rw,nosuid,nodev,noexec
│ │ ├─/sys/fs/cgroup/blkio      cgroup          cgroup    rw,nosuid,nodev,noexec
│ │ ├─/sys/fs/cgroup/hugetlb    cgroup          cgroup    rw,nosuid,nodev,noexec
```

Figure 3.22: Using the findmnt command to find mount points

Adding the **-D** parameter will show you the size of the filesystem and the amount of space that is available:

```
[student@server1 ~]$ findmnt -D
SOURCE                    FSTYPE      SIZE   USED   AVAIL USE% TARGET
devtmpfs                  devtmpfs    477M      0    477M   0% /dev
tmpfs                     tmpfs     487.6M      0  487.6M   0% /dev/shm
tmpfs                     tmpfs     487.6M   6.8M  480.9M   1% /run
tmpfs                     tmpfs     487.6M      0  487.6M   0% /sys/fs/cgroup
/dev/mapper/centos-root   xfs         12G   1.4G   10.6G  12% /
```

Figure 3.23: Listing the file size and available space with the findmnt -D command

The `findmnt` command is a great way to find out where a device is mounted, for instance:

```
findmnt /dev/sda1
```

If a directory is not a mount point, use the **-T** parameter:

```
findmnt -T /usr
```

In *Chapter 5, Advanced Linux Administration*, the different filesystems, and how to mount and automatically mount local and remote filesystems, are covered in detail.

Finding Files on the Filesystem

Searching for files on the filesystem can be done with the `find` command. Unfortunately, if you are not already familiar with this command, the man page may be overwhelming and not very easy to read. However, if you understand the basics of this command, the man page will help you add parameters to search every property of a file or directory, or both.

The first possible parameters of the `find` command are options. These affect the behavior of the `find` command, that is, whether it should follow symbolic links and debug and speed optimization options. Options are optional—most of the time you don't need them.

After the options, the next parameter tells the `find` command where to start the search process. It is not a very good idea to start at the root (**/**) directory; it takes too much time and can consume too much CPU activity on large filesystems. Remember the FHS—for instance, if you want to search configuration files, start searching in the **/etc** directory:

```
find /etc
```

The preceding command will show you all the files in **/etc**.

After the location, the next parameter is an expression containing one or more tests. To list the most common tests, use the following:

- **-type**, **f** for file, **d** for directory, **b** for block device
- **-name <pattern>**
- **-user** and **-group**
- **-perm**
- **-size**
- **-exec**

You can perform a combination of these tests. For instance, to search for files with filenames that end in **conf**, use the following:

```
find /etc -type f -name '*conf'
```

For some tests, such as **size** and **atime**, it's possible to add a so-called comparison with a provided parameter:

- **+n**: Greater than **n**
- **-n**: Less than **n**
- **n**: Exactly **n**

The **find** command searches for files and directories and compares them to the value of **n**:

```
find / -type d -size +100M
```

This example will search for directories with content that exceeds 100 MB.

The last parameter is the action that should be executed on the files that were found. Examples include:

- **-ls**, output is similar to the **ls** command.
- **-print** to print the filenames.
- **-printf** to format the output of the **-print** command.
- **-fprintf** to write the formatted output to a file.

The **-printf** parameter can be extremely useful. For instance, this command will search for files and list their size in bytes and the filename. After that, you can use the **sort** command to sort files by size:

```
find /etc -name '*conf' -printf '%s,%p\n' | sort -rn
```

There are some more dangerous actions as well, such as **-delete** to remove the files found and **-exec** to execute an external command. Be very sure of the result of your search action before using these parameters. Most of the time, performance-wise, you are better off using the **xargs** utility anyway. This utility takes the results and converts them into arguments to a command. An example of such a command is as follows; the **grep** utility is being used to search the content of the result:

```
find /etc/ -name '*' -type f| xargs grep "127.0.0.1"
```

Process Management

In the previous section, we discussed the filesystem in Linux. From a system administrator's perspective, managing processes is crucial. There will be scenarios where you'll need to start, stop, or even kill processes. Also, to avoid throttling your machine, you need to be cautious about the processes running on the system. Let's take a closer look at process management in Linux.

Processes are run by the Linux kernel, started by a user, or created by other processes. All processes are child processes of process number one, which will be covered in the next chapter. In this section, we'll learn to identify processes and how to send a signal to a process.

View Processes

If you start a program, a **process ID** (**PID**) is assigned to the process and a corresponding directory is created in **/proc**.

In Bash, you can find the PID of the current shell with:

```
echo $$
```

You can also find the PID of the parent shell:

```
echo $PPID
```

To find the PID of a program on your filesystem, use the **pidof** utility:

```
pidof sshd
```

You might see multiple PIDs returned by the shell. If you want to return only one PID, use the **-s** parameter, which stands for single shot:

```
pidof -s sshd
```

Let's have a look in the **proc** directory of the current shell:

```
[root@localhost ~]# cd /proc/$$
[root@localhost 1226]# ls
attr                cpuset    limits      net            projid_map  stat
autogroup           cwd       loginuid    ns             root        statm
auxv                environ   map_files   numa_maps      sched       status
cgroup              exe       maps        oom_adj        schedstat   syscall
clear_refs          fd        mem         oom_score      sessionid   task
cmdline             fdinfo    mountinfo   oom_score_adj  setgroups   timers
comm                gid_map   mounts      pagemap        smaps       uid_map
coredump_filter     io        mountstats  personality    stack       wchan
```

Figure 3.24: proc directory of the current shell

You can see all the properties of this process. Let's look at some of them:

- **cmdline**: The command that is executed to create this process

- **environ**: The environment variables that are available to this process

- **status**: The status of the file, the **UID** (**User Identifier**), and the **GID** (**Group Identifier**) of the user/group that owns the process

If you execute **cat environ**, the output is difficult to read because the end-of-line character is **\0** instead of **\n**. You can fix this using the **tr** command to translate the **\0** into **\n**:

```
cat /proc/$$/environ | tr "\0" "\n"
```

The **proc** directory is very interesting for troubleshooting, but there are also many tools that use this information to produce more human-friendly output. One of these utilities is the **ps** command. There is something strange about this command; it supports three different types of parameters:

- **Unix style**: Preceded by a dash. Commands can be grouped. **ps -ef** is the same as **ps -e -f**.

- **BSD style**: Not preceded by a dash. Commands can be grouped. **ps ax** is the same as **ps a x**.

- **GNU style**: Preceded by a double dash and a long-named option. Commands cannot be grouped.

The output formatting for the three styles is not the same, but you can modify the behavior with options. A comparison follows:

```
[root@localhost ~]# ps -ef | head -5
UID          PID   PPID  C STIME TTY          TIME CMD
root           1      0  0 02:15 ?        00:00:01 /usr/lib/systemd/systemd --swi
tched-root --system --deserialize 21
root           2      0  0 02:15 ?        00:00:00 [kthreadd]
root           3      2  0 02:15 ?        00:00:00 [ksoftirqd/0]
root           5      2  0 02:15 ?        00:00:00 [kworker/0:0H]
[root@localhost ~]# ps aux | head -5
USER       PID %CPU %MEM    VSZ   RSS TTY      STAT START   TIME COMMAND
root         1  0.0  0.6 128168  6836 ?        Ss   02:15   0:01 /usr/lib/syste
md/systemd --switched-root --system --deserialize 21
root         2  0.0  0.0      0     0 ?        S    02:15   0:00 [kthreadd]
root         3  0.0  0.0      0     0 ?        S    02:15   0:00 [ksoftirqd/0]
root         5  0.0  0.0      0     0 ?        S<   02:15   0:00 [kworker/0:0H]
```

Figure 3.25: Using the ps utility with its parameters

The processes between square brackets are kernel processes.

You can query for specific values, for instance:

```
ps -q $$ -o comm
```

This is the same as:

```
cat /proc/$$/cmdline
```

Another utility that can help you search for a process is **pgrep**. It searches on values such as the name and user and shows the PID by default. The output can be formatted using parameters such as **-l** to list the process name, or **-o** to add the full command to the output.

An interactive way to monitor processes uses the **top** command:

```
top - 03:12:45 up 57 min,  5 users,  load average: 0.00, 0.01, 0.05
Tasks: 104 total,   1 running, 103 sleeping,   0 stopped,   0 zombie
%Cpu(s):  0.0 us,  0.3 sy,  0.0 ni, 99.7 id,  0.0 wa,  0.0 hi,  0.0 si,  0.0 st
KiB Mem :   998636 total,   668612 free,   165676 used,   164348 buff/cache
KiB Swap:  2097148 total,  2097148 free,        0 used.   657180 avail Mem

  PID USER      PR  NI    VIRT    RES    SHR S %CPU %MEM     TIME+ COMMAND
 2042 root      20   0  157584   2132   1500 R  0.3  0.2   0:00.03 top
    1 root      20   0  128168   6836   4068 S  0.0  0.7   0:01.95 systemd
    2 root      20   0       0      0      0 S  0.0  0.0   0:00.00 kthreadd
    3 root      20   0       0      0      0 S  0.0  0.0   0:00.06 ksoftirqd/0
```

Figure 3.26: Monitoring processes using the top command

The values in the columns for a process visible in **top** are the same as in **ps**. In the man page of **top**, you can find a good explanation of what they mean. Some of them will be covered in later chapters.

The **top** command, or the fancier **htop** command, can help you to quickly identify processes taking too much memory or CPU and send a signal to the process. If you want detailed and advanced process monitoring and troubleshooting, it's better to use the tooling available in Azure. This is covered in *Chapter 11, Troubleshooting and Monitoring Your Workloads*.

Sending Signals to a Process

In the real world, you might encounter an issue where a particular process is consuming a lot of memory. At this point, you might want to send a kill signal to the process. Likewise, you may encounter different scenarios while dealing with processes. In this section, we will be exploring different signals that can be sent to the process. On the man page for signals, section 7, you can find more info about signals. A signal is a message to a process, for instance, to change the priority or to kill it. There are many different signals described in this manual, but only a few are really important:

- **Signal 1**: This hangs the process; it will reload everything that is attached to a process. Commonly used to reread a changed configuration file.

- **Signal 2**: This is the same as *Ctrl + C* and *Ctrl + Break*.

- **Signal 3**: Normal quitting of a process; the same as *Ctrl + D*.

- **Signal 15**: Default signal, used to terminate a command, giving the terminal time to clean up everything nicely.

- **Signal 9**: Kill a command without cleanup. This is dangerous and can make your system unstable and sometimes even vulnerable.

If you would like to see the list of signals that can be sent to a process, run:

```
kill -l
```

To send a signal to a process, you can use the **top** (shortcut **k**) or **kill** command:

```
kill -HUP <PID>
```

There is a nice utility you can use to grep a process or group of processes; it sends a signal at once: **pkill**. It's similar to **pgrep**. Selection is possible on values such as **name** and **uid**.

Discretionary Access Control

Now that we have covered the filesystem and process management, there should be a way to restrict permissions to the files that you are creating. In other words, you shouldn't grant everyone access to everything and most organizations follow the principle of giving the most granular permissions. **Discretionary Access Control (DAC)** is a security implementation that restricts access to objects such as files and directories. A user or a group of users gets access based on ownership and the permissions on the objects.

In cloud environments, user and group management may not be a part of your daily job. It's often delegated to identity management systems such as **Active Directory (AD)**, and you don't need many user accounts; authentication and authorization at an application level are more important nowadays. But it's still a good idea to be able to verify users and know how the underlying system works.

User Management

If you deploy a VM in Azure, in the wizard you'll specify a user, which will be created by the Azure Agent user management in the VM—for instance, if you deploy a VM with PowerShell:

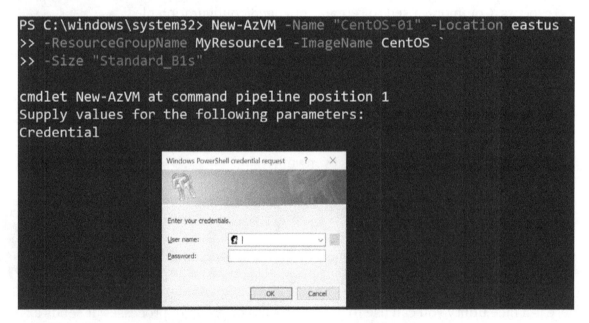

Figure 3.27: Deploying a VM with PowerShell

You can use this account to log in. It's a normal user, also called an unprivileged user, which doesn't have administrative privileges. To gain administrative privileges, you need the **sudo** command; **sudo** means superuser do (or do as superuser). Without parameters, the **su** command switches your current user to another user, root–the administrator account in Linux.

> **Note**
>
> If you want root privileges, in some Linux images in Azure you can't use the **su** command. It's disabled by default. To get a root shell, you can use **sudo -s**. By default, the **sudo** command will ask you for your password.

To get more information about this user account, use the **getent** command to get an entity from the **passwd** database, where the user information is stored. This **passwd** database can be local, stored in a **/etc/passwd** file, or can be remote, where a remote server will grant authorization by checking the user database, **Lightweight Directory Access Protocol** (**LDAP**) for example:

```
sudo getent passwd <username>
```

To get the details for the **linvirt** user:

```
[linvirt@CentOS-01 ~]$ sudo getent passwd linvirt
[sudo] password for linvirt:
linvirt:x:1000:1000::/home/linvirt:/bin/bash
```

Figure 3.28: Using getent to get details of linvirt

The output of this command is a colon-separated list:

- User account name
- Password
- User ID
- Group ID
- **General Electric Comprehensive Operating System** (**GECOS**) field for extra account information
- Home directory for this user
- Default shell

In the early days of the Unix operating system family, the password was stored in the **/etc/passwd** file, but for security reasons the hashed password was moved to **/etc/shadow**. The password can be changed with:

```
sudo passwd <username>
```

If you want to change the password of the current user, you don't need to use **sudo**, and don't need to specify the username. You can view the entry in the **/etc/shadow** file with **getent**:

```
[linvirt@CentOS-01 ~]$ sudo getent shadow linvirt
linvirt:$
                                1:17645:0:99999:7:::
```

Figure 3.29: Checking password entry using the getent command

The columns after the hashed password contain aging information that can be viewed (and changed) with the **chage** command. The notation in the shadow database is notated by the number of days since epoch (the virtual birthday of Unix: January 1, 1970). The **chage** command translates it into a more human-readable form:

```
[linvirt@CentOS-01 ~]$ chage -l linvirt
Last password change                                    : Apr 24, 2018
Password expires                                        : never
Password inactive                                       : never
Account expires                                         : never
Minimum number of days between password change          : 0
Maximum number of days between password change          : 99999
Number of days of warning before password expires       : 7
```

Figure 3.30: Using the chage command to get aging information

Let's go back to the **passwd** database. The numbering of the user ID is defined in the **/etc/login.defs** file. ID **0** is reserved for the root account. IDs **1** to **200** are reserved for **admin** accounts that are not in use any longer in modern Linux systems. In Red Hat–based distributions, the range 201–999 is reserved for system accounts, and daemons run under these accounts. The range for unprivileged accounts is between 1,000 and 60,000 for local users and >60,000 for remote users (for example, AD or LDAP users). There are small differences between Linux distributions. Let's summarize the values:

User IDs	User Type
0	Root
1–200	Admin accounts
201–999	System accounts
1,000–60,000	Local users
60,000+	Remote users

Figure 3.31: User IDs with their reserved user types

Many distributions are configured with the so-called **User Private Group (UPG)** scheme, thanks to the directive in the **/etc/login.defs** file:

```
USERGROUPS_ENAB  yes
```

This means that if you create a user, a primary group is automatically created with the same name as the login. If you disable this functionality, a newly created user becomes a member of another group automatically, defined in **/etc/default/useradd**:

```
GROUP=100
```

The GECOS field can be changed with the **chfn** command:

```
[linvirt@CentOS-01 ~]$ sudo chfn linvirt
[sudo] password for linvirt:
Changing finger information for linvirt.
Name []: Jane Roe
Office []: 112
Office Phone []: 00-01
Home Phone []: 00-02
```

Figure 3.32: Changing GECOS field with the chfn command

Note:

The **chfn** (change finger) command refers to an old utility, **finger**, which is not installed by default but is still available in repositories. A **finger** daemon that makes the GECOS information available via the network is available as well, but it's considered a security risk.

The default shell while creating a user is defined in **/etc/default/useradd**. You can change the default shell to another using the **chsh** command. The shell must be listed in the **/etc/shells** file:

```
chsh -s /bin/tcsh linvirt
```

For the purpose of this book, keep Bash as the default shell.

In this section, you learned how to verify and change the properties of an existing local user. Of course, you can add additional users as well:

```
sudo useradd <username>
```

The **useradd** command has a lot of customization options. You can learn more about this using **man useradd**. Alternatively, you can use the **adduser** command:

```
▢  / adduser john
Adding user `john' ...
Adding new group `john' (1001) ...
Adding new user `john' (1001) with group `john' ...
Creating home directory `/home/john' ...
Copying files from `/etc/skel' ...
Enter new UNIX password:
Retype new UNIX password:
passwd: password updated successfully
Changing the user information for john
Enter the new value, or press ENTER for the default
        Full Name []: John Doe
        Room Number []: 11
        Work Phone []: 000-000-0000
        Home Phone []: 000-000-0000
        Other []:
Is the information correct? [Y/n] y
▢  /
```

Figure 3.33: Adding a user with the adduser command

Group Management

As discussed in the previous chapter, a user will be part of a primary group. When you create a user, if you don't specify a group, a group will be created with the same name as the username. If you check the previous screenshot, you can see a group named **john** for the user **john**.

Besides being a member of a primary group, additional group memberships can be added. This is necessary to get access to a group directory/share or to delegate privileges in the **sudo** configuration. You can add existing additional groups with the **--groups** parameter of the **useradd** command during the creation of a user, or afterward with **usermod** or **groupmems**.

Let's create a new user and a new group and verify the results:

```
sudo useradd student

sudo passwd student

sudo getent passwd student

sudo groupadd staff

sudo getent group staff
```

Make the **student** user a member of the **staff** group:

```
sudo groupmems -g staff -a student
```

Alternatively:

```
sudo usermod -aG staff student

sudo groupmems -g staff -l

sudo getent group staff
```

You can change your primary group temporarily with **switch group** (**sg**):

```
su student

id -g

sg staff
```

> **Note:**
>
> It's not very common, but you can add a password to a group account using the **gpasswd** command. This way, a user that is not a member of this group can still use **sg** and enter the password for the group.

A very special group is the **wheel** group. In the **sudo** configuration, a user that is a member of this group is able to execute commands that need administrative privileges. In Ubuntu, this group is not available; instead, there is a group called **sudo** that can be used for the same purpose.

Login Management

In an enterprise environment, administrators are required to collect information such as the number of users logged in, the number of invalid logins, and whether any authorized users tried to log in for security auditing purposes. In this chapter, we'll cover login management in Linux, which is crucial from a security standpoint.

Any login into a Linux system is registered, tracked, and managed by a service called **systemd-logind** and a corresponding command: **loginctl**. This command is available for all Linux distributions; however, if you are using **Windows Subsystem for Linux** (**WSL**), due to the lack of systemd, this will not be available.

The parameters of this command are divided into sections for users, sessions, and seats. To do some exercises with these parameters, open a second **ssh** session to your VM using the credentials of the student account. Execute the commands in the first **ssh** session.

First, list the sessions:

```
loginctl list-sessions
```

Note down the session ID(s) and the details of a particular session:

```
loginctl show-session <session number>
```

In my case, the session ID is **27**, so we will be checking the session details using **loginctl**:

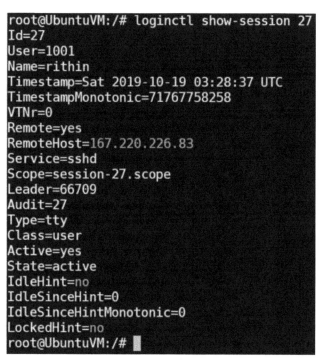

Figure 3.34: Checking the session details for session ID 27

View the user properties:

```
loginctl show-user <username>
```

Switch to the second SSH session and execute **man man**.

Now switch login management back to the first SSH session and view the status of the student using the **user-status** parameter:

```
student (1001)
            Since: Tue 2018-04-24 12:16:08 UTC; 14min ago
            State: active
         Sessions: *43
             Unit: user-1001.slice
                  └─session-43.scope
                     ├─37090 sshd: student [priv]
                     ├─37097 sshd: student@pts/1
                     ├─37098 -bash
                     ├─37475 man man
                     └─37487 less -s
```

Figure 3.35: Using the user-status parameter

Finally, terminate the session:

```
sudo loginctl terminate-session <session id>
```

There is also a **terminate-user** parameter that can be handy if there are multiple users in one session.

Summary

This chapter was a sort of crash course on how to survive in Linux if you are unfamiliar with the operating system. This chapter was not about how to become a senior Linux administrator.

In your daily life as an administrator in Azure, you may not use everything in this chapter. For instance, you might not create users in a VM. But you should be able to verify users configured in an identity management system such as AD and verify that they are able to log in.

This chapter was all about using shells, the structure of the filesystem, and finding files. We looked at the role of text files in Linux and how to process and edit them. We worked with processes and saw how to view and kill them. And, last but not least, we looked at user and group management.

In the next chapter, we will discuss managing resources in Azure.

Questions

In this chapter, instead of answering some questions, I want you to do an exercise:

1. Create the users `Lisa`, `John`, `Karel`, and `Carola`.

2. Set the passwords for these users to `welc0meITG`.

3. Verify the existence of these users.

4. Create `finance` and `staff` groups.

5. Make the users `Lisa` and `Carola` members of `finance`, and `Karel` and `John` members of `staff`.

6. Create the /home/staff and /home/finance directories and set the group ownership of these directories to staff and home, respectively.

7. Give the staff group read access to the finance directory.

8. Make sure that newly created files receive the correct group ownership and permissions.

Further Reading

There are many books that are published for users that are new to the Linux operating system. Here are a few of my personal favorites.

Working with Linux - Quick Hacks for the Command Line (ISBN 978-1787129184) by Petru Işfan and Bogdan Vaida is a strange collection of nice tips and tricks, and sometimes that is all you need.

If you are able to read German, all the books by Michael Kofler (https://kofler.info) should be on your bookshelf, even if you are an experienced Linux user!

The Microsoft website hosts very good documentation on regular expressions: https://docs.microsoft.com/en-us/dotnet/standard/base-types/regular-expressions. And I do like http://regexone.com if you want to practice using regular expressions.

The **awk** utility comes with a big manual (https://www.gnu.org/software/gawk/manual/gawk.html), but it's maybe not the best place to start. Shiwang Kalkhanda did a very good job in *Learning AWK Programming* (ISBN 978-1788391030), producing a very readable book. Don't be afraid of the word *Programming* in this title, especially if you are not a developer; you should read this book.

4

Managing Azure

In *Chapter 2, Getting Started with the Azure Cloud*, we took our first steps on a journey into the world of Azure. We discovered that there are many ways to manage an Azure environment and that these include the Azure portal and command-line interfaces. You can use the command-line interfaces within the Azure portal to run them on your workstation. Later in this book, we'll see that there are other great possibilities using automation and orchestration solutions. At the end of *Chapter 3, Basic Linux Administration*, we created a Linux VM and explored the basics of the Linux environment.

Before we continue our journey, covering more advanced topics, this chapter covers components of the Azure infrastructure that are needed for our workloads, VMs, and containers. We discussed the filesystem in Linux, but how will we add more data disks to the VM? As a system administrator, you might need to allow or deny traffic to your VM based on your business requirements, but how this can be done in Azure? There will be scenarios where you need to have multiple network interfaces attached to the VM. How will you accomplish that? This section will answer all your questions on how to manage Azure resources that are related to your VM. We're talking about components that we've already used in previous chapters, sometimes even without knowing that we did.

Basically, this chapter is about Azure resources. And, remember, they are all part of a resource group, a logical container into which resources are deployed and managed. The following are some of the key takeaways from this chapter:

- Managing storage resources in Azure and different storage options available
- Managing networking resources in Azure and understanding their role in VMs
- Using handy commands in PowerShell and the Azure CLI to manage resources in Azure

> **Note**
>
> In this book, we try to be as agnostic as possible regarding the available interfaces. Because this chapter is more about the theory than the interfaces, we'll use PowerShell as an example.

Managing Azure Resources Using the Azure CLI and PowerShell

In this chapter, we will see how we can manage Azure resources using PowerShell and the Azure CLI. Every task that we are going to do here can also be done from the Azure portal. However, as a system administrator who is performing day-to-day tasks from the terminal, you should be able to manage your resources using the CLI or PowerShell. Almost every command in this chapter is written in PowerShell; however, at the end of this chapter, you will find the Azure CLI equivalent command for every command in PowerShell. The list of commands is way too long, so it's better to refer to the official Microsoft documentation or use the respective help commands.

In some instances, even in upcoming chapters, we will use the Azure portal. This is to simplify the process and to get you all introduced to an alternate method. You can use the portal if you prefer, but when it comes to automating tasks and orchestrating deployment, the CLI or PowerShell experience is a prerequisite. So, we would encourage you all to follow the PowerShell commands in this chapter and invest your time in testing the equivalent commands using the Azure CLI.

Here are some of the technical requirements to complete the tasks in this chapter.

Technical Requirements

For this chapter, basic knowledge of storage and networking is required. In the *Further reading* section, you can find some suggestions to prepare yourself.

It's not necessary, but it's a good idea to have at least one VM up and running. This way, you will not only be able to create new resources in this chapter but also look at the properties of an existing VM. In this section, we will create an Ubuntu VM named **ubuntu01** in the **chapter4** resource group for the examples.

Set the variables for the resource group and the location:

```
$myRG = "chapter4"

$myLocation = "westus"

$myTestVM = "ubuntu01"
```

Create the resource group:

```
New-AzResourceGroup -Name $myRG -Location $myLocation
```

Create the VM:

```
New-AzVm '
  -ResourceGroupName $myRG '
  -Name $myTestVM '
  -ImageName UbuntuLTS '
  -Location $myLocation '
  -VirtualNetworkName "$myTestVM-Vnet" '
  -SubnetName $myTestVM-Subnet '
  -SecurityGroupName "$myTestVM-NSG" '
  -PublicIpAddressName $myTestVM-pip
```

For now, the parameters used in this example are not important; at the end of this chapter, you'll be able to understand them all.

Not a real requirement, but nice to have, is the Azure Storage Explorer utility, which is available for free at https://azure.microsoft.com/en-us/features/storage-explorer. This is a standalone utility to install on your workstation. This utility will help you upload, download, and manage Azure blobs, files, queues, and tables. It also supports Azure Cosmos DB and Azure Data Lake. Another advantage is you can access the disks attached to VMs. Storage Explorer is also available as an option in the Azure portal.

Managing Storage Resources

Microsoft's cloud solution for handling data storage is Azure Storage. Azure Storage offers high availability, security, scalability, and accessibility. In Azure, we have different types of data or storage services. They are:

- Azure Blobs
- Azure Files
- Azure Queue
- Azure Table

Let's take a closer look at each of these and understand what they are:

- **Azure Blobs**: Optimized objects for storing massive amounts of unstructured data, such as text or binary data. They're often used to make data available to other resources, for instance, to store VHD files that can be used to create virtual disks. Another use case is to use them as storage for audio and video files. Making a blob publicly accessible, it's even possible to stream data.

- **Azure Files**: Azure Files are file shares hosted in Azure that can be accessed via **Server Message Block** (**SMB**) and can be mounted to your local computer. You might wonder how these are different from normal file shares. The added advantage here is that the URL that will be generated will include a **shared access signature** (**SAS**) and the file share will be able to be accessed from anywhere in the world.

- **Azure Queue**: Used for passing messages from one resource to another, especially for serverless services such as Azure Web Apps and Functions. It can also be used to create a backlog of work to process asynchronously.

- **Azure Table**: This is for the Azure Cosmos DB service.

- **Azure Disk**: This is for managed disk storage and unmanaged disks.

In this chapter, we will only cover Blob storage, Azure Files, and disk storage, because Queue and Table storage are for specific solutions that are only important for application developers.

> **Note**
>
> If you have an enormous amount of data you want to store in the cloud, uploading can take too much time. Microsoft has a service called Azure Data Box Disk. It lets you send encrypted SSDs to your datacenter, copy the data, and send it back. For more information, visit https://docs.microsoft.com/en-gb/azure/databox/data-box-disk-overview.

Storage Accounts

A storage account provides a namespace that is unique across Azure to contain storage objects such as blobs, files, tables, queues, and so on. An account is needed to access the storage. It also defines the type of storage that is being used.

There are three different kinds of storage accounts:

- **Storage**: This old type of deprecated storage account doesn't support all features (for instance, there is no archive option). It's often more expensive than the newer V2.

- **StorageV2**: This is a newer type of storage account. It supports all types of storage and the latest features for blobs, files, queues, and tables.

- **BlobStorage**: This has not been deprecated yet, but there is no reason to use it any longer. The biggest problem with this account type is that you can't store files such as VHDs.

> **Note**
>
> You don't need to create a storage account for managed disks. However, if you want to store VM boot diagnostic data, you'll need one. A boot diagnostic account is very useful if your VMs go to non-bootable state. The logs stored in this account can be used to find the root cause for the non-booting state of the VM. For testing, this is not a mandatory option, but for production workloads it is recommended to enable boot diagnostics, which will help you to understand what went wrong during a failure.

Another property is the SKU, as covered in *Chapter 2, Getting Started with the Azure Cloud*. It specifies what type of replication applies to the storage account. Here are the available types and, if you recall, we've already discussed what they are:

- **Standard_LRS**: Locally redundant storage accounts storage accounts
- **Premium_LRS**: The same as LRS but supports FileStorage and BlockBlobStorage
- **Standard_GRS**: Geo-redundant storage accounts
- **Standard_RAGRS**: Read-access geo-redundant storage accounts
- **Standard_ZRS**: Zone-redundant storage accounts

The last important property is the access tier; it specifies the optimization of the storage. There are three types available:

- **Hot storage tier**: Data that needs to be accessed frequently will be stored in the hot tier.
- **Cool storage tier**: Data that is accessed infrequently and is stored for at least 30 days.
- **Archive storage tier**: Data that is rarely accessed and is stored for a period of at least 180 days with flexible latency requirements.

Setting an object-level access tier is only supported for Standard LRS, GRS, RA-GRS BlobStorage, and General Purpose V2 accounts. **General Purpose V1 (GPv1)** accounts don't support tiering.

The choice made for the access tier also affects the cost; for instance, archive storage offers the lowest storage costs but also the highest access costs.

The storage account name must be between three and 24 characters in length and must use only numbers and lowercase letters. Storage account names must be unique in Azure. Microsoft suggests using a globally unique name and a random number:

```
New-AzStorageAccount '
  -ResourceGroupName <resource group> '
  -SkuName <sku> '
  -Location <location> '
  -Kind StorageV2 '
  -AccessTier <access tier> '
  -name <storage account>
```

Let's create a storage account with redundancy as Standard_LRS:

```
$mySA = New-AzStorageAccount '
  -ResourceGroupName $myRG '
  -SkuName Standard_LRS '
  -Location $myLocation '
  -Kind StorageV2 '
  -AccessTier Hot '
  -name chapter4$(Get-Random -Minimum 1001 -Maximum 9999)
```

Check the available storage accounts in your subscription:

```
Get-AzStorageAccount | Select StorageAccountName, Location
```

```
> Get-AzStorageAccount | Select StorageAccountName, Location

StorageAccountName  Location
------------------  --------
chapter42298        westus
linvirtcloudsh2019  westeurope
loastorage          westus2
```

Figure 4.1: Available storage accounts

In the screenshot, you can see that there are three storage accounts available in three different regions for this subscription.

Storage accounts are protected by keys. You'll need the key if you want access to a storage account. A set of two keys are automatically created during the creation of an account. If you are still in the same session as when you created the account, you can receive the key:

```
$mySA | Get-AzStorageAccountKey | Format-Table -Wrap
```

Otherwise, you can use the following:

```
Get-AzStorageAccountKey '
  -ResourceGroupName <resource group>'
  -Name <storage account name>
```

In the following screenshot, the **chapter42298** storage account available in the **$MyRG** resource group has a set of protected keys:

```
> Get-AzStorageAccountKey -ResourceGroupName $myRG -Name chapter42298

KeyName Value
------- -----
key1    fd5RuIJkUG/sQX2L65PnxaIe9hk+MCQB8NhmW0Ay0o4zpk2Gx3XOLoaDDoUr2XcCvWL55Q...
key2    tjW9hjpr/PAW3QjN7WEcLbs6wv/BSf67RiSVVDqRtaXzpExY/gugNORILoOYG7GtsPXWDd...
```

Figure 4.2: Fetching keys for chapter42298 storage account

Managed Disks

Earlier, when we deployed a VM, we needed to create a storage account where we could save the **virtual hard disk** (**VHD**) of the VM. Later, Microsoft introduced **Managed Disks** where we can simply create a disk and Microsoft takes care of the underlying storage account. On top of that, customers get added advantages such as easy resizing, more encryption options, and better performance.

When you create a VM with a managed disk, two disks will be attached to the VM: an OS disk and a temporary disk. All the disks are in VHD format. The data stored on the temporary disk will be cleared when you restart the VM, so Microsoft doesn't recommend storing important data on the temporary disk as it is not persistent.

You can also add extra managed data disks. First, create the disk configuration:

```
New-AzDiskConfig -Location <location>'
   -DiskSizeGB <size> -OsType Linux -SkuName <sku>  '
   -CreateOption empty
```

Let's see how to create a sample disk configuration with a size of 5 GB and redundancy as Standard_LRS:

```
$diskconfig = New-AzDiskConfig -Location $myLocation '
   -DiskSizeGB 5 -OsType Linux -SkuName Standard_LRS '
   -CreateOption empty
```

Now, you can create the actual disk:

```
New-AzDisk -ResourceGroupName <resource group name> '
   -DiskName <disk name> -Disk <disk configuration>
```

For example, here's an implementation of the preceding command:

```
$Disk01 = New-AzDisk -ResourceGroupName $myRG '
    -DiskName 'Disk01' -Disk $diskconfig
```

By executing the **$Disk01** command, you'll see the newly created disk. In the following screenshot, the output is limited to make it more readable:

Figure 4.3: Output of the $Disk01 command

The next step is to attach the managed datadisk. To do this, we'll need the disk ID. So, we'll run the following command using the disk name to find the ID:

```
Get-AzDisk -DiskName <disk name> | select Id
```

Add the data disk:

```
Add-AzVMDataDisk -VM $myVM -Name <disk name> '
    -ManagedDiskId <disk id> -Lun <lun number> -CreateOption Attach
```

A **Logical Unit Number** (**LUN**) is a number used to identify the storage in the VM. You can start numbering at zero. Finally, update the VM settings:

```
Update-AzVM '
    -ResourceGroupName <resource group> '
    -VM <virtual machine>
```

You can now add the data disk to the VM. To summarize with a complete example, first you'll need all the properties of the VM. To get the properties of the VM, we will use the following command and save the properties to a variable, **$myVM**:

```
$myVM = Get-AzVM -ResourceGroupName $myRG -Name $myTestVM
```

The next command is to add the disk that was created earlier on to the VM:

```
Add-AzVMDataDisk -VM $myVM -Name Disk01 '
    -ManagedDiskId $Disk01.Id -Lun 1 -CreateOption Attach
```

The preceding command will show you the configured properties of the VM, as shown in this screenshot:

```
> $myVM = Get-AzVM -ResourceGroupName $myRG -Name $myTestVM
> Add-AzVMDataDisk -VM $myVM -Name Disk01 `
>>     -ManagedDiskId $Disk01.Id -Lun 1 -CreateOption Attach


ResourceGroupName : chapter4
Id                : /subscriptions/                              /resourc
eGroups/chapter4/providers/Microsoft.Compute/virtualMachines/ubuntu01
VmId              : 0ddc62e9-dda1-4e44-9cf7-fb9dce986e50
Name              : ubuntu01
Type              : Microsoft.Compute/virtualMachines
Location          : westus
Tags              : {}
HardwareProfile   : {VmSize}
NetworkProfile    : {NetworkInterfaces}
OSProfile         : {ComputerName, AdminUsername, LinuxConfiguration, Secrets,
AllowExtensionOperations}
ProvisioningState : Succeeded
StorageProfile    : {ImageReference, OsDisk, DataDisks}
```

Figure 4.4: Adding the created disk on the VM

As we can see from the output, the information is added to the **StorageProfile**, but the change is not active yet.

To make it active, use **Update-AzVM**. The output should give you the **StatusCode** as **OK**:

```
Update-AzVM -ResourceGroupName $myRG -VM $myVM
```

As you can see in the following screenshot, **IsSuccessStatusCode** is telling you that the request was received. **StatusCode** is the result of the request:

```
> Update-AzVM -ResourceGroupName $myRG -VM $myVM

RequestId IsSuccessStatusCode StatusCode ReasonPhrase
--------- ------------------- ---------- ------------
                         True         OK OK
```

Figure 4.5: Using the Update-AzVM command to update the StatusCode

Verify the result:

```
$myVM.StorageProfile.DataDisks
```

Or, even better, instead of reusing the variables, just query all the information in this one-liner:

```
$(Get-AzVM -Name $myTestVM '
  -ResourceGroupName $myRG).StorageProfile.DataDisks
```

You can see the name, size, and LUN:

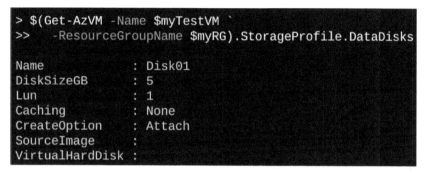

Figure 4.6: Disk storage profile

Azure Files

Instead of adding data disks to a VM, you can use **Azure Files**. If you recall, we discussed Azure Files at the very beginning of this chapter and mentioned that it's different from a normal file share. Azure Files is a fully managed file shares in the cloud, which can be accessed via **Server Message Block** (**SMB**), and this can be mounted to Linux, Windows, and macOS.

Azure Files needs a storage account and supports Standard_LRS, Standard_ZRS, Standard_GRS, and Standard_ZRS (only on selected regions) SKU types. There are no premium storage or other access tiers than the standard (hot) available. (At the time of writing this book, sources at Microsoft state that there is no timeline available for the introduction of these features.)

Please note that you will really require the SMB 3.0 protocol for performance reasons. This means that you need a recent Linux distribution such as one of these listed here:

- RHEL-based distributions 7.5 or higher
- Ubuntu 16.04 or higher
- Debian 9
- SUSE SLE 12 SP3 / OpenSUSE LEAP 42.3 or higher

You also need to force version 3 with the mount option: **vers=3.0**.

The first step involves creating the Azure Files share:

```
New-AzStorageShare '
   -Name <share name> -Context <storage account context>
```

For the storage account context, you can use the variable that was used to create the storage account or create the variable again:

```
$mySA = (Get-AzStorageAccount | Where-Object {$_.StorageAccountName -Like
"chapter*"})
```

Let's implement this and create a new file share:

```
$myShare01 = New-AzStorageShare '
   -Name "myshare01-staff" -Context $mySA.Context
```

Let's check the value of **$myShare01**. The output clearly shows you the URL of the storage, when you created it, and whether snapshots are available or not:

```
> $myShare01 = New-AzStorageShare `
>>    -Name "myshare01-staff" -Context $mySA.Context
> $myShare01


   File End Point: https://chapter42298.file.core.windows.net/
Name                                                        LastM IsSn Snap
                                                            odifi apsh shot
                                                            ed      ot Time
----                                                        ----- ---- ----
myshare01-staff                                             8/20… Fal…
```

Figure 4.7: Output of myShare01

To review the properties of the created share, execute the following command:

```
(Get-AzStorageShare -Context $mySA.Context).Uri
```

As you can see in the following screenshot, it will give you the same output with a little bit more information, which is not important at all for our purposes:

```
> (Get-AzStorageShare -Context $mySA.Context).Uri

AbsolutePath    : /myshare01-staff
AbsoluteUri     : https://chapter42298.file.core.windows.net/myshare01-staff
LocalPath       : /myshare01-staff
Authority       : chapter42298.file.core.windows.net
HostNameType    : Dns
IsDefaultPort   : True
IsFile          : False
IsLoopback      : False
PathAndQuery    : /myshare01-staff
Segments        : {/, myshare01-staff}
IsUnc           : False
Host            : chapter42298.file.core.windows.net
Port            : 443
Query           :
Fragment        :
Scheme          : https
OriginalString  : https://chapter42298.file.core.windows.net:443/myshare01-staff
DnsSafeHost     : chapter42298.file.core.windows.net
IdnHost         : chapter42298.file.core.windows.net
IsAbsoluteUri   : True
UserEscaped     : False
UserInfo        :
```

Figure 4.8: Properties of the created share

In Linux, you can mount the file share manually with the following code:

```
mount -t cifs \
  -o vers=3.0,username=<storage account>,password=<storage key>\
  //<storage account name>.file.core.windows.net/<share> \
  /<mount point>
```

Please note that we're not using the HTTPS scheme because CIFS is not using URIs. Azure will take care of the mapping between the different schemes.

Let's go ahead and mount the file share. Your password and storage file share will be different from the example as the name is unique across Azure:

```
mkdir /mnt/staff


mount -t cifs -o vers=3.0,username=chapter42585,password=.... \
  //chapter42585.file.core.windows.net/myshare-01.staff /mnt/staff
```

Also, you can use the connect option in the Azure portal (https://portal.azure.com/) for the file share and Azure will generate the commands for mounting the share to Linux as well as Windows and macOS systems.

In the following screenshot, you can see that upon clicking **Connect**, Azure generates the code to connect the file share to the Linux system. You can copy this code and paste this to your Linux system:

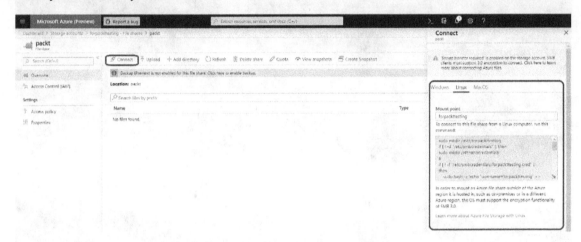

Figure 4.9: Connecting the file share to the Linux system

More information about Azure Files about mounting shares is available in *Chapter 5, Advanced Linux Administration*, in the *Mounting Remote Filesystems* section. The following is an example of a mount unit for Azure Files:

```
[Unit]
Description = Staff Share
[Mount]
What = //chapter42585.file.core.windows.net/myshare-01.staff
Where = /mnt/staff
Type = cifs
Options = vers=3.0,credentials=/root/.staff
```

Here, the **/root/.staffs** file contains the following entries:

```
username=<storage account>
password=<key>
```

Another great way to verify the share and manage the content is with Azure Storage Explorer. Start Azure Storage Explorer on your workstation and connect your Azure account. If you don't want to add the entire account, you also have the option to add just the storage account using the SAS key. Storage Explorer will show different types of resources on the left side, as shown in this screenshot:

Figure 4.10: Azure Storage Explorer

Azure Blob

Azure Blob storage is a storage service that stores unstructured data (images, video, audio, backup data, and so on that doesn't adhere to a data model) in the cloud as objects. Blob is object-based storage that can store any type of data.

Inside a storage account, you can have containers; containers are very similar to directories or folders on your computer. For example, if you are storing your favorite music files in Azure, you can set the account name as *Music* and inside that, you can create a container based on the genre or artists, and the actual music files are the blobs. A storage account can have an unlimited number of containers and a container can have an unlimited number of blobs.

Azure file shares are a great way to keep your data out of a VM. But they're file-based, and that's not the fastest choice for every data type. For instance, streaming from Azure Files, while possible, does not perform very well; uploading very big files can also be very challenging. Blob storage is a solution for this problem, and it scales much better: 5 TB for an Azure file share and 500 TB for a single blob container.

To be able to upload a blob, you have to create a container first:

```
New-AzStorageContainer -Name <container name> '
  -Context <context of storage account> -Permission blob
```

Here is an example of creating a container list:

```
$myContainer = New-AzStorageContainer '
  -Name container01 '
  -Context $mySA.context -Permission blob
```

```
> $myContainer = New-AzStorageContainer `
>>    -Name container01 `
>>    -Context $mySA.context -Permission blob
>
> $myContainer


   Blob End Point: https://chapter42298.blob.core.windows.net/
Name                    PublicAccess          LastModified
----                    ------------          ------------
container01             Blob                  8/20/19 2:07:07 PM +00:00
```

Figure 4.11: Creating a container list

There are three types of permissions available when creating a container:

- **Container**: Provides full read access to a container and its blobs. Clients can enumerate blobs in the container through anonymous requests; other containers are not visible.

- **Blob**: Provides read access to blob data throughout a container through anonymous requests but does not provide access to container data. Other blobs are not visible.

- **Off**: Restricts access to just the storage account owner.

You can use Azure Storage Explorer again to view the container:

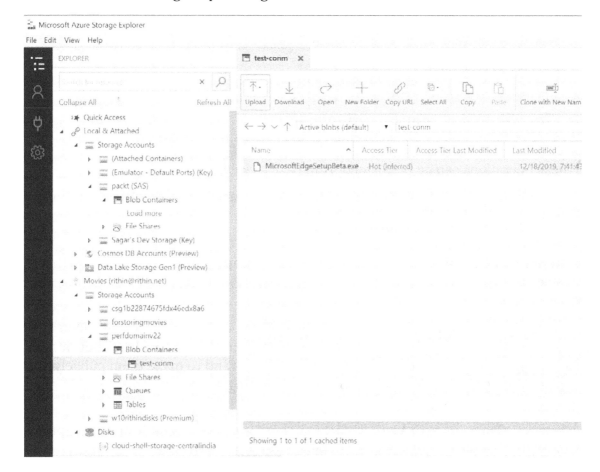

Figure 4.12: Viewing container using Azure storage explorer

Using PowerShell, you can create a blob:

```
Set-AzStorageBlobContent -File <filename> '
  -Container <container> -Blob <blobname> '
  -Context $mySA.context
```

You can verify the result using the following command:

```
Get-AzStorageBlob -Container <container name> '
  -Context $mySA.context | select Name
```

Now you can upload a file to the container, making it into a blob, for instance:

```
Set-AzStorageBlobContent -File "/Pictures/image.jpg" '
  -Container $myContainer.Name ' -Blob "Image1.jpg" '
  -Context $mySA.context
```

You can also list the result:

```
Get-AzStorageBlob -Container <container> '
  -Context $mySA.context | select Name
```

All these operations can be performed from Bash as well.

You can mount the blob from the Linux Blobfuse reference link using **Blobfuse**; for more information, visit https://github.com/Azure/azure-storage-fuse and https://docs. microsoft.com/en-us/azure/storage/blobs/storage-how-to-mount-container-linux.

An alternative solution to copy data into a blob is **AzCopy** (more information on this is available at https://docs.microsoft.com/en-us/azure/storage/common/storage-use-azcopy-linux).

But, honestly, most of the time, this is not the way you will use Blob storage. Blob storage is not something you want access to on an operating system level, but rather on an application level, to store objects such as images and to make them publicly available. Microsoft provides great examples for getting started at https://github.com/Azure-Samples?q=storage-blobs.

In *Chapter 7, Deploying Your Virtual Machine*, there is a good example of an exception: uploading a VHD file to create a custom image using that VHD.

Managing Network Resources

As discussed earlier, in *Chapter 3 Basic Linux Administration*, networking is very important. Azure Virtual Network is an Azure service that provides the following:

- Connectivity to your workload
- Connectivity from your workload to the outside world
- Connectivity between VMs
- Other connectivity options, such as VPN tunnels
- Traffic filtering
- Advanced routing options, including BGP routes through a VPN tunnel

Virtual Network

In Azure, the most important component of virtual networking is the **virtual network**, or **VNet** for short. A virtual network is crucial as it provides a highly secure isolated environment for your VMs to run in.

The following process might appear a little confusing and lengthy, but the intent here is to make you understand the process and commands. Let's start with the creation of a virtual network:

```
AzVirtualNetwork -Name <vnet name> '
  -ResourceGroupName <resource group> -Location <location>'
  -AddressPrefix <network>
```

So, if we wanted to create a virtual network with the name `MyVirtualNetwork` with the address space `10.0.0.0/16`, we would use:

```
$myVnet = New-AzVirtualNetwork -Name MyVirtualNetwork '
  -ResourceGroupName $myRG -Location $myLocation '
  -AddressPrefix "10.0.0.0/16"
```

Executing the variable you just created will show you all the properties:

```
> $myVnet

Name                   : MyVirtualNetwork
ResourceGroupName      : chapter4
Location               : westus
Id                     : /subscriptions/                              re
                         sourceGroups/chapter4/providers/Microsoft.Network/virt
                         ualNetworks/MyVirtualNetwork
Etag                   : W/"75fa3114-cfc1-4378-9b17-8d8bab493a15"
ResourceGuid           : 963201a2-83c5-4ecc-8a03-829d0c41e443
ProvisioningState      : Succeeded
Tags                   :
AddressSpace           : {
                             "AddressPrefixes": [
                               "10.0.0.0/16"
                             ]
                         }
DhcpOptions            : {}
Subnets                : []
VirtualNetworkPeerings : []
EnableDdosProtection   : false
DdosProtectionPlan     : null
```

Figure 4.13: Virtual network properties

The **AddressSpace** or address is the network that can be used by one or more subnets. It's possible to add additional address spaces.

Subnets

As stated, a subnet is created in a virtual network. All traffic between different subnets in the same network is routed in Azure so the subnets are able to reach one another. Of course, you can modify that behavior, for instance, when you want to use a load balancer.

Again, we'll take the simplest command possible for the same reason as for virtual networks:

```
Add-AzVirtualNetworkSubnetConfig '
  -AddressPrefix <subnet> -Name <subnet> '
  -VirtualNetwork <vnet>
```

To create a subnet with the name **MySubnet** with the address pool as **10.0.1.0/24**, execute the following command:

```
$mySubnet = Add-AzVirtualNetworkSubnetConfig '
  -AddressPrefix 10.0.1.0/24 -Name MySubnet '
  -VirtualNetwork $myVnet
```

> **Note**
>
> It is possible that you'll get a warning that some objects are deprecated. You can safely ignore it.

If you execute **$mysubnet**, you'll see that the subnet is added:

```
>   $myVnet.Subnets

Name                                   : MySubnet
Id                                     :
Etag                                   :
ProvisioningState                      :
AddressPrefix                          : {10.0.1.0/24}
IpConfigurations                       : null
ResourceNavigationLinks                : null
ServiceAssociationLinks                : null
NetworkSecurityGroup                   : null
RouteTable                             : null
NatGateway                             : null
ServiceEndpoints                       : null
ServiceEndpointPolicies                : null
PrivateEndpoints                       : null
PrivateEndpointNetworkPolicies         : Enabled
PrivateLinkServiceNetworkPolicies      : Enabled
```

Figure 4.14: Subnet details

As you can see in the preceding screenshot, we didn't use the full network, only a part of it.

Alternatively, verification can be done using the following command:

```
Get-AzVirtualNetworkSubnetConfig '
  -VirtualNetwork $myVnet -Name MySubnet
```

The output will be exactly the same as the preceding screenshot.

The first IP address of the subnet is the gateway for network traffic coming from the VM; it provides the following:

- A default gateway, with **Source Network Address Translation** (**SNAT**) to gain internet access. To be able to do so, a public IP address must be configured. SNAT allows you to send the traffic generated from your VM (or any resource) in the private network to the internet via the gateway.

- The DNS server, if not configured otherwise.

- The DHCP server.

The last part of the virtual network configuration involves attaching the newly created subnet:

```
Set-AzVirtualNetwork -VirtualNetwork $myVnet
```

From the output, among some other information, you can see the address space and the subnet within:

```
AddressSpace  : {
                    "AddressPrefixes": [
                      "10.0.0.0/16"
                    ]
                }
    Subnets   : [
                    {
                      "Delegations": [],
                      "Name": "MySubnet",
                      "Etag":
                "W/\"7abef25b-b16f-4b23-97a3-2585b2d338aa\"",
                      "Id": "/subscriptions/
                cd539e69/resourceGroups/chapter4/providers/Microsoft.N
                etwork/virtualNetworks/MyVirtualNetwork/subnets/MySubn
                et",
                      "AddressPrefix": [
                        "10.0.1.0/24"
                      ],
```

Figure 4.15: Attaching the newly created subnet

Network Security Group

Network security group (**NSG**) is the next component we need to take care of. It is essentially access control lists that are associated with a subnet. It also provides port forwarding to the VMs or containers. The rules are applied to all interfaces that are attached to the subnet.

The first step is to create an NSG:

```
New-AzNetworkSecurityGroup '
  -ResourceGroupName <resource group>'
  -Location <location> -Name <nsg name>
```

For example, you can create an NSG this way:

```
$myNSG = New-AzNetworkSecurityGroup '
  -ResourceGroupName $myRG -Location $myLocation -Name myNSG1
```

In the enormous output, you will find several sections; one of the sections is named **Default Security Rules**. This section contains a set of rules, given in order of priority:

- Allow inbound traffic from all VMs in the virtual network (**AllowVnetInBound**)

- Allow inbound traffic from Azure Load Balancer (**AllowAzureLoadBalancerInBound**)

- Deny all inbound traffic (**DenyAllInBound**)

- Allow outbound traffic from all VMs to all VMs in the virtual network (**AllowVnetOutBound**)

- Allow outbound traffic from all VMs to the internet (**AllowInternetOutBound**)

- Deny all outbound traffic (**DenyAllOutBound**)

Before going into the rules, let's associate the subnet with the NSG:

```
Set-AzVirtualNetworkSubnetConfig -Name <subnet name> '
  -VirtualNetwork <vnet> -NetworkSecurityGroupID <nsg id> '
  -AddressPrefix <subnet>
```

For example, here's an implementation of the preceding command:

```
$NSGSubnet = Set-AzVirtualNetworkSubnetConfig '
  -Name $myVnet.Subnets.Name '
  -VirtualNetwork $myVnet '
  -NetworkSecurityGroupID $myNSG.Id '
  -AddressPrefix 10.0.1.0/24
```

It's possible that you'll get the same deprecation warnings as you saw before. You can ignore them again. Attach the NSG to the network:

```
$NSGSubnet | Set-AzVirtualNetwork
```

The output of this command will be in JSON and is lengthy because of all the parameters. If you look at the output, you will see that **NetworkSecurityGroup** is mentioned as **myNSG1**, which is the NSG we created:

```
"NetworkSecurityGroup": {
    "Id": "/subscriptions/8852                    e
            /resourceGroups/chapter4/providers/Microsoft
.Network/networkSecurityGroups/myNSG1"
    },
```

Figure 4.16: NSG attached to the network

If we want access to our VM using SSH, then we need to add a security rule:

```
$myNSG | Add-AzNetworkSecurityRuleConfig -Name SSH '
   -Description "Allow SSH" '
   -Access Allow -Protocol Tcp -Direction Inbound '
   -Priority 100 '
   -SourceAddressPrefix Internet -SourcePortRange * '
   -DestinationAddressPrefix * '
   -DestinationPortRange 22 | Set-AzNetworkSecurityGroup
```

The **-SourceAddressPrefix** parameter is a sort of a shorthand for everything that is outside the virtual network and reachable by public internet. Other values are as follows:

- **VirtualNetwork**: Everything within this virtual network and other connected networks.

- **AzureLoadBalancer**: If you are using Azure Load Balancer, this provides access to your VMs.

- *****: Everything.

Priority ranges from **100** to **4096**. Higher numbers are created by Azure and can be overruled. The lower the priority number, the higher is the priority of the rule.

The output of the previous command may have too much information, which is a bit confusing to interpret. In order to confirm whether port **22** traffic is allowed, we will filter the output using the following command:

```
$myNSG | select SecurityRules
```

```
$myNSG.SecurityRules
```

The output, as shown in the following screenshot, verifies that TCP port **22** is open for inbound traffic. This port has a priority of **100**, but since it's the only rule, that doesn't matter:

```
PS C:\windows\system32> $myNSG | select SecurityRules

SecurityRules
-------------
{SSH}


PS C:\windows\system32> $myNSG.SecurityRules


Name                                    : SSH
Id                                      : /subscriptions/548f

Etag                                    : W/"6ccc50b2-c620-44
ProvisioningState                       : Succeeded
Description                             :
Protocol                                : Tcp
SourcePortRange                         : {*}
DestinationPortRange                    : {22}
SourceAddressPrefix                     : {*}
DestinationAddressPrefix                : {*}
SourceApplicationSecurityGroups         : []
DestinationApplicationSecurityGroups    : []
Access                                  : Allow
Priority                                : 1000
Direction                               : Inbound
```

Figure 4.17: Listing the security rules set for the NSG

Alternatively, you can use the following command:

```
$myNSG | Get-AzNetworkSecurityRuleConfig
```

As you can see, the output is the same.

Public IP Address and Network Interface

To be able to access the VM from the internet, a public IP address is needed along with a DNS label, which is the DNS name given to our VM.

The public IP can be static or dynamic. In the case of a dynamic public IP, whenever you deallocate and then restart the VM, the IP will be released and disassociated from the VM. Next time you start the VM, a new public IP will be associated with the VM. So, every time you deallocate and then restart the VM, you have to check the public IP from the CLI or the portal to connect to the VM.

Here comes the important part about the DNS label: if you have already added a DNS label to your VM, you can always use that to connect to the VM, irrespective of the public IP the VM has. The DNS label doesn't change when you deallocate and restart the VM. Also, the DNS label is unique across Azure.

In the case of a static public IP, the IP will be reserved for you. Even if you deallocate and then restart the VM, the IP will not change. Having a static IP assigned to the VM will not stop you from adding a DNS label. If that's needed, you can add the label as well.

Create a new dynamic public IP with the following command:

```
$pip = New-AzPublicIpAddress '
  -ResourceGroupName $myRG '
  -Location $myLocation -AllocationMethod Dynamic '
  -Name "$(Get-Random)"
```

Verify it by viewing the content of the **$pip** variable. If the allocation method is **Dynamic**, the IP address is not allocated until the IP address is assigned to a network interface:

```
PS C:\windows\system32> $pip = New-AzPublicIpAddress `
>> -ResourceGroupName $myRG `
>> -Location $myLocation -AllocationMethod Dynamic `
>> -Name "$(Get-Random)"
PS C:\windows\system32> $pip


Name                      : 1839463744
ResourceGroupName         : chapter4
Location                  : westus
Id                        : /subscriptions/548f7d26-b5b
Etag                      : W/"a1854475-cb1b-431f-a9cd-
ResourceGuid              : eff3b1e3-bfaa-43d6-898d-4ff
ProvisioningState         : Succeeded
Tags                      :
PublicIpAllocationMethod  : Dynamic
IpAddress                 : Not Assigned
PublicIpAddressVersion    : IPv4
IdleTimeoutInMinutes      : 4
IpConfiguration           : null
DnsSettings               : null
Zones                     : {}
Sku                       : {
                                "Name": "Basic"
                            }
```

Figure 4.18: Verifying the new dynamic public IP

So, that's why in the preceding screenshot, the **IpAddress** field states **Not Assigned**.

To create the network interface, use the following command:

```
$nic = New-AzNetworkInterface -Name myNic `
  -ResourceGroupName $myRG -Location $myLocation `
  -SubnetId $myVnet.Subnets[0].Id -PublicIpAddressId $pip.Id `
  -NetworkSecurityGroupId $myNSG.Id
```

If you get an error on the **SubnetId**, try to set the **myVnet** variable again and run the following command:

```
$myVnet = Get-AzVirtualNetwork -Name $myVnet.Name '
    -ResourceGroupName $myRG
```

To verify the result, execute the following command:

```
$nic.ipConfigurations
```

```
PS C:\windows\system32> $nic


Name                        : ipconfig1
ResourceGroupName           : chapter4
Location                    :
Id                          :                                    2ac
Etag                        : W/"2f0ef320-bbe4-4683-935f-2eaaba8b8f94"
ResourceGuid                : c846c95c-aad1-4b0c-827c-b5b696aed3e7
ProvisioningState           : Succeeded
Tags                        :
VirtualMachine              : null
IpConfigurations            : [
                                {
                                    "Name": "ipconfig1",
                                    "Etag": "W/\"2f0ef320-bbe4-4683-935f-2eaab
                                    "Id": "/subscriptions/
                              nfig1/ipConfigurations/ipconfig1",
                                    "PrivateIpAddress": "10.1.0.4",
                                    "PrivateIpAllocationMethod": "Dynamic",
                                    "Subnet": {
                                      "Delegations": [],
                                      "Id": "/subscriptions/
                              /subnets/default",
                                      "ServiceAssociationLinks": []
                                    },
                                    "ProvisioningState": "Succeeded",
                                    "PrivateIpAddressVersion": "IPv4",
```

Figure 4.19: Checking the IP address allocated to the network interface

In the output, as you can see in the preceding screenshot, an IP address is allocated, which is **10.0.1.4** this time.

Managing Compute Resources

Let's sum up the components covered in this chapter that you need as a requirement, before you can deploy a VM. In the case of the storage account, it's not a real requirement, but do you want to work without being able to receive boot diagnostics in times of trouble? As mentioned earlier, a boot diagnostics account is very useful if your VMs go into a non-bootable state. The logs stored in this account can be used to find the root cause of the non-booting state of the VM. For testing, this is not a mandatory option, but for production workloads, it is recommended to enable boot diagnostics, which will help you understand what went wrong during a failure.

> **Note**
>
> Every resource mentioned here is also used by Azure Container Service and Azure Kubernetes Service.

If you remember, in the *Technical requirements* section, we looked at PowerShell code to create a new VM, where most of the variables were not defined. Here is the code again:

```
New-AzVm '
-ResourceGroupName $myRG '
-Name $myTestVM '
-ImageName UbuntuLTS '
-Location $myLocation '
-VirtualNetworkName "$myTestVM-Vnet" '
-SubnetName $myTestVM-Subnet '
-SecurityGroupName "$myTestVM-NSG" '
-PublicIpAddressName $myTestVM-pip
```

Now, I hope you are able to understand what each of these parameters stands for and how they are crucial for your VM.

Virtual Machine Resources

In this section, we'll provide a few tables with the necessary components and the corresponding commands in PowerShell and Bash. It can be used together with the help available in PowerShell (`help <cmdlet>`), the Azure CLI (add the `--help` parameter to the command), or the Azure online documentation.

Azure Profile

The Azure profile comprises the settings needed to describe your Azure environment:

Requirement	PowerShell	Azure CLI
Subscription ID	Get-AzSubscription	az account list
Tenant ID	Get-AzSubscription	az account list

Figure 4.20: Azure profile settings commands

Resource Group

The resource group is needed to contain and manage resources:

Requirement	PowerShell	Azure CLI
Create resource group	New-AzResourceGroup	az group create
View resource group	Get-AzResourceGroup	az group list az group show

Figure 4.21: Azure resource group commands

Storage Account

The storage account is needed if you want to store data outside your VM/container:

Requirement	PowerShell	Azure CLI
Create storage account	New-AzStorageAccount	az storage account create
View storage account	Get-AzStorageAccount	az storage account show az storage account list
View storage account keys	Get-AzStorageAccountKey	az storage account keys list

Figure 4.22: Azure storage account commands

Virtual Networks

Virtual networking is needed for communication between VMs/containers and communication with the outside world:

Requirement	PowerShell	Azure CLI
Create virtual network	New-AzVirtualNetwork	az network vnet create
Create subnet	Add-AzVirtualNetworkSubnetConfig Set-AzVirtualNetworkSubnetConfig	az network vnet subnet create
View virtual network	Get-AzVirtualNetwork	az network vnet list az network vnet show
View subnet	Get-AzVirtualNetworkSubnetConfig	az network vnet subnet list az network vnet subnet show

Figure 4.23: Azure virtual network commands

Network Security Group

The NSG consists of **Access Control Lists** (**ACL**) to protect your workloads and allow access where needed. It is, together with the public IP address, also needed for port forwarding to the VM/container:

Requirement	PowerShell	Azure CLI
Create NSG	New-AzNetworkSecurityGroup	az network nsg create
Associate subnet with NSG	Set-AzVirtualNetworkSubnetConfig	az network vnet subnet update
Add NSG rule	Add-AzNetworkSecurityRuleConfig Set-AzNetworkSecurityGroup	az network nsg rule create
View components, for virtual machineNSG	Get-AzNetworkSecurityGroup	az network nsg show az network nsg list
View NSG rules	Get-AzNetworkSecurityRuleConfig	az network nsg rule show az network nsg rule list

Figure 4.24: Azure NSG commands

Public IP Address and Network Interface

The public IP address provides access from the outside world into the VM/container. It's necessary for Port Address Translation (PAT) and SNAT:

Requirement	PowerShell	Azure CLI
Create public IP address	New-AzPublicIpAddress	az network public-ip create
Create NIC	New-AzNetworkInterface	az network nic create
List public IP address	Get-AzPublicIpAddress	az network public-ip show az network public-ip list

Figure 4.25: Azure public IP address and network interface commands

Summary

With the knowledge gained in this chapter, you should now have a better understanding of the things you encountered in *Chapter 2, Getting Started with the Azure Cloud*.

In this chapter, we explored all the Azure components that are needed before you can create your workload in Azure:

- You'll need a storage account for the VM boot diagnostic extension.

- You'll want a storage account to store data outside your VM.

- Networking components are needed to be able to communicate with your VM, enable communication between your machines, and for the VM to be able to reach the internet.

The steps we have discussed so far will be very useful for you to understand the components related to VMs and also how each of those components is deployed in Azure. We started with storage solutions in Azure and then covered networking as well. We hope this gave you an idea of how these components come together to provide service delivery.

In the next chapter, we will be using the knowledge we gained from this chapter to identify and configure network and storage components in the Linux operating system. Besides network and storage topics, we'll explore other system administration tasks, such as software and service management.

Questions

1. Which resources are required before you can create your VM?

2. Which resources are recommended for a VM?

3. In the examples, a random number generator was used several times—why?

4. What is the purpose of `AddressPrefix` on a network?

5. What is the purpose of `AddressPrefix` on a subnet?

6. What is the purpose of the NSG?

7. Why is the public IP address needed for communication with the outside world?

8. What is the difference between a static and a dynamically allocated public IP address?

Further Reading

The book *Implementing Microsoft Azure Infrastructure Solutions* from Microsoft Press is intended as a reference guide for studying the 70-533 exam; even though the exam is deprecated, the content is still good for reference. It explains every part of the Azure infrastructure in detail, using the Azure portal and the command-line interfaces.

If you are new to networking, another recommended book, which is also written as a study guide for an exam, is the *Comptia Network+ Certification Guide* by Glen D. Singh and Rishi Latchmepersad.

Much older and more difficult to read is the freely available *TCP/IP Redbook* from IBM (https://www.redbooks.ibm.com/redbooks/pdfs/gg243376.pdf); it covers much more than you need to know, but if you are interested in the topic, it's a must-read. Even if you are not interested in taking the Cisco ICND1 exam, Neil Anderson recorded a video at https://www.packtpub.com, which provides, besides the Cisco part, a very good introduction to networking.

> **Note**
>
> Please be aware that the Azure environment is continuously changing, especially regarding storage and networking; it is important to validate sources against the documentation available on the Microsoft website. The date of publishing is perhaps the first thing you will want to check.

Advanced Linux Administration

In *Chapter 3, Basic Linux Administration*, some basic Linux commands were covered, and you learned how to find your way in the Linux environment. After that, in *Chapter 4, Managing Azure*, we took a deep dive into the Azure architecture.

With the knowledge gained from these two chapters, we're now ready to continue our journey in Linux. Let's go ahead and explore the following topics:

- Software management, where we will see how new packages can be added to a Linux machine and how to update existing ones.

- Storage management. In the previous chapter, we discussed attaching data disks to your **virtual machine** (**VM**) from Azure, but now we will discuss the management of these disks in Linux.

- Network management. Previously, we talked about adding a **network interface card** (**NIC**) to a VM and how networking resources are managed in Azure. In this chapter, we'll discuss how these resources are managed in Linux.

- System management, where we'll discuss how to manage services and system essentials.

Technical Requirements

For the purpose of this chapter, you'll need to deploy a Linux VM in Azure, with the distribution of your choice.

In terms of sizing, you'll need at least 2 GB of temporary storage, and the ability to add a minimum of three extra disks. For instance, the B2S VM size is a good starting point. In this chapter, I have shared the steps for Ubuntu, Red Hat, and SUSE systems; you can choose which distribution to follow.

Software Management

In any operating system, we need to install some software that will help us to do our day-to-day work. For example, if you are writing scripts, the stock software or application that comes with the operating system might not be enough. In that case, you need to install software such as Visual Studio Code to make your work easier. Likewise, in a corporate environment, you might need to add new software or even update existing software to meet your business requirements.

In the old days, installing software was a matter of extracting an archive to a filesystem. There were several problems associated with this approach, however:

- It was difficult to remove the software if the files were copied into directories also used by other software.

- It was difficult to upgrade software; maybe the files were still in use, or they were renamed for whatever reason.

- It was difficult to handle shared libraries.

That's why Linux distributions invented software managers. Using these software managers, we can install the packages and applications that are required to complete our tasks. Here are a few software managers:

- RPM
- YUM
- DNF
- DPKG
- APT
- ZYpp

Let's take a closer look at each of these and understand how they can be used to manage the software in your Linux system.

The RPM Software Manager

In 1997, Red Hat released the first version of their package manager, RPM. Other distributions, such as SUSE, adopted this package manager. RPM is the name of the **rpm** utility, as well as the name of the format and the filename extension.

The RPM package contains the following:

- A **CPIO** (**Copy In, Copy Out**) archive of packaged binaries and configuration files. CPIO is a utility used to combine multiple files and create an archive.

- Metadata with information about the software, such as a description and dependencies.

- Scriptlets for pre- and post-installation scripts.

In the past, Linux administrators used the **rpm** utility to install, update, and remove software on a Linux system. If there was a dependency, the **rpm** command could tell you exactly what other packages you'd need to install. The **rpm** utility is not able to fix dependencies or possible conflicts between packages.

Nowadays, we no longer use the **rpm** utility to install or remove software even though it's available; instead, we use more advanced software installers. Following the installation of software with **yum** (in Red Hat/CentOS) or **zypper** (in SUSE), all the metadata goes into a database. Querying this **rpm** database with the **rpm** command can be very handy.

Here is a list of the most common **rpm** query parameters:

Parameter	Description
-qa	Lists all installed packages.
-qi <software>	Lists information about the rpm package.
-qc <software>	Lists installed configuration files.
-qd<software>	Lists installed documentations and examples.
-ql<software>	Lists all installed files.
-qf<filename>	Shows the package that installed this file.
-V <software>	Verifies the integrity/changes following the installation of a package; uses -va to do this for all installed software.
-qp	Uses this parameter together with other parameters if the package is not already installed. It is especially useful if you combine this parameter with --**script** to investigate the pre- and post-installation scripts in the package.

Figure 5.1: Common **rpm** query parameters

The following screenshot is an example of getting information about the installed SSH server package:

```
[student@EL8 ~]$ rpm -qa | grep openssh
openssh-clients-7.8p1-4.el8.x86_64
openssh-server-7.8p1-4.el8.x86_64
openssh-7.8p1-4.el8.x86_64
[student@EL8 ~]$ rpm -qc openssh-server
/etc/pam.d/sshd
/etc/ssh/sshd_config
/etc/sysconfig/sshd
[student@EL8 ~]$ rpm -qd openssh-server
/usr/share/man/man5/moduli.5.gz
/usr/share/man/man5/sshd_config.5.gz
/usr/share/man/man8/sftp-server.8.gz
/usr/share/man/man8/sshd.8.gz
```

Figure 5.2: SSH server package information

The output of the **-V** parameter can tell us about the changes that are made to installed software. Let's make a change to the **sshd_config** file:

```
sudo cp /etc/ssh/sshd_config /tmp
```

```
sudo sed -i 's/#Port 22/Port 22/' /etc/ssh/sshd_config
```

If you verify the installed package, there is an **S** and a **T** added to the output, indicating that the timestamp is changed and the file size is different:

```
[student@EL8 ~]$ rpm -V openssh-server
S.?....T.  c /etc/ssh/sshd_config
..?......  c /etc/sysconfig/sshd
```

Figure 5.3: S and T indicating change in timestamp and file size

Other possible characters in the output are as follows:

S	File size
M	Mode (permissions)
5	Checksum
D	Major/minor numbers used to convey info to device drivers
L	Readlink mismatch
U	User ownership
G	Group ownership
T	Modification time
P	Capabilities

Figure 5.4: Possible output characters and their description

For text files, the **diff** command can help show the differences between the backup in the **/tmp** directory and the configuration in the **/etc/ssh** directory:

```
sudo diff /etc/ssh/sshd_config /tmp/sshd_config
```

Restore the original file as follows:

```
sudo cp /tmp/sshd_config /etc/ssh/sshd_config
```

Software Management with YUM

Yellowdog Updater Modified (**YUM**) is a modern software management tool that was introduced by Red Hat in Enterprise Linux version 5, replacing the **up2date** utility. It is currently in use in all Red Hat-based distributions but will be replaced with **dnf**, which is used by Fedora. The good news is that **dnf** is syntax-compatible with **yum**.

YUM is responsible for the following:

- Installing software, including dependencies
- Updating software
- Removing software
- Listing and searching for software

The important basic parameters are as follows:

Command	Description
yum search	Searches for software based on a package name/summary
yum provides	Searches for software based on a filename in a package
yum install	Installs software
yum info	Information and status
yum update	Updates all software
yum remove	Removes software

Figure 5.5: Basic YUM parameters

You can also install patterns of software; for instance, the *File and Print Server* pattern or group is a very convenient way to install the **Network File Share** (**NFS**) and Samba file servers together with the Cups print server instead of installing the packages one by one:

Command	Description
yum groups list	Lists the available groups.
yum groups install	Installs a group.
yum groups info	Gets information about a group, including the group names that are in use by the Anaconda installer. This information is important for unattended installations.
yum groups update	Updates software within a group.
yum groups remove	Removes the installed group.

Figure 5.6: YUM group commands and their description

Another nice feature of **yum** is working with history:

Command	Description
yum history list	Lists the tasks executed by **yum**.
yum history info <number>	Lists the content of a specific task.
yum history undo <number>	Undoes the task; a redo is also available.

Figure 5.7: YUM history commands and their description

The **yum** command uses repositories to be able to do all the software management. To list the currently configured repositories, use the following command:

```
yum repolist
```

To add another repository, you'll need the **yum-config-manager** tool, which creates and modifies the configuration files in **/etc/yum.repos.d**. For instance, if you want to add a repository to install Microsoft SQL Server, use the following command:

```
yum-config-manager --add-repo \

  https://packages.microsoft.com/config/rhel/7/\

  mssql-server-2017.repo
```

The **yum** functionality can be extended with plugins, for instance, to select the fastest mirror, enabling the filesystem / LVM snapshots, and running **yum** as a scheduled task (cron).

Software Management with DNF

In Red Hat Enterprise Linux 8, and all the distributions based on this distribution and also on Fedora, the **yum** command is replaced by DNF. The syntax is the same, so you only need to replace three characters. Regarding the **yum-config-manager** command, it is replaced with **dnf config-manager**.

Instead of a separate utility, it is integrated with the **dnf** command itself.

There is also new functionality. RHEL 8 comes with software modularity, also known as **AppStreams**. As a packaging concept, it allows system administrators to select the desired software version from multiple available versions. By the way, it is possible that at this moment, only one version is available, but newer versions will come! For example, one of the available AppStreams is the Ruby programming interpreter. Let's take a look at the module:

```
sudo dnf module list ruby
```

```
Name   Stream    Profiles     Summary
ruby   2.5 [d]   common [d]   An interpreter of object-oriented scripting language

Hint: [d]efault, [e]nabled, [x]disabled, [i]nstalled
```

Figure 5.8: Ruby programming interpreter module

From the preceding output, you can observe that at the time of writing this book, only version 2.5 is available; more versions will be added in time. This is the default version, but is not enabled and not installed.

To enable and install AppStreams, execute the following commands:

```
sudo dnf module enable ruby:2.5
sudo dnf module install ruby
```

If you list AppStreams again, the output is changed:

```
Name Stream      Profiles     Summary
ruby 2.5 [d][e] common [d] [ An interpreter of object-oriented scripting languag
             i]           e

Hint: [d]efault, [e]nabled, [x]disabled, [i]nstalled
```

Figure 5.9: Ruby 2.5 installed and enabled

Tip: to know what packages are installed by AppStreams, you can use the following command:

```
sudo dnf module info ruby
```

> **Note**
>
> To find out more about Subscription Manager, please visit https://access.redhat.com/ecosystem/ccsp/microsoft-azure.

The DPKG Software Manager

The Debian distribution doesn't use the RPM format; instead, it uses the DEB format, invented in 1995. The format is in use on all Debian- and Ubuntu-based distributions.

A DEB package contains the following:

- A file, **debian-binary**, with the version of the package.

- An archive file, **control.tar**, with metadata (package name, version, dependencies, and maintainer).

- An archive file, **data.tar**, containing the actual software.

Management of DEB packages can be done with the **dpkg** utility. Like **rpm**, the **dpkg** utility is no longer in use for installing software even though that functionality is available. Instead, the more advanced **apt** command is used. Nevertheless, it's good to know the basics of dpkg commands.

All the metadata goes into a database that can be queried with **dpkg** or **dpkg-query**.

The important parameters of **dpkg-query** are as follows:

-l	Lists all packages without parameters; you can use wildcards, for example, **dcpkg -l *ssh***
-L \<package\>	Lists files in an installed package
-p \<package\>	Shows information about a package
-s \<package\>	Shows the state of a package

Figure 5.10: Important **dpkg-query parametres**

The first column from the output of **dpkg -l** also shows whether the package is installed or not, or unpacked, or half-installed, and so on:

```
linvirt@debian:~$ dpkg -l xxd
Desired=Unknown/Install/Remove/Purge/Hold
| Status=Not/Inst/Conf-files/Unpacked/halF-conf/Half-inst/trig-aWait/Trig-pend
|/ Err?=(none)/Reinst-required (Status,Err: uppercase=bad)
||/ Name            Version        Architecture Description
+++-===============-==============-============-=====================================
ii  xxd             2:8.0.0197-4   amd64        tool to make (or reverse) a hex d
```

Figure 5.11: Output of **dpkg -l** command

The first character in the first column is the desired action, the second is the actual state of the package, and a possible third character indicates an error flag (**R**). **ii** means that the package is installed.

Possible desired states are as follows:

- **u**: Unknown
- **i**: Install
- **h**: Hold
- **r**: Remove
- **p**: Purge

Important package states are as follows:

- **n**: Not—the package is not installed.
- **i**: Inst—the package is successfully installed.
- **c**: Cfg-files—the configuration files are present.
- **u**: Unpacked—the package is still unpacked.
- **f**: Failed-cfg—failed to remove the configuration files.
- **h**: Half-inst—the package is only partially installed.

Software Management with apt

In Debian-/Ubuntu-based distributions, software management is done via the **apt** utility, which is a recent replacement for the **apt-get** and **apt-cache** utilities.

The most frequently used commands include the following:

Command	Description
`apt list`	Lists packages
`apt search`	Searches in descriptions
`apt install`	Installs a package
`apt show`	Shows package details
`apt remove`	Removes a package
`apt update`	Updates the catalog of available packages
`apt upgrade`	Upgrades the installed software
`apt edit-sources`	Edits the repository configuration

Figure 5.12: Common `apt commands and their description`

Repositories are configured in the **/etc/apt/sources.list** directory and files in the **/etc/apt/sources.list.d/** directory. Alternatively, the **apt-add-repository** command is available:

```
apt-add-repository \
  'deb http://myserver/path/to/repo stable'
```

The **apt** repositories have the concept of release classes, some of which are listed here:

- **oldstable**: The software was tested in the previous version of a distribution, but has not been tested again for the current one.

- **stable**: The software is officially released.

- **testing**: The software is not yet **stable**, but it's in the pipeline.

- **unstable**: The software development is happening and is mainly run by developers.

The repositories also have the concept of components, which are also known as main repositories:

- **main**: Tested and provided with support and updates

- **contrib**: Tested and provided with support and updates, but there are dependencies that are not in main and are instead, for instance, in **non-free**

- **non-free**: Software that isn't compliant with the Debian Social Contract Guidelines (https://www.debian.org/social_contract#guidelines)

Ubuntu adds several extra components, or repositories:

- **Universe**: Community-provided, no support, updates possible

- **Restricted**: Proprietary device drivers

- **Multiverse**: Software restricted by copyright or legal issues

Software Management with ZYpp

SUSE, like Red Hat, uses RPM for package management. But instead of using **yum**, they use another toolset with ZYpp (also known as libzypp) as a backend. Software management can be done with the graphical configuration software YaST, or the command-line interface tool, Zypper.

> **Note**
>
> YUM and DNF are also available in the SUSE software repositories. You can use them to manage (limited to installing and removing) software on your local system, but that's not why they are available. The reason is Kiwi: an application to build OS images and installers.

The important basic parameters are as follows:

Command	Description
`zypper search`	Searches for software
`zypper install`	Installs software
`zypper remove`	Removes software
`zypper update`	Updates software
`zypperdist-upgrade`	Performs a distribution upgrade
`zypper info`	Shows information

Figure 5.13: Important Zypper commands and their description

There is a search option to search for a command, **what-provides**, but it's very limited. If you don't know the package name, there is a utility called **cnf** instead. Before you can use **cnf**, you'll need to install **scout**; this way, the package properties can be searched:

```
sudo zypper install scout
```

After that, you can use **cnf**:

```
linvirt@suse01:~> sudo cnf finger

The program 'finger' can be found in the following package:
  * finger [ path: /usr/bin/finger, repository: zypp (openSUSE-Leap-42.3-Oss) ]

Try installing with:
    zypper install finger

linvirt@suse01:~> sudo zypper install finger
Loading repository data...
Reading installed packages...
Resolving package dependencies...

The following NEW package is going to be installed:
  finger

1 new package to install.
Overall download size: 18.9 KiB. Already cached: 0 B. After the operation,
additional 31.6 KiB will be used.
Continue? [y/n/...? shows all options] (y): 
```

Figure 5.14: Using the cnf utility

If you want to update your system to a new distribution version, you have to modify the repositories first. For instance, if you want to update from SUSE LEAP 42.3, which is based on **SUSE Linux Enterprise Server** (**SLES**), to version 15.0, which is based on **SUSE Linux Enterprise** (**SLE**), execute the following procedure:

1. First, install the available updates for your current version:

    ```
    sudo zypper update
    ```

2. Update to the latest version in the 42.3.x releases:

    ```
    sudo zypper dist-upgrade
    ```

3. Modify the repository configuration:

    ```
    sudo sed -i 's/42.3/15.0/g' /etc/zypp/repos.d/*.repo
    ```

4. Initialize the new repositories:

    ```
    sudo zypper refresh
    ```

5. Install the new distribution:

    ```
    sudo zypper dist-upgrade
    ```

Of course, you have to reboot following the distribution upgrade.

Besides installing packages, you can install the following:

*   **patterns**: Groups of packages, for instance, to install a complete web server including PHP and MySQL (also known as LAMP)

*   **patches**: Incremental updates for a package

*   **products**: Installation of an additional product

To list the available patterns, use the following command:

```
zypper patterns
```

To install them, use the following command:

```
sudo zypper install --type pattern <pattern>
```

The same procedure applies to patches and products.

Zypper uses online repositories to view the currently configured repositories:

```
sudo zypper repos
```

You can add repositories with the **addrepo** parameter; for instance, to add a community repository for the latest PowerShell version on LEAP 15.0, execute the following command:

```
sudo zypper addrepo \
  https://download.opensuse.org/repositories\
  /home:/aaptel:/powershell-stuff/openSUSE_Leap_15.0/\
  home:aaptel:powershell-stuff.repo
```

If you add a repository, you always need to refresh the repositories:

```
sudo zypper refresh
```

> **Note**
>
> SUSE has the concept of repositories that can be trusted or untrusted. If a vendor is not trusted, you need to add the **--from** parameter to the **install** command. Alternatively, you can add a configuration file to **/etc/vendors.d**, as here:
>
> **[main]**
>
> **vendors = suse,opensuse,obs://build.suse.de**
>
> The vendor of a package can be found with **zypper info**.

Now that you know how to manage the software in your distribution, let's go ahead and discuss networking. In the previous chapter, we discussed networking resources in Azure; it's now time to learn about Linux networking.

Networking

In Azure, the network settings, such as your IP address and DNS settings, are provided via **Dynamic Host Configuration Protocol** (**DHCP**). The configuration is very similar to the configuration of physical machines or VMs running on another platform. The difference is that the configuration is provided by Azure and normally shouldn't be changed.

In this section, you'll learn to identify the network configuration in Linux and how to match that information with the settings in Azure that were covered in the previous chapter.

Identifying the Network Interfaces

During the boot process and afterward, the Linux kernel is responsible for hardware identification. When the kernel identifies the hardware, it hands the collected information over to a process, a running daemon (background process), called **systemd-udevd**. This daemon does the following:

- Loads the network driver if necessary.

- It can assume responsibility for device naming.

- Updates **/sys** with all the available information.

The **udevadm** utility can help you to show the hardware identified. You can use the **udevadm info** command to query the **udev** database for device information:

```
[linvirt@CentOS-01 ~]$ sudo udevadm info -p /sys/class/net/eth*
P: /devices/LNXSYSTM:00/device:00/PNP0A03:00/device:08/VMBUS:01/vmbus_15/net/eth0
E: DEVPATH=/devices/LNXSYSTM:00/device:00/PNP0A03:00/device:08/VMBUS:01/vmbus_15/net/eth0
E: ID_NET_DRIVER=hv_netvsc
E: ID_NET_NAME_MAC=enx000d3a3ae27f
E: ID_OUI_FROM_DATABASE=Microsoft Corp.
E: ID_PATH=acpi-VMBUS:01
E: ID_PATH_TAG=acpi-VMBUS_01
E: IFINDEX=2
E: INTERFACE=eth0
E: SUBSYSTEM=net
E: SYSTEMD_ALIAS=/sys/subsystem/net/devices/eth0
E: TAGS=:systemd:
E: USEC_INITIALIZED=135398
E: net.ifnames=0
```

Figure 5.15: Using the **udevadm info** command to retrieve device information

Instead of using **udevadm**, you can also reach the **/sys/class/net** directory and view the **cat** command with the available files, but that's not a very user-friendly method and normally, there is no need to do it this way because there are utilities that parse all the available information.

The most important utility is the **ip** command. Let's start with listing the available network interfaces and the information related to that:

```
ip link show
```

The preceding command should give you the following output:

```
[linvirt@CentOS-01 ~]$ ip link show
1: lo: <LOOPBACK,UP,LOWER_UP> mtu 65536 qdisc noqueue state UNKNOWN mode DEFAULT
 qlen 1
    link/loopback 00:00:00:00:00:00 brd 00:00:00:00:00:00
2: eth0: <BROADCAST,MULTICAST,UP,LOWER_UP> mtu 1500 qdisc pfifo_fast state UP mo
de DEFAULT qlen 1000
    link/ether 00:0d:3a:3a:e2:7f brd ff:ff:ff:ff:ff:ff
[linvirt@CentOS-01 ~]$ ip link show dev eth0
2: eth0: <BROADCAST,MULTICAST,UP,LOWER_UP> mtu 1500 qdisc pfifo_fast state UP mo
de DEFAULT qlen 1000
    link/ether 00:0d:3a:3a:e2:7f brd ff:ff:ff:ff:ff:ff
```

Figure 5.16: Using ip link show to list available network interfaces

Once the available network interfaces are listed, you can be more specific:

```
ip link show dev eth0
```

The meaning of all the status flags, such as **LOWER_UP**, can be found in **man 7 netdevice**.

Identifying the IP Address

After learning the name of the network interface, the **ip** utility can be used to show the IP address configured on the network interface, as shown in the following screenshot:

```
[linvirt@CentOS-01 ~]$ ip addr show
1: lo: <LOOPBACK,UP,LOWER_UP> mtu 65536 qdisc noqueue state UNKNOWN qlen 1
    link/loopback 00:00:00:00:00:00 brd 00:00:00:00:00:00
    inet 127.0.0.1/8 scope host lo
       valid_lft forever preferred_lft forever
    inet6 ::1/128 scope host
       valid_lft forever preferred_lft forever
2: eth0: <BROADCAST,MULTICAST,UP,LOWER_UP> mtu 1500 qdisc pfifo_fast state UP ql
en 1000
    link/ether 00:0d:3a:3a:e2:7f brd ff:ff:ff:ff:ff:ff
    inet 192.168.1.4/24 brd 192.168.1.255 scope global eth0
       valid_lft forever preferred_lft forever
    inet6 fe80::20d:3aff:fe3a:e27f/64 scope link
       valid_lft forever preferred_lft forever
[linvirt@CentOS-01 ~]$ ip addr show eth0
2: eth0: <BROADCAST,MULTICAST,UP,LOWER_UP> mtu 1500 qdisc pfifo_fast state UP ql
en 1000
    link/ether 00:0d:3a:3a:e2:7f brd ff:ff:ff:ff:ff:ff
    inet 192.168.1.4/24 brd 192.168.1.255 scope global eth0
       valid_lft forever preferred_lft forever
    inet6 fe80::20d:3aff:fe3a:e27f/64 scope link
       valid_lft forever preferred_lft forever
```

Figure 5.17: Using ip utility to retrieve configured ip address

Showing the Route Table

A route table is a structure that is stored in the Linux kernel with the information on how to route the packets. You can configure the route table and make the packets take a route based on a rule or condition. For example, you can declare that if the destination of the packet is 8.8.8.8, it should be sent to the gateway. The route table can be shown per device or per subnet:

```
[linvirt@CentOS-01 ~]$ ip route show dev eth0
default via 192.168.1.1
168.63.129.16 via 192.168.1.1  proto static
169.254.0.0/16  scope link  metric 1002
169.254.169.254 via 192.168.1.1  proto static
192.168.1.0/24  proto kernel  scope link  src 192.168.1.4
[linvirt@CentOS-01 ~]$ ip route show 0.0.0.0/0
default via 192.168.1.1 dev eth0
```

Figure 5.18: Displaying the route table

Another nice feature is that you can query what device and gateway are used to reach a specific IP:

```
[linvirt@CentOS-01 ~]$  ip route get 9.9.9.9
9.9.9.9 via 192.168.1.1 dev eth0  src 192.168.1.4
    cache
```

Figure 5.19: Querying device and gateway used for specific IP

Network Configuration

Now that we know how to identify the IP address of the interface and the routes defined for the interface, let's see how these IP addresses and routes are configured on the Linux system.

The **ip** command is mainly used to verify settings. The persistent configuration is normally managed by another daemon. Different distributions have different daemons for managing the network:

- RHEL distributions use **NetworkManager**.

- In SLE and OpenSUSE LEAP, **wicked** is used.

- In Ubuntu 17.10 and later, **systemd-networkd** and **systemd-resolved** are used, and earlier versions of Ubuntu completely rely on the DHCP client configured in **/etc/network/interfaces.d/*cfg** files.

In Ubuntu, the Azure Linux Guest Agent creates two files in the **/run/system/network** directory. One is a link file named **10-netplan-eth0.link** to preserve the device name, based on the MAC address:

```
[Match]
MACAddress=00:....

[Link]
Name=eth0
WakeOnLan=off
```

The other is **10-netplan-eth0.network** for the actual network configuration:

```
[Match]
MACAddress=00:...
Name=eth0

[Network]
DHCP=ipv4

[DHCP]
UseMTU=true
RouteMetric=100
```

If you have more than one network interface, multiple sets of files are created.

In SUSE, the Azure Linux Guest Agent creates a file, **/etc/sysconfig/network/ifcfg-eth0**, with the following content:

```
BOOTPROTO='dhcp'
DHCLIENT6_MODE='managed'
MTU=''
REMOTE_IPADDR=''
STARTMODE='onboot'
CLOUD_NETCONFIG_MANAGE='yes'
```

The **wicked** daemon reads this file and uses it for the network configuration. As in Ubuntu, multiple files are created if you have more than one network interface. The status of the configuration can be viewed with the **wicked** command:

```
linvirt@suse:/etc/sysconfig/network> sudo wicked show eth0
eth0            up
        link:       #2, state up, mtu 1500
        type:       ethernet, hwaddr 00:0d:3a:2a:89:29
        config:     compat:suse:/etc/sysconfig/network/ifcfg-eth0
        leases:     ipv4 dhcp granted
        leases:     ipv6 dhcp requesting
        addr:       ipv4 10.1.0.4/24 [dhcp]
        route:      ipv4 default via 10.1.0.1 proto dhcp
        route:      ipv4 168.63.129.16/32 via 10.1.0.1 proto dhcp
        route:      ipv4 169.254.169.254/32 via 10.1.0.1 proto dhcp
```

Figure 5.20: Checking configuration status using the wicked show command

In RHEL and CentOS, the **ifcfg-** files are created in the **/etc/sysconfig/network-scripts** directory:

```
DEVICE=eth0

ONBOOT=yes

BOOTPROTO=dhcp

TYPE=Ethernet

USERCTL=no

PEERDNS=yes

IPV6INIT=no

NM_CONTROLLED=no

DHCP_HOSTNAME=...
```

If **NM_CONTROLLED** is set to **no**, then **NetworkManager** will not be able to control the connection. Most Azure Linux machines have this set to **yes**; nevertheless, you can verify it from the **ifcfg-** files in the **/etc/sysconfig/network-scripts** directory. You can use the **nmcli** command to show the device settings, but you can't use the command to modify those settings:

```
[linvirt@CentOS-01 network-scripts]$ nmcli device show eth0
GENERAL.DEVICE:                        eth0
GENERAL.TYPE:                          ethernet
GENERAL.HWADDR:                        00:0D:3A:3A:E2:7F
GENERAL.MTU:                           1500
GENERAL.STATE:                         10 (unmanaged)
GENERAL.CONNECTION:                    --
GENERAL.CON-PATH:                      --
WIRED-PROPERTIES.CARRIER:              on
IP4.ADDRESS[1]:                        192.168.1.4/24
IP4.GATEWAY:                           192.168.1.1
IP4.ROUTE[1]:                          dst = 168.63.129.16/32, nh = 192.168.1.1
, mt = 0
IP4.ROUTE[2]:                          dst = 169.254.0.0/16, nh = 0.0.0.0, mt =
 1002
IP4.ROUTE[3]:                          dst = 169.254.169.254/32, nh = 192.168.1
.1, mt = 0
IP6.ADDRESS[1]:                        fe80::20d:3aff:fe3a:e27f/64
IP6.GATEWAY:
```

Figure 5.21: Using the nmcli command to show the device settings

Changes in the Network Configuration

As stated before, every network setting is provided by the Azure DHCP server. Everything we've learned until now was about the verification of the network settings configured in Azure.

If you changed something in Azure, you need to restart the network in Linux.

In SUSE and CentOS, you can do this with the following command:

```
sudo systemctl restart network
```

In the latest version of Ubuntu Server, use the following commands:

```
sudo systemctl restart systemd-networkd
```

```
sudo systemctl restart systems-resolved
```

Hostname

The current hostname of the VM can be found with the **hostnamectl** utility:

```
[linvirt@CentOS-01 ~]$ hostnamectl status
   Static hostname: CentOS-01
         Icon name: computer-vm
           Chassis: vm
        Machine ID: e8abe05b1d42472d882942fe2bdfc47e
           Boot ID: 3d2a68fc99a346349fa0656f5184cf0f
    Virtualization: microsoft
  Operating System: CentOS Linux 7 (Core)
       CPE OS Name: cpe:/o:centos:centos:7
            Kernel: Linux 3.10.0-514.26.2.el7.x86_64
      Architecture: x86-64
```

Figure 5.22: Fetching the hostname using **hostnamectl** utility

The hostname is provided by the DHCP server in Azure; to view the configured hostname in Azure, you can use the Azure portal, Azure CLI, or PowerShell. As an example, in PowerShell, use the following command:

```
$myvm=Get-AzVM -Name CentOS-01 '
   -ResourceGroupName MyResource1
$myvm.OSProfile.ComputerName
```

In Linux, you can change the hostname with the **hostnamectl** utility:

```
sudo hostnamectl set-hostname <hostname>
sudo systemctl restart waagent #RedHat & SUSE
sudo systemctl restart walinuxagent  #Ubuntu
```

This should change your hostname. If it doesn't work, check the configuration file of the Azure Linux VM agent, **/etc/waagent.conf**:

```
Provisioning.MonitorHostName=y
```

If it is still not working, edit the **/var/lib/waagent/ovf-env.xml** file, and change the **HostName** parameter. Another possible cause is the **DHCP_HOSTNAME** line in the **ifcfg-<interface>** file; just remove it and restart **NetworkManager**.

DNS

The DNS settings are also provided via the Azure DHCP server. In Azure, the settings are attached to the virtual network interface. You can view them in the Azure portal, PowerShell (**Get-AZNetworkInterface**), or Azure CLI (**az vm nic show**).

You can, of course, configure your own DNS settings. In PowerShell, declare the VM and identify the network interface:

```
$myvm = Get-AzVM -Name <vm name> '
  -ResourceGroupName <resource group>
$nicid = $myvm.NetworkProfile.NetworkInterfaces.Id
```

The last command will give you the complete ID of the required network interface; the last part of this ID is the interface name. Let's now strip it from the output and request the interface properties:

```
$nicname = $nicid.split("/")[-1]
$nic = Get-AzNetworkInterface '
  -ResourceGroupName <resource group> -Name $nicname
$nic
```

If you look at the value of the **$nic** variable, you can see that it has all the information we need:

```
PS C:\windows\system32> $nic

Name                     :  ipconfig1
ResourceGroupName        :  chapter4
Location                 :
Id                       :  /subscriptions/                              /resourceGroups/
Etag                     :  W/"2f0ef320-bbe4-4683-935f-2eaaba8b8f94"
ResourceGuid             :  c846c95c-aad1-4b0c-827c-b5b696aed3e7
ProvisioningState        :  Succeeded
Tags                     :
VirtualMachine           :  null
IpConfigurations         :  [
                              {
                                "Name": "ipconfig1",
                                "Etag": "W/\"2f0ef320-bbe4-4683-935f-2eaaba8b8f94\"",
                                "Id": "/subscriptions,                            /resourceGroups/
                            nfig1/ipConfigurations/ipconfig1",
                                "PrivateIpAddress": "10.1.0.4",
                                "PrivateIpAllocationMethod": "Dynamic",
                                "Subnet": {
                                  "Delegations": [],
                                  "Id": "/subscriptions/                         /resourceGroups/
                            /subnets/default",
                                  "ServiceAssociationLinks": []
                                },
                                "ProvisioningState": "Succeeded",
                                "PrivateIpAddressVersion": "IPv4",
```

Figure 5.23: Getting interface properties using $nic variable

The last step is to update the DNS nameserver settings. For the purpose of this book, we are using **9.9.9.9**, which is a public, freely available DNS service called Quad9. You can also use the DNS service of Google (**8.8.8.8** and **8.8.4.4**):

```
$nic.DnsSettings.DnsServers.Add("9.9.9.9")

$nic | Set-AzNetworkInterface

$nic | Get-AzNetworkInterface | '
  Select-Object -ExpandProperty DnsSettings
```

The method that uses the Azure CLI is similar but involves fewer steps. Search for the network interface name:

```
nicname=$(az vm nic list \
  --resource-group <resource group> \
  --vm-name <vm name> --query '[].id' -o tsv | cut -d "/" -f9)
```

Update the DNS settings:

```
az network nic update -g MyResource1 --name $nicname \
  --dns-servers 9.9.9.9
```

And then verify the new DNS settings:

```
az network nic show --resource-group <resource group> \
  --name $nicname --query "dnsSettings"
```

In the Linux VM, you have to renew the DHCP lease to receive the new settings. In order to do this, you can run **systemctl restart NetworkManager** in RHEL or **dhclient -r** in Ubuntu. The settings are saved in the **/etc/resolv.conf** file.

In Linux distributions that use the network implementation of **systemd**, such as Ubuntu, the **/etc/resolv.conf** file is a symbolic link to a file in the **/run/systemd/resolve/** directory, and the **sudo systemd-resolve --status** command shows you the current settings:

```
link 2 (eth0)
      Current Scopes: DNS
       LLMNR setting: yes
MulticastDNS setting: no
      DNSSEC setting: no
    DNSSEC supported: no
         DNS Servers: 9.9.9.9
          DNS Domain: reddog.microsoft.com
```

To test the DNS configuration, you can use **dig**, or the simpler **host** utility, as here:

```
dig www.google.com A
```

Storage

In the previous chapter, we discussed how to create disks and attach them to the VM, but our job doesn't end there. We have to partition or mount the disk to the Linux machine. In this section, we will be discussing storage management in Linux. There are two types of storage available in Azure: virtual disks that are attached to the VM, and Azure file shares. In this chapter, both types will be covered. We will be discussing the following topics:

- Adding a single virtual disk to a VM

- Working with filesystems

- Working with multiple virtual disks using the **Logical Volume Manager** (**LVM**) and RAID software

Storage Provided by Block Devices

Local and remote storage can be delivered by block devices. In Azure, it's almost always a virtual hard disk that is attached to the VM, but it is possible to use **internet Small Computer System Interface** (**iSCSI**) volumes as well, delivered by Microsoft Azure StorSimple or third parties.

Every disk attached to a VM is identified by the kernel, and, after identification, the kernel hands it over to a daemon called **systemd-udevd**. This daemon is responsible for creating an entry in the **/dev** directory, updating **/sys/class/block**, and, if necessary, loading a driver to access the filesystem.

The device file in **/dev** provides a simple interface to the block device and is accessed by an SCSI driver.

There are multiple methods to identify available block devices. One possibility involves using the **lsscsi** command:

```
linvirt@ubuntu02:~$ sudo lsscsi
[0:0:0:0]    disk    Msft       Virtual Disk       1.0    /dev/sda
[1:0:1:0]    disk    Msft       Virtual Disk       1.0    /dev/sdb
[5:0:0:0]    cd/dvd  Msft       Virtual CD/ROM     1.0    /dev/sr0
```

Figure 5.24: Using the **lsscsi** command to identify block devices

The first available disk is called **sda**—SCSI disk A. This disk is created from the image disk used during the provisioning of the VM and is also known as the root disk. You can access this disk via **/dev/sda** or **/dev/disk/azure/root**.

Another way to identify the available storage is to use the **lsblk** command. It can provide more information about the content of the disk:

```
linvirt@ubuntu02:~$ sudo lsblk
NAME       MAJ:MIN RM   SIZE RO TYPE MOUNTPOINT
sda          8:0    0    30G  0 disk
|-sda1       8:1    0  29.9G  0 part /
|-sda14      8:14   0     4M  0 part
`-sda15      8:15   0   106M  0 part /boot/efi
sdb          8:16   0     4G  0 disk
`-sdb1       8:17   0     4G  0 part /mnt
sr0         11:0    1   628K  0 rom
```

Figure 5.25: Identifying available storage using the lsblk command

In this example, there are two partitions created on **/dev/sda, sda1** and **sda2** (or **/dev/disk/azure/root-part1** and **root-part2**). The major number in the second column, **8**, means that this is an SCSI device; the minor part is just numbering. The third column tells us that the device is not removable, indicated by a **0** (it's a **1** if it is removable), and the fifth column tells us that the drives and partitions aren't read-only: again, a **1** for read-only and a **0** for read-write.

Another disk is available, the resource disk, **/dev/sdb (/dev/disk/azure/resource)**, which is a temporary disk. This means that data is not persistent and is gone after a reboot and is used for storing data such as a page or swap file. Swap is like virtual memory in Windows, which is used when the physical RAM is full.

Adding a Data Disk

In this section, we will recollect what we have done in the previous chapter to continue with the exercise and help you to become familiar with the commands. If you already have a VM with data disks added, you can skip this section.

You can add an extra virtual disk to a VM using the Azure portal or via PowerShell. Let's add a disk:

1. First, declare how we want to name our disk and where the disk should be created:

    ```
    $resourcegroup = '<resource group>'
    $location = '<location>'
    $diskname = '<disk name>'

    $vm = Get-AzVM '
      -Name <vm name> '
      -ResourceGroupName $resourcegroup
    ```

2. Create the virtual disk configuration—an empty, standard managed disk of 2 GB in size:

    ```
    $diskConfig = New-AzDiskConfig '
      -SkuName 'Standard_LRS' '
      -Location $location '
      -CreateOption 'Empty' '
      -DiskSizeGB 2
    ```

3. Create the virtual disk using this configuration:

    ```
    $dataDisk1 = New-AzDisk '
      -DiskName $diskname '
      -Disk $diskConfig '
      -ResourceGroupName $resourcegroup
    ```

4. Attach the disk to the VM:

    ```
    $vmdisk = Add-AzVMDataDisk '
      -VM $vm -Name $diskname '
      -CreateOption Attach '
      -ManagedDiskId $dataDisk1.Id '
      -Lun 1

    Update-AzVM '
      -VM $vm '
      -ResourceGroupName $resourcegroup
    ```

5. Of course, you can use the Azure CLI as well:

```
az disk create \
  --resource-group <resource group> \
  --name <disk name> \
  --location <location> \
  --size-gb 2 \
  --sku Standard_LRS \


az vm disk attach \
  --disk <disk name> \
  --vm-name <vm name> \
  --resource-group <resource group> \
  --lun <lun number>
```

> **Note**
>
> LUN is the abbreviation of Logical Unit Number, a number or identifier used for the labeling of storage (in our case, virtual storage), which will help users to distinguish storage. You can start the numbering at zero.

After creation, the virtual disk is visible in the VM as **/dev/sdc** (**/dev/disk/azure/scsi1/lun1**).

Tip: if it's not available, execute the **rescan-scsi-bus** command, which is part of the **sg3_utils** package.

Look again at the output of **lssci**:

```
[5:0:0:1]    disk    Msft    Virtual Disk    1.0  /dev/sdc
```

The first column is formatted:

```
<hostbus adapter id> :  <channel id> : <target id> : <lun number>
```

hostbus adapter is the interface to the storage and is created by the Microsoft Hyper-V virtual storage driver. The channel ID is always **0**, unless you have configured multi-pathing. The target ID identifies an SCSI target on a controller; this is always zero for direct-attached devices in Azure.

Partitioning

Before you can use the block device, you'll need to partition it. There are multiple tools available for partitioning, and some distributions come with their own utilities to create and manipulate partition tables. SUSE, for instance, has one in its YaST configuration tool.

In this book, we will use the **parted** utility. This is installed by default on every Linux distribution and can handle all known partition layouts: **msdos**, **gpt**, **sun**, and so on.

You can use **parted** in a scripted way from the command line, but, if you're new to **parted**, it's easier to use the interactive shell:

```
parted /dev/sdc
  GNU Parted 3.1
  Using /dev/sdc
  Welcome to GNU Parted! Type 'help' to view a list of commands.
```

1. The first step is to show the information available regarding this device:

    ```
    (parted) print
      Error: /dev/sdc: unrecognised disk label
      Model: Msft Virtual Disk (scsi)
      Disk /dev/sdc: 2147MB
      Sector size (logical/physical): 512B/512B
      Partition Table: unknown
      Disk Flags:
    ```

    The important line here is **unrecognised disk label**. This means that there was no partition layout created. Nowadays, the most common layout is **GUID Partition Table** (**GPT**).

    > **Note**
    >
    > **parted** supports autocompletion after a question mark—press *Ctrl + I* twice.

2. Change the partition label to **gpt**:

    ```
    (parted) mklabel
      New disk label type? gpt
    ```

3. Verify the result by printing the disk partition table again:

```
(parted) print
  Model: Msft Virtual Disk (scsi)
  Disk /dev/sdc: 2147MB
  Sector size (logical/physical): 512B/512B
  Partition Table: gpt
  Disk Flags:
  Number Start  End  Size File system  Name  Flags
```

4. The next step is to create a partition:

```
(parted) mkpart
  Partition name?  []? lun1_part1
  File system type?  [ext2]? xfs
  Start? 0%
  End? 100%
```

Filesystems will be covered later in this chapter. For sizing, you can use percentages or fixed sizes. In general, in Azure, it makes more sense to use the whole disk.

5. Print the disk partition table again:

```
(parted) print
  Model: Msft Virtual Disk (scsi)
  Disk /dev/sdc: 2147MB
  Sector size (logical/physical): 512B/512B
  Partition Table: gpt
  Disk Flags:
  Number Start   End    Size   File system Name      Flags
  1      1049kB 2146MB 2145MB             lun1_part1
```

Please note that the filesystem column is still empty, because the partition is not formatted.

6. Use *Ctrl* + D, or **quit**, to exit **parted**.

Filesystems in Linux

Filesystems have their mechanism for organizing the data, and this will differ from one filesystem to another. If we compare the available filesystems, we see that some are fast, some are designed for larger storage, and some are designed to handle smaller chunks of data. Your choice of filesystem should depend upon the end requirements and what kind of data you are storing. Linux supports many filesystems—native Linux filesystems, such as ext4 and XFS, and third-party filesystems, such as FAT32.

Every distribution supports the native filesystems, ext4 and XFS; on top of that, SUSE and Ubuntu have support for a very modern filesystem: BTRFS. Ubuntu is one of the few distributions that have support for the ZFS filesystem.

After formatting the filesystem, you can mount it to the root filesystem. The basic syntax of the `mount` command is as follows:

```
mount <partition> <mountpoint>
```

A partition can be named with the device name, label, or **universally unique identifier** (**UUID**). ZFS can be mounted with the `mount` command or via the `zfs` utility.

Another important filesystem is the swap filesystem. Besides the normal filesystems, there are also other special filesystems: devfs, sysfs, procfs, and tmpfs.

Let's start with a short description of the filesystems and the utilities around them.

The ext4 Filesystem

ext4 is a native Linux filesystem, developed as the successor to ext3, and it was (and, for some distributions, still is) the default filesystem for many years. It offers stability, high capacity, reliability, and performance while requiring minimal maintenance. On top of that, you can resize (increase/decrease) the filesystem without a problem.

The good news is that it can offer this with very low requirements. There is, of course, also bad news: it's very reliable, but it cannot completely guarantee the integrity of your data. If data is corrupted while already on disk, ext4 has no way of either detecting or repairing such corruption. Luckily, because of the underlying architecture of Azure, this will not happen.

ext4 is not the fastest filesystem around, but, for many workloads, the gap between ext4 and the competition is very small.

The most important utilities are as follows:

- **mkfs.ext4**: Formats the filesystem
- **e2label**: Changes the label of the filesystem
- **tune2fs**: Changes the parameters of the filesystem
- **dump2fs**: Shows the parameters of the filesystem
- **resize2fs**: Changes the size of the filesystem
- **fsck.ext4**: Checks and repairs the filesystem
- **e2freefrag**: Reports on defragmentation
- **e4defrag**: Defrags the filesystem; normally not needed

To create an ext4 filesystem, use the following command:

```
sudo mkfs.ext4 -L <label> <partition>
```

The label is optional, but makes it easier to recognize a filesystem.

The XFS Filesystem

XFS is a highly scalable filesystem. It can scale to 8 EiB (exbibyte = 2^60 bytes) with online resizing; the filesystem can grow as long as there is unallocated space and it can span multiple partitions and devices.

XFS is one of the fastest filesystems around, especially in combination with RAID volumes. However, this does come at a cost: you'll need at least 1 GB of memory in your VM if you want to use XFS. And if you want to be able to repair the filesystem, you'll need at least 2 GB of memory.

Another nice feature of XFS is that you can quiesce the traffic to the filesystem to create consistent backups of, for instance, a database server.

The most important utilities are as follows:

- **mkfs.xfs**: Formats the filesystem
- **xfs_admin**: Changes the parameters of the filesystem
- **xfs_growfs**: Decreases the size of the filesystem
- **xfs_repair**: Checks and repairs the filesystem
- **xfs_freeze**: Suspends access to an XFS filesystem; this makes consistent backups easier
- **xfs_copy**: Fast copies the content of an XFS filesystem

To create an XFS filesystem, use the following command:

```
sudo mkfs.xfs -L <label> <partition>
```

The label is optional, but makes it easier to recognize a filesystem.

The ZFS Filesystem

ZFS is a combined filesystem and logical volume manager developed by SUN, owned by Oracle since 2005. It's very well known for its excellent performance and rich features:

- Volume management and RAID

- Protection against data corruption

- Data compression and deduplication

- Scalable to 16 exabytes

- Able to export filesystems

- Snapshot support

ZFS can be implemented on Linux with a user-space driver (FUSE) or with a Linux kernel module (OpenZFS). In Ubuntu, it's better to use the kernel module; it performs better and doesn't have some of the limitations of the FUSE implementation. For instance, if you use FUSE, you can't export the filesystem with NFS.

The main reason why OpenZFS is not widely adopted is licensing. OpenZFS's **Common Development and Distribution License** (**CDDL**) license is incompatible with the Linux kernel's General Public License. Another reason is that ZFS can be a real memory hog; your VM requires 1 GB of memory extra per TB of storage, meaning 16 TB of storage requires 16 GB of RAM for applications. For ZFS, at least 1 GB of memory is recommended. But the more the better, as ZFS uses a lot of memory.

The most important utilities are as follows:

- **zfs**: Configures the ZFS filesystem

- **zpool**: Configures the ZFS storage pools

- **zfs.fsck**: Checks and repairs the ZFS filesystem

In this book, only the basic functionality of ZFS is covered.

Ubuntu is the only distribution with ZFS support. To be able to use ZFS in Ubuntu, you have to install the ZFS utilities:

```
sudo apt install zfsutils-linux
```

Following installation, you can start using ZFS. Let's assume that you added three disks to a VM. It is a good idea to use RAID 0 because it offers better performance and throughput than a single disk.

As a first step, let's create a pool with two disks:

```
sudo zpool create -f mydata /dev/sdc /dev/sdd
sudo zpool list mydata
sudo zpool status mydata
```

Let's now add the third disk, to show how to extend the pool:

```
sudo zpool add mydata /dev/sde
sudo zpool list mydata
sudo zpool history mydata
```

You can use this pool directly, or you can create datasets in it for more fine-grained control over features such as quotas:

```
sudo zfs create mydata/finance
sudo zfs set quota=5G mydata/finance
sudo zfs list
```

Last but not least, you'll need to mount this dataset to be able to use it:

```
sudo zfs set mountpoint=/home/finance mydata/finance
findmnt /home/finance
```

This mount will be persistent across reboots.

The BTRFS Filesystem

BTRFS is a relatively new filesystem, mainly developed by Oracle, but with contributions from SUSE and companies such as Facebook.

It's very similar to ZFS in terms of features, but it is in heavy development. This means that not all the features are considered to be stable. Before using this filesystem, please visit https://btrfs.wiki.kernel.org/index.php/Status.

The memory requirements are the same as XFS: 1 GB of memory in your VM. You don't need extra memory if you want to repair the filesystem.

In this book, only the basic functionality of BTRFS is covered. You can use BTRFS on all distributions, but please be aware that on RHEL and CentOS, the filesystem is labeled as deprecated and, in RHEL 8, it's removed. For more information, please visit https://access.redhat.com/solutions/197643.

The most important utilities are as follows:

- `mkfs.btrfs`: Formats devices with this filesystem

- `btrfs`: Manages the filesystem

Let's assume that you added three disks to a VM. It is a good idea to use RAID 0 to improve performance and allow for improved throughput compared to using just a single disk.

As a first step, let's create a BTRFS filesystem with two underlying disks:

```
sudo mkfs.btrfs -d raid0 -L mydata /dev/sdc /dev/sdd
```

Of course, you can extend the filesystem with the third disk, but before you can do that, you have to mount the filesystem:

```
sudo mkdir /srv/mydata
sudo mount LABEL=mydata /srv/mydata
sudo btrfs filesystem show /srv/mydata
```

Now, add the third disk:

```
sudo btrfs device add /dev/sde /srv/mydata
sudo btrfs filesystem show /srv/mydata
```

Like ZFS, BTRFS has the concept of datasets, but in BTRFS, they are called **subvolumes**. To create a subvolume, execute the following command:

```
sudo btrfs subvolume create /srv/mydata/finance

sudo btrfs subvolume list /srv/mydata
```

You can mount a subvolume independently of the root volume:

```
sudo mkdir /home/finance

sudo mount -o subvol=finance LABEL=mydata /home/finance
```

You can see the ID **258** in the output of the **findmnt** command:

```
linvirt@suse01:~> sudo btrfs subvolume list /srv/mydata
ID 258 gen 8 top level 5 path finance
linvirt@suse01:~> findmnt /home/finance
TARGET          SOURCE                FSTYPE OPTIONS
/home/finance /dev/sdc[/finance] btrfs  rw,relatime,space_cache,subvolid=258,sub
```

Figure 5.26: Creating a subvolume

The swap Filesystem

If you do not enough memory available for your application, you can use swap. It's always a good practice to use swap, even if you have an ample amount of RAM on the machine.

Idle memory is memory that was used before but is not currently needed by an application. If this idle memory is not used for an extended period of time, it will be swapped to make more memory available for more frequently used applications.

To improve the overall performance, it's a good idea to add some swap space to your Linux installation. It is a good idea to use the fastest storage available, preferably on the resource disk.

> **Note**
>
> In Linux, you can use swap files and swap partitions. There is no difference in performance. In Azure, you can't use swap partitions; this will make your system unstable, which is caused by the underlying storage.

Swap in Azure is managed by the Azure VM Agent. You can verify whether the **ResourceDisk.EnableSwap** parameter is set to **y** to confirm that the swap is enabled in **/etc/waagent.conf**. Also, you can check the swap size in **ResourceDisk.SwapSizeMB**:

```
# Create and use swapfile on resource disk.
ResourceDisk.EnableSwap=y
# Size of the swapfile.
ResourceDisk.SwapSizeMB=2048
```

In general, a **swapfile** of 2,048 MB of memory is more than enough to increase the overall performance. If the swap was not enabled, to create a swap file, you can update the **/etc/waagent.conf** file by setting the following three parameters:

- **ResourceDisk.Format=y**
- **ResourceDisk.EnableSwap=y**
- **ResourceDisk.SwapSizeMB=xx**

And to restart the Azure VM Agent, for Debian/Ubuntu, execute the following command:

```
sudo systemctl restart walinuxagent
```

For Red Hat/CentOS, execute the following command:

```
service waagent restart
```

Verify the result:

```
ls -lahR /mnt | grep -i swap


swapon -s
```

If you find that the swap file is not created, you can go ahead and restart the VM. To do this, use either of the following commands:

```
shutdown -r now
init 6
```

Linux Software RAID

Redundant Array of Independent Disks (**RAID**), originally known as Redundant Array of Inexpensive Disks, is a redundancy technique where the same data is stored in different disks, which will help you recover data in the case of disk failure. There are different levels available for RAID. Microsoft officially states at https://docs.microsoft. com/en-us/azure/virtual-machines/linux/configure-raid that you'll need RAID 0 for optimal performance and throughput, but this is not a mandatory implementation. If your current infrastructure demands RAID, then you can implement it.

If your filesystem doesn't support RAID, you can use Linux Software RAID to create a RAID 0 device. You'll need to install the **mdadm** utility; it's available on every Linux distribution, but is probably not installed by default.

Let's assume you added three disks to your VM. Let's create a RAID 0 device called **/dev/md127** (just a random number that is not yet in use):

```
sudo mdadm --create /dev/md127 --level 0 \
   --raid-devices 3 /dev/sd{c,d,e}
```

Verify the configuration as follows:

```
cat /proc/mdstat


sudo mdadm --detail /dev/md127
```

The preceding commands should give you the following output:

```
[linvirt@centos ~]$ cat /proc/mdstat
Personalities : [raid0]
md127 : active raid0 sde[2] sdc[1] sdd[0]
        15716352 blocks super 1.2 512k chunks

unused devices: <none>
[linvirt@centos ~]$ sudo mdadm --detail /dev/md127
/dev/md127:
            Version : 1.2
      Creation Time : Wed Jun  6 15:24:36 2018
         Raid Level : raid0
         Array Size : 15716352 (14.99 GiB 16.09 GB)
       Raid Devices : 3
      Total Devices : 3
        Persistence : Superblock is persistent

        Update Time : Wed Jun  6 15:24:36 2018
              State : clean
     Active Devices : 3
    Working Devices : 3
     Failed Devices : 0
      Spare Devices : 0
```

Figure 5.27: Verifying the RAID configuration

Make the configuration persistent:

```
mdadm --detail --scan --verbose >> /etc/mdadm.conf
```

Now, you can use this device and format it with a filesystem, as here:

```
mkfs.ext4 -L BIGDATA /dev/md127
```

Stratis

Stratis is newly introduced in RHEL 8 and is used to create a multi-disk, multi-tiered storage pool, to monitor the pool and manage it with ease, and with a minimal amount of manual intervention. It does not provide RAID support, but it converts multiple block devices into one pool with a filesystem on top of it. Stratis uses already existing technology: LVM and the XFS filesystem.

If Stratis is not installed on your RHEL, this can be easily installed by executing the following command:

```
sudo dnf install stratis-cli
```

Enable the daemon with the following command:

```
sudo systemctl enable --now stratisd
```

Let's assume that you added two data disks to your VM: **/dev/sdc** and **/dev/sdd**. Create the pool:

```
sudo stratis pool create stratis01 /dev/sdc /dev/sdd
```

Verify using this command:

```
sudo stratis pool list
```

The output shows the total amount of storage; in the example above, 64 GB. 104 MiB of it is already occupied by metadata required for pool management:

```
[rithin@rhel8 ~]$ sudo stratis pool list
Name          Total Physical Size  Total Physical Used
stratis01               64 GiB                104 MiB
```

Figure 5.28: Storage details of stratis pool

To get more details about the disks in the pool and the usage, execute the following command:

```
sudo stratis blockdev list
```

As you can see in the following screenshot, we get the same output, but with more details about the disks in the pool and usage. In the following output, you can see the pool name and the status:

```
[rithin@rhel8 ~]$ sudo stratis blockdev list
Pool Name  Device Node  Physical Size  State  Tier
stratis01  /dev/sdc           32 GiB  InUse  Data
stratis01  /dev/sdd           32 GiB  InUse  Data
```

Figure 5.29: Pool name and status

Here, the storage is used for data, because it's also possible to have a disk configured as a read/write cache. Stratis forms a filesystem (which is xfs, by default) on top of the newly created pool:

```
sudo stratis filesystem create stratis01 finance
```

The filesystem is labeled **finance** and is accessible via the device name (**/stratis/stratis01/finance**) or UUID.

With this information, you can mount it as you would do for any other filesystem, like with systemd mounts, as we'll discuss later in this chapter.

After creating a filesystem, you can create snapshots, which are basically copies of the original filesystem. A snapshot can be added by executing this command:

```
sudo stratis filesystem snapshot stratis01 finance finance_snap
```

To list the filesystem, we can execute the following command:

```
sudo stratis filesystem
```

And you have to mount it as a normal filesystem!

Adding a read/write cache can improve performance, especially if you use a disk with better performance than the standard SSD disks (or even non-SSD disks). Let's say that this disk is **/dev/sde**:

```
sudo sudo stratis pool add-cache stratis01 /dev/sde
```

And verify it the same way, with the **blockdev** parameter as we did before:

```
[student@rhel8 ~]$ sudo sudo stratis pool add-cache stratis01 /dev/sde
[student@rhel8 ~]$ sudo stratis blockdev list
Pool Name  Device Node    Physical Size   State    Tier
stratis01  /dev/sdc             32 GiB   In-use   Data
stratis01  /dev/sdd             32 GiB   In-use   Data
stratis01  /dev/sde             32 GiB   In-use   Cache
```

Figure 5.30: Adding a cache to **/dev/sde disk**

To conclude the section, we have discussed various filesystems; your choice of them will depend on your requirements. First, you need to make sure that the filesystem is compatible with your distribution; for example, BTRFS is removed in RHEL 8. So, it's always best to check compatibility before choosing.

systemd

After the Linux kernel boots, the first Linux process begins the first process. This process is known as an **init** process. In modern Linux systems, this process is **systemd**. Have a look at the following screenshot, which shows the running process in a tree format:

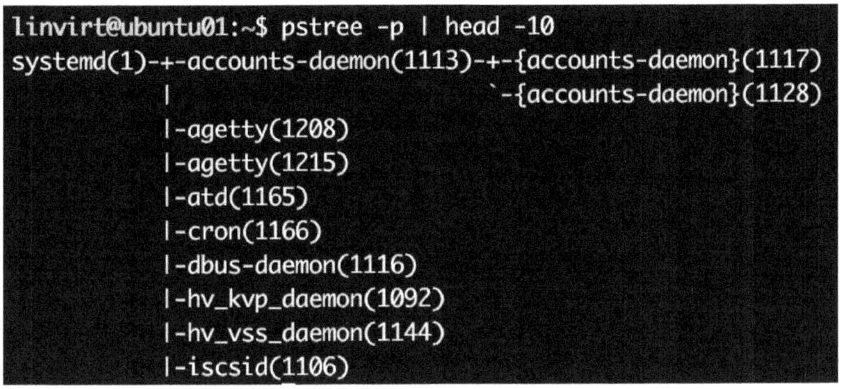

```
linvirt@ubuntu01:~$ pstree -p | head -10
systemd(1)-+-accounts-daemon(1113)-+-{accounts-daemon}(1117)
           |                       `-{accounts-daemon}(1128)
           |-agetty(1208)
           |-agetty(1215)
           |-atd(1165)
           |-cron(1166)
           |-dbus-daemon(1116)
           |-hv_kvp_daemon(1092)
           |-hv_vss_daemon(1144)
           |-iscsid(1106)
```

Figure 5.31: A view of the running processes in a tree format

systemd is responsible for starting all processes in parallel during the boot process, except the processes that are created by the kernel. After that, it activates services, among other things, on demand. It also tracks and manages mount points, and it manages system-wide settings such as the hostname.

systemd is an event-driven system. It communicates with the kernel and will react to an event such as a point in time or a user who introduces a new device or who presses *Ctrl + Alt + Del*.

Working with Units

systemd works with units, which are entities that are managed by systemd and encapsulate information about every object that is relevant to systemd.

The unit files are configuration files that contain configuration directives, describing the unit and defining its behavior. These files are stored as follows:

File	Description
service	Script or daemon
mount	Mounts filesystems
automount	Mounts remote NFS or Common Internet File System (CIFS) shares
timer	Scheduled tasks
path	Monitors a file or directory for events and uses them for service unit execution
target	Collection of other units

Figure 5.32: Unit files and their description

Units are manageable via the **systemctl** utility. If you want to see all the available types, execute the following command:

```
systemctl --type help
```

To list all installed unit files, use the following command:

```
sudo systemctl list-unit-files
```

To list the active units, use the following command:

```
sudo systemctl list-units
```

Both the **list-unit-files** and **list-units** parameters can be used in combination with **--type**.

Services

The service units are there to manage scripts or daemons. Let's have a look at the SSH service:

> **Note**
>
> The screenshots are taken from Ubuntu 18.04. The names of services may be different on other distributions.

```
linvirt@ubuntu01:~$ systemctl status sshd.service
● ssh.service - OpenBSD Secure Shell server
   Loaded: loaded (/lib/systemd/system/ssh.service; enabled; vendor preset: enab
led)
   Active: active (running) since Thu 2018-06-07 07:34:44 UTC; 58min
ago
 Main PID: 1291 (sshd)
    Tasks: 1 (limit: 1051)
   CGroup: /system.slice/ssh.service
           └─1291 /usr/sbin/sshd -D

Jun 07 07:34:44 ubuntu01 systemd[1]: Starting OpenBSD Secure Shell server...
Jun 07 07:34:44 ubuntu01 sshd[1291]: Server listening on 0.0.0.0 port 22.
Jun 07 07:34:44 ubuntu01 sshd[1291]: Server listening on :: port 22.
```

Figure 5.33: ssh service details

Using the **status** parameter of **systemctl**, you can see that the unit is loaded, enabled at boot, and that it's the default value. If it's not enabled, you can enable it with this command; enabling will add the service to the autostart chain:

```
sudo systemctl enable <service name.service>
```

To see the status of the service, you can execute this command:

```
sudo systemctl status <service name>
```

In the output, you can see that the SSH service is running and that the last entries in the logging are shown:

```
[rithin@rhel8 ~]$ sudo systemctl status sshd
● sshd.service - OpenSSH server daemon
   Loaded: loaded (/usr/lib/systemd/system/sshd.service; enabled; vendor preset: enabled)
   Active: active (running) since Fri 2019-12-20 05:37:11 UTC; 5h 26min ago
     Docs: man:sshd(8)
           man:sshd_config(5)
 Main PID: 1385 (sshd)
    Tasks: 1 (limit: 12003)
   Memory: 8.9M
   CGroup: /system.slice/sshd.service
           └─1385 /usr/sbin/sshd -D -oCiphers=aes256-gcm@openssh.com,chacha20-poly1305@openssh.co>

Dec 20 10:07:28 rhel8 sshd[12071]: pam_unix(sshd:auth): check pass; user unknown
Dec 20 10:07:28 rhel8 sshd[12071]: pam_unix(sshd:auth): authentication failure; logname= uid=0 eu>
Dec 20 10:07:29 rhel8 sshd[12070]: Failed password for invalid user pi from 116.86.166.93 port 46>
Dec 20 10:07:29 rhel8 sshd[12071]: Failed password for invalid user pi from 116.86.166.93 port 46>
Dec 20 10:07:30 rhel8 sshd[12070]: Connection closed by invalid user pi 116.86.166.93 port 46074 >
Dec 20 10:07:30 rhel8 sshd[12071]: Connection closed by invalid user pi 116.86.166.93 port 46078 >
Dec 20 10:56:41 rhel8 sshd[13988]: Accepted password for rithin from 137.97.45.178 port 44866 ssh2
Dec 20 10:56:41 rhel8 sshd[13988]: pam_unix(sshd:session): session opened for user rithin by (uid>
Dec 20 10:56:43 rhel8 sshd[14008]: Accepted password for rithin from 137.97.45.178 port 48766 ssh2
Dec 20 10:56:44 rhel8 sshd[14008]: pam_unix(sshd:session): session opened for user rithin by (uid>
```

Figure 5.34: Service status and entries

To look into the content of the **unit** file, execute the following command:

```
sudo systemctl cat <service name.service>
```

A **unit** file always has two or three sections:

- **[Unit]**: Description and dependency handling
- **[<Type>]**: Configuration of the type
- **[Install]**: Optional section if you want to be able to enable the service at boot time

To handle the dependencies, there are several directives available; the most important ones are these:

- **before**: The specified unit is delayed until this unit is started.
- **after**: The specified unit is started before this unit is started.
- **requires**: If this unit is activated, the unit listed here will be activated as well. If the specified unit failed, this one will fail as well.
- **wanted**: If this unit is activated, the unit listed here will be activated as well. There are no consequences if the specified unit fails.

> **Note**
>
> If you don't specify **before** or **after**, the listed unit or units (comma separated) will be started at the same time as the unit starts.

An example of an **ssh** service is as follows:

```
[Unit]
Description=OpenSSH Daemon After=network.target


[Service]
EnvironmentFile=-/etc/sysconfig/ssh

ExecStartPre=/usr/sbin/sshd-gen-keys-start

ExecStart=/usr/sbin/sshd -D $SSHD_OPTS

ExecReload=/bin/kill -HUP $MAINPID KillMode=process

Restart=always


[Install]
WantedBy=multi-user.target
```

Most options in the **Service** section speak for themselves; if not, just look into the man pages of **systemd.unit** and **systemd.service**. For the **[Install]** section, the **WantedBy** directive states that if you enable this service, it will become a part of the **multi-user. target** collection, which is activated at boot.

Before going into the targets, the last thing to cover is how to create overrides. systemd units can have many different directives; many are default options. To show all possible directives, execute the following command:

```
sudo systemctl show
```

If you want to change one of the defaults, use the following command:

```
sudo systemctl edit <service name.service>
```

An editor is started. Add the entry, for instance, as follows:

```
[Service]
ProtectHome=read-only
```

Save the changes. You need to reload the systemd configuration files and restart the service:

```
sudo systemctl daemon-reload


sudo systemctl restart sshd
```

Review the changes with `systemctl cat sshd.service`. Log in again and try to save something in your home directory.

> **Note**
>
> If you want another editor for `systemctl edit`, add a variable, **SYSTEMD_EDITOR**, to the **/etc/environment** file, for instance, **SYSTEMD_EDITOR=/usr/bin/vim**.

Targets

A target is a collection of units. There are two types of targets:

- **Non-isolatable**: A normal collection of units; for instance, the `timers.target`, which contains all scheduled tasks.

- **Isolatable**: If you execute `systemctl isolate <target name.target>`, this will shut down all processes that are not part of the target and start all those that are part of it. Examples include the `rescue.target` and `graphical.target` units.

To see the content of a target, use the following command:

```
systemctl list-dependencies <target name.target>
```

Scheduled Tasks

systemd can be used to schedule tasks. An example of a timer unit file follows:

```
[Unit]
Description=Scheduled backup task

[Timer]
OnCalendar=*-*-* 10:00:00

[Install]
WantedBy=timers.target
```

If you save the content of this file to **/etc/systemd/system/backup.timer**, you'll need a corresponding file, **/etc/systemd/system/backup.service**, for example, with the following content:

```
[Unit]
Description = backup script


[Service]
Type = oneshot
ExecStart = /usr/local/bin/mybackup.sh
```

Enable and activate the timer:

```
sudo systemctl enable --now backup.timer
```

To find out about the scheduled tasks, use the following command:

```
sudo systemctl list-timers
```

> **Note**
>
> Read **man 7 systemd.time** to learn more about the syntax of the calendar events. There is a special section on this man page for it.

If the scheduled task is not a recurring one, you can use the following command:

```
sudo systemd-run --on-calendar <event time> <command>
```

For example, if we want to echo **done** to a file **/tmp/done** on October 11, 2019, 12:00 AM, we must do as shown in the following screenshot:

```
[rithin@rhel8 ~]$ sudo systemd-run --on-calendar '2019-10-11 12:00' /bin/bash \
> -c 'echo done > /tmp/done'
Running timer as unit: run-r082253503fb74c07a0bd684db303549e.timer
Will run service as unit: run-r082253503fb74c07a0bd684db303549e.service
[rithin@rhel8 ~]$
```

Figure 5.35: Running a scheduled task by providing event time

Mounting Local Filesystem

The mount unit is available to mount filesystems. There is something special about the name of the mount unit: it must correspond to the mount point. For instance, if you want to mount on **/home/finance**, the mount unit file becomes **/etc/systemd/system/home-finance.mount**:

```
[Unit]
Description = Finance Directory


[Mount]
What = /dev/sdc1
Where = /home/finance
Type = xfs
Options = defaults


[Install]
WantedBy = local-fs.target
```

Use **systemctl start home-finance.mount** to start mounting, and **systemctl enable home-finance.mount** to mount at boot time.

Mounting Remote Filesystem

If a filesystem is not local but remote, for instance, if it's an NFS share, the best way to mount it is using **automount**. If you are not using automount (the **autofs** service), you have to manually mount the remote share; the advantage here is that if you have accessed the remote share, autofs will automatically mount. It will mount the share, and if you lose the connection to the share, it will try to automount the share on demand.

You have to create two files. Let's take an NFS mount on **/home/finance** as an example. First, create **/etc/systemd/system/home-finance.mount** with the following content:

```
[Unit]
Description = NFS Finance Share


[Mount]
What = 192.168.122.100:/share
Where = /home/finance
Type = nfs
Options = vers=4.2
```

Create a file named **/etc/systemd/system/home-finance.automount**:

```
[Unit]
Description = Automount NFS Finance Share


[Automount]
Where = /home/finance


[Install]
WantedBy = remote-fs.target
```

Start the automount unit, and not the mount unit. Of course, you can enable it at boot.

Summary

In this chapter, we took a deep dive into Linux, explaining the fundamental tasks of every Linux system administrator: managing software, the network, storage, and services.

Of course, as a Linux system administrator, this is not something you're going to do on a daily basis. Most likely, you're not going to do it manually, but automate or orchestrate it. But to be able to orchestrate it, you'll need to understand how it works and be able to verify and troubleshoot the configuration. This will be covered in *Chapter 8, Exploring Continuous Configuration Automation*.

In the next chapter, we will explore the options available in Linux that limit access to the system:

- Mandatory access control
- Network access control lists
- Firewalls

We'll also cover how to join Linux machines to the domain using Azure Active Directory Domain Services.

Questions

1. What is responsible for the recognition of hardware?
2. What is responsible for device naming?
3. What are the methods for identifying network interfaces?
4. Who maintains the network configuration?
5. What are the methods for identifying locally attached storage?
6. Why do we use RAID 0 in Azure?
7. What are the options for implementing RAID 0 in Azure?
8. Try to implement a RAID 0 device using three disks; format it with XFS. Mount it, and make sure that it's mounted at boot time.

Further Reading

In one way, this chapter was a deep dive, but there is much more to learn in relation to all the topics covered in this chapter. I strongly suggest that you read the man pages of all the commands used.

For storage, besides the documentation on the Azure website, some filesystems have their own websites:

- **XFS**: https://xfs.org
- **BTRFS**: https://btrfs.wiki.kernel.org
- **ZFS**: http://open-zfs.org
- **Stratis**: https://stratis-storage.github.io

Lennart Poettering, one of the main developers of systemd, has a nice blog with lots of tips and background information: http://0pointer.net/blog. And, in addition, documentation is available at https://www.freedesktop.org/wiki/Software/systemd.

As the `systemctl status` command doesn't provide you with enough information, we will be discussing more regarding logging in *Chapter 11, Troubleshooting and Monitoring Your Workloads*.

Managing Linux Security and Identities

In the previous chapter, we discussed handling storage, along with network and process management. However, as a system administrator, your primary goal is to secure your Linux machine to deny any unauthorized access or limit access to users. In an enterprise environment, security breaches are a massive concern. In this chapter, we'll be covering security—the protection of your workload at the operating system level; for example, if your organization is a financial institution where you will be dealing with workloads that deal with monetary commitments and even the **personally identifiable information** (**PII**) of customers, it's critical that you secure the workload to avoid any breaches. Of course, Azure already provides you with services to protect your VMs in many ways and at many levels. The following are a few of these services:

- Azure Resource Manager, which provides security, auditing, and tagging features

- Web Application Firewall, which protects against many attacks, such as SQL injection

- The stateful packet filtering feature of network security groups

- Azure Firewall, which provides a stateful firewall tightly integrated with the monitoring functions of Azure

You can also subscribe to the Azure Security Center service for unified security management with a number of attractive features, such as continuous security assessment.

With all these possibilities, do we still need protection at the operating system level? In our opinion, multi-level protection is a good idea. It will cost a hacker more effort and time, and this will make it easier to detect the hacker. There is no such thing as bug-free software: if an application is vulnerable, at least the operating system should be protected.

Identity management is a topic that is certainly related to security. You can integrate Linux with **Azure Active Directory** (**Azure AD**) to centralize your login accounts, make access fine-grained by using role-based access control, revoke access, and enable multi-factor authentication.

By the end of this chapter, you'll be able to:

- Implement a **mandatory access control** (**MAC**) system, such as SELinux or AppArmor.

- Understand the basics of **discretionary access control** (**DAC**).

- Use the identity management systems available in Azure.

- Enhance Linux security with the firewall daemon and systemd.

Linux Security Tips

Before we deep dive into all the great security measures you can take, here are some tips regarding security.

Security implementation on multiple levels is, in general, a good idea. This way, a hacker requires different approaches to gain access, and this costs them time. Because of this time, and hopefully also because of logging and monitoring, you have a greater chance of detecting unauthorized access.

For files and directories, **DAC** is still a very good foundation. Make the permissions on files and directories as strict as possible. Check the owner and group ownership and use **access control lists** (**ACLs**) instead of permissions for unauthorized users. Try to avoid using the `suid/sgid` bit as much as possible. Are there users who need to change their own password? No? Then remove that bit from the `passwd` command.

Use partitioning, especially for directories such as **/tmp**, **/var**, **/var/tmp**, and **/home**, and mount them with the **noexec**, **nodev**, and **nosuid** flags:

- In general, it's not a good idea for a user to be able to execute programs from these locations. Luckily, if you can't set the owner to root, you can copy a program with the **suid** bit to your own directory as a normal user.

- The **suid** and **sgid** permissions on files in these directories are very, very dangerous.

- Do not allow the creation or existence of characters or special devices on this partition.

To access the VM, use SSH key-based authentication, not passwords. Limit access to certain IPs, using ACLs or a firewall. Limit users and allow no remote access for root (use the **PermitRootLogin no** parameter and **AllowUsers** to only allow one or two accounts access). Use **sudo** to execute commands as root. Perhaps create special users, or groups of users, for special tasks in the **sudo** configuration.

Do not install too much software on a VM, especially when it comes to network services, such as web servers and email servers. Use the **ss** command from time to time to review the open ports and compare them with the ACLs and/or firewall rules.

Another tip is not to disable SELinux on your system, which is a security module in the Linux kernel. Don't worry about this now, as we have a dedicated section on SElinux.

Keep your system up to date; there is a reason why Linux vendors provide you with updates. Do it manually or with an automation/orchestration tool. Just do it!

Technical Requirements

For the purposes of this chapter, you'll need to deploy RedHat/CentOS 7 and an Ubuntu 18.04 VM. Another option is to use SUSE SLE 12 or openSUSE LEAP instead of the CentOS and Ubuntu VMs. SUSE supports all options discussed in this chapter.

DAC

DAC is also known as user-dictated access control. You may already be familiar with the classic permissions in Linux and ACLs. These combine to form DAC. Classic permissions check the **user ID** (**UID**) and **group ID** (**GID**) of the current process. Classic permissions match the UID and GID of the user trying to access the file with the UID and GID set to the file. Let's see how DAC was introduced and what level of permission you have in Linux. However, we will not be discussing this in detail as the main intention is to get you familiarized with permissions in Linux.

Introduction to DAC

The majority of operating systems, such as Linux, macOS, flavors of Unix, and even Windows, are based on DAC. MAC and DAC were defined in the **Trusted Computer System Evaluation Criteria** (**TCSEC**), also known as the Orange Book, published by the US **DoD** (**Department of Defense**). We'll be discussing MAC in the next section. As the name suggests, DAC allows the owners or creators of files to decide what level of access they need to give to other users for the same file.

Although we see DAC implemented in all systems, it is also regarded as weak. For example, if we grant read access to a user, it will be transitive in nature. So, there is nothing that will stop the user from copying the content of someone else's file to an object that the user has access to. In other words, the distribution of information is not administered in DAC. In the next section, we will take a quick look at file permissions.

File Permissions in Linux

Every file and directory in Linux is treated as an object and has three types of owner: user, group, and other. Going forward, we will generally refer to files and directories as objects. First, let's understand the three different types of owners:

- **User**: The user is the person who creates the object. By default, this person will become the owner of the object.

- **Group**: A group is a collection of users. All users who are part of the same group will have the same access levels in relation to the object. The concept of a group makes it easier for you to assign permissions to multiple users at the same time. Think of a scenario where you will be creating a file and you want your team members to access the file as well. If you are part of a large team and assigning permissions to each user, this will be hectic. Instead, you can add the users to a group and define the permission for the group, meaning that all the users in the group inherit access.

- **Other**: This refers to any other user who is not the owner (creator) of the object or who is not part of the user group who could own the object. In other words, think of a set containing the creator and all users in the group that has permission; "other" refers to a user who is not an element of this set.

As stated earlier, each object has three types of owner. Each owner (user, group, owner) will have three permissions on an object. These are as follows:

- **Read**: Read permission will give permission to read or open a file. Read permission on a directory means that the user will be able to list the content of the directory.

- **Write**: If applied to a file, this will give permission to alter the content of the file. Adding this permission to a directory will grant the authority to add, remove, and rename files in the directory.

- **Execute**: This permission is mandatory for running an executable program or script. For example, if you have a bash script and you have read/write permission, this means you will be able to read and alter the code. To execute the code, however, you need this permission.

Here is a pictorial representation of owners and the associated permissions:

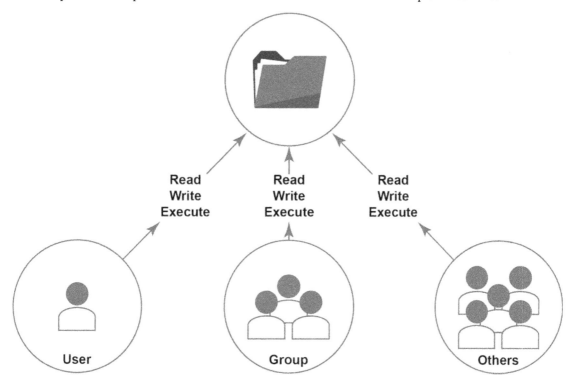

Figure 6.1: Owner types and access permissions

Let's move on and understand how we can figure out the permissions from the Linux Terminal.

To list the contents of a directory, execute **ls -lah**.

The output will be different based on the content you have in the directory you're listing from:

```
 ?  linux ls -lah
total 0
drwxr-xr-x 1 root    root    4.0K Nov 21 17:52 .
drwxr-xr-x 1 rithin  rithin  4.0K Nov 21 18:26 ..
drwxr-xr-x 1 rithin  rithin  4.0K Nov 21 17:50 data
-rw-r--r-- 1 rithin  rithin     0 Nov 21 17:52 external.png
lrwxrwxrwx 1 root    root      13 Nov 21 17:52 home -> /home/rithin/
```

Figure 6.2: Listing the contents of a directory

If you observe the **data** line, the first letter is **d**, which implies that it is a directory. As regards **external.png**, it's showing **-**, which stands for a file, and there is **l** for **home**, which means a link (more like a shortcut).

Let's take a closer look:

```
drwxr-xr-x 1 rithin rithin 4.0K Nov 21 17:50 data
```

Figure 6.3: Data line of the directory output

First, **rwx** denotes that the user/owner has read, write, and execute permissions.

Second, **r-x** denotes that the group has read and execute permissions. However, write permission is not there.

Third, **r-x** denotes that all others have read and execute access, but no write access.

Similarly, you can understand the permissions assigned to other objects.

These will already be written in the order **read(r)**, **write(w)**, and **execute**. If a letter is missing, that means that the permission is not there. Here is a table explaining what these letters signify:

R	Read
W	Write
X	Execute
-	Nopermission

Figure 6.4: Symbols for access permissions

You might be wondering who the owner of this file is and which group is getting access. This is answered in the output itself:

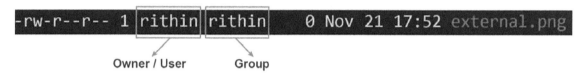

Figure 6.5: Owner and group details

In this case:

- The user has read and write permission, but no execute permission.

- The group has read permission only, and no write and execute permission.

- All others have read permission only.

The following diagram will help you to understand how to differentiate between permissions for each owner:

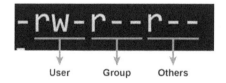

Figure 6.6: Differentiating between permissions for each owner

You can change the permissions of a file or folder using the **chmod** command. The general syntax is:

```
chmod permissions filename/directory
```

However, applying a permission to the directory doesn't inherit the same to the sub-folders and files therein. If you would like the permissions to be inherited, you can use the **-R** parameter, which stands for *recursive*.

Also, this command doesn't give any output; that is, it doesn't return any output irrespective of whether it applied the permissions or not. You can use the **-v** parameter to get verbose output.

There are two ways in which you can pass permissions to the **chmod** command:

- Symbolic method
- Absolute method/numeric model

Symbolic Method

In the symbolic method, we will use the operator and user denotations. The following is a list of operators:

Operator	Purpose
=	Set permission, and this overrides the current permission
+	Add permission
-	Remove permission

Figure 6.7: Operators in symbolic method

And here is a list of user denotations:

Denotation	Explanation
u	owner/user
g	group
o	others
a	all

Figure 6.8: User denotations

Let's now examine how we can combine the operator and denotation to change permission. We will be using the **-v** parameter to understand what's changed.

Let's recall the permissions we had for the **external.png** file:

```
-rw-r--r-- 1 rithin rithin     0 Nov 21 17:52 external.png
```

Figure 6.9: Permissions for external.png file

As of now, the user doesn't have execute permissions. To add these, execute the following command:

```
chmod -v u+x external.png
```

In the output, you can see that the value changed from **rw-r--r--** to **rwxr--r--**:

```
 linux chmod -v u+x external.png
mode of 'external.png' changed from 0644 (rw-r--r--) to 0744 (rwxr--r--)
```

Figure 6.10: Adding execute permissions

You will see some numbers here. We will discuss what these are when we discuss the absolute method.

Next, let's try to write and execute permissions for the group by executing the following command:

```
chmod -v g+wx external.png
```

So, adding **wx(write, execute)** to **g(group)** will give you an output similar to the following. You can clearly understand the change from the output:

```
 linux chmod -v g+wx external.png
mode of 'external.png' changed from 0744 (rwxr--r--) to 0774 (rwxrwxr--)
```

Figure 6.11: Adding write and execute permissions to a group

Until now, we have been adding permissions. Now, let's see how to remove the existing read permissions of others.

Execute the following:

```
chmod -v o-r external.png
```

This will remove the read permission, which is evident from the following output:

```
 linux chmod -v o-r external.png
mode of 'external.png' changed from 0774 (rwxrwxr--) to 0770 (rwxrwx---)
```

Figure 6.12: Removing the read permission

Let's set read, write, and execute permissions for everyone (user, group, and other).

Execute the following command:

```
chmod -v a=rwx external.png
```

The output shows that the permissions changed to **rwxrwxrwx**:

```
⊡  linux chmod -v a=rwx external.png
mode of 'external.png' changed from 0770 (rwxrwx---) to 0777 (rwxrwxrwx)
```

Figure 6.13: Setting read, write and execute permissions to everyone

Another example involves combining the permissions for each owner and passing these in a single shot, as shown here:

```
chmod -v u=rw,g=r,o=x external.png
```

Here, user permission is set to read and write, group permission to read-only, and other permission to execute-only. Likewise, you can separate the permissions using commas and use the necessary operators to grant permissions.

Absolute (Numeric) Node

In this method, we will be using a three-digit octal number to set the permission. The following is a table of values and their corresponding permissions:

Number	PermissionType	Symbol
0	NoPermission	---
1	Execute	--x
2	Write	-w-
3	Execute+Write	-wx
4	Read	r--
5	Read+Execute	r-x
6	Read+Write	rw-
7	Read+Write+Execute	rwx

Figure 6.14: Numeric values and their corresponding permissions

Let's take an example. Check the permissions of the **new-file** file, which is located in our current directory. Execute **ls -lah**:

```
-rw-r--r-- 1 rithin rithin    0 Nov 21 19:47 new-file
```

Figure 6.15: Checking permissions of new-file

Now, let's use numeric mode and assign permissions. We will change the user permission to **rwx**, so 4 + 2 + 1 = 7, and then change the group permission to **rw**, so 4 + 2 + 0 = 6, and only execute for others, so 0 + 0 + 1 = 1.

Combining these three numbers, we get 761, so that is the value we need to pass to **chmod**.

Execute the following command:

```
chmod -v 761 new-file
```

The output will be as follows:

```
  data chmod -v 761 new-file
mode of 'new-file' changed from 0644 (rw-r--r--) to 0761 (rwxrw---x)
```

Figure 6.16: Assigning permissions using the 3-digit octal code

Now, we can relate the numbers we got in previous outputs when we were testing using the symbolic method.

Here is a pictorial representation of the value:

7	6	1
Read, Write, Execute (rwx)	Read, Write, (rw-)	Execute (--x)
4 + 2 + 1 = 7	4 + 2 + 0 = 6	0 + 0 + 1 = 1

Figure 6.17: Pictorial representation of the 3-digit octal code

You may have noticed that there is an extra digit before the permission we assigned (for example, 0761). This 0 is for advanced file permissions. If you recall the tips, we had "*The suid and sgid permissions on files in these directories are very, very dangerous*" and "*Try to avoid using the suid/sgid bit as much as possible*". These **suid/sgid** values are passed via an additional digit. It's better not to use this and stick to the basic permission as these are very dangerous and can be complex.

Now we know how to change permission, but how will we change the owning user and group? For this, we will be using the **chown** command. The syntax is as follows:

```
chown user:group filename/directory
```

This will change the owner and group of the file. If you want to change the owner only, you can use this:

```
chown user filename/directory
```

If you want to change just the group, use the **chgrp** command:

```
chgrp group filename/directory
```

As explained in the case of the **chown** command, this command is also not recursive. If you want to make the change inherited to the subfolder and files of a directory, use the **-R** (recursive) parameter. You also have a verbose (**-v**) option as we saw in **chmod**.

Now that we know about handling permissions, let's go to the next section about MAC. DAC was all about permission checks using the UID and GID. On the other hand, MAC is policy-based access control. Let's now take a closer look at MAC.

MAC

In MAC, a system limits access to specific resources depending on the authorization and sensitivity of the specific resource. It's more policy-based and is implemented using **Linux Security Modules** (**LSM**).

Security labels are at the heart of MAC. Every subject is given a level of security clearance (for example, secret or confidential) and each data object gets a security classification. For instance, a user with a security clearance level of confidential who is trying to retrieve a data object with a security classification of top secret is denied access, because their clearance is lower than the classification of the object.

Hence, it is quite obvious that you can use the MAC model mostly in those environments where confidentiality is of the utmost importance (government institutions, and so on).

SELinux and AppArmor are examples of MAC-based commercial systems.

LSM

LSM is a framework for providing an interface for adding MAC on top of DAC. This extra layer of security can be added with SELinux (Red Hat–based distributions and SUSE), AppArmor (Ubuntu and SUSE), or the lesser-known Tomoyo (SUSE). In this section, we'll cover SELinux and AppArmor.

DAC is a model that provides access control based on users who are a member of a group and permissions on files and devices. MAC restricts access to resource objects such as the following:

- Files

- Processes

- TCP/UDP ports

- Users and their roles

MAC, as implemented by SELinux, works by assigning a classification label, also known as a context label, to every resource object, whereas AppArmor is path-based. In either case, if one resource object requires access to another object, it needs clearance. So, even if a hacker makes it into your web application, for instance, the other resources are still protected!

SELinux

As we mentioned earlier, SELinux is a security module in Linux and, by way of a security tip, it's recommended that it not be disabled. SELinux was developed by the NSA and Red Hat. The initial release was on December 22, 2000, and, at the time of writing this book, the stable release available is 2.9, released in 2019. It can be used on every Red Hat–based distribution and SUSE. This book will cover implementation on Red Hat. If you want to use it on SUSE, visit the SUSE documentation at https://doc.opensuse. org/documentation/leap/security/html/book.security/cha-selinux.html to install and enable SELinux. After that, the procedures are the same. In the past, some effort was made to make it work on Ubuntu but, at the moment, there is no active development and the packages are broken.

All access must be explicitly granted but, on the distributions that utilize SELinux, many policies are already in place. This covers almost every resource object. On top of the list already mentioned in the documentation, it covers the following:

- The complete network stack, including IPsec
- Kernel capabilities
- **Inter-process communication** (**IPC**)
- Memory protection
- File descriptor (communication channels) inheritance and transfer

For container virtualization solutions such as Docker, SELinux can protect the host and offers protection between containers.

SELinux Configuration

SELinux is configured via the **/etc/selinux/config** file:

```
#  This file controls the state of SELinux on the system.
#  SELINUX= can take one of these three values:
#  enforcing - SELinux security policy is enforced.
#  permissive - SELinux prints warnings instead of enforcing.
#  disabled - No SELinux policy is loaded.
SELINUX=enforcing
```

The status should be in **enforcing** mode in a production environment. Policies are enforced and, if access is restricted, auditing can be done to be able to fix the problems caused by SELinux. The **permissive** mode can become handy if you are a software developer or packager and you need to create SELinux policies for your software.

It's possible to switch between the **enforcing** and **permissive** modes using the **setenforce** command. Use **setenforce 0** to switch to the permissive mode and **setenforce 1** to go back to the enforcing mode. The **getenforce** command is available to view the current status:

```
#  SELINUXTYPE= can take one of these three values:
#  targeted - Targeted processes are protected,
#  minimum - Modification of targeted policy.
#  Only selected processes are protected.
#  mls - Multi Level Security protection.
SELINUXTYPE=targeted
```

The default policy–**targeted**, protects all resources and provides enough protection for most workloads. **Multi-level security** (**MLS**) offers additional security by using levels of clearance provided by categories and sensitivities (such as confidential, secret, and top secret) together with SELinux users and roles. This can be very useful for file servers that offer file shares.

If the **minimum** type is selected, then only the bare minimum is protected; you need to configure everything else yourself if you want more protection. This type can be useful if there are difficulties in protecting a multi-process application (typically, very old applications) and a generated policy removes too many restrictions. In this scenario, it's better to leave the specific application unprotected, and protect the rest of the system. In this section, I'll only discuss **SELINUXTYPE=targeted**, which is the most widely used option.

To show the state of SELinux, you can use the **sestatus** command. The output should be similar to the following screenshot:

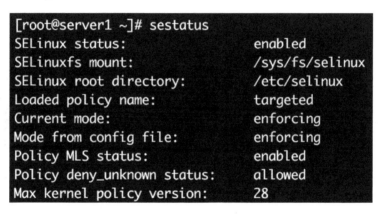

Figure 6.18: SELinux state

Before we explore SELinux, you'll need to add the necessary packages to your system to be able to audit SELinux. Please execute the following command:

```
sudo yum install setroubleshoot
```

After this, you'll need to reboot the VM:

```
sudo systemctl reboot
```

After the reboot, we're ready to use and troubleshoot SELinux:

```
SELinux context on ports
```

Let's start with an easy example involving the SSH service. As stated earlier, all processes are labeled with a context label. To make this label visible, many utilities, such as **ls**, **ps**, and **lsof**, have the **-Z** parameter. First, you have to find the main process ID of this service:

```
systemctl status sshd | grep PID
```

Using this process ID, we can ask for the context label:

```
ps -q <PID> -Z
```

The context label is **system_u**, **system_r**, **sshd_t**, and **s0-s0, c0.c1023**. Because we're using the targeted SELinux type, we only take care of the SELinux type part: **sshd_t**.

SSH is running on port 22. Let's now investigate the label on the port:

```
ss -ltn sport eq 22 -Z
```

You will establish that the context label is **system_u**, **system_r**, **sshd_t**, **s0-s0**, and **c0.c1023**, in other words, exactly the same. It's not difficult to understand that the **sshd** process does indeed have permission to run on this port with the same label:

```
[rithin@rhel8 ~]$ sudo systemctl status sshd | grep PID
 Main PID: 1385 (sshd)
[rithin@rhel8 ~]$ ps -q 1385 -Z
LABEL                            PID TTY          TIME CMD
system_u:system_r:sshd_t:s0-s0:c0.c1023 1385 ?   00:00:00 sshd
[rithin@rhel8 ~]$ ss -ltn sport eq 22 -Z
State      Recv-Q     Send-Q           Local Address:Port          Peer Address:Port
LISTEN     0          128                    0.0.0.0:22                 0.0.0.0:*
LISTEN     0          128                       [::]:22                    [::]:*
```

Figure 6.19: Context label for sshd process

It's not always that simple, but before going into a more complex scenario, let's modify the port that the SSH server is listening on to port 44. To do so, edit the **/etc/ssh/sshd_config** file:

```
sed -i 's/#Port 22/Port 44/' /etc/ssh/sshd_config
```

Then, restart the SSH server:

```
sudo systemctl restart sshd
```

This will fail:

```
Job for sshd.service failed because the control process exited with error code.

See systemctl status sshd.service and journalctl -xe for details.
```

If you execute the **journalctl -xe** command, you will see the following message:

```
SELinux is preventing /usr/sbin/sshd from name_bind access

on the tcp_socket port 44.
```

There are multiple methods for troubleshooting SELinux. You can use the log file, **/var/log/audit/audit.log**, directly, or with the **sealert -a /var/log/audit/audit.log** command, or use the **journalctl** command:

```
journalctl --identifier setroubleshoot
```

The logging entry also states the following:

```
For complete SELinux messages run: sealert -l <audit id>
```

Execute this command (and maybe redirect the output to a file or pipe it through **less** or **more**), and it will not only show you the same SELinux message again, but it will also come with a suggestion for how to fix it:

```
If you want to allow /usr/sbin/sshd to bind to network port 44

Then you need to modify the port type.

Do

# semanage port -a -t PORT_TYPE -p tcp 44

where PORT_TYPE is one of the following: ssh_port_t, vnc_port_t, xserver_
port_t.
```

Before going into this solution, SELinux works with multiple databases that contain the resource object, and the context label, that is, **/**, should be applied to the resource object. The **semanage** tool is available to modify the database and add entries to it; in our scenario, the database port. The output of the logging suggests adding a context label for TCP port 44 to the database. There are three possible contexts; all of them will fix your problem.

Another important aspect is the fact that there are sometimes other possible solutions. There is a confidence rating to make the choice easier for you. But even then, you still have to read carefully. Especially with files, sometimes, you want to add a regular expression instead of doing it for every file over and over again.

You can take a pragmatic approach and state "I am not using **vnc** and **xserver**, so I choose **ssh_port_t**" or you can use the **sepolicy** utility, part of the **policycoreutils-devel** package. If you're getting an error message, install **policycoreutils-devel** using **sudo yum install -y policycoreutils-devel**:

```
sepolicy network -a /usr/sbin/sshd
```

Search in the output for the TCP **name_bind**, because SELinux access is preventing **/usr/sbin/sshd** from having **name_bind** access to **tcp_socket port 44**.

Now that you know where the suggestion comes from, look into the current label of port 22:

```
sepolicy network -p 22
```

The label is **ssh_port_t**.

> **Note**
>
> You can use **semanage port -l** and **grep** on port 22.

It really makes sense to use the same label. Not convinced? Let's generate man pages:

```
sepolicy manpage -a -p /usr/share/man/man8/
mandb
```

The **ssh_selinux** man page tells you in the **port types** section that the correct label is **ssh_port_t**.

Finally, let's fix the problem:

```
semanage port -a -t ssh_port_t -p tcp 44
```

You don't have to restart the **sshd** service; **systemd** will restart this service automatically within 42 seconds. By the way, the **sshd_config** file already has a comment that describes this fix. It is explicitly stated in the line before **#Port 22**:

```
If you want to change the port on a SELinux system, you have to tell:
# SELinux about this change.
# semanage port -a -t ssh_port_t -p tcp #PORTNUMBER
```

It's a good idea to undo the configuration change and configure it back to port 22; otherwise, you might be locked out of the test system.

SELinux Context on Files

After our first meeting with SELinux and investigating context labels on ports, it's time to investigate context labels on files. As an example, we're going to use an **FTP** (**File Transfer Protocol**) server and client. Install **vsftpd** and an FTP client:

```
sudo yum install vsftpd ftp
```

Then, create a directory called **/srv/ftp/pub**:

```
sudo mkdir -p /srv/ftp/pub
chown -R ftp:ftp /srv/ftp
```

And then create a file in **/srv/ftp**:

```
echo WELCOME > /srv/ftp/README
```

Edit the configuration file, **/etc/vsftpd/vsftpd.conf**, and add the following beneath the **local_enable=YES** line:

```
anon_root=/srv/ftp
```

This makes **/srv/ftp** the default root directory for the **vsftpd** service for anonymous users. Now you are ready to start the service:

```
sudo systemctl start vsftpd.service

sudo systemctl status vsftpd.service
```

Using the **ftp** utility, try to log into the FTP server as the user **anonymous**, without a password:

```
ftp localhost
```

```
Trying ::1...

Connected to localhost (::1).

220 (vsFTPd 3.0.2)

Name (localhost:root): anonymous

331 Please specify the password.

Password:

230 Login successful.

Remote system type is UNIX.

Using binary mode to transfer files.

ftp> ls

229 Entering Extended Passive Mode (|||57280|).

150 Here comes the directory listing.

-rw-r--r-- 1 14 50 8 Jul 16 09:47 README

drwxr-xr-x 2 14 50 6 Jul 16 09:44 pub

226 Directory send OK.

Try to get the file:

get README
```

And it works! Why is this possible? Because there is already an entry in the database for **/srv/ftp/README** with the correct label:

```
semanage fcontext -l | grep /srv
```

The preceding command shows the following line:

```
/srv/([^/]*/)?ftp(/.*)? all files system_u:object_r:public_content_t:s0
```

It's applied while creating a new file:

```
stat -c %C /srv/ftp/README
```

```
ls -Z /srv/ftp/README
```

Both commands tell you that the type is **public_content_t**. The man page of **ftpd_ selinux** has two sections that are important here: **standard file context** and **sharing files**. The man page states that the **public_content_t** type only allows you to read (download) files, but that you are not allowed to write (upload) files with this type. You need another type, **public_content_rw_t**, to be able to upload files.

Create an upload directory:

```
mkdir -m 2770 /srv/ftp/incoming
```

```
chown -R ftp:ftp /srv/ftp/incoming
```

View the current label and change it:

```
ls -dZ /srv/ftp/incoming
```

```
semanage fcontext -a -t public_content_rw_t "/srv/ftp/incoming(/.*)?"
```

```
restorecon -rv /srv/ftp/incoming
```

```
ls -dZ /srv/ftp/incoming
```

First, you have to add the policy to the **fcontext** database; after that, you can apply the policy to the already existing directory.

> **Note**
>
> Read the man page of **selinux-fcontext**. In addition to describing all the options, there are also some nice examples.

SELinux Boolean

Using a single string, you can change the behavior of SELinux. This string is called **SELinux Boolean**. You can get a list of Booleans and their values using `getsebool -a`. Using `boolean allow_ftpd_anon_write`, we are going to change the way in which SELinux reacts. Connect anonymously to the FTP server again and try to upload a file:

```
ftp> cd /incoming

250 Directory successfully changed.

ftp> put /etc/hosts hosts

local: /etc/hosts remote: hosts

229 Entering Extended Passive Mode (||||12830|).

550 Permission denied.
```

The `journalctl --identifier setroubleshoot` command makes it very clear to you:

```
SELinux is preventing vsftpd from write access on the directory ftp.
```

The `sealert` command will provide you with the information necessary to fix the problem:

```
setsebool -P allow_ftpd_anon_write 1
```

So, what's happening here? Sometimes, simple rules for a port or file are not enough, for instance, if an NFS share has to be exported with Samba as well. In this scenario, it is possible to create your own complex SELinux policy or use the Boolean database with easy-to-use on/off switches. To do so, you can use the older `setsebool` utility or `semanage`:

```
semanage boolean --list | grep "ftpd_anon_write"

semanage boolean --modify ftpd_anon_write --on
```

Using `setsebool` without `-P` makes the change, but it is not persistent. The `semanage` utility doesn't have the option to change it non-permanently.

AppArmor

In Debian, Ubuntu, and SUSE distributions, AppArmor is available to implement MAC. Please be aware that there are some minor differences between the distributions, but, in general, a distribution can add fewer or more profiles and some extra tooling. In this section, we use Ubuntu 18.04 as an example.

Also, you must make sure that you keep your distribution up to date, especially with AppArmor; the packages in Debian and Ubuntu were plagued by bugs, which sometimes led to unexpected behavior.

Make sure that the necessary packages are installed:

```
sudo apt install apparmor-utils apparmor-easyprof \
   apparmor-profiles apparmor-profiles-extra apparmor-easyprof
```

There are some fundamental differences compared with SELinux:

- By default, only the bare minimum is protected. You have to apply security for each application.

- You can mix enforcing and complaining modes; you can decide in relation to each application.

- When AppArmor development started, the scope was quite limited: processes and files. Nowadays, you can use it for **role-based access control** (**RBAC**), MLS, login policies, and other aspects besides.

In this chapter, we'll cover the initial scope: processes that need access to files.

AppArmor Status

The first thing to do is to check whether the AppArmor service is up and running:

```
sudo systemctl status apparmor
```

Alternatively, execute the following command:

```
sudo aa-enabled
```

And after that, view the status in greater detail with the following command:

```
sudo apparmor_status
```

Here is an alternative to the preceding command:

```
sudo aa-status
```

The following screenshot shows the status of AppArmor, derived using the **apparmor_status** command:

```
linvirt@ubuntu01:~$ sudo apparmor_status
apparmor module is loaded.
15 profiles are loaded.
15 profiles are in enforce mode.
   /sbin/dhclient
   /usr/bin/lxc-start
   /usr/bin/man
   /usr/lib/NetworkManager/nm-dhcp-client.action
   /usr/lib/NetworkManager/nm-dhcp-helper
   /usr/lib/connman/scripts/dhclient-script
   /usr/lib/snapd/snap-confine
   /usr/lib/snapd/snap-confine//mount-namespace-capture-helper
   /usr/sbin/tcpdump
   lxc-container-default
   lxc-container-default-cgns
   lxc-container-default-with-mounting
   lxc-container-default-with-nesting
   man_filter
   man_groff
0 profiles are in complain mode.
0 processes have profiles defined.
0 processes are in enforce mode.
0 processes are in complain mode.
0 processes are unconfined but have a profile defined.
```

Figure 6.20: AppArmor status

Generating AppArmor Profiles

Each application you want to protect requires a profile, provided by the **apparmor-profiles** or **apparmor-profiles-extra** packages, the application package, or you. The profiles are stored in **/etc/apparmor.d**.

Let's install the nginx web server as an example:

```
sudo apt install nginx
```

If you browse through the **/etc/apparmor.d** directory, there is no profile for nginx. Create a default one:

```
sudo aa-autodep nginx
```

A profile is created: **/etc/apparmor.d/usr.sbin.nginx**. This file is almost empty, and only includes some basic rules and variables, called abstractions, and the following line:

```
/usr/sbin/nginx mr,
```

The **mr** value defines the access mode: **r** means read mode, and **m** allows a file to be mapped into memory.

Let's enforce the mode for nginx:

```
sudo aa-enforce /usr/sbin/nginx

sudo systemctl restart nginx
```

nginx will not start. The output of the preceding commands is as follows:

```
sudo journalctl --identifier audit
```

This points very clearly in the direction of AppArmor:

```
sudo journalctl -k | grep audit
```

To fix the problem, set the complain mode for this profile. This way, it doesn't enforce the policy, but complains about every violation of the security policy:

```
sudo aa-complain /usr/sbin/nginx

sudo systemctl start nginx
```

Make an **http** request, using a browser or a utility, for instance, **curl**:

```
curl http://127.0.0.1
```

The next step is to scan the **logfile** and approve or reject every action:

```
sudo aa-logprof
```

Read very carefully and select the correct option with the arrow keys (if needed):

```
Profile:    /usr/sbin/nginx
Capability: dac_override
Severity:   9


  1 - #include <abstractions/lxc/container-base>
  2 - #include <abstractions/lxc/start-container>
 [3 - capability dac_override,]
(A)llow / [(D)eny] / (I)gnore / Audi(t) / Abo(r)t / (F)inish
```

Figure 6.21: Configuring the profile for nginx

LXC (**Linux Containers**) is a container technology, and we are just configuring the profile for a web server. Something to fix with DAC seems to be a good choice:

```
Profile:  /usr/sbin/nginx
Path:     /var/log/nginx/error.log
New Mode: w
Severity: 8


  1 - #include <abstractions/lxc/container-base>
  2 - #include <abstractions/lxc/start-container>
 [3 - /var/log/nginx/error.log w,]
```

Figure 6.22: Fixing DAC for nginx

The audit suggests a new mode: w means write access to the **/var/log/nginx/error.log** file.

In addition, you can block access to the following directories:

- Read access to **/etc/ssl/openssl.conf**. This is a difficult one, but the abstraction for **ssl** sounds right.

- Read access to **/etc/nginx/nginx.conf**. Again, not a container, so the owner of the file must be OK.

- In general, the owner of the file is a good choice.

Now, it is time to save the changes and try again:

```
sudo aa-enforce /usr/sbin/nginx
sudo systemctl restart nginx
curl http://127.0.0.1
```

Everything seems to work now, at least for a request to a simple website. As you can see, it's all largely based on educated guesses. The alternative is a deep dive into all the suggested abstractions.

The created file, **/etc/apparmor.d/usr.sbin.nginx**, is relatively easy to read. It starts with all the tunable variables that should be available for every profile:

```
#include <tunables/global>
```

The file is then followed by other abstractions, such as the following:

```
#include <abstractions/nameservice
```

To know what they are doing, just view the file. For instance, the **/etc/apparmor.d/abstractions/nameservice** file states the following:

```
/usr/sbin/nginx flags=(complain) {
  #include <abstractions/base>
  #include <abstractions/nameservice>
  #include <abstractions/openssl>
  #include <abstractions/web-data>
```

> **Note**
>
> Many programs wish to perform name service–like operations, such as looking up users by name or ID, groups by name or ID, and hosts by name or IP. These operations may be performed through DNS, NIS, NIS+, LDAP, hesiod, and wins files. Allow all of these options here.

The next section is about Posix capabilities; refer to **man 7 capabilities** for more information:

```
capability dac_override,
```

The final section is the permissions; for a complete list, refer to the **Access Mode** section in **man 5 apparmor.d**:

```
/var/log/nginx/error.log w,

  owner /etc/nginx/modules-enabled/ r,

  owner /etc/nginx/nginx.conf r,

  owner /run/nginx.pid w,

  owner /usr/lib/nginx/modules/ngx_http_geoip_module.so mr,

  owner /usr/share/nginx/modules-available/mod-http-geoip.conf r,

  owner /usr/share/nginx/modules-available/mod-http-image-filter.conf r,

  owner /var/log/nginx/access.log w,

}
```

aa-logprof, in particular, can be a little bit overwhelming when you start using it. But the profile is not that difficult to read; every option is in the two man pages, and the abstractions included are documented by comments.

firewalld and systemd

In *Chapter 5*, *Advanced Linux Administration*, systemd was covered as a system and service manager. In systemd, there are several options to add an extra layer of protection to your daemons and filesystem.

To be honest, in our opinion, it really makes sense to use Azure Firewall on top of Azure network security groups. It is easy to set up, provides central administration, and requires almost no maintenance. It provides security between VMs, virtual networks, and even different Azure subscriptions.

> **Note**
>
> There is an additional cost if you want to use this firewall. However, a Linux firewall doesn't incur any charges as it is a security measure installed on your machine.

The choice between Azure Firewall and a Linux firewall depends on many things:

- Cost

- Deployment and orchestration of your VMs and applications

- Different roles: is there one administrator for everything?

I hope that after covering one of the Linux firewall implementations, it becomes clear that a Linux firewall is in no way a complete replacement for Azure Firewall. It can only provide security for incoming traffic to the VM, and yes, it is possible to configure this firewall to block outgoing traffic as well, but that's quite complex. On the other hand, if it's configured on top of Azure network security groups, in many cases, that is more than enough.

There are different types of firewall solutions available for Linux, including firewalld and iptables. In this book, we'll be following firewalld on account of the configuration options available and its popularity. Please make sure that the firewalld software is installed and that other firewall software is removed from the system to avoid conflicts. In RHEL/CentOS-based distributions, this is already the case. In Ubuntu, use the following commands:

```
sudo apt remove ufw
sudo apt install firewalld
```

In SUSE-based distributions, use the following commands:

```
sudo zypper install susefirewall2-to-firewalld
sudo susefirewall2-to-firewalld -c
```

There are multiple firewall implementations for Linux; some of them are even developed for a specific distribution, such as SuSEfirewall2. In this chapter, we'll cover firewalld, which is available on every distribution.

firewalld consists of a daemon that manages all the components of the firewall:

- Zones

- Interfaces

- Sources

- Direct rules for iptables and ebtables (not covered in this book) firewalld utilizes kernel modules: iptables/IP6 tables for IPv4 and IPv6 traffic, and ebtables for the filtering of network traffic passing through a Linux bridge. In more recent distributions, such as RHEL 8, the **nftables** module is used.

To configure the firewalld rules, there is a command-line utility available: **firewall-cmd**. Rules can be runtime-only or persistent. There are two important reasons for this behavior: this way, it's not necessary to reload all the rules, implying a temporary security risk. You can dynamically add and remove rules. If you make a mistake, and you are not able to log in again because of this; just reboot as a quick solution. We can also use the **systemd-run --oncalendar** command to create a scheduled task that executes **firewall-cmd --reload**, which is an even better solution:

```
sudo systemd-run --on-calendar='2018-08-20 13:00:00' \
  firewall-cmd --reload
```

```
sudo systemctl list-timers
```

Don't forget to stop and disable the timer if the firewall rules were correct (and you did not lock yourself out).

You can also configure the daemon with orchestration tools that talk to the daemon or push XML files to the host.

> **Note**
>
> The ports are only open for the VMs connected to the virtual machine network, unless you open the ports in the network security group!

It is important to know that Azure Service Fabric (the infrastructure) will add, if necessary, extra rules to your firewall configuration. It's recommended not to remove these rules as they are important, given that they are used by the Azure platform. You can see this if you search in the logging database with the **journalctl** command:

```
sudo journalctl | grep "Azure fabric firewall"
```

Use the **iptables-save** command to view all the active firewall rules, or if your distribution is using **nftables**:

```
sudo nft list ruleset
```

firewalld Zones

One of the most important concepts of firewalld is the zone. A zone consists of a default rule, called a target, a network interface or network source, and additional services, ports, protocols, and rich rules.

A zone is only active if a network interface is attached to the interface or a network source.

To list the zones available, use the following command:

```
sudo firewall-cmd --get-zones
```

These zones are configured in **/usr/lib/firewalld/zones**. You should not make changes to these files. New zones or changes to a zone are written into the **/etc/firewalld/zones** directory.

The default zone is the public zone:

```
sudo firewall-cmd --get-default-zone
```

To list the zone configuration of the public zone, use the following command:

```
sudo firewall-cmd --zone public --list-all
```

The zone configuration will be as shown here:

```
public
    target: default
    icmp-block-inversion: no
    interfaces:
    sources:
    services: ssh dhcpv6-client
    ports:
    protocols:
    masquerade: no
    forward-ports:
    source-ports:
    icmp-blocks:
    rich rules:
```

The public zone has the target policy **default**, which means that everything incoming is blocked by default, except the configured services, ports, and protocols.

The corresponding **/usr/lib/firewalld/zones/public.xml** file of this zone is as follows:

```
<?xml version="1.0" encoding="utf-8"?>

<zone>

 <short>Public</short>

 <description>For use in public areas. You do not trust the other computers
on networks to not harm your computer. Only selected incoming connections
are accepted.</description>

 <service name="ssh"/>

 <service name="dhcpv6-client"/>

</zone>
```

There are also options for configuring masquerading and port forwarding. Rich rules are advanced firewall rules, as described in the **firewalld.richlanguage** man page.

Execute **man firewalld.richlanguages** as shown in the following screenshot:

```
FIREWALL-CMD(1)                      firewall-cmd                    FIREWALL-CMD(1)

NAME
       firewall-cmd - firewalld command line client

SYNOPSIS
       firewall-cmd [OPTIONS...]

DESCRIPTION
       firewall-cmd is the command line client of the firewalld daemon. It provides
       interface to manage runtime and permanent configuration.

       The runtime configuration in firewalld is separated from the permanent
       configuration. This means that things can get changed in the runtime or
       permanent configuration.

OPTIONS
       Sequence options are the options that can be specified multiple times, the
       exit code is 0 if there is at least one item that succeeded. The
       ALREADY_ENABLED (11), NOT_ENABLED (12) and also ZONE_ALREADY_SET (16) errors
       are treated as succeeded. If there are issues while parsing the items, then
       these are treated as warnings and will not change the result as long as
```

Figure 6.23: Output of **man firewalld.richlanguages** command

Depending on the distribution that you're using, you may have additional service names. For example, if you are using RHEL 8, you might see **cockpit** listed as a service. **cockpit** is a web-based interface used to administer RHEL machines.

You may have noticed that in the public zone, it says **target: default**. The target is the default behavior. The possible values are as follows:

- **default**: Don't do anything, accept every ICMP packet, and reject everything else.

- **%%REJECT%%**: This sends a reject response to the client via the ICMP protocol.

- **DROP**: This sends a TCP SYN/ACK, as on an open port, but all other traffic is dropped. There is no ICMP message to inform the client.

- **ACCEPT**: Accept everything.

In Ubuntu, by default, there is no network interface attached. Please don't reboot the VM before an interface is attached! Execute the following command:

```
sudo firewall-cmd --add-interface=eth0 --zone=public
```

```
sudo firewall-cmd --add-interface=eth0 --zone=public --permanent
```

```
sudo firewall-cmd --zone=public --list-all
```

If you modify a zone, the file is copied from **/usr/lib/firewalld/zones** to **/etc/firewalld/zones**. The next modification will create a backup of the zone with the file extension **.old** and create a new file with the modifications in it.

firewalld Services

A service is an application-centric configuration to allow one or more ports. To receive a list of the services available, use the following command:

```
sudo firewall-cmd --get-services
```

If you want to add a service, for instance, MySQL, execute the following commands:

```
sudo firewall-cmd --add-service=mysql --zone=public
```

```
sudo firewall-cmd --add-service=mysql --zone=public \
  --permanent
```

If you want to remove a service from a zone, use the **--remove-service** parameter.

The services are configured in the **/usr/lib/firewalld/services** directory. Again, you shouldn't modify these files. You can change them or create your own by copying them to the **/etc/firewalld/services** directory.

It is possible to add single ports as well, but, in general, that's not a good idea: can you still remember after a while which ports are in use by which application? Instead, if the service is not already defined, create your own service.

Let's now create a service file for the Microsoft PPTP firewall protocol, **/etc/firewalld/ services/pptp.xml**:

```
<?xml version="1.0" encoding="utf-8"?>

<service>

 <short>PPtP</short>

 <description>Microsoft VPN</description>

 <port protocol="tcp" port="1723"/>

</service>
```

In the preceding file, you can see that TCP port **1723** is allowed. You can add as many port rules as you want. For example, if you want to add TCP port **1724**, then the line item will be as follows:

```
<port protocol="tcp" port="1724" />
```

After reloading the firewall with **firewalld-cmd --reload**, the service is available. This is not enough: the **GRE** (**Generic Routing Encapsulation**) protocol is not allowed. To allow this protocol, use the following commands:

```
sudo firewall-cmd --service=pptp --add-protocol=gre \

   --permanent


sudo firewall-cmd --reload
```

This will add the following line to the service file:

```
<protocol value="gre"/>
```

You can remove the protocol using the **--remove-protocol** parameter.

firewalld Network Sources

A zone is only active when a network interface is attached to it, or a network source. It doesn't make sense to add a network interface to the drop zone. The drop zone is where all the incoming packets are dropped with no reply; however, outgoing connections are allowed. So, as I mentioned, if you add the network interface to the drop zone, all incoming packets will be dropped by firewalld, which doesn't make any sense at all.

However, it does make sense to add a network source. A source consists of one or more entries: a media access control address, IP addresses, or IP ranges.

For instance, for whatever reason, say you want to block all traffic from Bermuda. The website http://ipdeny.com can provide you with a list of IP addresses:

```
cd /tmp

wget http://www.ipdeny.com/ipblocks/data/countries/bm.zone
```

There are several types of **ipset**. To view the list of supported **ipset** types, execute the following command:

```
sudo firewall-cmd --get-ipset-types
```

In our scenario, we want the type for **hash:net** IP ranges:

```
sudo firewall-cmd --new-ipset=block_bermuda --type=hash:net --permanent

sudo firewall-cmd --reload
```

Now, we can add entries to **ipset** using the downloaded file:

```
sudo firewall-cmd --ipset=block_bermuda --add-entries-from-file=/tmp/bm.zone

sudo firewall-cmd --ipset=block_bermuda --add-entries-from-file=/tmp/bm.zone \
   --permanent

sudo firewall-cmd --reload
```

The final step involves adding **ipset** as a source to the zone:

```
sudo firewall-cmd --zone=drop --add-source=ipset:block_bermuda

sudo firewall-cmd --zone=drop --add-source=ipset:block_bermuda --permanent

sudo firewall-cmd --reload
```

The purpose of the drop zone is to drop all traffic without letting the client know that the traffic is dropped. Adding **ipset** to this zone makes it active, and all the traffic coming from Bermuda will be dropped:

```
sudo firewall-cmd --get-active-zones

drop

  sources: ipset:block_bermuda

public

  interfaces: eth0
```

Now that we know how firewalld works, and how we can secure our machine using zones, let's jump to the next section.

systemd Security

As mentioned in the previous chapter, systemd is responsible for starting all processes in parallel during the boot process, except those processes that are created by their kernel. After that, it's a question of activating services, among other things, on demand. systemd units can also provide an extra layer of security. You can add several options to your unit file to make your unit more secure.

Just edit the unit file using **systemctl edit** and add the security measures. For example, execute the following command:

```
sudo systemctl edit sshd
```

Then, add the following lines:

```
[Service]

ProtectHome=read-only
```

Save the file, re-read the **systemctl** configuration, and restart **sshd**:

```
sudo systemctl daemon-reload

sudo systemctl restart sshd
```

Now, log in again with your SSH client and try to save a file in your home directory. This will fail because it's a read-only filesystem:

```
linvirt@ubuntu01:~$ echo test > ~/test
-bash: /home/linvirt/test: Read-only file system
linvirt@ubuntu01:~$ findmnt -T ~
TARGET  SOURCE            FSTYPE  OPTIONS
/home   /dev/sda1[/home]  ext4    ro,relatime,discard,data=ordered
```

Figure 6.24: Log in failed as unit file changed to read-only

Restricting Access to the Filesystem

The **ProtectHome** parameter is a very interesting one. The following values are available:

- **true**: The directories **/home**, **/root**, and **/run/user** are not accessible by the unit, and show empty for processes starting within the unit.

- **read-only**: These directories are read-only.

Another very similar parameter is **ProtectSystem**:

- **true**: **/usr** and **/boot** are mounted as read-only.

- **full**: **/etc** is mounted as read-only, along with **/usr** and **/boot**.

- **strict**: The full filesystem is read-only, except **/proc**, **/dev**, and **/sys**.

Instead of **ProtectHome** and **ProtectSystem**, additionally, you can use the following parameters: **ReadWritePaths** to whitelist directories, **ReadOnlyPaths**, and **InaccessiblePaths**.

Some daemons use the **/tmp** directory for temporary storage. The problem with this directory is that it's world-readable. The **PrivateTmp=true** parameter sets up a new temporary filesystem for the process, which is only accessible by the process.

There are also kernel-related parameters: the **ProtectKernelModules=true** parameter makes it impossible to load modules, and the **ProtectKernelTunables=true** parameter makes it impossible to change kernel parameters with the **sysctl** command or manually in the **/proc** and **/sys** directory structure.

Last, but not least, the **SELinuxContext** and **AppArmorProfile** parameters force the context for the unit.

Restricting Network Access

systemd can also be used to restrict network access, as in you can list those IP addresses that can be allowed or denied. Newer versions of systemd, after version 235, such as those used by Ubuntu 18.04, SLE 15 SP1, and RHEL 8, also support IP accounting and access lists to restrict network access.

IPAccounting=yes allows a unit to collect and analyze network data. To view the results, you can use the **systemctl** command:

```
systemctl show <service name> -p IPIngressBytes \
 -p IPIngressPackets \
 -p IPEgressBytes -p IPEgressPackets
```

As with every parameter, you can use this with **systemd-run** as well:

```
root@ubuntu01:~# systemd-run -p IPAccounting=yes ping -c5 9.9.9.9
Running as unit: run-rfd0ca0d359ee4f77aefa7b6e1fcfe43f.service
root@ubuntu01:~#
root@ubuntu01:~# systemctl show run-rfd0ca0d359ee4f77aefa7b6e1fcfe43f.service -p
 IPIngressBytes -p IPIngressPackets \
> -p IPEgressBytes -p IPEgressPackets
IPIngressBytes=18446744073709551615
IPIngressPackets=18446744073709551615
IPEgressBytes=18446744073709551615
IPEgressPackets=18446744073709551615
```

Figure 6.25: Using systemd-run and systemctl to collect and analyze network data

You can use **IPAddressDeny** to deny an IP address or an IP range. An exception can be made with **IPAddressAllow**. It's even possible to deny everything system-wide and whitelist on a per-service basis:

```
sudo systemctl set-property sshd.service IPAddressAllow=any
sudo systemctl set-property waagent.service IPAddressAllow=10.0.0.1
```

> **Note**
>
> If you are using Ubuntu, the service name is **walinuxagent**.

```
sudo systemctl set-property system.slice IPAddressAllow=localhost
sudo systemctl set-property system.slice IPAddressAllow=10.0.0.1
sudo systemctl set-property system.slice IPAddressDeny=any
```

The changes are saved in the **/etc/systemd/system.control** directory structure:

```
[root@rhel8 system.control]# ls -R
.:
sshd.service.d

./sshd.service.d:
50-IPAddressAllow.conf
```

Figure 6.26: Saving the changes in system.control directory

Here are some remarks:

- Of course, you have to change the IP range to your virtual subnet, and you have to allow access to the first IP address of your subnet for the Azure agent and network service, such as **DHCP** (**Dynamic Host Configuration Protocol**).

- It's also a very good idea to restrict SSH access to the IP address of your own network.

- View the systemd journal very carefully, to find out whether you need more ports to open.

The systemd access list feature is perhaps not as advanced as firewalld, but it is a very good alternative for restrictions on the application level (hosts allow directives in the configuration files of the daemon, or **/etc/hosts.allow** and **/etc/hosts.deny** for applications that are compiled with **libwrap** support). And, in our opinion, in Azure, you don't need more than this. If only all distributions had a recent version of systemd.

> **Note**
>
> We won't cover the **libwrap** library in this book, because more and more applications are no longer using this option, and some vendors, such as SUSE, are busy removing the complete support for this library.

Identity and Access Management in Azure – IAM

Up to now, we have been discussing how to manage security in Linux. Since we are deploying in Azure, Azure also provides some added security to our Linux VMs. For example, earlier, we discussed Azure Firewall and network security groups, which help in controlling traffic, limiting access to unwanted ports, and filtering traffic originating from unknown locations. On top of this, there are other services in Azure, such as Azure AD Domain Services, which will let you join a Linux VM to a domain. Recently, Microsoft launched an option by which Azure AD users can sign in to the Linux VM. The advantage of this is that you don't have to use other usernames; instead, you can use Azure AD credentials. Let's take a closer look at these services and understand how we can make use of them to increase the security of our Linux VMs.

Azure AD Domain Services

Until now, we have been discussing what can be done inside the Linux VM. Since we are on Azure, we should take advantage of **Azure AD Domain Services**, by which you can domain join your Linux machines and enforce your organization's policies. Azure AD Domain Services is a domain controller as a service that provides you with a DNS service and identity management. Central identity management is always an important part of security solutions. It enables the user to access resources. On top of that, you can enforce policies and enable multi-factor authentication.

In this section, we will focus on how to set up a service and how to join a domain.

Setting up Azure AD Domain Services

The easiest way to set up Azure AD Domain Services is via the Azure portal. In the left-hand bar, select **Create a resource** and search for *Domain Services*. Select **Azure AD Domain Services** and click on the **Create** button.

In the wizard, you will be asked for some settings:

- **Domain name**: You can use your own or use a built-in domain name that ends with `.onmicrosoft.com`. For the purposes of this book, that is sufficient.

- **Virtual network**: It's a good idea to create a new virtual network and a new subnet. Labeling doesn't matter.

- **Administrators**: A group will be made called `AAD DC Administrators`. To be able to join a domain with a user, the user must be a member of this group, using the **Active Directory** section in the left-hand bar in the Azure portal.

Now you are ready to deploy the service. This will take a while; in my personal experience, it can take 20 to 30 minutes.

When you are finished, go to the **Virtual Networks** section in the left-hand bar and enter the newly created virtual network. You will find two newly created network interfaces and their IP addresses. You'll need this information, so make a note of it.

It is a good idea to create a new subnet in this virtual network, but it's not necessary.

Linux Configuration

You have to deploy the Linux VM in the same virtual network or on a peered network where Azure AD Directory Services is deployed. As stated, it is a good idea to attach it to another subnet. Here, we are not following the secure LDAP.

Hostname

Change the hostname with the `hostnamectl` utility to the correct `fqdn`:

```
sudo hostnamectl set-hostname ubuntu01.frederikvoslinvirt.onmicrosoft.com
```

Then edit the **/etc/hosts** file. Add an entry such as the following:

```
127.0.0.1 ubuntu01.frederikvoslinvirt.onmicrosoft.com ubuntu01
```

DNS Servers

In the left-hand bar of the Azure portal, go to **Virtual Networks** and navigate to the subnet where the Azure AD Domain Services network interfaces are located. Select **DNS servers** and use the custom options to set the IP addresses of the Azure AD Domain Services network interfaces. By doing so, whenever DNS resolution of the hostname is required, it will be pointed to Azure AD Domain Services.

Alternatively, if your Azure AD Domain Services is a new deployment, in the **Overview** pane of the Azure portal, it will ask you to change the DNS servers. Just clicking the **Configure** button would change the DNS servers in the virtual network to point to Azure AD Domain Services.

Normally, restarting the network in the VM should suffice, but it's a better idea to reboot now. From time to time, the old and new settings both survive.

In RHEL, Ubuntu, and SUSE, view the content of the **/etc/resolv.conf** file to verify the result. Then, look into the settings for `eth0`.

Installing Dependencies

There are some important components and dependencies that are required in order to be able to use Azure AD Domain Services:

- A Kerberos client, for authorization
- SSSD, a backend that is responsible for the configuration and utilization of features such as using and caching credentials
- Samba libraries, to be compatible with Windows features/options
- Some utilities to join and manage the domain, such as **realm**, **adcli**, and the **net** command

Install the necessary software to be able to join the domain.

For RHEL/CentOS-based distributions, execute the following command:

```
sudo yum install realmd sssd krb5-workstation krb5-libs samba-common-tools
```

In Ubuntu, execute the following command:

```
sudo apt install krb5-user samba sssd sssd-tools libnss-sss libpam-sss
realmd adcli
```

In SLE/OpenSUSE LEAP, dependencies will be handled by YaST.

Joining the Domain – Ubuntu and RHEL/CentOS

In Ubuntu- and RHEL/CentOS-based distributions, the **realm** utility is available to join the domain. First, discover the domain:

```
sudo realm discover <your domain>
```

The output should be similar to this:

```
linvirt@ubuntu01:~$ sudo realm discover frederikvoslinvirt.onmicrosoft.com
frederikvoslinvirt.onmicrosoft.com
  type: kerberos
  realm-name: FREDERIKVOSLINVIRT.ONMICROSOFT.COM
  domain-name: frederikvoslinvirt.onmicrosoft.com
  configured: no
  server-software: active-directory
  client-software: sssd
  required-package: sssd-tools
  required-package: sssd
  required-package: libnss-sss
  required-package: libpam-sss
  required-package: adcli
  required-package: samba-common-bin
```

Figure 6.27: Discovering the domain

Now, you are ready to join the domain:

```
sudo realm join <your domain> -U <username@domain>
```

Use the username you added earlier on as a member of the Azure AD Domain Services administrator group. If you get a message saying **Necessary packages are not installed**, but you are certain that they are installed, add the **--install=/** parameter to the **realm** command.

To verify the result, execute the following command:

```
sudo realm list
```

The output should be similar to the following:

```
frederikvoslinvirt.onmicrosoft.com
  type: kerberos
  realm-name: FREDERIKVOSLINVIRT.ONMICROSOFT.COM
  domain-name: frederikvoslinvirt.onmicrosoft.com
  configured: kerberos-member
  server-software: active-directory
  client-software: sssd
  required-package: sssd-tools
  required-package: sssd
  required-package: libnss-sss
  required-package: libpam-sss
  required-package: adcli
  required-package: samba-common-bin
  login-formats: %U@frederikvoslinvirt.onmicrosoft.com
  login-policy: allow-realm-logins
```

Figure 6.28: Joining the domain

You should be able to do things such as the following:

```
id <user>@<domain>
```

```
su <user>@<domain>
```

Log in remotely with **ssh** with this user.

> **Note**
>
> If this doesn't work, and the join was successful, reboot the VM.

Joining the Domain – SUSE

In SUSE SLE and LEAP, the best way to join the domain is by using YaST.

Start the YaST utility:

```
sudo yast
```

From the YaST main window, start the **User Logon Management** module and click on **Change Settings**. Click on **Join Domain** and fill in the domain name. After that, you will be able to enroll in the domain successfully. If necessary, dependencies will be installed.

A new window will appear to manage the domain user logons. You need at least the following: **Allow Domain User Logon** and **Create Home Directory**. All the other options are not yet possible in Azure AD Domain Services.

YaST will give you a colorful GUI-like interface on the shell, the use of which means you can join the machine to the domain. Once you run **sudo yast**, you will get a screen as shown here. From the list, use the arrow keys to select **Network Services** and then **Windows Domain Membership**:

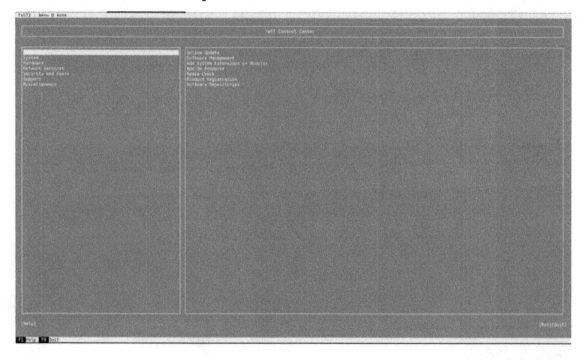

Figure 6.29: YaST interface on the Shell

The best part is that if any dependencies are missing, YaST will prompt you to install them, so please go ahead and complete the dependency installation. Right after installation, you can enter your domain name and, once you save, you will be prompted to enter the username and password, as shown in the following screenshot:

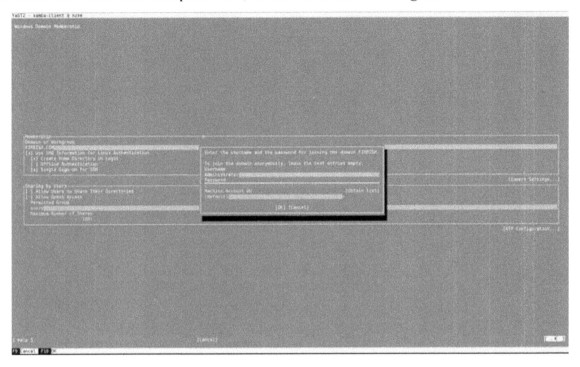

Figure 6.30: Providing credentials to register the machine

Enter your credentials in the format **user@domain** and then your password. Once you complete the process, the SUSE machine will reach out to Azure AD Domain Services and register your machine. If joining is successful, you will get a message on your screen as shown here:

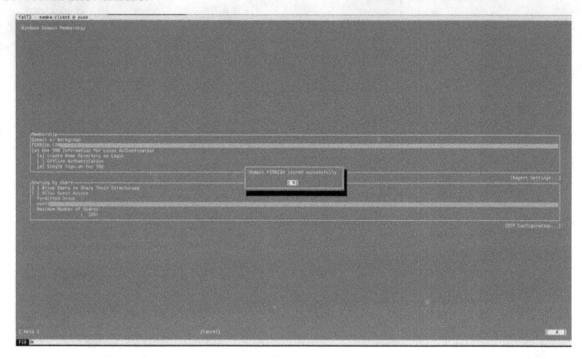

Figure 6.31: Domain join successful

You can verify by switching the current user to your AD username using the **su** command, as shown in the following screenshot:

Figure 6.32: Verifying the domain join

Finally, we have completed joining our Linux machine to Azure AD Domain Services. Recently, Microsoft added support for Azure AD sign-in to Linux VMs without the need to join the machines to the domain. An agent will be installed on the machine to complete the authorization. This will be discussed in the next section.

Logging in with Azure AD Credentials to the Linux VM

Another form of identity management is possible with Azure AD. This is a completely different identity management system, without LDAP and Kerberos, as discussed in the preceding section. In Linux, Azure AD will allow you to use your Azure credentials to log into your VM, but has no support at an application level. At the time of writing this book, this feature is still in preview. Also, this feature is not available in SUSE.

To be able to use Azure AD, you have to deploy a VM extension, for instance, using the Azure CLI:

```
az vm extension set \
    --publisher Microsoft.Azure.ActiveDirectory.LinuxSSH \
    --name AADLoginForLinux \
    --resource-group myResourceGroup \
    --vm-name myVM
```

After this, you have to assign a role, either the **Virtual Machine Administrator Login** (with root privileges) or **Virtual Machine User Login** (unprivileged user) role, to your Azure AD account, with the scope limited to this VM:

```
az role assignment create \
    --role "Virtual Machine Administrator Login" \
    --assignee <ad user name> \
    --scope <your vm>
```

Here, you can set the scope at the subscription level, **--scope / subscriptions/<subcription ID>**. By doing so, the role will be inherited by all resources in the subscription.

If you want granular-level access only to a particular VM, you can execute the following command (in PowerShell):

```
$vm = Get-AzVM -Name <VM Name> -ResourceGroup <resource group>
```

$vm.Id will give you the scope of the VM.

In bash, execute the following command:

```
az vm show --name<name> --resource-group <resource group> --query id
```

This command will query the ID of the VM and is the scope for role assignment.

You can log in using your AD credentials:

```
ssh <ad user>@<ad domain>@<ip address>
```

Finally, you will be able to see that you are logged into the Linux VM using your Azure AD credentials.

Other Security Solutions in Azure

In this chapter, we have discussed how to increase the Linux security level and incorporate certain Azure services to improve security. Having said that, the list of Azure services that can be used to increase security is very long. Some of them are highlighted here:

- Azure AD Managed Identity: Using this, you can create managed identities for VMs, which can be used to authenticate any service that supports Azure AD authentication (https://docs.microsoft.com/en-us/azure/active-directory/managed-identities-azure-resources/overview). Formerly, this service was known as **Managed Service Identity** (**MSI**) which is now called as **managed identities for Azure resources**.

- Key Vault: This can be used to store your keys securely. For example, in Azure Disk Encryption, the key will be stored in a key vault and accessed whenever required (https://docs.microsoft.com/en-us/azure/key-vault/basic-concepts).

- Azure Disk Encryption: Disk encryption will help you encrypt the operating system disk, as well as the data disk, so as to have additional security for the data stored (https://docs.microsoft.com/en-us/azure/virtual-machines/linux/disk-encryption-overview).

- RBAC: RBAC in Azure gives you the ability to assign granular permission to your VMs. There are lots of in-built roles available in Azure and you can assign one depending upon your security requirements. Also, you can create custom RBAC roles to give more granular permissions (https://docs.microsoft.com/en-us/azure/role-based-access-control/overview).

- **Azure Security Center** (**ASC**): ASC is a unified infrastructure security management system designed to consolidate your security (https://docs.microsoft.com/en-us/azure/security-center/security-center-intro).

- Azure Policy Guest Configuration: This can be used to audit settings inside your Linux VM. It has been discussed in detail in *Chapter 8, Exploring Continuous Configuration Automation.*

We would recommend that you go through the Microsoft documentation pertaining to these services in order to have a better insight into how these can be used in your environment to strengthen the overall security aspect.

Summary

Security is a very important topic nowadays. Many reports, books, and so on have been written on this subject. In this chapter, we covered several options in Linux to increase security levels. All of them come on top of the basic security already provided by Azure through network security groups. They are relatively easy to implement and will make a big difference!

Central identity management is not only a way of providing users with access to the VM, but it's also a part of reducing the security risks. Azure AD Domain Services provides, via LDAP and Kerberos, an identity management solution for all operating systems and applications that have support for these protocols.

Chapter 8, Exploring Continuous Configuration Automation, will cover automation and orchestration. Please note that all the security measures covered in this chapter can be easily orchestrated. Orchestration makes central configuration management possible. One of its big advantages is the prevention of mistakes and unmanageable configurations. This way, even orchestration is a part of your security plan!

And it would be nice if you are going to create your own VMs, especially if you're going to build your own images. We will discuss in the next chapter how to build your own images. Also, we will consider the security aspects of pushing these images and deploying them in your environment.

Questions

1. If you are going to implement firewalld, what are the methods for configuring this firewall?

2. What is the reason for using the `--permanent` parameter of `firewall-cmd`?

3. What other options are available to restrict network access?

4. Explain the difference between DAC and MAC.

5. Why is it important to utilize Linux security modules in a VM running on Azure?

6. Which MAC system is available for which distribution?

7. What is the main difference between AppArmor and SELinux?

8. What are the requirements to be able to join Azure AD Domain Services in regards to dependencies and Linux configuration?

Further Reading

Similar to the previous chapter, I strongly suggest you visit *Chapter 11, Troubleshooting and Monitoring Your Workloads*, to read about logging in Linux, because often, the `systemctl status` command doesn't provide you with enough information. I have also already pointed to the blog by Lennart Poettering, and the systemd website.

For Linux security in general, you can start reading the book *Mastering Linux Security and Hardening*, by Donald A. Tevault. Many of the topics covered in this chapter, and many more besides, are explained in great detail.

The firewalld daemon has a project website, https://firewalld.org, with a blog and excellent documentation. For older distributions, the wiki of Arch Linux is a good place to start to learn more: https://wiki.archlinux.org/index.php/iptables. And since iptables is utilized by firewalld, it's a good start before diving into the man page of `firewalld.richlanguage`.

All the details regarding SELinux are covered in guides provided by Red Hat: https://access.redhat.com/documentation/en-us/red_hat_enterprise_linux/7/html/selinux_users_and_administrators_guide/ And although it's slightly out of date, it's a very good idea to watch this video of a Red Hat Summit on YouTube relating to SELinux: https://www.youtube.com/watch?v=MxjenQ31b70.

However, it's more difficult to find good information about AppArmor. There is project documentation available at https://gitlab.com/apparmor/apparmor/wikis/Documentation, and the Ubuntu server guide is a good start. This is available at https://help.ubuntu.com/lts/serverguide/apparmor.html.en.

Deploying Your Virtual Machines

It's easy to deploy a single **virtual machine** (**VM**) in Azure, but as soon as you want to deploy more workloads in a single, reproducible way, you need some sort of automation.

In Azure, you can use **Azure Resource Manager** (**ARM**) to deploy VMs using template configuration files together with the Azure CLI, PowerShell, Ruby, and C#. Other third-party tools used to create images for VMs, such as Packer and Vagrant, are discussed later in this chapter.

All these deployment methods or image creation methods use images from Azure, but it's also possible to create your own custom VMs with custom images.

Before going into the configuration of all the possible options, it is important to be aware of the different deployment options and why you should or shouldn't use them. You must ask yourself several questions first:

- When are you going to deploy your application?

- Which parts of the workload should be reproducible?

- Which parts of the configuration of the workload should be done during deployment?

All these questions will be answered by the end of this chapter. These are the key takeaways from this chapter:

- We will be discussing automated deployment options in Azure.

- We will see how deployment can be automated using the Azure CLI and PowerShell.

- We will be covering Azure ARM templates for deployment and how they can be reused for redeployment.

- VM image creation tools such as Packer and Vagrant will be discussed.

- Finally, we will explain how to use custom images and bring our own **VHD** (**Virtual Hard Disks**) to Azure.

Deployment Scenarios

The three questions mentioned in the introduction are very important; these can differ per company, per application, and during the development stage. The following are examples of a few deployment scenarios:

- Applications are developed in-house, maybe even on your local computer. Once finished, applications are deployed in Azure. Updates will be applied to the running workload.

- This is the same scenario, but now the updates will be done by deploying a new VM.

- Applications are delivered by another vendor.

These three examples are very common and can affect the way that you want to deploy your workload.

What Do You Need?

Before jumping into the deployment, you should know what you need or, in other words, what resources are required to make your application work properly. Additionally, everything in Azure has a limit and a quota. Some limits are hard, and some can be increased by reaching out to Microsoft Support. To see the complete list of Azure limits and quotas, visit https://docs.microsoft.com/en-us/azure/azure-subscription-service-limits.

Prior to deployment, we need to plan and make sure that our subscription limits won't block our project. If there is a restriction or limitation, reach out to Microsoft Support and increase the quota. However, if you are on a free trial, quota requests will not be approved. You may have to move the deployment to a region where you have enough quota to fulfill the deployment. These are the key resources that we'll be deploying:

- A resource group
- A storage account (unmanaged) or a managed disk
- A network security group
- A virtual network
- A subnet for the virtual network
- A network interface attached to the VM

Regarding the VM, you need to specify and think about the following:

- VM sizing
- Storage
- VM extensions
- Operating system
- Initial configuration
- The deployment of your application

If you take a look at these lists, you might be wondering whether automated deployment or automation is necessary or required. The answer is not easy to find. Let's look at the scenarios again and try to find the answer. We could decide to do the following:

1. Create a script in PowerShell or Bash to prepare the Azure environment for the workload

2. Create a second script to deploy the VM based on an offer in Azure and use an Azure VM extension to configure the initial configuration

3. Deploy the application with a software manager such as Yum

There is nothing wrong with deciding to do this; it could be the best solution for you! However, whether you like it or not, there are dependencies:

- You deploy your operating system based on an image. This image is made available by a publisher. What happens if the image is updated to a version that is not supported by your application?

- How much initial configuration is already done in this image? How much is needed, and who is in control of the image?

- Is this image compliant with your security policies?

- If you want to leave Azure for whatever reason, can you move your application to somewhere else?

Automated Deployment Options in Azure

After this long introduction, it's time to have a look at the feature options that make it possible to automate the deployment of your workload:

- Scripting

- Azure Resource Manager

- Ansible

- Terraform

We will be discussing Ansible and Terraform in *Chapter 8, Exploring Continuous Configuration Automation*.

Scripting

Automation can be done with scripts. In Azure, there are many options supported by Microsoft:

- Bash with the Azure CLI

- PowerShell with the Az module

- Python, with the complete SDK available at https://docs.microsoft.com/en-us/azure/python/python-sdk-azure-install

- Ruby, with a preview SDK available at https://azure.microsoft.com/en-us/develop/ruby

- Go, with a complete SDK available at https://github.com/Azure/azure-sdk-for-go

- And there are libraries available for Node.js

Also, you can use programming languages such as Java and C#. There are community projects as well; for instance, https://github.com/capside/azure-sdk-perl is an attempt to build a full Azure SDK for Perl.

All languages are valid options; choose a language you are already familiar with. Please be aware that the Ruby SDK was in preview at the time that this book was written. During the preview state, the syntax can change.

Scripting is especially good for preparing an Azure environment. You can also use scripting to deploy your VMs, and you can even include the initial configuration using VM extensions. The question of whether it's a good idea is dependent on your scripting abilities, the base image of the operating system, and the versions of software installed in it.

The biggest argument against using scripts is that it is time-consuming to write them. Here are some tips that can help you write scripts efficiently:

- Use as many variables as possible. This way, if you have changes to make in the script, all you have to do is change the variables' values.

- Use recognizable variable names in loops, not something like **for i in**.

- Especially for bigger scripts, declare functions that you can reuse.

- Sometimes, it makes sense to put variables (such as the one that provides authentication) and functions in separate files. One task per script is often a good idea.

- Include the timestamp of the modification in your code, or, even better, use a version control system such as Git.

- Include tests. For instance, only create this resource if it doesn't already exist. Use human-readable exit codes. If the script failed to deploy a resource, use something like *not able to create $resource*, so that whoever is running the script will understand that the script failed to create the resource.

- Include sufficient comments. If you need to debug or reuse the script after some time, you'll still know what it does. Don't forget to include a description in the header as well.

- Spend some time on the layout; use indentation to keep the code readable. Use two spaces for indentation, not tabs!

It's now time for a short example. This example will give you an idea of how to create scripts to provide the things needed in Azure before deploying a VM.

First, declare the variables. You can also add the variables to a file and make PowerShell load the variables. It is recommended to store them in the same script so that you can always go back and update them when required:

```
#Declare Variables
$myResourceGroup = "LinuxOnAzure"
$myLocation = "West Europe"
$myNSG = "NSG_LinuxOnAzure"
$mySubnet = "10.0.0.0/24"
$myVnet= "VNET_LinuxOnAzure"
```

Next, write a script to create a resource group. If the resource already exists, the script will skip the creation part. As mentioned earlier, adding comments is the best practice to make the script readable, so make use of comments marked by **#** so that you understand what the code block does:

```
# Test if the Resource Group already exists, if not: create it.

Get-AzResourceGroup -Name $myResourceGroup -ErrorVariable notPresent
-ErrorAction SilentlyContinue | out-null

if ($notPresent)

  {

    # ResourceGroup doesn't exist, create it:

    New-AzResourceGroup -Name $myResourceGroup -Location $myLocation

    Write-Host "The Resource Group $myResourceGroup is created in the
location $myLocation"

  }

else

  {

    Write-Host "The Resource Group $myResourceGroup already exists in the
location $myLocation"

  }
```

Create the virtual network and configure the subnet:

```
#Test if the vnet name not already exists:

Get-AzVirtualNetwork -Name $myVnet -ResourceGroupName $myResourceGroup
-ErrorVariable notPresent -ErrorAction SilentlyContinue | out-null

if ($notPresent)

  {

    # vnet doesn't exist, create the vnet


    $virtualNetwork = New-AzVirtualNetwork -ResourceGroupName
$myResourceGroup -Location $myLocation -Name $myVnet -AddressPrefix
10.0.0.0/16
```

```
    # add subnet configuration
    $subnetConfig = Add-AzVirtualNetworkSubnetConfig -Name default
-AddressPrefix $mySubnet -VirtualNetwork $virtualNetwork

    # Associate the subnet to the virtual network
    $virtualNetwork | Set-AzVirtualNetwork

     Write-Host "The virtual network $myVnet with $mySubnet configured is
created in the location $myLocation"
 }
else
  {
    Write-Host "The Resource Group $myVnet already exists in the location
$myLocation"
 }
```

Here is an example of creating a network security group:

```
# Create NSG
# Test if the Network Security Group does not already exist:


Get-AzNetworkSecurityGroup -ResourceGroupName $myResourceGroup -Name $myNSG
-ErrorVariable notPresent -ErrorAction SilentlyContinue | out-null

if ($notPresent)

{
# create the NSG
$nsg = New-AzNetworkSecurityGroup -ResourceGroupName $myResourceGroup
-Location $myLocation -Name $myNSG

# create the rules for SSH and HTTP

$nsg | Add-AzNetworkSecurityRuleConfig -Name "allow_http" -Description "Allow
HTTP" -Access Allow '

    -Protocol "TCP" -Direction Inbound -Priority 1002 -SourceAddressPrefix
"*" -SourcePortRange * '

    -DestinationAddressPrefix * -DestinationPortRange 80
```

```
$nsg | Add-AzNetworkSecurityRuleConfig -Name "allow_ssh" -Description "Allow
SSH" -Access Allow '

    -Protocol "TCP" -Direction Inbound -Priority 1001 -SourceAddressPrefix
"*" -SourcePortRange * '

    -DestinationAddressPrefix * -DestinationPortRange 22

# Update the NSG.

  $nsg | Set-AzNetworkSecurityGroup

Write-Host "The NSG: $myNSG is configured is created with rules for SSH and
HTTP in the resource group $myResourceGroup"

}

else

{

Write-Host "The NSG $myNSG already existed in the resource group
$myResourceGroup"

}
```

By now, you should have a pretty good idea of how you can create a script and a virtual network. As mentioned at the beginning of this section, scripting is not the only resort to automate a deployment; there are other methods. In the next section, we'll be discussing how to use Azure Resource Manager templates to automate deployment.

Automated Deployment with Azure Resource Manager

In *Chapter 2, Getting Started with the Azure Cloud*, we defined **<u>Azure Resource Manager</u>** (**<u>ARM</u>**) as follows:

"Basically, the Azure Resource Manager enables you to work with resources such as storage and VMs. To do so, you have to create one or more resource groups so you can execute life cycle operations, such as deploying, updating, and deleting all the resources in the resource group in a single operation."

From the Azure portal or with scripting, you are able to do all the things stated. But that's only a small part of it. You can deploy Azure resources through ARM by using templates. There are hundreds of quick-start templates provided by Microsoft, available at https://azure.microsoft.com/en-us/resources/templates

When you create a VM via the Azure portal, you can download that VM as a template even before you create it. If you refer to the following screenshot, you can see that even before creating the VM, we have an option to download the template for automation:

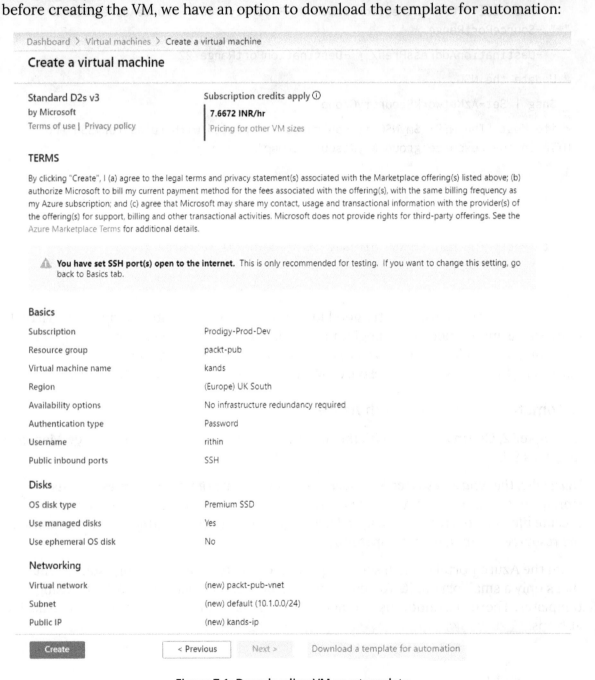

Figure 7.1: Downloading VM as a template

If you click on **Download a template for automation**, you'll get the following screen:

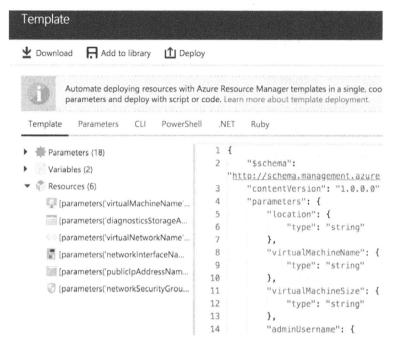

Figure 7.2: VM template pane

As you can see, you can add the script to your library in Azure or you can download this file to your local computer. You will also get a **Deploy** option, with which you can change the parameters and deploy directly to Azure.

In the **Scripts** pane, Azure gives you links on how to deploy using PowerShell and the CLI.

You can easily change the parameters and deploy a new VM or redeploy exactly the same VM. It is not that different than using your own scripts, but it's less time-consuming in development terms.

This is not the only thing you can do with ARM; you can configure every aspect of Azure resources. For example, if you are deploying a Network Security Group via an ARM template, you define everything, such as the rule, port range, and the priority of the rule, in the same way as you would create from the Azure portal or via the CLI. It's not that difficult to create your own ARM template. You'll need the ARM reference guide, which can be found at https://docs.microsoft.com/en-us/azure/templates. Together with these examples, it's a great resource to get started.

Another way of getting started is by using the Visual Studio Code editor, which is available for Windows, Linux, and macOS at https://code.visualstudio.com. The **Azure Resource Manager Tools** extension is a must-have if you are going to start using ARM, together with some other extensions, such as **Azure Account and Sign-In**, **Azure Resource Manager snippets**, and **Azure CLI Tools**. You can start using existing templates, and can even upload them to Cloud Shell, execute them, and debug them.

To install the Azure Resource Manager Tools extension, follow these steps:

1. Open Visual Studio Code.

2. Select **Extensions** from the left menu. Or, from the **View** menu, select **Extensions** to open the **Extensions** pane.

3. Search for **Resource Manager**.

4. Select **Install** under **Azure Resource Manager Tools**.

Here is the screen where you find the **Install** option:

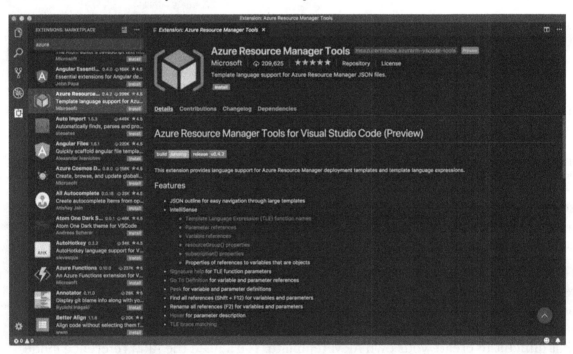

Figure 7.3: Installing Azure Resource Manager Tools

Another nice feature in Azure is the ARM Visualizer, which you can find at http://armviz.io. It's still in the early stages of development. This is a tool that can help you to get a quick insight into the purpose of the ARM template you downloaded from the Quickstart Templates website.

Instead of downloading templates, it's also possible to save them to a library:

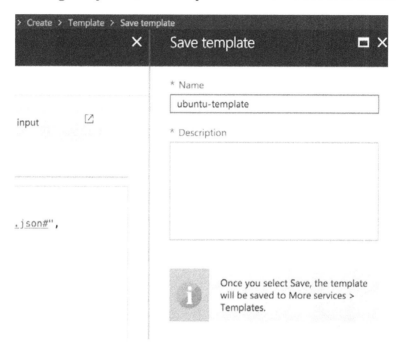

Figure 7.4: Saving templates to the library

As stated in this pane, you can easily navigate in the Azure portal by using **All resources** in the left-hand navigation bar and searching for templates:

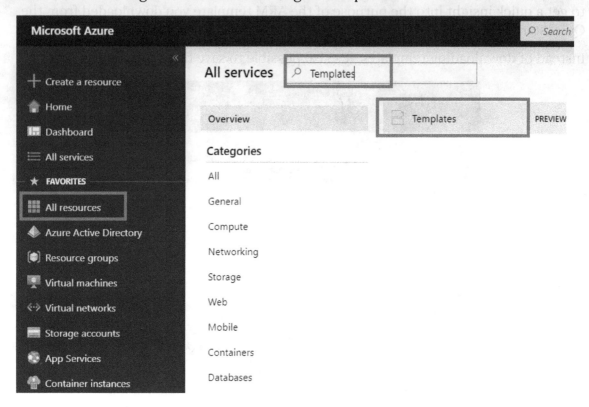

Figure 7.5: Navigating to the templates on the Azure portal

You can still edit your template here! Another nice feature is that you can share your template with other users of your tenant. This can be very useful, as you can create a user who is only allowed to use this template for deployment.

Now that we know how to deploy a template from the Azure portal, let's see how we can deploy ARM templates using PowerShell and Bash.

Deploying ARM Templates Using PowerShell

First, to validate whether the template format is right, execute the following command:

```
Test-AzResourceGroupDeployment -ResourceGroupName ExampleResourceGroup'
-TemplateFile c:\MyTemplates\azuredeploy.json '

-TemplateParameterFile  c:\MyTemplates\storage.parameters.json
```

Then go ahead with the deployment:

```
New-AzResourceGroupDeployment -Name <deployment name> -ResourceGroupName
<resource group name> -TemplateFile c:\MyTemplates\azuredeploy.json

-TemplateParameterFile c:\MyTemplates\storage.parameters.json
```

Deploying ARM Templates Using Bash

You can also validate your template and parameter file prior to deployment to avoid any unexpected errors:

```
az group deployment validate \

--resource-group ResourceGroupName \

    --template-file template.json \

    --parameters parameters.json
```

To deploy, execute the following command:

```
az group deployment create \

   --name DeploymentName \

   --resource-group ResourceGroupName \

   --template-file template.json \

   --parameters parameters.json
```

Now that we have deployed a new VM, we can keep the **templates.json** and **parameters. json**, which can be reused by changing the variable values.

Let's assume we have deleted the VM and you want it to be redeployed. All you need is the JSON files. As explained earlier, if you have stored the template in Azure, you can find an option to redeploy there:

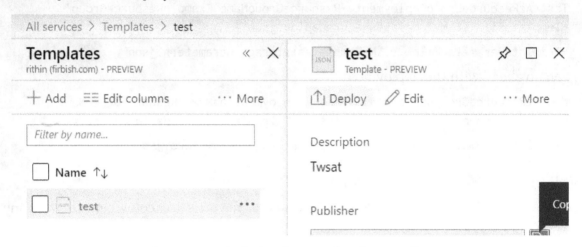

Figure 7.6: Redeploying the VM using the JSON files

If you prefer to accomplish the same task via the Azure CLI or PowerShell, run the commands we used earlier and your VM will be ready with the same configuration as mentioned in the ARM template.

Initial Configuration

Following the deployment of your workload, post-deployment configuration is needed. If you want to do this as a part of your automation solution, then there are two options:

- The custom script extension, which can be used at any time after the deployment.
- `cloud-init` is available during boot.

Initial Configuration with the Custom Script Extension

After the deployment of the VM, it is possible to execute post-deployment scripts using the custom script extension. In the previous example, we were deploying a VM using ARM templates. What if you want to run a script after deployment? This is the role of the custom script extension. For example, let's assume you want to deploy a VM, and after deployment, you want to install Apache on it without logging in to the VM. In this case, we will write a script to install Apache and Apache will be installed after deployment using the custom script extension.

This extension will work on all Microsoft-endorsed Linux operating systems, except CoreOS and OpenSUSE LEAP. Change the **apt-get** command in the script to the software manager supported by your distribution if you are using a distribution other than Debian or Ubuntu.

You can use PowerShell to configure the extension:

```
$myResourceGroup = "<resource group name>"

$myLocation = "<location>"

$myVM = "<vm name>"

$Settings = @{ "commandToExecute" = "apt-get -y install nginx";};


Set-AzVMExtension -VMName $myVM '

-ResourceGroupName $myResourceGroup'

-Location $myLocation '

-Name "CustomscriptLinux" -ExtensionType "CustomScript" '

-Publisher "Microsoft.Azure.Extensions" '

-typeHandlerVersion "2.0" -InformationAction SilentlyContinue '

-Verbose -Settings $Settings
```

The PowerShell output will give you the status after the configuration, that is, whether it was OK or something went wrong. After running the script, you can verify whether the installation was successful in the logs of the VM. Since we are following this on an Ubuntu VM, you can verify the installation of nginx by checking the **/var/log/apt/history.log** file. The output confirms that nginx and all other dependencies have been installed:

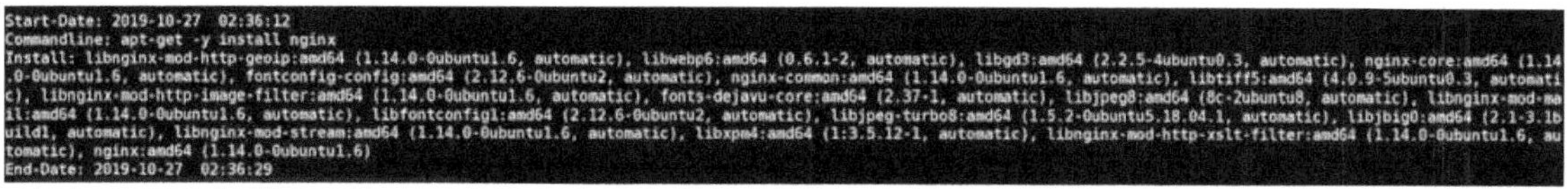

Figure 7.7: Checking logs to verify nginx installation

Instead of a command, you can also provide a script.

Let's create a very simple script:

```
#!/bin/sh
apt-get install -y nginx firewalld
firewall-cmd --add-service=http
firewall-cmd --add-service=http --permanent
```

Now, the script must be encoded using the **base64** command. You can do this on any Linux VM you have, or you can use **WSL** (**Windows Subsystem for Linux**) to create the **base64** string:

```
cat nginx.sh| base64
```

> **Note**
>
> On some versions of base64, you have to add the **-w0** parameter to disable word wrapping. Just make sure that it is one line!

The **$Settings** variable will be as follows:

```
$Settings = @{"script" = "<base64 string>";};
```

As we have already installed nginx using the first script, you can either remove ngnix using **apt purge nginx** or you can create a new VM altogether. As we did before, we can go and check the history log:

```
Start-Date: 2019-10-27  02:44:02
Commandline: apt-get install -y nginx firewalld
Install: ipset:amd64 (6.34-1, automatic), python3-slip-dbus:amd64 (0.6.5-2, automatic), libipset3:amd64 (6.34-1, aut
decorator:amd64 (4.1.2-1, automatic), firewalld:amd64 (0.4.4.6-1), python3-selinux:amd64 (2.7-2build2, automatic), n
End-Date: 2019-10-27  02:44:12
```

Figure 7.8: Checking the history log

The log entry clearly shows that `apt install -y nginx firewalld` has been executed. Since we are looking at the apt history, we will not be able to confirm whether the firewalld HTTP rule was added. To confirm that, you can run `firewall-cmd -list-services`:

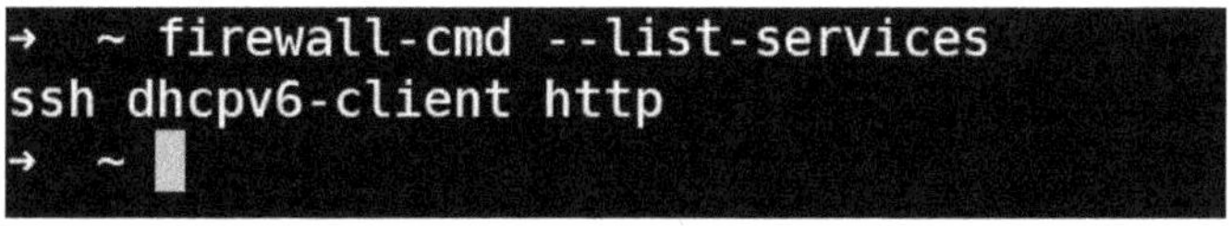

Figure 7.9: Checking whether the firewalld HTTP rule is added

Scripts can be compressed or uploaded to a storage blob if you want.

Of course, you can use the Azure CLI to make the initial configuration. In that scenario, you have to provide a JSON file similar to this one:

```
{
    "autoUpgradeMinorVersion": true,
    "location": "<location>",
    "name": "CustomscriptLinux",
    "protectedSettings": {},
    "provisioningState": "Failed",
    "publisher": "Microsoft.Azure.Extensions",
    "resourceGroup": "<resource group name>",
    "settings": {
      "script": "<base64 string"
    },
    "tags": {},
    "type": "Microsoft.Compute/virtualMachines/extensions",
    "typeHandlerVersion": "2.0",
    "virtualMachineExtensionType": "CustomScript"
  }
```

Then, execute the following **az** command:

```
az vm extension set --resource-group <resource group> \
   --vm-name <vm name> \
   --name customScript --publisher Microsoft.Azure.Extensions \
   --settings ./nginx.json
```

> **Note**
>
> The JSON file can be included in an ARM template.

If you are using PowerShell or the Azure CLI for debugging purposes, the **/var/log/azure/custom-script** directory contains the log of your actions.

Initial Configuration with cloud-init

A problem with the custom VM extension is that scripts can be very distribution-specific. You can already see that in the examples used. If you use different distributions, you'll need multiple scripts or you'll have to include distribution checks.

Another way to do some initial configuration after the deployment of your VM is by using cloud-init.

cloud-init is a Canonical project that was created to provide a cloud solution and a Linux-distribution-agnostic approach for customizing cloud images. In Azure, it can be used with images to prepare the operating system during the first boot, or while creating the VM.

Not every Microsoft-endorsed Linux distribution is supported; Debian and SUSE are not supported at all and it always takes some time before the latest version of a distribution can be used.

cloud-init can be used to run Linux commands and create files. There are modules available in cloud-init to configure the system, for instance, to install software or do some user and group management. If a module is available, then it's the best way to do it. It is not only easier (the hard work is done for you), but it's also distribution agnostic.

cloud-init uses YAML; please be aware that indentation is important! The purpose of the script is to install the **npm**, **nodejs**, and **nginx** packages, then configure nginx, and finally, display a message, **Hello World from host $hostname**, where **$hostname** is the name of the VM. To start with, let's create a YAML file with the following content, and name it **cloudinit.yml**:

```
#cloud-config

groups: users

users:

  - default

  - name: azureuser

  - groups: users

  - shell: /bin/bash

package_upgrade: true

packages:

  - nginx

  - nodejs

  - npm

write_files:

  - owner: www-data:www-data

  - path: /etc/nginx/sites-available/default

    content: |

      server {

        listen 80;

        location / {

          proxy_pass http://localhost:3000;

          proxy_http_version 1.1;

          proxy_set_header Upgrade $http_upgrade;

          proxy_set_header Connection keep-alive;

          proxy_set_header Host $host;

          proxy_cache_bypass $http_upgrade;

        }

      }
```

```
    - owner: azureuser:users
    - path: /home/azureuser/myapp/index.js
      content: |
        var express = require('express')

        var app = express()

        var os = require('os');

        app.get('/', function (req, res) {

          res.send('Hello World from host ' + os.hostname() + '!')

        })

        app.listen(3000, function () {

          console.log('Hello world app listening on port 3000!')

        })
  runcmd:
    - systemctl restart nginx
    - cd "/home/azureuser/myapp"
    - npm init
    - npm install express -y
    - nodejs index.js
```

If you look at this configuration file, you can use some of the following modules in action:

- **users** and **groups**: User management
- **packages** and **package_upgrade**: Software management
- **write_files**: File creation
- **runcmd**: Run commands that are not possible with modules

You can also create a VM:

```
az vm create --resource-group <resource group> \
    --name <vm name> --image UbuntuLTS \
    --admin-username linuxadmin \
    --generate-ssh-keys --custom-data cloudinit.txt
```

After deployment, it will take some time before everything is done. Logging is done in the VM in the **/var/log/cloud-init.log** and **/var/log/cloud-init-output.log** files.

Change the network security group rules to permit traffic on port **80**. After that, open your browser to the IP address of the VM. If everything is OK, it will show the following: `Hello World from host ubuntu-web!`

> **Note**
>
> There is no support for cloud-init in the Az cmdlets.

Vagrant

Until now, we used solutions provided by Microsoft; maybe we should call them native solutions. That's not the only way to deploy your workload in Azure. Many vendors have created solutions to automate deployments in Azure. In this section, we want to cover a solution from a company called HashiCorp (https://www.hashicorp.com). Later on in this chapter, we'll cover another product from this company: Packer. There are several reasons why we have chosen these products:

- The products are very popular and well-known.

- There is an excellent relationship between Microsoft and HashiCorp; they work very hard together to implement more and more features.

- And the most important reason: HashiCorp has different products that you can use for different implementation scenarios. This will make you think again about what method you want to choose in different use cases.

Vagrant is a tool you can use for deployment if you are a developer. It helps you to set up an environment in a standardized way that you can redeploy over and over again.

Installing and Configuring Vagrant

Vagrant is available for several Linux distributions, Windows, and macOS and can be downloaded from https://www.vagrantup.com/downloads.html:

1. To install the software in Ubuntu, use the following commands:

    ```
    cd /tmp
    ```

    ```
    wget \ https://releases.hashicorp.com/vagrant/2.1.2/vagrant_2.1.2_x86_64.deb
    sudo dpkg -i vagrant_2.1.2_x86_64.deb
    ```

    In RHEL/CentOS, use the following command:

    ```
    sudo yum install \
     https://releases.hashicorp.com/vagrant/2.1.2/ \
     vagrant_2.1.2_x86_64.rpm
    ```

    If you deploy it on a separate VM or workstation, make sure that you install the Azure CLI as well.

    Log in to Azure:

    ```
    az login
    ```

    Create a service principal account that Vagrant can use to authenticate:

    ```
    az ad sp create-for-rbac --name vagrant
    ```

    From the output, you need the **appID**, also known as the **Client ID**, and the password, which is the same as the **Client Secret**.

2. Execute the following command to get your tenant ID and subscription ID:

    ```
    az account show
    ```

    In the output of this command, you can see your tenant ID and your subscription ID.

3. Create a file with the following content and save it to ~/.azure/vagrant.sh:

```
AZURE_TENANT_ID="<tenant id>"
AZURE_SUBSCRIPTION_ID="<account id>"
AZURE_CLIENT_ID="<app id>"
AZURE_CLIENT_SECRET="<password>"

export AZURE_TENANT_ID AZURE_SUBSCRIPTION_ID AZURE_CLIENT_ID\
    AZURE_CLIENT_SECRET
```

4. These variables must be exported before you can use Vagrant. In macOS and Linux, you can do that by executing the following command:

```
source <file>
```

5. An SSH key pair must be available. If this has not already been done, create a key pair with this command:

```
ssh-keygen
```

6. The last step involves the installation of the Azure plugin for Vagrant:

```
vagrant plugin install vagrant-azure
```

7. Verify the installation:

```
vagrant version
```

```
student@azure01:~$ vagrant version
Installed Version: 2.1.2
Latest Version: 2.1.2

You're running an up-to-date version of Vagrant!
```

Figure 7.10: Verifying the vagrant installation

Now that we have confirmed Vagrant is up and running, let's go ahead and deploy a VM using Vagrant.

Deploying a VM with Vagrant

To deploy a VM with Vagrant, you'll need to create a new working directory where we will create the **Vagrantfile**:

```
Vagrant.configure('2') do |config|

config.vm.box = 'azure'

# use local ssh key to connect to remote vagrant box  config.ssh.private_key_
path = '~/.ssh/id_rsa'

config.vm.provider :azure do |azure, override|

azure.tenant_id = ENV['AZURE_TENANT_ID']

azure.client_id = ENV['AZURE_CLIENT_ID']

azure.client_secret = ENV['AZURE_CLIENT_SECRET']    azure.subscription_id =
ENV['AZURE_SUBSCRIPTION_ID']

end

end
```

The configuration file starts with a statement that we need the Azure plugin for Vagrant that we installed earlier. After that, the configuration of the VM starts. To be able to provide a workload with Vagrant, a dummy VM is needed. It's almost an empty file: it only registers Azure as a provider. To get this dummy VM, execute the following command:

```
vagrant box add azure-dummy\

  https://github.com/azure/vagrant-azure/raw/v2.0/dummy.box\

  --provider azure
```

Normally, a lot of the options, for example, **vm_image_urn**, will be embedded in a box file and you just have to provide minimal options in the **Vagrantfile**. Since we're using a dummy box, there are no pre-configured defaults. **az.vm_image_urn** is the actual image offered by Azure with the following syntax:

```
<publisher>:<image>:<sku>:<version>
```

Besides using standard images, it is possible to use custom **virtual hard disk** (**VHD**) files using these directives:

- **vm_vhd_uri**

- **vm_operating_system**

- **vm_vhd_storage_account_id**

Later in this chapter, we will discuss these custom VHD files in more detail.

Another important value is the name of the VM; it's also used as a DNS prefix. This must be unique! Otherwise, you'll get this error: **DNS record <name>.<location>.cloudapp.azure.com is already used by another public IP.**

Deploy the Vagrant box, the VM:

```
vagrant up
```

Here is what the output should look like:

```
student@azure01:~/ubuntu_lts$ vagrant up
Bringing machine 'default' up with 'azure' provider...
==> default: Launching an instance with the following settings...
==> default:   -- Management Endpoint: https://management.azure.com
==> default:   -- Subscription Id:
==> default:   -- Resource Group Name: vagrant
==> default:   -- Location: westus
==> default:   -- Admin Username: vagrant
==> default:   -- VM Name: linvirt001
==> default:   -- VM Storage Account Type: Premium_LRS
==> default:   -- VM Size: Standard_B1s
==> default:   -- Image URN: Canonical:UbuntuServer:18.04-LTS:latest
==> default:   -- DNS Label Prefix: linvirt001
==> default:   -- Create or Update of Resource Group: vagrant
==> default:   -- Starting deployment
==> default:   -- Finished deploying
==> default: Waiting for SSH to become available...
Enter passphrase for /home/student/.ssh/id_rsa:
==> default: Machine is booted and ready for use!
```

Figure 7.11: Deploying the vagrant box

When the machine is ready to use, you can log in using this command:

```
vagrant ssh
```

The contents of your work directory are copied to **/vagrant** in the VM. This can be a very nice way to have your files available in the VM.

Clean up your work with this command:

```
vagrant destroy
```

> **Note**
>
> It's possible to create multi-machine boxes as well.

Vagrant Provisioners

Providing an easy way to deploy a VM is not the most important feature of Vagrant. The main reason to use Vagrant is to have a complete environment up and running; after deployment, VMs need configuration. There are provisioners to do the after-work. The purpose of provisioners is to make configuration changes, automatically install packages, and more. You can use the shell provisioner, which helps to upload and execute scripts in the guest VM, and the file provisioner to run commands and copy files to the VM.

Another possibility is to use Vagrant provisioners for orchestration tools, such as Ansible and Salt. The next chapter will discuss those tools. In this chapter, together with the provisioners' documentation on the Vagrant website (https://www.vagrantup.com/docs/provisioning/), we will configure the shell provisioners and the file provisioner. Let's go ahead start configuring the provisioners by adding the following code block to the **Vagrantfile**.

Add this to the bottom of the **Vagrantfile**:

```
# Configure the Shell Provisioner
config.vm.provision "shell", path: "provision.sh"
end # Vagrant.config
```

We have referenced a file, **provision.sh**, in the shell provisioner. So let's create a short **provision.sh** script with some simple commands:

```
#!/bin/sh
touch /tmp/done
touch /var/lib/cloud/instance/locale-check.skip
```

Deploy the VM again, and you can see that Vagrant has taken the SSH key we created and has started the provisioning:

```
Enter passphrase for key '/home/student/.ssh/id_rsa':
==> default: Running provisioner: shell...
    default: Running: /tmp/vagrant-shell20180807-2269-1i5pqjq.sh
```

Figure 7.12: Vagrant has started provisioning

Execute this code to verify whether the **/tmp/done** directory has been created in the VM as we instructed in the **provision.sh** file:

```
vagrant ssh -c "ls -al /tmp/done"
```

Packer

It's important for a developer, especially if there are many people working on the same application, to have a standardized environment. If you are not using container technology (refer to *Chapter 9, Container Virtualization in Azure*, and *Chapter 10, Working with Azure Kubernetes Service*, to find out more about this technology), Vagrant is a great tool that helps developers with this and manages the life cycle of a VM to get things running very quickly in a reproducible way. It provisions the setup based on image offerings or a custom VHD. It's everything you need if you want to develop your application in the cloud.

But if you want more complex environments, building your own images, multi-machine deployments, cross-cloud environments, and so on, it's not completely impossible, but as soon as you try, you will see that Vagrant is not made for those scenarios.

This is where another HashiCorp product comes in handy: Packer. In this section, we're going to use Packer with a very similar configuration to the one we used before with Vagrant.

Installing and Configuring Packer

Packer is available for macOS, Windows, several Linux distributions, and FreeBSD. Packages are available to download at https://www.packer.io/downloads.html.

Download a package, unzip it, and you're ready to go. In Linux, it's a good idea to create a ~/.bin directory and unzip it there:

```
mkdir ~/bin
cd /tmp
wget wget https://releases.hashicorp.com/packer/1.2.5/\
  packer_1.2.5_linux_amd64.zip
unzip /tmp/packer*zip
cp packer ~/bin
```

Log out and log in again. Almost every distribution adds the **~/bin** directory to the **PATH** variable as soon it's available, but you have to log out and log in again.

Check the **PATH** variable by executing **$PATH**. If you are not able to see the **bin** folder in your home directory added to the path, execute the following:

```
export PATH=~/bin:$PATH
```

Verify the installation:

```
packer version
```

If the installation was successful, the command will return the version of Packer, as you can see in this screenshot:

```
student@azure01:~$ packer version
Packer v1.2.5
```

Figure 7.13: Verifying packer installation through Packer version

For the configuration of Packer, we'll need the same information as for Vagrant:

- Azure tenant ID (**az account show**)

- Azure subscription ID (**az account show**)

- The ID of the service principal account (if you want to use the same one as in Vagrant, use the **az app list --display-name vagrant** command)

- The secret key to this account (if needed, you can use the **az ad sp reset-credentials** command to generate a new one)

- The existing resource group in the correct location; in this example, we are using **LinuxOnAzure** as the resource group name and **West Europe** as the location (created with the **az group create --location "West Europe" --name "LinuxOnAzure"** command)

Create a file (for instance, **/packer/ubuntu.json**) with the following content:

```json
{
    "builders": [{
      "type": "azure-arm",
      "client_id": "<appId>",
      "client_secret": "<appPassword>",
      "tenant_id": "<tenantId>",
      "subscription_id": "<subscriptionID>",
      "managed_image_resource_group_name": "LinuxOnAzure",
      "managed_image_name": "myPackerImage",
      "os_type": "Linux",
      "image_publisher": "Canonical",
      "image_offer": "UbuntuServer",
      "image_sku": "18.04-LTS",
      "location": "West Europe",
      "vm_size": "Standard_B1s"
    }],
    "provisioners": [{
    "type": "shell",
    "inline": [
    "touch /tmp/done",
    "sudo touch /var/lib/cloud/instance/locale-check.skip"
    ]
    }]
}
```

Validate the syntax:

```
packer validate ubuntu.json
```

Then, build the image as follows:

```
packer build ubuntu.json
```

```
⏸  /tmp packer build ubuntu.json
azure-arm output will be in this color.

==> azure-arm: Running builder ...
    azure-arm: Creating Azure Resource Manager (ARM) client ...
==> azure-arm: Creating resource group ...
==> azure-arm:  -> ResourceGroupName : 'packer-Resource-Group-c11v0gttsw'
==> azure-arm:  -> Location          : 'West Europe'
==> azure-arm:  -> Tags              :
==> azure-arm: Validating deployment template ...
==> azure-arm:  -> ResourceGroupName : 'packer-Resource-Group-c11v0gttsw'
==> azure-arm:  -> DeploymentName    : 'pkrdpc11v0gttsw'
==> azure-arm: Deploying deployment template ...
==> azure-arm:  -> ResourceGroupName : 'packer-Resource-Group-c11v0gttsw'
==> azure-arm:  -> DeploymentName    : 'pkrdpc11v0gttsw'
==> azure-arm: Getting the VM's IP address ...
==> azure-arm:  -> ResourceGroupName  : 'packer-Resource-Group-c11v0gttsw'
==> azure-arm:  -> PublicIPAddressName : 'pkripc11v0gttsw'
==> azure-arm:  -> NicName            : 'pkrnic11v0gttsw'
==> azure-arm:  -> Network Connection  : 'PublicEndpoint'
==> azure-arm:  -> IP Address         : '104.40.247.200'
==> azure-arm: Waiting for SSH to become available...
==> azure-arm: Connected to SSH!
==> azure-arm: Provisioning with shell script: /tmp/packer-shell943526308
==> azure-arm: Querying the machine's properties ...
==> azure-arm:  -> ResourceGroupName : 'packer-Resource-Group-c11v0gttsw'
==> azure-arm:  -> ComputeName       : 'pkrvmc11v0gttsw'
==> azure-arm:  -> Managed OS Disk   : '/subscriptions/71766a1b-baf2-43e0-aa09-72
==> azure-arm: Querying the machine's additional disks properties ...
==> azure-arm:  -> ResourceGroupName : 'packer-Resource-Group-c11v0gttsw'
==> azure-arm:  -> ComputeName       : 'pkrvmc11v0gttsw'
==> azure-arm: Powering off machine ...
==> azure-arm:  -> ResourceGroupName : 'packer-Resource-Group-c11v0gttsw'
==> azure-arm:  -> ComputeName       : 'pkrvmc11v0gttsw'
==> azure-arm: Capturing image ...
==> azure-arm:  -> Compute ResourceGroupName : 'packer-Resource-Group-c11v0gttsw'
==> azure-arm:  -> Compute Name              : 'pkrvmc11v0gttsw'
==> azure-arm:  -> Compute Location          : 'West Europe'
==> azure-arm:  -> Image ResourceGroupName   : 'LinuxOnAzure'
==> azure-arm:  -> Image Name                : 'myPackerImage'
==> azure-arm:  -> Image Location            : 'westeurope'
==> azure-arm: Deleting resource group ...
==> azure-arm:  -> ResourceGroupName : 'packer-Resource-Group-c11v0gttsw'
==> azure-arm:
==> azure-arm: The resource group was created by Packer, deleting ...
```

Figure 7.14: Building the image using Packer build command

It takes a few minutes for Packer to build the VM, run the provisioners, and clean up the deployment.

Once the build is complete, Packer will give you a summary of what was built, such as the resource group, where the VM was deployed, the name of the image, and the location:

```
==> Builds finished. The artifacts of successful builds are:
--> azure-arm: Azure.ResourceManagement.VMImage:

ManagedImageResourceGroupName: LinuxOnAzure
ManagedImageName: myPackerImage
ManagedImageLocation: westeurope
```

Figure 7.15: Image summary

The build will create an image but not a running VM. From the image Packer created, you can deploy a machine using this command:

```
az vm create \
--resource-group LinuxOnAzure \
 --name mypackerVM \
--image myPackerImage \
--admin-username azureuser \
--generate-ssh-keys
```

To clean up the environment and delete the image created by Packer, execute the following command:

```
az resource delete --resource-group LinuxOnAzure --resource-type images \
   --namespace Microsoft.Compute --name myPackerImage
```

The JSON file that I provided earlier in this chapter is sufficient to create an image. It is very similar to what we did with Vagrant, but to make it into a deployable image, we have to generalize the VM, which means allowing it to be imaged for multiple deployments. Adding **/usr/sbin/waagent -force -deprovision+user & export HISTSIZE=0 && sync** to the code will generalize the VM. Don't worry about this code – you will see it again when we generalize the VM via the Azure CLI in the next section.

Locate the following code:

```
"provisioners": [{
    "type": "shell",
    "inline": [
        "touch /tmp/done",
        "sudo touch /var/lib/cloud/instance/locale-check.skip"
    ]
```

This needs to be replaced with the following code:

```
    "provisioners": [{
    "type": "shell",
    "execute_command": "echo '{{user 'ssh_pass'}}' | {{ .Vars }} sudo -S -E
sh '{{ .Path }}'",
    "inline": [
     "touch /tmp/done",
     "touch /var/lib/cloud/instance/locale-check.skip",
      "/usr/sbin/waagent -force -deprovision+user && export HISTSIZE=0 &&
sync"
    ]
    }]
  }
```

execute_command is a command used to execute the script as the correct user.

Validate the template using the **packer validate** command, as we did before, to avoid any errors and build the image again.

So far, we have created the image using Packer, but this can also be done using the Azure CLI and Powershell. The next section is all about this.

Custom Virtual Machines and VHDs

In the previous section, we used standard VM offerings in Azure and used two different methods to do some configuration work afterward. However, as stated before, there are reasons why a default image might not be the solution for you. Let's summarize the reasons one more time.

The native image offerings by Azure are a good starting point to deploy VMs. Some of the benefits of using native images are as follows:

- Created and supported by Linux distribution vendors or a trusted partner

- Fast to deploy, both manually and orchestrated, and, of course, you can customize them afterward

- Easy-to-extend functionality and options with Azure extensions

If you are going with the native offerings there are some disadvantages or, in other words, some drawbacks:

- If you want more hardening than the standard image, then you have to rely on hardened image versions from the Marketplace, which is expensive for some.

- The standard image is not compliant with, for example, company standards, especially when it comes to partitioning.

- The standard image is not optimized for a certain application.

- Some Linux distributions aren't supported, such as Alpine and ArchLinux.

- Questions about reproducible environments: how long is a certain image version available?

So we need custom images, with which we can customize the image and mitigate the issues or drawbacks. We are not suggesting that the native offers are not secure or can't accomplish the task, but in an enterprise environment, there are scenarios such as bring-your-own-subscription for RHEL/SLES VMs and third-party **Independent Software Vendor** (**ISV**) software packaged as images with which you have to go with the custom images. Let's go ahead and see how we can use custom images in Azure.

Creating a Managed Image

In the previous section, we investigated Packer. A VM was created, and after that, it was transformed into an image. This image can be used to deploy a new VM. This technique is also called **capturing a VM image**.

Let's find out whether we can do it step by step the manual way using the Azure CLI:

1. Create a resource group:

   ```
   myRG=capture
   myLocation=westus

   az group create --name $myRG --location $myLocation
   ```

2. Create a VM:

   ```
   myVM=ubuntudevel
   AZImage=UbuntuLTS
   Admin=linvirt

   az vm create --resource-group $myRG  --name $myVM \
     --image $AZImage \
     --admin-username linvirt  --generate-ssh-keys
   ```

3. Log in to the VM and deprovision it using the Azure VM Agent. It generalizes the VM by removing user-specific data:

   ```
   sudo waagent -deprovision+user
   ```

   Once you execute the command, the output will show warnings about the data that is going to be deleted. You can proceed by entering **y**, as shown here:

```
linvirt@ubuntudevel:~$ sudo waagent -deprovision+user
WARNING! The waagent service will be stopped.
WARNING! Cached DHCP leases will be deleted.
WARNING! root password will be disabled. You will not be able to login as root.
WARNING! /etc/resolvconf/resolv.conf.d/tail and /etc/resolvconf/resolv.conf.d/original will be deleted.
WARNING! linvirt account and entire home directory will be deleted.
Do you want to proceed (y/n)y
```

Figure 7.16: Deprovisioning the VM

Type **exit** to leave the SSH session.

4. Deallocate the VM:

```
az vm deallocate --resource-group $myRG --name $myVM
```

5. Mark it as being generalized. This means allowing it to be imaged for multiple deployments:

```
az vm generalize --resource-group $myRG --name $myVM
```

6. Create an image from the VM in this resource group:

```
destIMG=customUbuntu

az image create --resource-group $myRG --name $destIMG --source $myVM
```

7. Verify the result:

```
az image list -o table
```

The output will show the list of images in a table format:

Figure 7.17: Azure image list

8. You can deploy a new VM with this image:

```
az vm create --resource-group <resource group> \
  --name <vm name> \
  --image $destIMG \
  --admin-username <username> \
  --generate-ssh-key
```

If you are in PowerShell, this is also possible. Let's go very quickly through the first step. The process is very similar; the only difference is that we are using PowerShell cmdlets:

```
$myRG="myNewRG"
$myLocation="westus"
$myVM="ubuntu-custom"
$AZImage="UbuntuLTS"

#Create resource group
New-AzResourceGroup -Name $myRG -Location $myLocation

#Create VM
New-AzVm '
-ResourceGroupName $myRG '
-Name $myVM '
-ImageName $AZimage '
-Location $myLocation '
-VirtualNetworkName "$myVM-Vnet" '
-SubnetName "$myVM-Subnet" '
-SecurityGroupName "$myVM-NSG" '
-PublicIpAddressName "$myVM-pip"
```

PowerShell may prompt you to enter credentials. Proceed with entering the credentials to access your VM. After that, we will proceed with the deallocation of the VM:

```
Stop-AzureRmVM -ResourceGroupName <resource group>'
  -Name <vm name>
```

As we did before, now we have to mark the VM as generalized:

```
Set-AzVm -ResourceGroupName <resource group> -Name <vm name> '
 -Generalized
```

Let's capture the VM information and save it to a variable, because we will need it to create the image's configuration:

```
$vm = Get-AzVM -Name <vm name> -ResourceGroupName <resource group name>
```

Now let's create the image's configuration:

```
$image = New-AzImageConfig -Location<location> -SourceVirtualMachineId $vm.Id
```

Since we have the configuration stored in **$image**, use that to create the image:

```
New-AzImage -Image $image -ImageName <image name> '
  -ResourceGroupName <resource group name>
```

Verify that the image has been created:

```
Get-AzImage -ImageName <Image Name>
```

Running the preceding command will give you an output similar to the following, with the details of the image you created:

```
PS C:\windows\system32> Get-AzImage -ImageName CustomUbuntuCore


ResourceGroupName    : MYNEWRG
SourceVirtualMachine : Microsoft.Azure.Management.Compute.Model
StorageProfile       : Microsoft.Azure.Management.Compute.Model
ProvisioningState    : Succeeded
HyperVGeneration     : V1
Id                   : /subscriptions/71766a1b-baf2-43e0-aa09-7
Name                 : CustomUbuntuCore
Type                 : Microsoft.Compute/images
Location             : westus
Tags                 : {}
```

Figure 7.18: Fetching image details

If you want to create a VM using the image we just created, execute the following command:

```
New-AzVm '
 -ResourceGroupName "<resource group name>" '
 -Name "<VM Name>" '
 -ImageName "<Image Name>" '
 -Location "<location>" '
 -VirtualNetworkName "<vnet name>" '
 -SubnetName "<subnet name>" '
 -SecurityGroupName "<nsg name>" '
 -PublicIpAddressName "<public IP name>"
```

To summarize what we did, we created a VM, generalized it, and created an image that can be further used to deploy multiple VMs. There is also an alternative method to create multiple VMs from a reference image, which is using "snaphots". This will be covered in the next section.

An Alternative Method Using Snapshots

If you want to keep the original VM, you can create a VM image from a snapshot. A snapshot in Azure is actually a complete VM!

Using PowerShell

1. Declare a variable, **$vm**, which will store the information about the VM we are going to take and create a snapshot:

```
$vm = Get-AzVm -ResourceGroupName <resource group> '
  -Name $vmName

$snapshot = New-AzSnapshotConfig '
  -SourceUri $vm.StorageProfile.OsDisk.ManagedDisk.Id '
  -Location <location> -CreateOption copy

New-AzSnapshot '
  -Snapshot $snapshot -SnapshotName <snapshot name> '
  -ResourceGroupName <resource group>
```

2. As we need the snapshot ID for a later step, we will reinitialize the snapshot variable:

```
$snapshot = Get-AzSnapshot -SnapshotName <Snapshot Name>
```

3. The next step involves creating the image configuration from the snapshot.

```
$imageConfig = New-AzImageConfig -Location <location>


$imageConfig = Set-AzImageOsDisk -Image $imageConfig '
  -OsState Generalized -OsType Linux -SnapshotId $snapshot.Id
```

4. Finally, create the image:

```
New-AzImage -ImageName <image name> '
  -ResourceGroupName <resource group> -Image $imageConfig
```

Using the Azure CLI

In the Azure CLI, things are easier; just get the ID of the snapshot and convert it to a disk:

1. Using the Azure CLI, create a snapshot:

    ```
    disk=$(az vm show --resource-group <resource group>\
      --name <vm name> --query "storageProfile.osDisk.name" -o tsv)

    az snapshot create --resource-group <resource group>\
      --name <snapshot name> --source $disk
    ```

2. Create the image:

    ```
    snapshotId=$(az snapshot show --name <snapshot name>\
      --resource-group <resource group> --query "id" -o tsv)

    az image create --resource-group <resource group> --name myImage \
      --source $snapshotID --os-type Linux
    ```

Don't forget to generalize the VM before you snapshot it. If you don't want to do that, create a disk from the snapshot and use that as a disk parameter with the **--attach-os-disk** command in the Azure CLI, or **Set-AzVMOSDisk** in PowerShell.

Custom VHDs

You can completely build your own image from scratch. In this scenario, you have to build your own VHD file. There are multiple ways to do this:

-   Create a VM in Hyper-V or in VirtualBox, which is a free hypervisor available for Windows, Linux, and macOS. Both products support VHD natively.

-   Create your VM in VMware Workstation or KVM and use it in Linux **qemu-img** to convert the image. For Windows, the Microsoft Virtual Machine Converter is available at https://www.microsoft.com/en-us/download/details.aspx?id=42497. This includes a PowerShell cmdlet, **ConvertTo-MvmcVirtualHardDisk**, to make the conversion.

> **Note**
>
> Azure only supports Type-1 VHD files and should have a virtual size aligned to 1 MB. At the time of writing this book, Type-2 is available in preview (https://docs.microsoft.com/en-us/azure/virtual-machines/windows/generation-2).

Azure runs on Hyper-V. Linux requires certain kernel modules to run in Azure. If the VM was created outside of Hyper-V, the Linux installers may not include the drivers for Hyper-V in the initial ramdisk (**initrd** or **initramfs**), unless the VM detects that it's running on a Hyper-V environment.

When using a different virtualization system (such as VirtualBox or KVM) to prepare your Linux image, you may need to rebuild the **initrd** so that at least the **hv_vmbus** and **hv_storvsc** kernel modules are available on the initial ramdisk. This known issue is for systems based on the upstream Red Hat distribution, and possibly others.

The mechanism for rebuilding the **initrd** or **initramfs** image may vary depending on the distribution. Consult your distribution's documentation or support for the proper procedure. Here is an example of rebuilding the **initrd** by using the **mkinitrd** utility:

1. Back up the existing **initrd** image:

   ```
   cd /boot
   sudo cp initrd-'uname -r'.img  initrd-'uname -r'.img.bak
   ```

2. Rebuild the **initrd** with the **hv_vmbus** and **hv_storvsc kernel** modules:

   ```
   sudo mkinitrd --preload=hv_storvsc --preload=hv_vmbus -v -f initrd-'uname
   -r'.img 'uname -r'
   ```

   It's almost impossible to describe every available option for each Linux distribution and each hypervisor. In general, the things you need to do are listed here. It's very important that we follow the steps accurately, otherwise, this task cannot be accomplished. We strongly recommend following the Microsoft documentation for this (https://docs.microsoft.com/en-us/azure/virtual-machines/linux/create-upload-generic).

3. Modify the kernel boot line in GRUB or GRUB2 to include the following parameters so that all console messages are sent to the first serial port. These messages can help Azure Support to debug any issues:

   ```
   console=ttyS0,115200n8 earlyprintk=ttyS0,115200 rootdelay=300
   ```

4. Microsoft also recommends removing the following parameters, if they exist:

   ```
   rhgb quiet crashkernel=auto
   ```

5. Install the Azure Linux Agent, because the agent is required for provisioning Linux images on Azure. You can install it using the **rpm** or **deb** file, or you can manually install it using the steps available in the Linux Agent Guide (https://docs.microsoft.com/en-us/azure/virtual-machines/extensions/agent-linux).

6. Make sure the OpenSSH server is installed and autostarts during boot.

7. Don't create swap. You can enable it later if required, as we discussed in the previous chapter.

8. Deprovision the VM as in the *Creating a Managed Image* section.

9. Shut down the VM, and your VHD is ready to be uploaded to the VM.

For simplicity, we are going to skip the preceding steps and download the official image from Ubuntu's cloud image repository, because the most important part is the uploading of the image to Azure. Download the cloud image from https://cloud-images. ubuntu.com/bionic/. This web page contains all the versions of Bionic, and you can navigate through the directories and download the tar.gz file for Azure. The filename will be similar to **bionic-server-cloudimg-amd64-azure.vhd.tar.gz**; however, this name may vary a little depending upon the version you are looking at.

Now we have to upload the VHD to Azure:

1. To start with, it's a good idea to have a separate storage account for images, so let's create a new storage account. Here, we are going with **Premium_LRS**, but if you wish, you can go for **Standard_LRS** as well to save some costs:

   ```
   az storage account create --location <location> \
     --resource-group <resource group> --sku Premium_LRS \
     --name <account name> --access-tier Cool --kind StorageV2
   ```

2. Save the output for later use. List the access keys:

   ```
   az storage account keys list --account-name <storage account name>\
     --resource-group <resource group>
   ```

3. Save the output again. The next thing we need is a container to store the files:

   ```
   az storage container create \
     --account-name <storage account>\
     --account-key <storage account key 1>
     --name <container name>
   ```

4. Now you can upload the VHD:

```
az storage blob upload --account-name <storage account>\
    --account-key <storage account key> \
    --container-name <container name> \
    --type page --file ./bionic-server-cloudimg-amd64.vhd \
    --name bionic.vhd
```

> **Note**
>
> You can also upload the file using the Azure portal or PowerShell. Other methods are Azure Storage Explorer (https://azure.microsoft.com/en-us/features/storage-explorer/) or the Azure VHD utils (https://github.com/Microsoft/azure-vhd-utils). The last one is amazingly fast!

5. Receive the blob URL:

```
az storage blob url --account-name <storage account> \
    --account-key <storage account key> \
    --container-name <container name> \
    --name bionic.vhd
```

6. It's now possible to create a disk from the upload:

```
az disk create --resource-group <resoure group> \
  --name bionic --source <blob url> --Location <location>
```

7. Create a VM image with this disk:

```
az image create --resource-group <resource group> \
    --name bionic --source <blob url> --os-type linux
    --location <location>
```

8. Finally, create a VM based on this image:

```
az vm create --resource-group <resource group> \
  --name <vm name> \
  --image bionic \
  --admin-username <username> \
  --generate-ssh-key \
  --location <location>
```

> **Note**
>
> You can make your VHD images public; a nice example of this is a lesser-known Linux distribution named NixOS. On their website, https://nixos.org/nixos/download.html, they describe a way to deploy their operating system in Azure!

Let's conclude what we've done. We took two approaches here. We created and uploaded a Linux VHD from an existing VM, and then we manually downloaded an Ubuntu VHD and used it. Either way, we will be uploading it to a storage account and will create an image using it. This image is reusable, and you can deploy as many VMs you want.

The automation process and the tools available for it is vast. In the next chapter, we will continue with the automation process and we will discuss the most widely used tools, which are Ansible and Terraform.

Summary

In this chapter, we started asking why and when we should use automation in Azure. Later on, we added questions regarding using the images offered by Azure.

With these questions in mind, we explored the options for automating our deployments:

- Scripting
- ARM templates
- Vagrant
- Packer
- Building and using your own images

Vagrant and Packer are examples of third-party solutions that are very popular tools that make it possible to easily create and recreate environments as an important part of your development process.

It's important to know that all the techniques described in this chapter can be combined into a complete solution. For instance, you can use cloud-init together with ARM, but also with Vagrant.

Automation and orchestration are closely related. In this chapter, we covered automation, especially as a part of development environments, to automate the deployment of VMs. Automation is often a difficult solution to maintain your workload following development and deployment. This is where orchestration kicks in, as covered in the next chapter.

Questions

1. What are the main reasons for using automated deployments in Azure?
2. What is the purpose of automation in development environments?
3. Can you describe the differences between scripting and automation?
4. Can you name some of the automated deployment options available in Azure?
5. What is the difference between Vagrant and Packer?
6. Why should you use your own image instead of an image offered by Azure?
7. What options are available to create your own image?

And perhaps you can find some time to finish the example script in the *Scripting* section, in the language of your choice.

Further Reading

Especially regarding the Azure CLI, PowerShell, and ARM, the Azure documentation contains a huge amount of valuable information, with many examples. And everything we wrote in the *Further reading* section of *Chapter 2, Getting Started with the Azure Cloud*, is important for this chapter as well.

Another resource provided by Microsoft is its blogs. If you visit https://blogs.msdn. microsoft.com/wriju/category/azure/, you'll find many interesting posts about automation, including more detailed examples.

In his blog at https://michaelcollier.wordpress.com, Michael S. Collier provides a lot of information regarding Azure. Almost every post includes scripting and automation possibilities.

There are not many recent books about Vagrant. We are sure you would really enjoy *Infrastructure as Code (IAC) Cookbook*, by Stephane Jourdan and Pierre Pomes, published a year ago. This book not only concerns Vagrant; it also covers other solutions, such as cloud-init and Terraform. The authors created a book that is not only a great introduction but managed to make it useable as a reference guide as well.

Can we suggest a book that has been recently published? *Hands-On DevOps with Vagrant: Implement End-to-End DevOps and Infrastructure Management Using Vagrant*, by Alex Braunton. His posts on YouTube regarding this topic are worth watching as well.

8
Exploring Continuous Configuration Automation

Until now, we have worked with single VMs, deploying and configuring them manually. This is nice for labs and very small environments, but if you have to manage bigger environments, this is a very time-consuming and even boring job. It's also very easy to make mistakes and forget things, such as the slight differences between VMs, not to mention the concomitant stability and security risks. For example, choosing the wrong version during deployment will result in consistency issues, and performing an upgrade later is a tedious process.

Automating deployment and configuration management is the ideal way to mitigate this boring task. However, after a while, you might notice some problems with that approach. There are so many reasons why there are problems, and some of the reasons for failure are listed here:

- The script fails because something changed, caused by, for instance, a software update.

- There is a newer version of a base image that is slightly different.

- Scripts can be hard to read and difficult to maintain.

- Scripts are dependent on other components; for instance, the OS, script language, and available internal and external commands.

- And, there is always that one colleague—the script works for you but, for some reason, it always fails when they execute it.

Of course, things have improved over time:

- Many script languages are multiplatform now, such as Bash, Python, and PowerShell. They are available on Windows, macOS, and Linux.

- In `systemd`, the `systemctl` utility with the `-H` parameter can execute commands remotely, and it works even if the remote host is another Linux distribution. The newer `systemd` version has more features.

- `firewalld` and `systemd` work with easy-to-deploy configuration files and overrides.

Automation is most likely not the answer in your quest to deploy, install, configure, and manage your workload. Luckily, there is another way: orchestration.

In musical terms, orchestration is the study of how to write music for an orchestra. You have to understand each instrument and know what sounds they can make. Then, you can start writing the music; to do this, you have to understand how the instruments sound together. Most of the time, you start with a single instrument, for instance, a piano. After that, you scale up to include the other instruments. Hopefully, the result will be a masterpiece and the members of the orchestra will be able to start playing it. It's not that important how the members start, but, in the end, the conductor makes sure that the results count.

There are many similarities to orchestration in computation. Before you can start, you have to understand how all the components work, how they fit together, and what the components do so that you can get the job done. After that, you can start writing the code to achieve the ultimate goal: a manageable environment.

One of the biggest advantages of a cloud environment is that really every component of the environment is written in software. Yes, we know, at the end of the line, there is still a datacenter with many hardware components, but as a cloud user, you don't care about that. Everything you need is written in software and has APIs to talk to. So, it's not only possible to automate the deployment of your Linux workloads, but you can automate and orchestrate the configuration of the Linux operating system and the installation and configuration of applications and keep everything up to date. You can also use orchestration tools to configure Azure resources, and it's even possible to create Linux VMs using these tools.

In orchestration, there are two different approaches:

- **Imperative**: Tell the orchestration tool what to do to reach this goal
- **Declarative**: Tell the orchestration tool what the goal you want to achieve is

Some orchestration tools can do both, but, in general, the declarative approach is the better approach in a cloud environment, where you have so many options to configure and you can declare each option and achieve the exact goal. The good news is that if it's becoming too complex for this method, for instance, when the orchestration tool is not able to understand the goal, you can always extend this method with a little bit of the imperative method using scripts.

A big part of this chapter is about Ansible, but we'll also cover PowerShell **Desired State Configuration** (**DSC**) and Terraform as examples of declarative implementations. The focus, in this chapter, is to understand orchestration and know enough to get started. And, of course, we'll discuss integration with Azure.

The key takeaways from this chapter are:

- Understanding the third-party automation tools such as Ansible and Terraform and how they can be used in Azure.

- Using Azure's native automation and PowerShell DSC to achieve the desired state of the machine.

- How to implement Azure Policy Guest Configuration and audit the settings in your Linux VMs.

- An overview of other solutions available on the market to automate deployments and configuration.

Technical Requirements

In practice, you'll need at least one VM as a control machine, or you can use your workstation running Linux or **Windows Subsystem for Linux** (**WSL**). Along with this, we need a node, which needs to be an Azure VM. However, in order to provide a better explanation, we've deployed three nodes. If you have budget constraints in your Azure subscription, feel free to proceed with one node. It doesn't matter which Linux distribution you're using. The examples in this section, to orchestrate the node, are for an Ubuntu node, but it's easy to translate them to other distributions.

In this chapter, multiple orchestration tools are explored. For every tool, you'll need a clean environment. So, when you are finished with the Ansible section in this chapter, remove the VMs and deploy new ones before going into Terraform.

Understanding Configuration Management

In the introduction of this chapter, you might have read the term *configuration management*. Let's understand this in more depth. Configuration management refers to how you want your VM to be configured. For example, you want an Apache webserver to host a website in a Linux VM; so, the configuration part of the VM involves:

- Installation of Apache package and dependencies

- Opening firewall ports for HTTP traffic or HTTPS traffic if you are using SSL (Secure Sockets Layer) certificates

- Enabling the service and bootstrapping it so the Apache service is started on boot

This example is for a very simple web server. Think about a complex scenario where you have a front-end web server and back-end databases, so the configuration involved is very high. So far, we've been talking about a single VM; what if you want multiple VMs with the same configuration? We are back to square one, where you have to repeat the configuration multiple times, which is a time-consuming and boring task. Here comes the role of orchestration, as we discussed in the introduction. We can make use of orchestration tools to deploy the VM with the state we want. The tools will take care of the configuration. Also, in Azure, we have Azure Policy Guest Configuration, which can be used to audit the settings. Using this policy, we can define a condition that the VM should be in. If the evaluation fails or the condition is not met, Azure will mark this machine as non-compliant.

A big part of this chapter is about Ansible, but we'll also cover PowerShell DSC and Terraform as examples of declarative implementations. The focus, in this chapter, is to understand orchestration and learn enough to get started. And, of course, we'll discuss integration with Azure.

Using Ansible

Ansible is minimal in nature, has almost no dependencies, and it doesn't deploy agents to nodes. Only OpenSSH and Python are required for Ansible. It's also highly reliable: changes can be applied multiple times without changing the result beyond the initial application and there shouldn't be any side effects on the rest of the system (unless you write really bad code). There is a strong focus on the reuse of code, which makes it even more reliable.

Ansible doesn't have a very steep learning curve. You can start with just a few lines of code and scale up afterward without breaking anything. In our opinion, if you want to try an orchestration tool, start with Ansible, and if you want to try another, the learning curve will be much less steep.

Installation of Ansible

In Azure Marketplace, a ready-to-go VM is available for Ansible. There are three versions of Ansible available in Azure Marketplace currently: Ansible Instance, Ansible Tower, and AWX, which is a Community edition of Ansible Tower. In this book, we will concentrate on the community project that is freely available; it's more than enough to learn and get started with Ansible. After that, you can go to the Ansible website to explore the differences, download the trial version of the enterprise edition of Ansible, and decide whether you need the enterprise version.

There are multiple ways to install Ansible:

- Using the repository of your distribution
- Using the latest release available at https://releases.ansible.com/ansible
- Using GitHub: https://github.com/ansible
- Using the Python installer, the preferred method, which works on every OS:

    ```
    pip install ansible[azure]
    ```

Python's **pip** is not available for installation in the standard repositories of Red Hat and CentOS. You have to use the extra EPEL repository:

```
sudo yum install epel-release
sudo yum install python-pip
```

After installing Ansible, check the version:

```
ansible --version
```

You don't have to install Ansible if you don't want to: Ansible is preinstalled in Azure Cloud Shell. At the time of writing this book, Cloud Shell supports Ansible version 2.9.0. However, to give a walk-through of the installation, we'll go for the local installation of Ansible on the VM. For integration with Azure, you also need to install the Azure CLI to get the information you'll need to provide to Ansible.

SSH Configuration

The machine where you installed Ansible is now called the ansible-master or, in other words, it's just a VM with Ansible, the Ansible configuration file, and the instructions for orchestration. Communication with the nodes is done using communication protocols. For Linux, SSH is used as a communication protocol. To make Ansible be able to communicate in a secure way with the nodes, use key-based authentication. If this has not already been done, generate an SSH key pair and copy the key to the VM you want to orchestrate.

To generate the SSHs key, use this command:

```
ssh-keygen
```

Once you generate the key, it will be saved to the home directory of the user in the **.ssh** directory by default. To display the key, use this command:

```
cat ~/.ssh/id_rsa.pub
```

Once we have the key, we have to copy this value to the node server. Follow these steps to copy the key:

1. Copy the contents of the **id_rsa.pub** file.

2. SSH to your node server.

3. Switch to superuser using the **sudo** command.

4. Edit the **authorized_keys** file in **~/.ssh/**.

5. Paste the key we copied from the Ansible server.

6. Save and close the file.

To verify whether the process was successful, go back to the machine where Ansible is installed (going forward, we'll call this ansible-master) and **ssh** to the node. It will ask for the passphrase if you used one while generating the key. Another method to automate the entire process of copying keys is to use the **ssh-copy-id** command.

Bare-Minimum Configuration

To configure Ansible, you'll need an **ansible.cfg** file. There are different locations where this configuration file can be stored, and Ansible searches in the following order:

```
ANSIBLE_CONFIG (environment variable if set)

ansible.cfg (in the current directory)

~/.ansible.cfg (in the home directory)

/etc/ansible/ansible.cfg
```

Ansible will process the preceding list and uses the first file found; all others are ignored.

Create the **ansible** directory in **/etc** if not available and add a file called **ansible.cfg**. This is where we are going to save our configuration:

```
[defaults]
inventory = /etc/ansible/hosts
```

Let's try the following:

```
ansible all -a "systemctl status sshd"
```

This command, called an ad hoc command, executes **systemctl status sshd** to all hosts defined in **/etc/ansiblehosts**. If you have multiple usernames for each host, you can also specify the username for these nodes in the format as shown in the following ansible hosts file:

```
<ip address>   ansible_ssh_user='<ansible user>'
```

So you can add the user to the inventory file line items as shown in the following screenshot, if needed, and the file will look like this for three nodes:

```
root@ansible-master:/etc/ansible# cat hosts
[nodepool]
10.0.0.5 ansible_ssh_user=rithin
10.0.0.6 ansible_ssh_user=rithin
10.0.0.7 ansible_ssh_user=rithin
```

Figure 8.1: Adding the user to the inventory file line items

Try again. Instead of your local username, the remote user is used. You're now able to log in and execute the command.

Inventory File

The Ansible inventory file defines the hosts and groups of hosts. Based on this, you can call out the host or group (group of hosts) and run a specific playbook or execute a command.

Here, we are going to call our group **nodepool** and add IPs of our nodes. Since all our VMs are in the same Azure VNet, we are using the private IP. If they are in different networks, you can add the public IP. Here, we are using three VMs to aid explanation. If you have only one node, just input that one.

Also, you can use the DNS name of the VMs, but they should be added to your **/etc/ hosts** file for resolution:

```
[nodepool]
10.0.0.5
10.0.0.6
10.0.0.7
```

Another parameter that will be useful is **ansible_ssh_user**. You can use this to specify the username used to sign in to the node. This scenario comes into the picture if you are using multiple usernames across your VMs.

Instead of using **all** in our example, you can use a group name that is **ansible-nodes**. It's also possible to use generic variables that are valid for every host and override them per server; for instance:

```
[all:vars]
ansible_ssh_user='student'


[nodepool]
<ip address> ansible_ssh_user='other user'
```

Sometimes, you'll need privileges to execute a command:

```
ansible nodepool-a "systemctl restart sshd"
```

This gives the following error message:

```
Failed to restart sshd.service: Interactive authentication required.
See system logs and 'systemctl status sshd.service' for details.non-zero
return code.
```

For ad hoc commands, just add the **-b** option as an Ansible parameter to enable privilege escalation. It will use the **sudo** method by default. In Azure images, you don't need to give your root password if you are using **sudo**. This is why the **-b** option works without a problem. If you configured **sudo** to prompt for a password, use **-K**.

We would suggest running other commands, such as **netstat** and **ping**, to understand how the commands are executed in these machines. Running **netstat** and grepping for **sshd** will give a similar output to this:

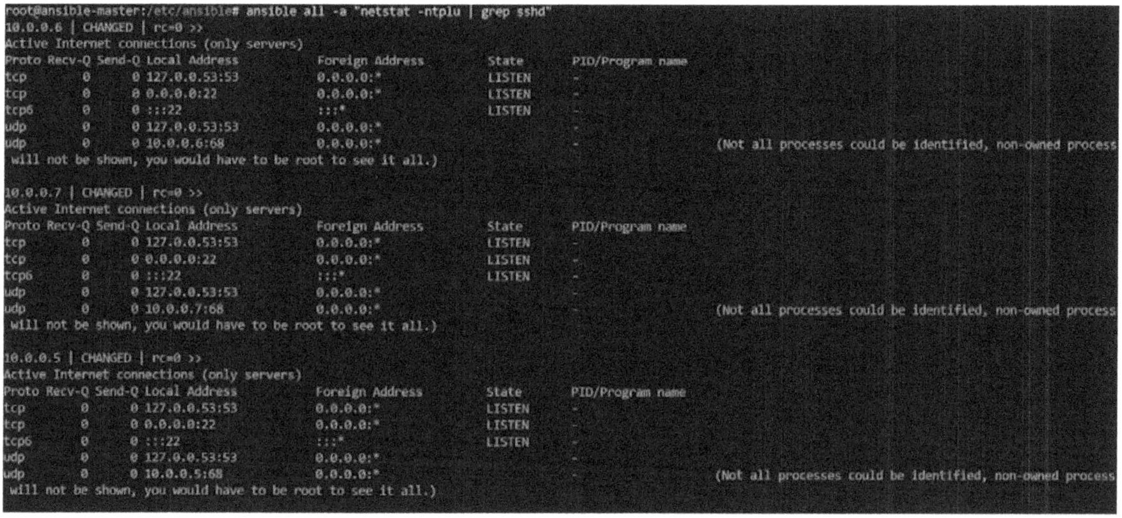

Figure 8.2: Running netstat and grepping for sshd

> **Note**
>
> You might get deprecation warnings when running the **ansible all** command. To suppress this, use **deprecation_warnings=False** in **ansible.cfg**.

Ansible Playbooks and Modules

Using ad hoc commands is an imperative method and is not any better than just using the SSH client to execute commands remotely.

There are two components that you need to make it into real, imperative orchestration: a playbook and a module. The playbook is the basis for the deployment, configuration, and maintenance of your system. It can orchestrate everything, even between hosts! A playbook is there to describe the state you want to reach. Playbooks are written in YAML and can be executed with the **ansible-playbook** command:

```
ansible-playbook <filename>
```

The second component is the module. The best way to describe a module is as follows: the task to be executed to reach the desired state. They are also known as task plugins or library plugins.

All the available modules are documented; you can find the documentation online and on your system.

To list all the available plugin documentation, execute the following command:

```
ansible-doc -l
```

This will take a while. We suggest that you redirect the result to a file. This way, it takes less time and it's easier to search for a module.

As an example, let's try to create a playbook that will create a user using the **user** module if the user doesn't already exist. In other words, the desired state is that a specific user exists.

Start by reading the documentation:

```
ansible-doc user
```

Create a file in the Ansible directory, for instance, **playbook1.yaml**, with the following content. Verify the parameters in the user documentation:

```
---


- hosts: all


  tasks:


- name: Add user Jane Roe
    become: yes
    become_method: sudo
    user:
      state: present
      name: jane
      create_home: yes
      comment: Jane Roe
```

```
generate_ssh_key: yes

group: users

groups:

  - sudo

  - adm

shell: /bin/bash

skeleton: /etc/skel
```

From the output, you can see that all hosts returned **OK** and the user was created:

```
root@ansible-master:/etc/ansible# ansible-playbook playbook1.yml

PLAY [all] *******************************************************************

TASK [Gathering Facts] ******************************************************
ok: [10.0.0.6]
ok: [10.0.0.7]
ok: [10.0.0.5]

TASK [Add user Jane Roe] ****************************************************
changed: [10.0.0.6]
changed: [10.0.0.7]
changed: [10.0.0.5]

PLAY RECAP ******************************************************************
10.0.0.5        : ok=2   changed=1   unreachable=0   failed=0   skipped=0   rescued=0   ignored=0
10.0.0.6        : ok=2   changed=1   unreachable=0   failed=0   skipped=0   rescued=0   ignored=0
10.0.0.7        : ok=2   changed=1   unreachable=0   failed=0   skipped=0   rescued=0   ignored=0
```

Figure 8.3: Running the Ansible playbook

Just to make sure that the user is created, we will check the **/etc/passwd** file in all the hosts. From the output, we can see that the user has been created:

```
root@ansible-master:/etc/ansible# ansible all -a "grep jane /etc/passwd"
10.0.0.5 | CHANGED | rc=0 >>
jane:x:1001:100:Jane Roe:/home/jane:/bin/bash

10.0.0.6 | CHANGED | rc=0 >>
jane:x:1001:100:Jane Roe:/home/jane:/bin/bash

10.0.0.7 | CHANGED | rc=0 >>
jane:x:1001:100:Jane Roe:/home/jane:/bin/bash
```

Figure 8.4: Verifying user creation using /etc/passwd

Make sure that the indentation is correct because YAML is a very strict language when it comes to indentation and white space. Using an editor such as vi, Emacs, or Visual Studio Code with YAML support really helps.

If you are required to run a command privilege escalation, **become** and **become_method** or **-b** can be used.

To check the Ansible syntax, use the following command:

```
ansible-playbook --syntax-check Ansible/example1.yaml
```

Let's go ahead and see how we can authenticate to Azure and start the deployment in Azure.

Authenticating to Microsoft Azure

To integrate Ansible with Microsoft Azure, you need to create a configuration file to provide the credentials for Azure to Ansible.

The credentials must be stored in your home directory in the **~/.azure/credentials** file. First, we have to collect the necessary information with the Azure CLI. Authenticate to Azure as follows:

```
az login
```

If you're successfully logged in, you will get an output similar to the following:

```
{
    "cloudName": "AzureCloud",
    "id": "                              e7",
    "isDefault": false,
    "name": "[PROD]           ",
    "state": "Enabled",
    "tenantId": "                              ",
    "user": {
      "name": "rithir           ",
      "type": "user"
    }
},
{
    "cloudName": "AzureCloud",
    "id": "7                            3f",
    "isDefault": false,
    "name": "Prod          v",
    "state": "Enabled",
    "tenantId": "                            ",
    "user": {
      "name": "rithir        :",
      "type": "user"
    }
}
```

Figure 8.5: Logging in to Azure with the az login command

This is already a part of the information you'll need. If you were already logged in, execute the following command:

```
az account list
```

Create a Service Principal:

```
az ad sp create-for-rbac --name <principal> --password <password>
```

The app ID is your **client_id**, and the password is your **secret**, which will be referenced in the credentials file we are going to create.

Create the **~/.azure/credentials** file with the following content:

```
[default]

subscription_id=xxxxxxx-xxxx-xxxx-xxxx-xxxxxxxxxxxx

client_id=xxxxxxx-xxxx-xxxx-xxxx-xxxxxxxxxxxx

secret=xxxxxxxxxxxxxxxx

tenant=xxxxxxx-xxxx-xxxx-xxxx-xxxxxxxxxxxx
```

Use **ansible-doc -l | grep azure** to find out which Ansible modules are available for Azure. Redirect the content to a file for reference.

Resource Group

Let's check everything works as expected. Create a new playbook named **resourcegroup. yaml** with the following content:

```
---

- hosts: localhost

  tasks:

  - name: Create a resource group
    azure_rm_resourcegroup:
      name: Ansible-Group
      location: westus
```

Please note that the hosts directive is localhost! Execute the playbook and verify whether the resource group is created:

```
az group show --name Ansible-Group
```

The output should be very similar to the following:

```
{
  "id": "/subscriptions/xxxx/resourceGroups/Ansible-Group",
  "location": "westus",
  "managedBy": null,
  "name": "Ansible-Group",
  "properties": {
  "provisioningState": "Succeeded"
  },
  "tags": null
}
```

Virtual Machine

Let's create a VM in Azure using Ansible. To do this, create a **virtualmachine.yaml** file with the following content. Examine the **name** field of each block to understand what the code does:

```
- hosts: localhost
  tasks:
  - name: Create Storage Account
    azure_rm_storageaccount:
      resource_group: Ansible-Group
      name: ansiblegroupsa
      account_type: Standard_LRS

      .

      .

      .
  - name: Create a CentOS VM
    azure_rm_virtualmachine:
      resource_group: Ansible-Group
```

```
    name: ansible-vm

    vm_size: Standard_DS1_v2

    admin_username: student

  admin_password:welk0mITG!

    image:

      offer: CentOS

      publisher: OpenLogic

      sku: '7.5'

      version: latest
```

Considering the length of the code, we have just shown a few lines here. You can download the entire **virtualmachine.yaml** file from the **chapter 8** folder in the GitHub repository of this book.

In the following screenshot, you can see that all the resources required for the VM are created by Ansible:

```
root@ansible-master:/etc/ansible# ansible-playbook xmk.yml

PLAY [localhost] ************************************************************
TASK [Gathering Facts] *****************************************************ok: [localhost]

TASK [Create a resource group] ********************************************changed: [localhost]

TASK [Create Storage Account] *********************************************changed: [localhost]

TASK [Create virtual network] *********************************************changed: [localhost]

TASK [Add subnet] *********************************************************changed: [localhost]

TASK [Create public ip] ***************************************************changed: [localhost]

TASK [Create security group that allows SSH] ******************************changed: [localhost]

TASK [Create NIC] *********************************************************changed: [localhost]

TASK [Create a CentOS VM] *************************************************changed: [localhost]

PLAY RECAP ****************************************************************localhost
    changed=8    unreachable=0    failed=0    skipped=0    rescued=0    ignored=0
```

Figure 8.6: Creating all the required resources for the VM with Ansible

You can find a full example for Azure VM deployment using Ansible in Ansible's Microsoft Azure Guide (https://docs.ansible.com/ansible/latest/scenario_guides/guide_azure.html).

Azure Inventory Management in Ansible

We have learned two ways to use Ansible in Azure:

- Using Ansible in an inventory file to connect to Linux machines. In fact, it doesn't matter whether it's running in Azure or somewhere else.

- Using Ansible to manage Azure resources.

In this section, we're going one step further. Instead of using a static inventory, we will ask Azure what is running in your environment using dynamic inventory scripts.

The first step is to download the dynamic inventory script for Azure. Execute with **sudo** if you are not a root user:

```
cd /etc/ansible
```

```
wget https://raw.githubusercontent.com/ansible/ansible/devel/contrib/
inventory/azure_rm.py

chmod +x /etc/ansible/azure_rm.py
```

Edit the **/etc/ansible/ansible.cfg** file and remove the **inventory=/etc/ansible/hosts** line.

Let's carry out the first step:

```
ansible -i /etc/ansible/azure_rm.py azure -m ping
```

It will probably fail on account of authentication problems:

```
[student@centos01 ~]$ ansible -i ~/Ansible/azure_rm.py azure -m ping
 [ERROR]: No handlers could be found for logger
"msrestazure.azure_active_directory"

ubuntu01 | UNREACHABLE! => {
    "changed": false,
    "msg": "Failed to connect to the host via ssh: Permission denied (publickey,
password).\r\n",
    "unreachable": true
}
CentOS03 | SUCCESS => {
    "changed": false,
    "ping": "pong"
}
```

Figure 8.7: Host connection failure due to authentication issues

If you have a different login for different VMs, you can always use the user directive per task. Here, we are using **azure** which means all VMs. You can always query for a machine using the VM name. For example, you can ping the **ansible-node3** VM using a user credential:

```
root@ansible-master:/etc/ansible# ansible -i azure_rm.py ansible-node3 -m ping --user=rithin
[WARNING]: Invalid characters were found in group names but not replaced, use -vvvv to see details

ansible-node3 | SUCCESS => {
    "ansible_facts": {
        "discovered_interpreter_python": "/usr/bin/python"
    },
    "changed": false,
    "ping": "pong"
}
```

Figure 8.8: Querying for the ansible-node3 VM

Ideally, Ansible expects you to use SSH keys instead of passwords. If you would like to use a password, you can use **-extra-vars** and pass the password. Please note that for this you need to install an application called **sshpass**. To ping a VM in Azure that uses a password via Ansible, execute the following command:

```
ansible -i azure_rm.py ansible-vm -m ping \

--extra-vars "ansible_user=<username> ansible_password=<password>"
```

Let's take the instance of the VM we created using Ansible in the previous example, where the username was **student** and the password was **welk0mITG!**. From the screenshot, you can see that the ping succeeds. You might see some warnings, but they can be safely ignored. However, further investigation is needed if the ping fails:

```
root@ansible-master:/etc/ansible# ansible -i azure_rm.py ansible-vm -m ping --extra-vars "ansible_user=student ansible_password=welk0mITG!"
[WARNING]: Invalid characters were found in group names but not replaced, use -vvvv to see details

ansible-vm | SUCCESS => {
    "ansible_facts": {
        "discovered_interpreter_python": "/usr/bin/python"
    },
    "changed": false,
    "ping": "pong"
}
```

Figure 8.9: Sending a ping for the username student

By creating an **azure_rm.ini** file in the same directory as the **azure_rm.py** directory, you can modify the behavior of the inventory script. Here is an example **ini** file:

```
[azure]

include_powerstate=yes

group_by_resource_group=yes

group_by_location=yes

group_by_security_group=yes

group_by_tag=yes
```

It works in a very similar way to the **hosts** file. The **[azure]** section means all VMs. You can also provide sections for the following:

- Location name
- Resource group name
- Security group name
- Tag key
- Tag key value

Another method for selecting one or more VMs is to use tags. To be able to tag a VM, you'll need the ID:

```
az vm list --output tsv
```

Now, you can tag the VM:

```
az resource tag --resource-group <resource group> \
   --tags webserver --id </subscriptions/...>
```

You can also tag the VM in the Azure portal:

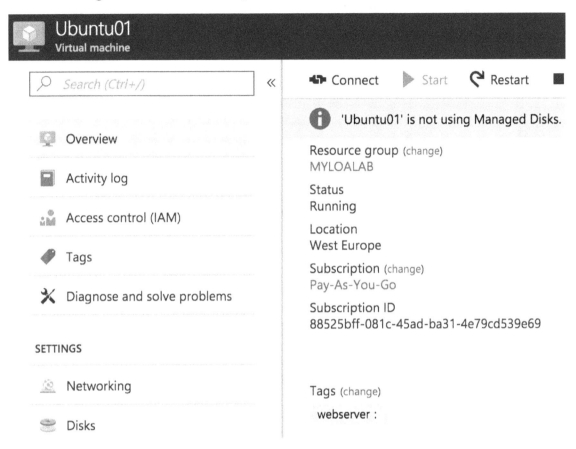

Figure 8.10: Tagging the VM in the Azure portal

Click on **change** and add a tag, with or without a value (you can use the value to filter the value too). To verify, use the tag name host:

```
ansible -i /etc/ansible/azure_rm.py webserver -m ping
```

Only the tagged VM is pinged. Let's create a playbook for this tagged VM, for instance, **/etc/ansible/example9.yaml**. The tag is, again, used in the **hosts** directive:

```
---


- hosts: webserver

  tasks:

  - name: Install Apache Web Server
    become: yes
    become_method: sudo
    apt:
      name: apache2
      install_recommends: yes
      state: present
      update-cache: yes
    when:
      - ansible_distribution == "Ubuntu"
      - ansible_distribution_version == "18.04"
```

Execute the playbook:

```
ansible-playbook -i /etc/ansible/azure_rm.py /etc/ansible/example9.yaml
```

Once the playbook has been run, if you check the VM, you can see that Apache is installed.

As mentioned earlier, Ansible is not the only tool. There is another popular one called Terraform. In the next section, will be discussing Terraform on Azure.

Using Terraform

Terraform is another **Infrastructure as Code** (**IaC**) tool that is developed by HashiCorp. You might wonder why it is called an IaC tool. The reason is you can define how your infrastructure needs to be using code, and Terraform will help you deploy it. Terraform uses **HashiCorp Configuration Language** (**HCL**); however, you can also use JSON. Terraform is supported in macOS, Linux, and Windows.

Terraform supports a wide range of Azure resources such as networks, subnets, storage, tags, and VMs. If you recall, we discussed the imperative and declarative ways of writing code. Terraform is declarative in nature, and it can maintain the state of the infrastructure. Once deployed, Terraform remembers the current state of the infrastructure.

As in every section, the first part of the process involves the installation of Terraform. Let's proceed with the Linux installation of Terraform.

Installation

Terraform's core executable can be downloaded from https://www.terraform.io/downloads.html and can be copied to one of the directories added to your **$PATH** variable. You can also use the **wget** command to download the core executable. To do this, first you have to find out the latest version of Terraform from the aforementioned link. At the time of writing, the latest version available is 0.12.16

Now that we have the version, we will download the executable using **wget** with the following command:

```
wget https://releases.hashicorp.com/terraform/0.12.17/terraform_0.12.17_
linux_amd64.zip
```

The ZIP will be downloaded to the current working directory. Now we will use the unzip tool to get the executable extracted:

```
unzip terraform_0.12.16_linux_amd64.zip
```

> **Note**
>
> **unzip** might not be installed by default. If it's throwing an error, install **unzip** using **apt** or **yum** depending on the distribution you are using.

The extraction process will get you the Terraform executable, and you can copy this to any location in your **$PATH**.

To verify whether the installation was successful, you can execute:

```
terraform --version
```

Now that we have confirmed that Terraform been installed, let's go ahead and set up the authentication to Azure.

Authenticating to Azure

There are multiple ways by which you can authenticate to Azure. You can use Azure CLI, Service Principal using a Client Certificate, Service Principal and Client Secret, and many more methods. For testing purposes, Azure CLI using the **az** login command is the right choice. However, if we want to automate deployment, this is not an ideal method. We should go for Service Principal and Client Secret, the same as we did in Ansible.

Let's start by creating a Service Principal for Terraform. If you already have a Service Principal created for the previous section, feel free to use that. To create a new Service Principal from Azure CLI, use this command:

```
az ad sp create-for-rbac -n terraform
```

At this point, you might be already familiar with the output, which contains the **appID**, password, and tenant ID.

Note down the values in the output, and we will be creating variables to store this value:

```
export ARM_CLIENT_ID="<appID>"

export ARM_CLIENT_SECRET="<password>"

export ARM_SUBSCRIPTION_ID="<subscription ID>"

export ARM_TENANT_ID="<tenant ID>"
```

So, we have stored all the values to variables that will be used by Terraform for authentication. Since we have dealt with authentication, let's write code in HCL with which we can deploy resources in Azure.

Deployment to Azure

You can use any code editor for this purpose. Since we are already on a Linux machine, you can use vi or nano. If you want, you can also use Visual Studio Code, which has extensions for Terraform and Azure, which will get you IntelliSense and syntax highlighting.

Let's create a terraform directory to store all our code, and inside the **terraform** directory, we will create further directories based on what we are going to deploy. In our first example, we will be using Terraform to create a resource group in Azure. Later, we will discuss how to deploy a VM in this resource group.

So, to create a **terraform** directory and to create a **resource-group** subfolder within this directory, execute the following command:

```
mkdir terraform

cd terraform && mkdir resource-group

cd resource-group
```

Next, create a main.tf file with the below content:

```
provider "azurerm" {
    version = "~>1.33"
}


resource "azurerm_resource_group" "rg" {
    name     = "TerraformOnAzure"
    location = "eastus"
}
```

The code is very simple. Let's take a closer look at each of the items.

The provider directive shows that we would like to use the version 1.33 of the **azurerm** provider. In other words, we are indicating that we are going to use version 1.33 of the Terraform Azure Resource Manager provider, which is one of the plugins available for Terraform.

The **resource** directive says that we are going to deploy an Azure resource of the **azurerm_resource_group** type with two parameters, **name** and **location**.

rg stands for the resource configuration. Resource names must be unique per type in each module. For example, if you want to create another resource group in the same template, you cannot use **rg** again as you have already used it; instead, you can go for anything other than **rg**, such as **rg2**.

Before we start the deployment using the template, we first need to initialize the project directory, which is our **resource-group** folder. To initialize Terraform, execute the following:

```
terraform init
```

During initialization, Terraform will download the **azurerm** provider from its repository and will show a similar output as the following:

```
▣   resource-group terraform init

Initializing the backend...

Initializing provider plugins...
- Checking for available provider plugins...
- Downloading plugin for provider "azurerm" (hashicorp/azurerm) 1.36.1...

Terraform has been successfully initialized!

You may now begin working with Terraform. Try running "terraform plan" to see
any changes that are required for your infrastructure. All Terraform commands
should now work.

If you ever set or change modules or backend configuration for Terraform,
rerun this command to reinitialize your working directory. If you forget, other
commands will detect it and remind you to do so if necessary.
```

Figure 8.11: Initializing Terraform to download the azurerm provider

Since we've already exported the Service Principal details to the variables, we can deploy using this command:

```
terraform apply
```

This command will connect Terraform to your Azure subscription and check whether the resource exists. If Terraform figures out that the resource doesn't exist, it will go ahead and create an execution plan to deploy. You will get the output shown in the following screenshot. To proceed with the deployment, type **yes**:

```
☐  resource-group terraform apply

An execution plan has been generated and is shown below.
Resource actions are indicated with the following symbols:
  + create

Terraform will perform the following actions:

  # azurerm_resource_group.rg will be created
  + resource "azurerm_resource_group" "rg" {
      + id       = (known after apply)
      + location = "eastus"
      + name     = "TerraformOnAzure"
      + tags     = (known after apply)
    }

Plan: 1 to add, 0 to change, 0 to destroy.

Do you want to perform these actions?
  Terraform will perform the actions described above.
  Only 'yes' will be accepted to approve.

  Enter a value:
```

Figure 8.12: Connecting Terraform to the Azure subscription

Once you have given the input, Terraform will start the resource creation. After creation, Terraform will show you a summary of everything that was created and how many resources were added and destroyed, as shown here:

```
  Enter a value: yes

azurerm_resource_group.rg: Creating...
azurerm_resource_group.rg: Creation complete after 5s [id=/subscriptions/1b228

Apply complete! Resources: 1 added, 0 changed, 0 destroyed.
```

Figure 8.13: Summary of the created resources

A state file named **terraform.tfstate** will be generated in the project directory from where we initialized Terraform. This file will have the state information and also the list of resources we deployed to Azure.

We have successfully created the resource group; in the next section, we will discuss how to create a Linux VM using Terraform.

Deploying a Virtual Machine

In the previous example, where we created the resource group, we used **azurerm_ resource_group** as the resource to be created. For each resource there will be a directive, for example, for a VM, it'll be **azurerm_virtual_machine**.

Also, we created the resource group using the **terraform apply** command. But Terraform also offers a way to work with an execution plan. So instead of deploying straight away, we can create a plan and see what changes will be made and then deploy.

To start with, you can go back to the **terraform** directory and create a new directory called **vm**. It's always a good idea to have separate directories for different projects:

```
mkdir ../vm

cd ../vm
```

Once you are in the directory, you can create a new **main.tf** file with the content shown in the following code block. Use the comments added to see the purpose of each block. Considering the length of the code, we are showing the truncated version of the code block. You can find the **main.tf** code file in the **chapter 8** folder of the GitHub repository of this book:

```
provider "azurerm" {

    version = "~>1.33"

}

#Create resource group

resource "azurerm_resource_group" "rg" {

    name      = "TFonAzure"

    location = "eastus"

}
.

.

.

#Create virtual machine, combining all the components we created so far
```

```
resource "azurerm_virtual_machine" "myterraformvm" {
    name                  = "tf-VM"
    location              = "eastus"
    resource_group_name   = azurerm_resource_group.rg.name
    network_interface_ids = [azurerm_network_interface.nic.id]
    vm_size               = "Standard_DS1_v2"


    storage_os_disk {
        name              = "tfOsDisk"
        caching           = "ReadWrite"
        create_option     = "FromImage"
        managed_disk_type = "Standard_LRS"
    }


    storage_image_reference {
        publisher = "Canonical"
        offer     = "UbuntuServer"
        sku       = "16.04.0-LTS"
        version   = "latest"
    }


    os_profile {
        computer_name  = "tfvm"
        admin_username = "adminuser"
        admin_password = "Pa55w0rD!@1234"
    }


    os_profile_linux_config {
    disable_password_authentication = false
  }


}
```

If you look at the section for **azurerm_virtual_network**, you can see that instead of writing down the resource name, we gave a reference in the format **type.resource_configuration.parameter**. In this case, instead of writing down the resource group name, the reference was given as **azurerm_resource_group.rg.name**. Likewise, throughout the code, we have taken references to make the deployment easy.

Before starting the deployment planning, we have to initialize the project using the following:

```
terraform init
```

As mentioned earlier, we will go with the execution plan. To create an execution plan and save it to a **vm-plan.plan** file, execute:

```
terraform plan -out vm-plan.plan
```

You will get a lot of warnings; they can be safely ignored. Make sure that the code doesn't show any errors. If the execution plan is successfully created, it will show the next step to be taken to execute the plan, as shown here:

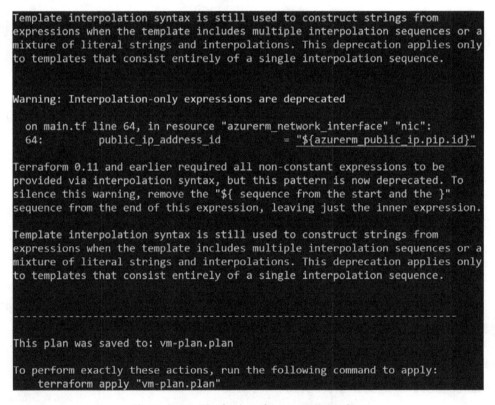

```
Template interpolation syntax is still used to construct strings from
expressions when the template includes multiple interpolation sequences or a
mixture of literal strings and interpolations. This deprecation applies only
to templates that consist entirely of a single interpolation sequence.


Warning: Interpolation-only expressions are deprecated

  on main.tf line 64, in resource "azurerm_network_interface" "nic":
  64:         public_ip_address_id            = "${azurerm_public_ip.pip.id}"

Terraform 0.11 and earlier required all non-constant expressions to be
provided via interpolation syntax, but this pattern is now deprecated. To
silence this warning, remove the "${ sequence from the start and the }"
sequence from the end of this expression, leaving just the inner expression.

Template interpolation syntax is still used to construct strings from
expressions when the template includes multiple interpolation sequences or a
mixture of literal strings and interpolations. This deprecation applies only
to templates that consist entirely of a single interpolation sequence.


-------------------------------------------------------------------------

This plan was saved to: vm-plan.plan

To perform exactly these actions, run the following command to apply:
    terraform apply "vm-plan.plan"
```

Figure 8.14: Displaying the execution plan

As suggested in the output, we will execute:

```
terraform apply "vm-plan.plan"
```

Now, the deployment will start and will show what resource it's deploying, how much time has elapsed, and so on, as shown in the output:

```
▢  terraform terraform apply "vm-plan.plan"
azurerm_resource_group.rg: Creating...
azurerm_resource_group.rg: Creation complete after 4s [id=/subscriptions/1b2
azurerm_virtual_network.vnet: Creating...
azurerm_public_ip.pip: Creating...
azurerm_network_security_group.nsg: Creating...
azurerm_network_security_group.nsg: Creation complete after 8s [id=/subscrip
ders/Microsoft.Network/networkSecurityGroups/tf-nsg]
azurerm_virtual_network.vnet: Creation complete after 9s [id=/subscriptions/
icrosoft.Network/virtualNetworks/tf-vnet]
azurerm_subnet.subnet: Creating...
azurerm_public_ip.pip: Creation complete after 9s [id=/subscriptions/1b22874
t.Network/publicIPAddresses/tf-pip]
azurerm_subnet.subnet: Creation complete after 3s [id=/subscriptions/1b22874
t.Network/virtualNetworks/tf-vnet/subnets/mySubnet]
azurerm_network_interface.nic: Creating...
azurerm_network_interface.nic: Creation complete after 10s [id=/subscription
/Microsoft.Network/networkInterfaces/tf-nic]
azurerm_virtual_machine.myterraformvm: Creating...
azurerm_virtual_machine.myterraformvm: Still creating... [10s elapsed]
azurerm_virtual_machine.myterraformvm: Still creating... [20s elapsed]
azurerm_virtual_machine.myterraformvm: Still creating... [30s elapsed]
azurerm_virtual_machine.myterraformvm: Still creating... [40s elapsed]
azurerm_virtual_machine.myterraformvm: Still creating... [50s elapsed]
azurerm_virtual_machine.myterraformvm: Still creating... [1m0s elapsed]
azurerm_virtual_machine.myterraformvm: Still creating... [1m10s elapsed]
azurerm_virtual_machine.myterraformvm: Still creating... [1m20s elapsed]
azurerm_virtual_machine.myterraformvm: Still creating... [1m30s elapsed]
azurerm_virtual_machine.myterraformvm: Still creating... [1m40s elapsed]
azurerm_virtual_machine.myterraformvm: Creation complete after 1m42s [id=/su
/providers/Microsoft.Compute/virtualMachines/tf-VM]
```

Figure 8.15: Resource deployment details

At the end, Terraform will give a summary of the number of resources deployed:

```
Apply complete! Resources: 7 added, 0 changed, 0 destroyed.

The state of your infrastructure has been saved to the path
below. This state is required to modify and destroy your
infrastructure, so keep it safe. To inspect the complete state
use the `terraform show` command.
```

Figure 8.16: Summary of the number of resources deployed

There is also another command, which is the **show** command. This will show the complete state of the deployment, as can be seen in the following screenshot:

```
 terraform terraform show
# azurerm_network_interface.nic:
resource "azurerm_network_interface" "nic" {
    applied_dns_servers              = []
    dns_servers                      = []
    enable_accelerated_networking    = false
    enable_ip_forwarding             = false
    id                               = "/subscriptions/1b228746-75
Interfaces/tf-nic"
    location                         = "eastus"
    name                             = "tf-nic"
    network_security_group_id        = "/subscriptions/1b228746-75
SecurityGroups/tf-nsg"
    private_ip_address               = "10.0.2.4"
    private_ip_addresses             = [
        "10.0.2.4",
    ]
    resource_group_name              = "TFonAzure"
    tags                             = {}

    ip_configuration {
        application_gateway_backend_address_pools_ids = []
        application_security_group_ids                = []
        load_balancer_backend_address_pools_ids       = []
        load_balancer_inbound_nat_rules_ids           = []
        name                                          = "myNicC
        primary                                       = true
        private_ip_address_allocation                 = "dynami
        private_ip_address_version                    = "IPv4"
        public_ip_address_id                          = "/subsc
soft.Network/publicIPAddresses/tf-pip"
        subnet_id                                     = "/subsc
soft.Network/virtualNetworks/tf-vnet/subnets/mySubnet"
    }
}
```

Figure 8.17: Displaying the complete state of the deployment

We have written a small piece of code that can deploy a VM in Azure. However, there are lots of arguments that can be added to the code by which advanced state configuration can be made. The complete list of arguments is available in the Terraform documentation (https://www.terraform.io/docs/providers/azurerm/r/virtual_machine.html) and the Microsoft documentation (https://docs.microsoft.com/en-us/azure/virtual-machines/linux/terraform-create-complete-vm).

As these templates are a bit advanced, they will be using variables instead of values that are repeating. Nevertheless, once you get used to this, you'll understand how powerful Terraform is.

Finally, you can destroy the entire deployment or project by executing:

```
terraform destroy
```

This will delete all the resources we mentioned in the **main.tf** file of the project. If you have multiple projects, you have to navigate to the project directory and execute the **destroy** command. On executing this command, you will be asked you to confirm the deletion; once you say **yes**, the resources will be deleted:

```
to templates that consist entirely of a single interpolation sequence.

Do you really want to destroy all resources?
  Terraform will destroy all your managed infrastructure, as shown above.
  There is no undo. Only 'yes' will be accepted to confirm.

  Enter a value: yes

azurerm_virtual_machine.myterraformvm: Destroying... [id=/subscriptions/1b228746-
soft.Compute/virtualMachines/tf-VM]
azurerm_virtual_machine.myterraformvm: Still destroying... [id=/subscriptions/1b2
elapsed]
azurerm_virtual_machine.myterraformvm: Still destroying... [id=/subscriptions/1b2
elapsed]
azurerm_virtual_machine.myterraformvm: Still destroying... [id=/subscriptions/1b2
elapsed]
azurerm_virtual_machine.myterraformvm: Still destroying... [id=/subscriptions/1b2
elapsed]
azurerm_virtual_machine.myterraformvm: Still destroying... [id=/subscriptions/1b2
elapsed]
azurerm_virtual_machine.myterraformvm: Still destroying... [id=/subscriptions/1b2
 elapsed]
azurerm_virtual_machine.myterraformvm: Still destroying... [id=/subscriptions/1b2
s elapsed]
azurerm_virtual_machine.myterraformvm: Still destroying... [id=/subscriptions/1b2
s elapsed]
azurerm_virtual_machine.myterraformvm: Still destroying... [id=/subscriptions/1b2
s elapsed]
azurerm_virtual_machine.myterraformvm: Still destroying... [id=/subscriptions/1b2
s elapsed]
azurerm_virtual_machine.myterraformvm: Still destroying... [id=/subscriptions/1b2
s elapsed]
azurerm_virtual_machine.myterraformvm: Still destroying... [id=/subscriptions/1b2
 elapsed]
azurerm_virtual_machine.myterraformvm: Still destroying... [id=/subscriptions/1b2
s elapsed]
azurerm_virtual_machine.myterraformvm: Still destroying... [id=/subscriptions/1b2
```

Figure 8.18: Deleting all the resources with the terraform destroy command

And finally, you will get a summary, as shown here:

```
azurerm_resource_group.rg: Destroying... [id=/subscriptions/1b2287
azurerm_resource_group.rg: Still destroying... [id=/subscriptions/
azurerm_resource_group.rg: Still destroying... [id=/subscriptions/
azurerm_resource_group.rg: Still destroying... [id=/subscriptions/
azurerm_resource_group.rg: Still destroying... [id=/subscriptions/
azurerm_resource_group.rg: Still destroying... [id=/subscriptions/
azurerm_resource_group.rg: Still destroying... [id=/subscriptions/
azurerm_resource_group.rg: Still destroying... [id=/subscriptions/
azurerm_resource_group.rg: Still destroying... [id=/subscriptions/
azurerm_resource_group.rg: Still destroying... [id=/subscriptions/
azurerm_resource_group.rg: Still destroying... [id=/subscriptions/
azurerm_resource_group.rg: Still destroying... [id=/subscriptions/
azurerm_resource_group.rg: Still destroying... [id=/subscriptions/
azurerm_resource_group.rg: Still destroying... [id=/subscriptions/
azurerm_resource_group.rg: Still destroying... [id=/subscriptions/
azurerm_resource_group.rg: Still destroying... [id=/subscriptions/
azurerm_resource_group.rg: Still destroying... [id=/subscriptions/
azurerm_resource_group.rg: Still destroying... [id=/subscriptions/
azurerm_resource_group.rg: Still destroying... [id=/subscriptions/
azurerm_resource_group.rg: Destruction complete after 3m12s

Destroy complete! Resources: 7 destroyed.
```

Figure 8.19: Summary of the destroyed resources

Now we are familiar with using Terraform on Azure and deploying a simple VM. Nowadays, Terraform is gaining a lot of popularity due to the usability and adoption of DevOps. Terraform has made the process of evaluating infrastructure and rebuilding it hassle-free.

Using PowerShell DSC

Like Bash, PowerShell is a shell with strong scripting possibilities. We might think that PowerShell is more of a scripting language and that can be used to carry out simple operations or to create resources as we have done so far. However, the capabilities of PowerShell are beyond that and extend all the way to automation and configuration.

DSC is an important but little-known part of PowerShell that, instead of automating scripts in the PowerShell language, provides declarative orchestration in PowerShell.

If you compare it to Ansible, support for Linux is very limited. But it is very useful for common administration tasks, and missing features can be compensated for with PowerShell scripts. Microsoft is very focused on getting it on a par with Windows Server. When that happens, it will be replaced by PowerShell DSC Core, a move very similar to what they did before with PowerShell | PowerShell Core. This will be finished by the end of 2019.

Another important note is that, for some reason, the Python scripts that come with DSC don't work—from time to time, you'll get a 401 error or even an undefined error. First, make sure that you have the latest version of the OMI server and DSC and just try again; sometimes, you have to try two or three times.

Azure Automation DSC

One way to use DSC is to use Azure Automation DSC. This way, you don't have to use a separate machine as a controller node. To be able to use Azure Automation DSC, you'll need an Azure Automation account.

Automation account

In the Azure portal, select **All Services** in the left-hand bar, navigate to **Management + governance**, and choose **Automation Accounts**. Create an automation account and make sure that you choose **Run As Account**.

Navigate again to **All Services**, **Management Tools**, and then select the **just-created account**:

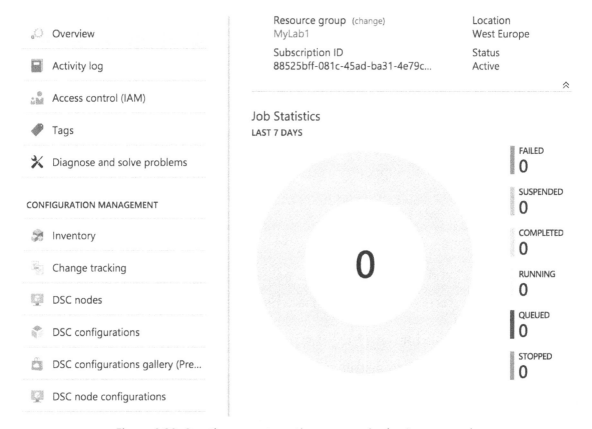

Figure 8.20: Creating an automation account in the Azure portal

Here, you can manage your nodes, configurations, and so on.

Please note that this service is not exactly free. Process automation is priced per job execution minute, while configuration management is priced per managed node.

To be able to use this account, you'll need the registration URL and the corresponding key of your **Run As Account**. Both values are available under **Account** and **Key Settings**.

Or, in PowerShell, execute the following command:

```
Get-AzAutomationRegistrationInfo '
  -ResourceGroup <resource group> '
  -AutomationAccountName <automation account name>
```

There is a VM extension available for Linux; this way, you can deploy VMs, including their configuration, fully orchestrated.

For more information, visit https://github.com/Azure/azure-linux-extensions/tree/master/DSC and https://docs.microsoft.com/en-us/azure/virtual-machines/extensions/dsc-linux.

Because we're going to play with Linux and DSC, we'll need a DSC module called **nx**. This module contains DSC resources for Linux. In the settings of your automation account, select **Shared Resources and Modules**. In the **Browse Gallery** tab, search for **nx** and import the module.

Installing PowerShell DSC on Linux

To be able to use PowerShell DSC on Linux, you'll need the Open Management Infrastructure Service. The supported versions of Linux distributions are as follows:

- Ubuntu 12.04 LTS, 14.04 LTS, and 16.04 LTS. Ubuntu 18.04 is not supported at the moment.

- RHEL/CentOS 6.5 and higher.

- openSUSE 13.1 and higher.

- SUSE Linux Enterprise Server 11 SP3 and higher.

The software is available for download at https://github.com/Microsoft/omi.

Installation on Red Hat–based distributions is as follows:

```
sudo yum install \
  https://github.com/Microsoft/omi/releases/download/\
  v1.4.2-3/omi-1.4.2-3.ssl_100.ulinux.x64.rpm
```

For Ubuntu, you can download the **deb** file from the GitHub repository using **wget** and install it using **dpkg**:

```
dpkg -i ./omi-1.6.0-0.ssl_110.ulinux.x64.deb
```

> **Note**
>
> Make sure you download the file that matches your SSL version. Your SSL version can be checked using the **openssl version** command.

After installation, the service is automatically started. Check the status of the service by using the following command:

```
sudo systemctl status omid.service
```

To show product and version information, including the configuration directories used, use the following command:

```
/opt/omi/bin/omicli id
```

```
[root@centos01 bin]# /opt/omi/bin/omicli id
instance of OMI_Identify
{
        [Key] InstanceID=2FDB5542-5896-45D5-9BE9-DC04430AAABE
        SystemName=centos01
        ProductName=OMI
        ProductVendor=Microsoft
        ProductVersionMajor=1
        ProductVersionMinor=4
        ProductVersionRevision=2
        ProductVersionString=1.4.2-3
        Platform=LINUX_X86_64_GNU
        OperatingSystem=LINUX
        Architecture=X86_64
        Compiler=GNU
        ConfigPrefix=GNU
        ConfigLibDir=/opt/omi/lib
        ConfigBinDir=/opt/omi/bin
        ConfigIncludeDir=/opt/omi/include
        ConfigDataDir=/opt/omi/share
        ConfigLocalStateDir=/var/opt/omi
        ConfigSysConfDir=/etc/opt/omi/conf
        ConfigProviderDir=/etc/opt/omi/conf
        ConfigLogFile=/var/opt/omi/log/omiserver.log
        ConfigPIDFile=/var/opt/omi/run/omiserver.pid
        ConfigRegisterDir=/etc/opt/omi/conf/omiregister
        ConfigSchemaDir=/opt/omi/share/omischema
        ConfigNameSpaces={root-omi, root-Microsoft-DesiredStateConfiguration, root-M
icrosoft-Windows-DesiredStateConfiguration}
```

Figure 8.21: Displaying the product and version information

Creating a Desired State

PowerShell DSC is not just a script or a code with parameters, like in Ansible. To start with PowerShell DSC, you'll need a configuration file that must be compiled into a **Management Object Format** (**MOF**) file.

But, first things first. Let's create a file, **example1.ps1**, with the following content:

```
Configuration webserver {

Import-DscResource -ModuleName PSDesiredStateConfiguration,nx


Node "ubuntu01"{

    nxPackage apache2

    {

        Name = "apache2"

        Ensure = "Present"

        PackageManager = "apt"

    }

 }

 }

webserver
```

Let's investigate this configuration. As stated, it's very similar to a function declaration. The configuration gets a label and is executed at the end of the script. The necessary modules are imported, the hostname of the VM is declared, and the configuration starts.

PowerShell DSC Resources

In this configuration file, a resource called **nxPackage** is used. There are several built-in resources:

- **nxArchive**: Provides a mechanism to unpack archive (**.tar**, **.zip**) files at a specific path.

- **nxEnvironment**: Manages environment variables.

- **nxFile**: Manages files and directories.

- **nxFileLine**: Manages lines in a Linux file.

- **nxGroup**: Manages local Linux groups.

- **nxPackage**: Manages packages on Linux nodes.

- **nxScript**: Runs scripts. Most of the time, this is used to switch temporarily to a more imperative orchestration approach.

- **nxService**: Manages Linux services (daemons).

- **nxUser**: Manages Linux users.

You can also write your own resources in the MOF language, C#, Python, or C/C++.

You can make use of the official documentation by visiting https://docs.microsoft.com/en-us/powershell/dsc/lnxbuiltinresources.

Save the script and execute it as follows:

```
pwsh -file example1.ps
```

As a result of the script, a directory is created with the same name as the configuration name. In it, there's a localhost file in MOF format. This is the language used to describe CIM classes (**CIM** stands for **Common Information Model**). CIM is an open standard for the management of a complete environment, including hardware.

We think that this description alone is enough to understand why Microsoft chooses this model and the corresponding language file for orchestration!

You can also upload the configuration file to Azure, under **DSC Configurations**. Press the **Compile** button to generate the MOF file in Azure.

Applying the Resources in Azure

If you want, you can apply the desired state locally, using scripts in **/opt/microsoft/dsc/Scripts**, which is, in our opinion, not as easy as it should be. And, because this chapter is about orchestration in Azure, we'll just move straight on to Azure.

Register the VM:

```
sudo /opt/microsoft/dsc/Scripts/Register.py \
    --RegistrationKey <automation account key> \
    --ConfigurationMode ApplyOnly \
    --RefreshMode Push --ServerURL <automation account url>
```

Check the configuration again:

```
sudo /opt/microsoft/dsc/Scripts/GetDscLocalConfigurationManager.py
```

The node is now visible in the **DSC Nodes** pane under your **Automation Account** settings. Now, you can link the uploaded and compiled DSC configuration. The configuration is applied!

Another way is to use the **Add Node** option and then select the DSC configuration.

To conclude, the primary use case scenario of PowerShell DSC is to write, manage, and compile DSC configurations, as well as import and assign these configurations to the target nodes in the cloud. Before using any tool, you need to understand the use case scenarios and how they fit into your environment to achieve the goal. So far, we have been configuring VMs; the next section is all about how to audit the settings inside the Linux VM using Azure Policy Guest Configuration.

Azure Policy Guest Configuration

Policies are mainly used for the governance of resources. Azure Policy is a service in Azure by which you can create, manage, and assign policies in Azure. These policies can be used for auditing and for compliance. For example, if you are hosting a secured application in the East US location and you want to limit the deployments in East US only, Azure Policy can be used to accomplish this.

Let's say you don't want to deploy SQL servers in a subscription. In Azure Policy, you can create a policy and specify the allowed services, and only they can be deployed in that subscription. Please note, if you are assigning a policy to a subscription that already has resources, Azure Policy can only act on resources that are created post assignment. However, if any of the existing resources before assignment don't comply with the policy, they will be marked as "non-compliant" so an administrator can rectify them if necessary. Also, Azure Policy will only kick in during the validation phase of the deployment.

Some of the built-in policies are:

- Allowed locations: Using this, you can enforce geo-compliance.

- Allowed virtual machine SKUs: Defines a set of virtual machine SKUs.

- Add a tag to resources: Adds a tag to the resource. If no value is passed, it will take the default tag value.

- Enforce a tag and its value: Used to enforce a required tag and its value to the resource.

- Not allowed resource types: Prevents the deployment of selected resources.

- Allowed storage account SKUs: We discussed different SKUs that are available for storage accounts in the previous chapter, such as LRS, GRS, ZRS, and RA-GRS. You can specify the allowed SKUs, and the rest of them are denied from being deployed.

- Allowed resource type: As we mentioned in the example, you can specify which resources are allowed in the subscription. For example, if you want only VMs and networking, you can accept the **Microsoft.Compute** and **Microsoft.Network** resource providers; all other providers are denied from deployment.

So far, we have discussed how Azure Policy can be used to audit Azure resources, but it can be also used to audit settings inside a VM. Azure Policy accomplishes this task using the Guest Configuration extension and client. The extension and client work hand-in-hand to confirm the configuration of the guest OS, the presence of an application, its state, and also the environmental settings of the guest OS.

Azure Policy Guest Configuration can only help you audit the guest VM. Applying configurations is not available at the time of writing.

Guest Configuration Extension for Linux

The guest policy configuration is done by the Guest Configuration extension and agent. The Guest Configuration agent on VMs is configured by using the Guest Configuration extension for Linux. As discussed earlier, they work hand-in-hand, allowing the user to run the in-guest policy on the VMs, which, in turn, helps the user to audit the policies on the VM. Chef InSpec (https://www.inspec.io/docs/) is the In-Guest policy for Linux. Let's see how to deploy the extension to a VM and use the commands supported by the extension.

Deployment to a Virtual Machine

To do this, you need to have a Linux VM. We will be deploying the Guest Configuration extension onto the VM by executing:

```
az vm extension set --resource-group <resource-group> \

--vm-name <vm-name> \

--name ConfigurationForLinux \

--publisher Microsoft.GuestConfiguration \

--version 1.9.0
```

You will get a similar output to this:

```
/ az vm extension set --resource-group ps-dsc --vm-name ps-dsc-node \
--name ConfigurationForLinux --publisher Microsoft.GuestConfiguration --version 1.9.0
{
  "autoUpgradeMinorVersion": true,
  "forceUpdateTag": null,
  "id": "/subscriptions/                              /resourceGroups/ps-dsc/providers/Microsoft.Compute/vi
/ConfigurationForLinux",
  "instanceView": null,
  "location": "eastus",
  "name": "ConfigurationForLinux",
  "protectedSettings": null,
  "provisioningState": "Succeeded",
  "publisher": "Microsoft.GuestConfiguration",
  "resourceGroup": "ps-dsc",
  "settings": null,
  "tags": null,
  "type": "Microsoft.Compute/virtualMachines/extensions",
  "typeHandlerVersion": "1.9",
  "virtualMachineExtensionType": "ConfigurationForLinux"
}
  /
```

Figure 8.22: Deploying the Guest Configuration extension onto the VM

Commands

The Guest Configuration extension supports the **install**, **uninstall**, **enable**, **disable**, and **update** commands. To execute these commands; you need to switch the current working directory to **/var/lib/waagent/Microsoft.GuestConfiguration. ConfigurationForLinux-1.9.0/bin**. After that, you can chain the available commands with the **guest-configuration-shim** script.

> **Note**
>
> Check whether the execute bit is enabled for the file. If not, use **chmod +x guest-configuration-shim** to set the execution permission.

The general syntax for executing any command is **./guest-configuration-shim <command name>**.

For example, if you want to install Guest Configuration Extension, you can use the **install** command. When the extension is already installed, **enable** will be called, which will extract the Agent package, which installs and enables the agent.

Similarly, **update** will update the Agent Service to the new agent, **disable** disables the agent, and, finally, **uninstall** will uninstall the agent.

The agent is downloaded to a path such as **/var/lib/waagent/Microsoft. GuestConfiguration.ConfigurationForLinux-<version>/GCAgent/DSC**, and the **agent** output is saved to the **stdout** and **stderr** files in this directory. If you encounter any issues, verify the contents of these files. Try to understand the error and then troubleshoot.

Logs are saved to **/var/log/azure/Microsoft.GuestConfiguration. ConfigurationForLinux**. You can use these to debug the issues.

Currently, these are the supported OS versions for Azure Policy Guest Configuration:

Publisher	Name	Versions
Canonical	Ubuntu Server	14.04, 16.04, 18.04
Credativ	Debian	8, 9
OpenLogic	CentOS	7.3, 7.4, 7.5
Red Hat	Red Hat Enterprise Linux	7.4, 7.5
Suse	SLES	12 SP3

Figure 8.23: OS versions supported for Azure Policy Guest Configuration

Azure Policy is written as a JSON manifest. As writing policies is not part of this book; you can refer the sample policy shared by Microsoft (https://github.com/ MicrosoftDocs/azure-docs/blob/master/articles/governance/policy/samples/ guest-configuration-applications-installed-linux.md). This sample is to audit if specific applications are installed inside Linux VMs.

If you investigate the sample, you will learn what the components are and how you can use the parameters in your context.

Other Solutions

Another big player in the orchestration market is Puppet. Until very recently, the support for Azure in Puppet was very limited, but that is changing very quickly. The Puppet module, **puppetlabs/azure_arm**, is still somewhat in its infancy, but **puppetlabs/azure** provides you with everything you'll need. Both modules need the Azure CLI to work. The integration of the Azure CLI in their commercial Puppet Enterprise product is amazingly good. Azure has a VM extension that's available for VMs that will become Puppet nodes.

More information can be found at https://puppet.com/products/managed-technology/microsoft-windows-azure.

You can also go for the Chef software, which provides an automation and orchestration platform that has been around for a long time. Its development started in 2009! The user writes "recipes" that describe how Chef manages the "kitchen" using tools such as a knife. In Chef, much of its terminology comes from the kitchen. Chef integrates very well with Azure, especially if you use Chef Automate from Azure Marketplace. There is also a VM extension available. Chef is intended for big environments and has a relatively steep learning curve, but it's worth trying it at least.

More information can be found at https://www.chef.io/partners/azure/.

Summary

We started this chapter with a short introduction to orchestration, the reasons to use orchestration, and the different approaches: imperative versus declarative.

After that, we covered the Ansible, Terraform, and PowerShell DSC platforms. Many details were covered about the following:

- How to install the platforms
- Working with resources at the OS level
- Integration with Azure

Ansible is by far the most complete solution, and maybe the one with the least steep learning curve. However, all of the solutions are very powerful and there are always ways around their limitations. And for all orchestration platforms, the future is promising in terms of even more features and capabilities.

Creating Linux VMs is not the only way to create a workload in Azure; you can also use container virtualization to deploy a platform for your application. In the next chapter, we're going to cover container technologies.

Questions

For this chapter, let's skip the normal questions. Fire up some VMs and choose the orchestration platform of your choice. Configure the network security groups to allow HTTP traffic.

Try to configure the following resources with Ansible, Terraform, or PowerShell DSC:

1. Create a user and make it a member of the group `wheel` (RH-based distributions) or `sudo` (Ubuntu).

2. Install an Apache web server, serve content from `/wwwdata`, secure it with AppArmor (Ubuntu) or SELinux (RHEL-based distributions), and serve a nice `index.html` page on this web server.

3. Restrict SSH to your IP address. HTTP ports must be open to the whole world. You can use systemd methods by providing override files or FirewallD.

4. Deploy a new VM with the distribution and version of your choice.

5. Create a new `/etc/hosts` file using variables. If you use PowerShell DSC, you'll need PowerShell as well for this task. For experts: use the hostnames and IP addresses of other machines in your resource group.

Further Reading

We really hope that you enjoyed this introduction to orchestration platforms. It was only a short introduction to make you curious to learn more. All the websites of the orchestration tools mentioned in this chapter are great resources and a pleasure to read.

Some extra resources to mention include the following:

- *Learning PowerShell DSC – Second Edition* by James Pogran.

- Ansible: We do think that *Learn Ansible* by Russ McKendrick, and other titles by the same author about Ansible, deserve a lot of credit. If you are too lazy to read the book, then you can refer to the Ansible documentation to start with. If you want some hands-on tutorials, you can use this GitHub repository: https://github.com/leucos/ansible-tuto.

- Terraform: **Terraform on Microsoft Azure – Part 1: Introduction** is a blog series written by Julien Corioland, who is a Senior Software Engineer at Microsoft. The blog includes a series of topics discussing Terraform on Azure. It's worth reading and trying out the tasks. The blog is available at https://blog.jcorioland.io/archives/2019/09/04/terraform-microsoft-azure-introduction.html.

- *Mastering Chef* by Mayank Joshi

- *Learning Puppet* by Jussi Heinonen

Container Virtualization in Azure

In *Chapter 2*, *Getting Started with the Azure Cloud*, we started our journey in Azure with the creation of our first workload in Azure: the deployment of a Linux VM. After that, we covered many aspects of the Linux operating system.

In *Chapter 7*, *Deploying Your Virtual Machines*, we explored several options to deploy your VMs, and *Chapter 8*, *Exploring Continuous Configuration Automation*, was all about what to do afterward in terms of configuration management using orchestration tooling.

Orchestration is a growing part of a movement called DevOps. DevOps is about breaking down the classic silos in an organization. The different teams involved in developing, testing, and deploying products must communicate and work together. DevOps is a combination of cultural philosophies, practices, and tools. And DevOps is a way to make deployments incremental, frequent, and routine events while constraining the impact of failure.

VMs are not the only way to deploy workloads: you can also deploy your workload in containers. It makes it possible, together with orchestration, to fulfill DevOps requirements.

So, before we actually learn about and implement containers in Azure, let's quickly have a look at what this chapter has to offer. By the end of this chapter, you will:

- Understand the history of containers and know the early adoptions of containerization.

- Be familiar with container tools such as **systemd-nspawn** and Docker.

- Be able to work with Docker Machine and Docker Compose.

- Be able to use Azure Container Instances and Azure Container Registry.

- Know about the new generation container tools such as Buildah, Podman, and Skopeo.

Now, we'll first understand what a container is and how it has evolved.

Introduction to Container Technology

In *Chapter 1, Exploring the Azure Cloud*, we had a short introduction to containers. So, let's go ahead and cover containers in more detail. We know that VMs are run on a hypervisor, and for each purpose, in most cases you have to create a separate VM to isolate the environments. VMs will have a guest OS, such as Linux, and on top of that we will install the software we require. There will be scenarios where you have to deploy a large number of VMs for testing. If you are using an on-premises infrastructure running Hyper-V, you have to think about resource utilization—that is, how much memory, CPU, and so on you will use for each VM. If you are deploying in Azure, you have to think about the cost as well. You might need some VMs only for a couple of hours just to test something, but the footprints of these VMs are large; they're complete computers that are running virtually. Another problem is compatibility issues. Let's assume you have an app that requires a dependency package such as Python 2.2. Now think about another app running in the same VM that has compatibility issues with Python 2.2 and can only work with Python 2.1. You would end up creating a new VM for the second app with Python 2.1. To overcome this, containers were introduced. Here is a pictorial representation of how containers differ from VMs:

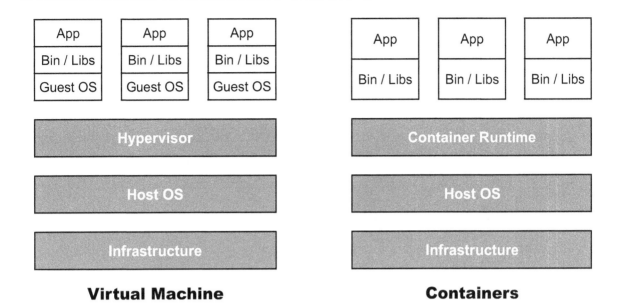

Figure 9.1: Representation of VMs and Containers

Like VMs, containers allow you to package your application along with all the dependencies and libraries. They are isolated environments like VMs and can be used to test and run applications without needing to create multiple VMs. Containers are also lightweight.

Instead of virtualizing each hardware component as with the VMs, containers virtualize at the OS level. This means that the containers have a smaller footprint than VMs. For example, an Ubuntu ISO image will have a size close to 2.4 GB; on the other hand, an Ubuntu container image is less than 200 MB. Let's consider the previous example, where we had dependency issues with Python 2.2 and ended up creating two VMs. With containers, we can have two containers with a much smaller footprint than two VMs. Also, the cost and resource utilization of the host OS is far less than that of two VMs. Containers are deployed using a container runtime; there are different runtimes available. In this chapter, we will take a look at the popular container runtimes.

A container is not the Holy Grail. It doesn't fix all your problems. However, you can consider the following scenarios, and if any of them match your requirements, you might want to containerize your application:

- There is a need for applications that often need updates with new features, preferably without downtime, driven by business needs.

- System engineers and developers can work together to address the business needs and have enough understanding and knowledge of each other's domains (without being a specialist in both), and have a culture of continual experimentation and learning.

- There is room for failure in order to make the application better.

- The application is not a single point of failure.

- The application is not a critical application in terms of availability and security.

One other little thing: if you have many different types of applications and there is almost no code shared between those applications, container technology is still an option, but it's possible that VMs are a better solution in this scenario.

We'll cover a little bit of the history of container technology to give you a better understanding of where it comes from. We'll explore some of the solutions available today: systemd-nspawn and Docker. There are more container virtualization implementations available, even some of the earliest implementations, such as LXC. In fact, it doesn't matter which containerization tool you're using: if you understand the ideas and concepts behind containers, it's easy to implement the same ideas and concepts with other tools. The only thing that changes is the command; the underlying concepts for all these tools are the same.

History of Containers

Containers are very popular nowadays. But they are not new; they didn't come out of the blue. It's not easy to point to an exact time when they started. We don't want to give you a history lesson, but history can give you an understanding of the technology and even give you a clue as to why or when you should use containers in your organization.

So, instead of focusing on an exact timeline, we'll only cover the important steps: the implementation of technologies that are important if you want to understand container technology as it is today.

The chroot Environment

In Linux, there is a root filesystem, as covered in *Chapter 5, Advanced Linux Administration*, and everything is mounted to that filesystem, which will be visible to the currently running processes and their children.

A process running in **chroot** has its own root filesystem, fully separated from the system-wide root, known as **chroot jail**. In chroot jail is a filesystem called `fs.chroot`. It is often used in development as the program running in **chroot** cannot access files or commands outside its root filesystem. To start a chroot jail from a directory, execute the following:

```
chroot /<directory>
```

In 1979, the **chroot** system call was introduced in version 7 of Unix, and in 1982, it was introduced in BSD Unix. Linux has implemented this system call since the early days of its existence.

OpenVZ

In 2005, almost at the same time that Solaris started its container technology, a company called Virtuozzo started the OpenVZ project.

They took the principle of the chroot environment and applied it to other resources. A chroot process will have the following:

- A root filesystem
- Users and groups
- Devices
- A process tree
- A network
- Interprocess communication objects

At that time, OpenVZ was seen as a lightweight alternative to virtualization based on a hypervisor, and also as a solid platform for developers. It still exists, and you can use it on top of every Linux operating system, running in the cloud or not.

Using OpenVZ is similar to using a VM: you create an image with a base installation of your favorite distribution and, if you want, after that you can use orchestration to install the application and maintain everything.

LXC

In 2006, engineers at Google started working on a feature in the Linux kernel called **cgroups** (**control groups**) to enable resource control on resources such as CPU, memory, disk I/O, and the network for collections of processes (resource groups).

A related feature of the Linux kernel is the concept of **namespace isolation**: the possibility to isolate resource groups so that they cannot see resources in other groups. So, **cgroups** became a namespace.

In 2008, **cgroups** was merged into the Linux kernel and a new namespace was introduced, the **user** namespace. Both technologies were then enabled for a new step forward for containers: LXC.

Other available namespaces are **pid**, **mount**, **network**, **uts** (own domain name), and **ipc**.

There is no longer any need to keep up to date with Linux kernel development: every component needed is available, and there is much better resource management.

Recently, Canonical developed a new container manager called the LXD, which has LXC in its backend and aims to provide an improved user experience for managing containers. Technically, LXD uses LXC through liblxc and its Go binding to achieve this aim. Some advantages of LXD are listed here:

- Secure
- Highly scalable
- Simplifies resource sharing

systemd-nspawn

systemd comes with a container solution. It started as an experiment, and then Lennart Poettering considered it ready for production. It is, in fact, the base for another solution, Rkt. At the time of writing this book, Rkt development has stopped. However, you can still access the Rkt GitHub repository (https://github.com/rkt/rkt).

systemd-nspawn is not very well known, but it is a powerful solution that is available on every modern Linux system. It is built on top of the kernel namespaces and systemd for management. It's a sort of chroot on steroids.

If you want to learn more about the underlying technologies of containers, systemd-nspawn is a good start. Here, every component is visible and can be configured manually if you want. The downside of systemd-nspawn is that you have to do everything on your own, from creating the image, to orchestration, to high availability: it's all possible, but you have to build it.

Containers can also be created using package managers such as **yum** and by extracting raw cloud images (several distributions provide such images, such as https://cloud.centos.org/centos/7/images and https://cloud-images.ubuntu.com/). You can even use Docker images!

As stated, there are multiple ways to create a container. As an example, we'll cover two of them: **debootstrap** and **yum**.

Creating a Container with debootstrap

The **debootstrap** utility is a tool that will install a Debian- or Ubuntu-based system into a subdirectory of another already installed system. It is available in the repositories of SUSE, Debian, and Ubuntu; on CentOS or other Red Hat–based distributions, you'll need to pull it from the **Extra Packages for Enterprise Linux** (**EPEL**) repository.

As an example, let's bootstrap Debian on a CentOS machine to create a template for our systemd containers.

For the purposes of this chapter, if you are running on CentOS, you have to change the security label for systemd-nspawn:

```
semanage fcontext -a -t virtd_lxc_exec_t /usr/bin/systemd-nspawn

  restorecon -v /usr/bin/systemd-nspawn
```

First, install debootstrap:

```
sudo yum install epel-release
sudo yum install debootstrap
```

Create a subdirectory:

```
sudo mkdir -p /var/lib/machines/releases/stretch
sudo -s
cd /var/lib/machines/releases
```

And bootstrap, for instance, from the US mirror of Debian:

```
debootstrap --arch amd64 stretch stretch \
  http://ftp.us.debian.org/debian
```

Creating a Container with yum

The **yum** utility is available in every repository and can be used to create a container with a Red Hat–based distribution.

Let's go through the steps to create a CentOS 7 container:

1. Create a directory in which we're going to install CentOS, and that will be used for our template:

   ```
   sudo mkdir -p /var/lib/machines/releases/centos7
   sudo -s
   cd /var/lib/machines/releases/centos7
   ```

   First, you have to download the **centos-release rpm** package at http://mirror. centos.org/centos-7/7/os/x86_64/Packages/.

2. Initialize the **rpm** database and install this package:

   ```
   rpm --rebuilddb --root=/var/lib/machines/releases/centos7
   rpm --root=/var/lib/machines/releases/centos7 \
     -ivh --nodeps centos-release*rpm
   ```

3. Now you are ready to install at least the bare minimum:

   ```
   yum --installroot=/var/lib/machines/releases/centos7 \
     groups install  'Minimal Install'
   ```

After the installation of the packages, a complete root filesystem is available, providing everything that is needed to boot the container. You can also use this root filesystem as a template; in that scenario, you need to modify the template to make sure that every container is unique.

systemd-firstboot

systemd-firstboot is a nice way to configure a few things if you start the container for the first time. You can configure the following parameters:

- System locale (**--locale=**)
- System keyboard map (**--keymap=**)
- System time zone (**--timezone=**)
- System hostname **(--hostname=)**
- Machine ID of the system (**--machine-id=**)
- Root user's password (**--root-password=**)

You can also use the **-prompt** parameter to ask for these parameters at first boot.

In the following example, we will be modifying the systemd-firstboot unit to pass a configuration that is going to be executed when the container is run for the first time.

Execute **chroot** in the container directory. Let's take our CentOS image as an example:

```
chroot /var/lib/containers/releases/centos7

passwd root
```

Fire up the image:

```
systemd-nspawn --boot -D centos7
```

Open the systemd-firstboot unit, **/usr/lib/systemd/system/systemd-firstboot.service**, and modify it:

```
[Unit]

Description=First Boot Wizard

Documentation=man:systemd-firstboot(1)

DefaultDependencies=no

Conflicts=shutdown.target

After=systemd-readahead-collect.service systemd-readahead-replay.service
systemd-remount-fs.service

Before=systemd-sysusers.service sysinit.target shutdown.target

ConditionPathIsReadWrite=/etc

ConditionFirstBoot=yes


[Service]

Type=oneshot

RemainAfterExit=yes

ExecStart=/usr/bin/systemd-firstboot --locale=en_US-utf8 --root-
password=welk0mITG! --timezone=Europe/Amsterdam

StandardOutput=tty

StandardInput=tty

StandardError=tty
```

Enable the service:

```
systemctl enable systemd-firstboot
```

Clean up the settings:

```
rm /etc/\
  {machine-id,localtime,hostname,shadow,locale.conf,securetty}
```

Exit the chroot environment with *Ctrl + D*.

Deploying the First Container

If you are using the BTRFS filesystem template directory as a subvolume, you can use the **--template** parameter of systemd-nspawn. Otherwise, it will create a new subvolume:

```
cd /var/lib/machines/releases
cp -rf centos7/ /var/lib/machines/centos01
```

It's time to boot our first container:

```
systemd-nspawn --boot -D centos01
```

Try to log in and kill it with *Ctrl +]]]*.

From now on, you can manage the containers with the **machinectl** command:

```
machinectl start <machine name>
```

Log in with the following:

```
machinectl login <machine name>
```

There are many other parameters of **machinectl** that are worth investigating! If you get a permission-denied message, think about SELinux troubleshooting! Also, **journalctl** has a **-M** parameter to see the logging within the container, or use the following:

```
journalctl _PID=<pid of container> -a
```

If you execute **hostnamectl** in the container, you'll see something similar to the following:

```
[root@centos01 ~]# hostnamectl
   Static hostname: n/a
Transient hostname: centos01
        Icon name: computer-container
          Chassis: container
       Machine ID: 75a8d3f58d9b47ce9e15f3f8e6aecae4
          Boot ID: e7374a2812ab4a64920accabb3753f7f
   Virtualization: systemd-nspawn
 Operating System: CentOS Linux 7 (Core)
     CPE OS Name: cpe:/o:centos:centos:7
           Kernel: Linux 3.10.0-862.3.3.el7.x86_64
     Architecture: x86-64
```

Figure 9.2: Output of the hostnamectl command

The kernel is the one of the host!

Enabling a Container at Boot Time

To make a container available at boot time, enable the target, **machines.target**:

```
sudo systemctl enable machines.target
```

Now create a **nspawn** file for our container: **/etc/systemd/nspawn/centos01.nspawn**. The filename must be the same as the container:

```
[Exec]
PrivateUsers=pick


[Network]
Zone=web
Port=tcp:80


[Files]
PrivateUsersChown=yes
```

[Network] also sets up port forwarding from TCP port **80** in the container to port **80** on the host. You have to configure an IP address on the network interface in the container and on the host on the virtual Ethernet interface in the subnet to make it work.

Now enable the VM:

```
sudo machinectl enable centos01
```

Now that you know how to work with systemd-nspawn and deploy your container, let's go ahead and discuss the most popular containerization tool: Docker. You might have heard a lot about Docker, so let's get started!

Docker

In March 2010, Solomon Hykes started the development of Docker. It started in France as an internal dotCloud. Thanks to the public release at a big Python conference in 2013 and the interest of Red Hat, Docker really took off. In the last quarter of that same year, the name of the company was changed to Docker Inc.

Docker was originally built on top of LXC but after a while, LXC was replaced by their own **libcontainer** library.

The architecture of Docker is quite complex: it consists of a client, Docker, and a daemon, **dockerd**. Another daemon, **containerd**, is an abstraction layer for the OS and the type of container technology that is being used. You can interact with **containerd** using the **docker- containerd-ctr** utility. The **containerd** daemon is responsible for the following:

- The registry (where you can store images)
- The image (building, metadata, and so on)
- Networking
- Volumes (to store persistent data)
- Signing (trust on content)

containerd communicates with RunC, which is responsible for the following:

- Life cycle management
- Runtime information
- Running commands within the container
- Generating the specs (image ID, tags, and so on)

There are two editions of Docker available—**Docker Community Edition** (**CE**) and **Docker Enterprise Edition** (**EE**). Docker EE was sold to Mirantis by Docker Inc in November 2019; however, Docker CE is still handled by Docker Inc. Docker EE adds Docker support, but also an integrated security framework, certified plugins, support for Docker Swarm (which is a container orchestration solution like Kubernetes), and support for RBAC/AD/LDAP. All of this comes at a price, though. If you feel like your environment needs these added advantages, it's worth paying for. On the other hand, Docker CE is open-source software that is available for free.

Docker Installation

There are multiple ways to install and use Docker CE in Azure. You can install a Linux distribution of your choice and install Docker on top of it. There are several VMs available in the Azure Marketplace, such as RancherOS, which is a very minimal Linux distribution that was specially created to run Docker. And, last but not least, there is the Docker for Azure template, which is provided by Docker at https://docs.docker.com/docker-for-azure and https://docs.docker.com/docker-for-azure.

For the purposes of this chapter, the Docker on Ubuntu Server VM is absolutely not a bad idea; it saves a lot of work! But there are several reasons not to use this VM:

- It really can help to understand things better if you configure everything yourself.

- The software used is relatively old.

- The Docker VM extension that is used to create the VM is deprecated and not in active development any longer.

The Docker for Azure template also installs and configures Docker Swarm, a Docker-native clustering system.

The Docker website provides excellent documentation about how to install Docker manually. If you would like to install using `apt` or `yum` without following the script, you can follow the official Docker documentation (https://docs.docker.com/v17.09/engine/installation/#supported-platforms). If you are following that, then you can skip the `cloud-init` script.

Here, we'll follow the installation via our script. Please note that this script is convenient for lab environments, but not for production environments.

It installs the latest version of Docker from the Edge channel, not from the Stable channel. In theory, this could be a little bit unstable.

However, for the purposes of this chapter, it's a good way to get started. To get things up and running very quickly, let's use the technique of cloud-init that we learned in *Chapter 7, Deploying Your Virtual Machines*.

Start by creating a new resource group, for instance, **Docker_LOA**:

```
az group create --name Docker_LOA --location westus
```

Create a cloud-init configuration file; in my example, the file is named **docker.yml** with the following content:

```
#cloud-config
package_upgrade: true
write_files:
- content: |
    [Service]
    ExecStart=
    ExecStart=/usr/bin/dockerd
  path: /etc/systemd/system/docker.service.d/docker.conf
- content: |
    {
      "hosts": ["fd://","tcp://127.0.0.1:2375"]
    }
  path: /etc/docker/daemon.json
runcmd:
  - curl -sSL https://get.docker.com/ | sh
  - usermod -aG docker <ssh user>
```

Don't forget to replace **<ssh user>** with the login name of the account you're using to execute the **az** command.

You might have noticed that we added **ExecStart** twice in the script. ExecStart allows you to specify what command needs to be run when a unit is started. It's a good practice to clear it by setting **ExecStart=** and then specifying the actual command in the second line. The reason is that when Docker is installed, it will have an **ExecStart** value initially and when we supply another value, it will lead to a conflict. This conflict will stop the service from starting. Let's go ahead and create a VM with Docker installed using the cloud-init file we created:

1. Create a VM with the distribution of your choice:

    ```
    az vm create --name UbuntuDocker --resource-group Docker_LOA \
      --image UbuntuLTS --generate-ssh-keys --admin-username <ssh-user> \
      --custom-data docker.yml
    ```

2. When the VM is ready, log in and execute the following:

   ```
   sudo systemctl status docker.service
   ```

   > **Note**
   >
   > If you get a message that says "**Warning: docker.service changed on disk,
   > run systemctl daemon-reload to reload docker.service**," be patient, cloud-
   > init is still busy. Also, if you see that **docker.service** is not found, allow some time
   > for cloud-init to finish the installation. You can always verify if the Docker CE is
   > installed by executing **dpkg -l | grep docker**.

3. Execute the following to receive even more information about the Docker daemon:

   ```
   docker info
   ```

4. It's time to download our first container and run it:

   ```
   docker run hello-world
   ```

In the following screenshot, you can see that the container was run successfully and
you received a **Hello from Docker!** message:

```
rithin@UbuntuDocker:~$ docker run hello-world
Unable to find image 'hello-world:latest' locally
latest: Pulling from library/hello-world
1b930d010525: Pull complete
Digest: sha256:c3b4ada4687bbaa170745b3e4dd8ac3f194ca95b2d0518b417fb47e5879d9b5f
Status: Downloaded newer image for hello-world:latest

Hello from Docker!
This message shows that your installation appears to be working correctly.

To generate this message, Docker took the following steps:
 1. The Docker client contacted the Docker daemon.
 2. The Docker daemon pulled the "hello-world" image from the Docker Hub.
    (amd64)
 3. The Docker daemon created a new container from that image which runs the
    executable that produces the output you are currently reading.
 4. The Docker daemon streamed that output to the Docker client, which sent it
    to your terminal.

To try something more ambitious, you can run an Ubuntu container with:
 $ docker run -it ubuntu bash

Share images, automate workflows, and more with a free Docker ID:
 https://hub.docker.com/

For more examples and ideas, visit:
 https://docs.docker.com/get-started/
```

Figure 9.3: Successful container execution

A Docker container is an executed image. To list the available images on your system, execute the following:

```
docker image ls
```

In the previous example, we ran **docker run hello-world**. So, the image is already pulled in and you can see that the **hello-world** image is listed when we use the **docker image ls** command:

```
rithin@UbuntuDocker:~$ docker image ls
REPOSITORY          TAG               IMAGE ID            CREATED           SIZE
hello-world         latest            fce289e99eb9        10 months ago     1.84kB
```

Figure 9.4: Listing the Docker image

If you execute **docker run hello-world** again, this time the image will not be downloaded. Instead, it will go for the image that was already stored or downloaded during the previous run.

Let's download another image:

```
docker run ubuntu
```

After that, we'll list all containers, even those that are not running:

```
docker ps -a
```

All containers have the **exited** status. If you want to keep the container running, you have to add the **-dt** parameters to the run command; **-d** means run as detached:

```
docker run -dt ubuntu bash
```

If you want an interactive shell to the Ubuntu container (as you SSH to a VM), you can add the **-i** parameter:

```
docker run -it ubuntu
```

Verify that it is running by viewing the process list again:

```
docker ps
```

Using the container ID or name, you can execute a command in a container and receive the standard output in your Terminal:

```
docker exec <id/name> <command>
```

For instance, you can execute the following command to see the OS release of the container image:

```
docker exec <id/name> cat /etc/os-release
```

Attach to the container to verify whether the content is as expected:

```
docker attach <id/name>
```

And detach using *Ctrl* + *P* and *Ctrl* + *Q*, which means that you will exit from the interactive shell and the container will start running in the background.

To conclude, if you have been following along, by this time, you will be able to run containers, run them as detached, execute commands to the container from the host machine, and also get an interactive shell to the container. So far, we have used images that are already available in Docker Hub. In the next section, we will learn how to build our own Docker images with custom configurations from a base image.

Building Docker Images

A Docker image contains layers. For every command you run to add a component to the container, a layer is added. Each container is an image with read-only layers and a writable layer on top of that. The first layer is the boot filesystem and the second is called the base; it contains the OS. You can pull images from the Docker Registry (you'll find out more about the Registry later on) or build them yourself.

If you want to build one yourself, you can do so in a similar way to what we saw earlier on, with systemd-nspawn containers, for instance, by using debootstrap. Most of the commands require root user access, so escalate your privileges as follows:

```
sudo -i
```

Let's take Debian as the base image here. This will help you understand the **docker import** command. Download and extract Debian Stretch:

```
debootstrap --arch amd64 stretch stretch \
    http://ftp.us.debian.org/debian
```

Create a tarball and import it directly into Docker:

```
tar -C stretch -c . | docker import - stretch
```

Verify it using the following command:

```
docker images
```

Docker also provides a very minimal base image called **scratch**.

A Docker image is built from a Dockerfile. Let's create a working directory to save the Dockerfile:

```
mkdir ~/my-image && cd ~/my-image
```

As the **stretch** image is already available in Docker Hub, it's a good idea to tag your image with a new name so that Docker will not try to pull the image, but rather go for the local image. To tag the image, use the following command:

```
docker tag stretch:latest apache_custom:v1
```

Then, create a Dockerfile by executing **vi Dockerfile** (you can use any text editor). The first line in this file adds the base image as a layer:

```
FROM apache_custom:v1
```

The second layer contains Debian updates:

```
RUN apt-get --yes update
```

The third layer contains the Apache installation:

```
RUN apt-get --yes install apache2
```

Add the latest layer and run Apache in this read/write layer. **CMD** is used to specify the defaults for executing the container:

```
CMD /usr/sbin/apachectl -e info -DFOREGROUND
```

Open port **80**:

```
EXPOSE 80
```

Save the file and your file entries will look like the following screenshot. Adding comments is a good practice; however, it's optional:

```
root@UbuntuDocker:~/my-image# cat Dockerfile
#Taking the base image
FROM apache_custom:v1
# Running an apt update
RUN apt-get --yes update
# Install Apache
RUN apt-get --yes install apache2
# Adding defaults to execute
CMD /usr/sbin/apachectl -e info -DFOREGROUND
# Exposing Port 80 for HTTP traffic
EXPOSE 80
```

Figure 9.5: Creating a Docker image

Build the container:

```
docker build -t apache_image .
```

If everything went well, the output should show something similar to the following:

```
Successfully built 62b3f7d66fe1
Successfully tagged apache_image:latest
```

Figure 9.6: Docker image built successfully

You can test the container:

```
docker run -d apache_image
```

Review the history of the build:

```
docker history <ID/name>
```

As shown in the following screenshot, you'll be able to see the history of the build for your container:

```
rithin@UbuntuDocker:~$ docker history apache_image:latest
IMAGE          CREATED          CREATED BY                                        SIZE      COMMENT
62b3f7d66fe1   2 minutes ago    /bin/sh -c #(nop)  EXPOSE 80                      0B
4c7b7a261c05   2 minutes ago    /bin/sh -c #(nop)  CMD ["/bin/sh" "-c" "/usr...   0B
0ea527b75cd2   2 minutes ago    /bin/sh -c apt-get --yes install apache2         136MB
c47f78bde563   4 minutes ago    /bin/sh -c apt-get --yes update                  79.4MB
45014a481afc   35 minutes ago                                                    258MB     Imported from -
```

Figure 9.7: Reviewing the history of the container built

Execute **docker ps** to get the ID of the container, and use that to collect information about the container:

```
docker inspect <ID/name> | grep IPAddress
```

In the output, you can find the IP address of the container:

```
rithin@UbuntuDocker:~$ docker inspect 65cd | grep IPAddress
            "SecondaryIPAddresses": null,
            "IPAddress": "172.17.0.3",
                    "IPAddress": "172.17.0.3",
```

Figure 9.8: Fetching the IP address of the Docker

Use **curl** to see whether the web server is really running:

```
curl <ip address>
```

You will be able to see the famous "It works" page in HTML as shown here:

```
rithin@UbuntuDocker:~$ curl 172.17.0.3

<!DOCTYPE html PUBLIC "-//W3C//DTD XHTML 1.0 Transitional//EN" "http://www.w3.org/TR/xhtml1/DTD/xhtml1-transitional.dtd">
<html xmlns="http://www.w3.org/1999/xhtml">
  <head>
    <meta http-equiv="Content-Type" content="text/html; charset=UTF-8" />
    <title>Apache2 Debian Default Page: It works</title>
    <style type="text/css" media="screen">
  * {
    margin: 0px 0px 0px 0px;
    padding: 0px 0px 0px 0px;
  }

  body, html {
    padding: 3px 3px 3px 3px;

    background-color: #D8DBE2;

    font-family: Verdana, sans-serif;
    font-size: 11pt;
    text-align: center;
  }
```

Figure 9.9: Using the curl command to test the web server

Now, we'll stop the container using the following command:

```
docker stop <ID>
```

Now run it again:

```
docker run -d <ID> -p 8080:80
```

This makes the website available on localhost port **8080**.

You can also use **acbuild** to build Docker containers.

Docker Machine

There is another way to create Docker containers: Docker Machine. This is a tool that creates VMs that will host Docker. It's something you should run on a development machine, physical or not, and you should execute everything remotely.

Please note that Docker Machine can be installed on macOS, Linux, and Windows machines. Refer to the Docker Machine documentation (https://docs.docker.com/machine/install-machine/) for macOS and Windows installation as we're following only the Linux installation.

Switch back to the Ubuntu machine where we installed Docker. Install the following dependency:

```
sudo apt install sshfs
```

Next, you need to download Docker Machine and then extract it to your **PATH**:

```
base=https://github.com/docker/machine/releases/download/v0.16.0 \
&& curl -L $base/docker-machine-$(uname -s)-$(uname -m) \
>/tmp/docker-machine && \
sudo mv /tmp/docker-machine /usr/local/bin/docker-machine \
&& chmod +x /usr/local/bin/docker-machine
```

Autocompletion can be very useful, and also make sure you run the following script as root, as the script will write to the **/etc/** directory:

```
base=https://raw.githubusercontent.com/docker/machine/v0.16.0
for i in docker-machine-prompt.bash docker-machine-wrapper.bash \
docker-machine.bash
do
  sudo wget "$base/contrib/completion/bash/${i}" -P \ /etc/bash_completion.d
source /etc/bash_completion.d/$i
done
```

Log out and log in again. In order to verify that **bash-completion** is working, you can tap the tab button to see available commands for **docker-machine** as shown in the following screenshot:

```
root@UbuntuDocker:~# docker-machine
active      env      ip     mount             restart   ssh      stop
config      help     kill   provision         rm        start    upgrade
create      inspect  ls     regenerate-certs  scp       status   url
```

Figure 9.10: Verifying that bash-completion is successful

Verify the version:

```
docker-machine version
```

Using Azure as a driver, you can now deploy a VM:

```
docker-machine create -d azure \
  --azure-subscription-id <subscription id> \
  --azure-ssh-user <username> \
  --azure-open-port 80 \
  --azure-size <size> <vm name>
```

There are other options, such as the public IP and the resource group name, that can be passed during deployment. You can see the complete list and default values for these options in the Docker documentation (https://docs.docker.com/machine/drivers/azure/). If we don't specify a value for a specific option, Docker will take the default value. Another thing to keep in mind is that the VM name should only contain lowercase alpha-numeric characters or hyphens if required; otherwise, you will get an error.

In the following screenshot, you can see that the deployment of a VM named **docker-machine-2** of size `Standard_A2` was successful and that Docker is running on the machine. For simplicity, we have saved our subscription ID to a variable, **$SUB_ID**, so that we don't have to check it every time; you can also do the same if required. Since we have already authenticated before, the driver is not asking us to sign in again. The driver remembers your credentials for up to two weeks, which means you don't have to sign in every time you deploy. You can also see what resources were deployed:

```
root@UbuntuDocker:~# docker-machine create -d azure --azure-subscription-id $SUB_ID --azure-ssh-user rithin --azure-open-port 80 --azure-size Standard_A2 docker-machine-2
Running pre-create checks...
(docker-machine-2) Completed machine pre-create checks.
Creating machine...
(docker-machine-2) Querying existing resource group.  name="docker-machine"
(docker-machine-2) Resource group "docker-machine" already exists.
(docker-machine-2) Configuring availability set.  name="docker-machine"
(docker-machine-2) Configuring network security group.  name="docker-machine-2-firewall" location="westus"
(docker-machine-2) Querying if virtual network already exists.  name="docker-machine-vnet" rg="docker-machine" location="westus"
(docker-machine-2) Virtual network already exists.  rg="docker-machine" location="westus" name="docker-machine-vnet"
(docker-machine-2) Subnet already exists.
(docker-machine-2) Creating public IP address.  name="docker-machine-2-ip" static=false
(docker-machine-2) Creating network interface.  name="docker-machine-2-nic"
(docker-machine-2) Using existing storage account.  name="vhds5fltiq7nm49xbp0zd4si" sku=Standard_LRS
(docker-machine-2) Creating virtual machine.  username="rithin" osImage="canonical:UbuntuServer:16.04.0-LTS:latest" name="docker-machine-2" location="westus" size="Standard_A2"
Waiting for machine to be running, this may take a few minutes...
Detecting operating system of created instance...
Waiting for SSH to be available...
Detecting the provisioner...
Provisioning with ubuntu(systemd)...
Installing Docker...
Copying certs to the local machine directory...
Copying certs to the remote machine...
Setting Docker configuration on the remote daemon...
Checking connection to Docker...
Docker is up and running!
To see how to connect your Docker Client to the Docker Engine running on this virtual machine, run: docker-machine env docker-machine-2
```

Figure 9.11: Deploying the docker-machine-2 VM

To tell Docker to use the remote environment instead of running containers locally, execute the following:

```
docker-machine env <vm name>
eval $(docker-machine env <vm name>)
```

To verify that the remote environment is being used, use the **info** command:

```
docker info
```

Among other information, the output shows you that you are using a specific VM running in Azure:

```
Kernel Version: 4.15.0-1061-azure
Operating System: Ubuntu 16.04.6 LTS
OSType: linux
Architecture: x86_64
CPUs: 2
Total Memory: 3.339GiB
Name: docker-machine-2
ID: EIFT:PLZL:CKYJ:QZRN:LX4B:ROAU:GTVX:HYXO:KUIR:L4KA:E67G:PLRL
Docker Root Dir: /var/lib/docker
Debug Mode: false
Registry: https://index.docker.io/v1/
Labels:
 provider=azure
Experimental: false
Insecure Registries:
 127.0.0.0/8
Live Restore Enabled: false
```

Figure 9.12: Fetching the docker information

And for Docker Machine, execute the following command:

```
docker-machine ls
```

The output should be similar to the following:

Figure 9.13: Listing docker-machine

Let's create an nginx container with the host port **80** mapped to container port **80**. This means that all traffic coming to the host VM's port **80** will be directed to port **80** of the container. This is given using the **-p** parameter. Execute the following command to create an nginx container:

```
docker run -d -p 80:80 --restart=always nginx
```

Find the IP address of the VM:

```
docker-machine ip <vm name>
```

Use that IP address in a browser to verify that nginx is running.

Docker Machine also allows us to copy files into the VM with the **scp** parameter, or even to mount the files locally:

```
mkdir -m 777 /mnt/test
```

```
docker-machine mount <vm name>:/home/<username> /mnt/test
```

Use **docker ps** to find the running instances, stop them, and remove them, so that they are ready for the next utility.

Docker Compose

Docker Compose is a tool for creating a multiple-container application, for instance, a web application that needs a web server and a database.

You can check for the latest or stable release of Docker Compose at https://github.com/docker/compose/releases and install it, replacing the version number in the command with the latest release:

```
sudo curl -L "https://github.com/docker/compose/releases/download/1.24.1/
docker-compose-$(uname -s)-$(uname -m)" -o /usr/local/bin/docker-compose
```

Now, apply executable permission to the binary we downloaded:

```
sudo chmod +x /usr/local/bin/docker-compose
```

Next, verify the installation:

```
docker-compose version
```

If the installation was successful, you will be able to see the version of Docker Compose installed:

```
root@vm-docker-host:~# docker-compose version
docker-compose version 1.8.0, build unknown
docker-py version: 1.9.0
CPython version: 2.7.13
OpenSSL version: OpenSSL 1.1.0l  10 Sep 2019
root@vm-docker-host:~#
```

Figure 9.14: Verifying Docker compose installation

> **Note**
>
> After installation, if the preceding command fails, then check your path or else create a symbolic link to **/usr/bin** or any other directory in your path. To find out what directories are in your **PATH**, execute **$PATH** in the shell.To create a symbolic link, execute **sudo ln -s /usr/local/bin/docker-compose /usr/bin/docker-compose**.

Create a file named **docker-compose.yml** with the following content:

```
wordpress:
  image: wordpress
  links:
    - db:mysql
  ports:
    - 80:80


db:
  image: mariadb
  environment:
    MYSQL_ROOT_PASSWORD: <password>
```

Replace **<password>** with the password of your choice. While still being connected to the Azure environment, using Docker Machine, execute the following:

```
docker-compose up -d
```

If the build is successful, two containers are running, which you can verify by using **docker ps** and opening a browser with the correct IP address (**docker-machine ip <vm name>**). The WordPress installer is waiting for you.

Docker Registry

Every time we executed **docker run** or **docker pull** (download only), images were fetched from the internet. Where did they come from? Run this command:

```
docker info | grep Registry
```

The output of the preceding command gives you the answer: https://index.docker.io/v1/. This URL is the official Docker Hub. Docker Hub, or Docker Store, also has a nice web interface available via https://hub.docker.com, and is an online repository of private and publicly available Docker images.

The **docker search** command can be used to search this repository. To limit the output of this command, you can add filters:

```
docker search --filter "is-official=true" nginx --no-trunc
```

Here's the output of the **docker search** command:

```
rithin@UbuntuDocker:~$ docker search --filter "is-official=true" nginx --no-trunc
NAME                DESCRIPTION              STARS        OFFICIAL           AUTOMATED
nginx               Official build of Nginx. 12180        [OK]
```

Figure 9.15: Output of the docker search command

Optionally, add the **--no-trunc** parameter to see the complete description of the image. In the output, there is also a star rating that can help us to select the best available image.

If you create your own account on the Docker Hub website, you can use **docker push** to upload your images to the registry. It is free of charge!

Log in with the following:

```
docker login -u <username> -p <password>
```

Build the image:

```
docker build -t <accountname>/<image>:versiontag .
```

You can also tag the image afterward:

```
docker tag <tag id> <accountname>/<image>:versiontag
```

For versioning, it is a good idea to use a string such as **v1.11.1.2019**, which means the first version was released on November 1, 2019. If you don't add the version, it is tagged as the latest version.

You can't see the tags using the **docker search** command. You'll need the web interface or to query the Docker API using **curl** (a tool to transfer data to and from a server) and **jq** (a tool similar to **sed** but specifically for JSON data):

```
wget -q https://registry.hub.docker.com/v1/repositories/<image>/tags -O - |
jq
```

> **Note**
>
> jq is not installed by default. You have to install it using **apt install jq**.

This output will be in JSON format. You can further query using **jq** and refine the output if needed. If you don't want to use jq for formatting JSON, you can use the native **sed**, **tr**, and **cut** commands to format output and get something cleaner:

```
wget -q https://registry.hub.docker.com/v1/repositories/<image name>/tags -O
- | sed -e 's/[][]//g' -e 's/"//g' -e 's/ //g' | tr '}' '\n' | cut -d ":"
-f3
```

If you would like to get all the tags for nginx, you can replace **<image name>** with **nginx**.

We have discussed Docker Hub and how to check available images. Similarly, Azure offers Azure Container Registry, where you can store your private images and pull them when required. Before we start Azure Container Registry, we need to understand Azure Container Instances, with which you can run containers without the hassle of managing the host machines. Let's go ahead and learn more.

Azure Container Instances

Now that we are able to run a container in a VM, we can go one step further: we can use the Azure Container Instances service to run it without managing servers.

You can do that using the Azure portal. In the left-hand navigation bar, select **All Services** and search for **Container instances**. Once you are in **Container instances**, click on **Add** to create a new container instance and the portal will redirect you to the following window:

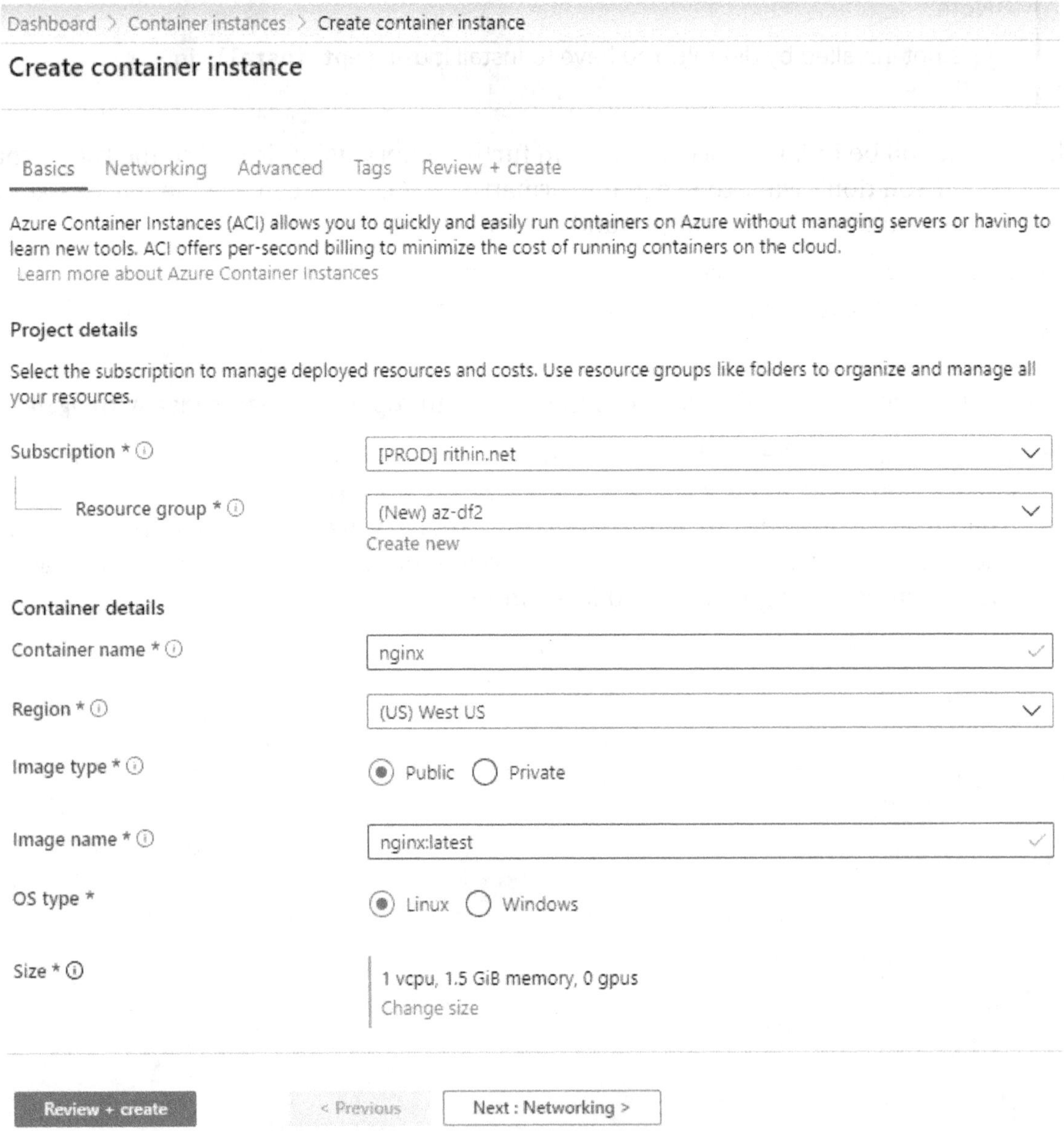

Dashboard > Container instances > Create container instance

Create container instance

Basics   Networking   Advanced   Tags   Review + create

Azure Container Instances (ACI) allows you to quickly and easily run containers on Azure without managing servers or having to learn new tools. ACI offers per-second billing to minimize the cost of running containers on the cloud.
Learn more about Azure Container Instances

Project details

Select the subscription to manage deployed resources and costs. Use resource groups like folders to organize and manage all your resources.

Subscription * ⓘ	[PROD] rithin.net
└─ Resource group * ⓘ	(New) az-df2
	Create new

Container details

Container name * ⓘ	nginx
Region * ⓘ	(US) West US
Image type * ⓘ	● Public ○ Private
Image name * ⓘ	nginx:latest
OS type *	● Linux ○ Windows
Size * ⓘ	1 vcpu, 1.5 GiB memory, 0 gpus
	Change size

Review + create   < Previous   Next : Networking >

Figure 9.16: Creating a Docker container instance

You can create a resource group or use an existing one. Set the container name to **nginx**, set **Image type** to `Public` because we are going to pull a public image, set the image name to **nginx:latest**, set **OS type** to `Linux`, and choose the desired resource requirement for the container. Hit **Next** and in the **Networking** section, we will expose **port 80** for HTTP traffic as shown in the following screenshot. Also, you can add a **DNS label** and opt for a public IP address if required:

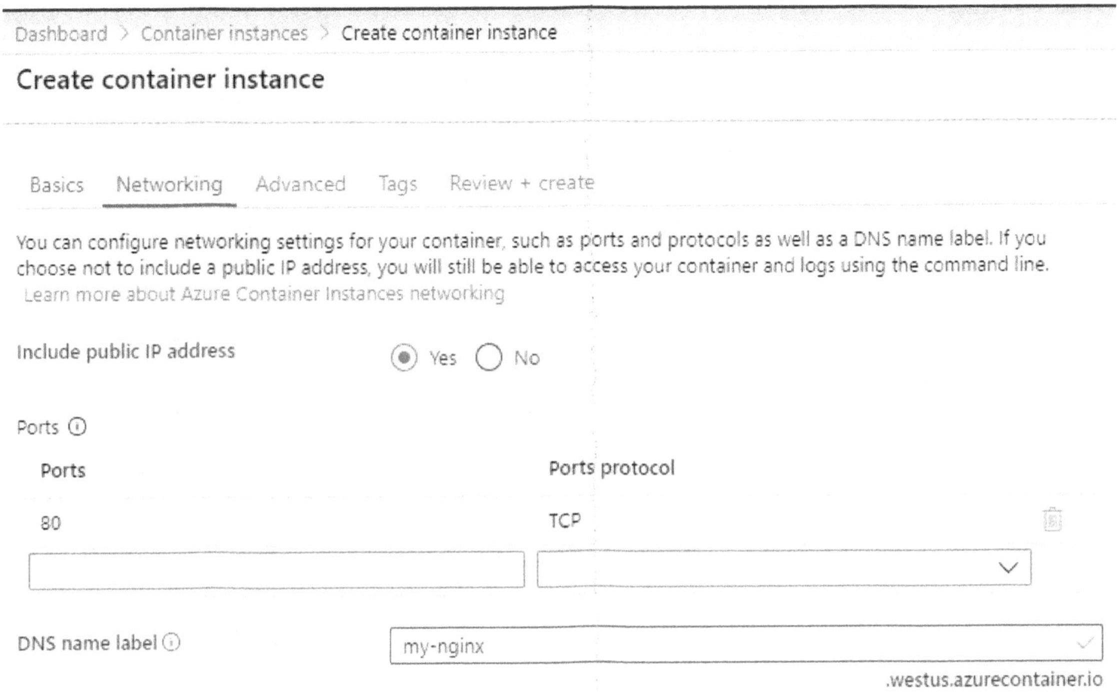

Figure 9.17: Adding networking details a container instance

This is enough for the validation and creation of the instance. You can skip the next sections and go to **Review+ Create**. However, Azure offers advanced options in the **Advanced** tab. These can be used to add environment variables, set the restart policy option, and use command override to include a set of commands that need to be executed when the container is initialized. If you want, you can configure this as well.

You can also create containers with the command line using the Azure CLI:

```
az container create --resource-group <resource group> --name nginx --image
nginx:latest --dns-name-label nginx-loa --ports 80
```

You can also use PowerShell:

```
New-AzContainerGroup -ResourceGroupName <resource group> '
   -Name nginx -Image nginx:latest r -OsType Linux '
   -DnsNameLabel nginx-loa2
```

Please note that the DNS label must be unique in your region.

In the output of the commands, the IP address of the instance is visible:

```
"ipAddress": {
  "dnsNameLabel": "nginx-loa",
  "fqdn": "nginx-loa.westus.azurecontainer.io",
  "ip": "13.83.150.22",
  "ports": [
    {
      "port": 80,
      "protocol": "TCP"
    }
  ],
  "type": "Public"
},
"location": "westus",
"name": "nginx",
"networkProfile": null,
"osType": "Linux",
"provisioningState": "Succeeded",
"resourceGroup": "Docker_LOA",
"restartPolicy": "Always",
"tags": {},
"type": "Microsoft.ContainerInstance/containerGroups",
"volumes": null
}
```

Figure 9.18: Creating containers using PowerShell

You should be able to access the web server on an FQDN and IP address. As shown in the screenshot, you can point your browser to the DNS label or IP address and you can see the **Welcome to nginx!** page:

Welcome to nginx!

If you see this page, the nginx web server is successfully installed and working. Further configuration is required.

For online documentation and support please refer to nginx.org. Commercial support is available at nginx.com.

Thank you for using nginx.

Figure 9.19: Output of the web server when the browser is pointed to the DNS label

To get the list of container instances, execute the following:

```
az container list
```

Alternatively, execute the following:

```
Get-AzContainerGroup | Format-List
```

So far, we have been relying on the Docker Registry to save, pull, and push images. Azure offers a private image registry where you can store your images so that they can be used when needed. This service is called Azure Container Registry. Let's learn about it.

Azure Container Registry

As mentioned, instead of the Docker Registry, you can use the private Azure Container Registry. This service is not free of charge! Using this Azure service has the advantage that you have all the features of Blob storage (reliability, availability, replication, and so on) and can keep all the traffic within Azure, which makes this registry an interesting option in terms of features, performance, and cost.

Using the Azure Portal

The easiest way to create a registry is by using the Azure portal. In the left-hand navigation bar, select **All Services** and search for **Container registries**. Click on **Add** and you should get the following screen. Don't forget to enable the **Admin user** option; by doing so, you can sign in to the container registry via **docker login** with the username as the registry name and the password as the access key:

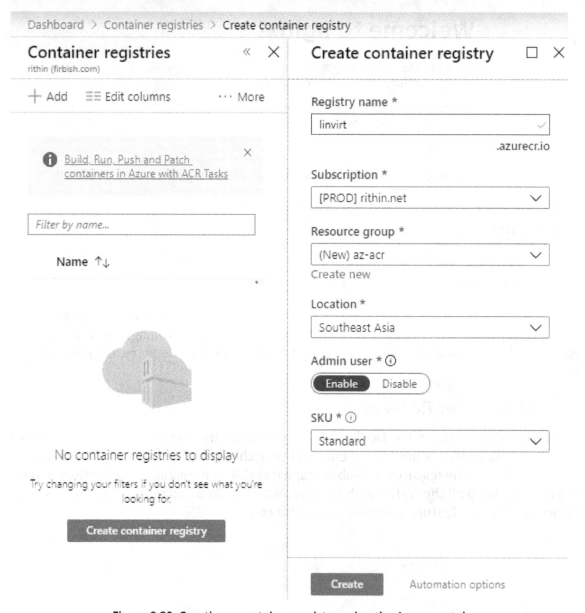

Figure 9.20: Creating a container registry using the Azure portal

If the registry is ready, there will be a popup saying that the job is finished and you will be able to see the resource. If you navigate to the **Access Keys blade**, you will find the login server and your username, which is the same as the registry name and the set of passwords:

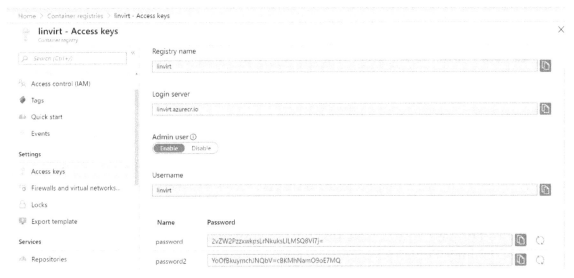

Figure 9.21: The Access key blade pane

Use this information to log into the repository, the same way you did with Docker Hub.

After pushing an image, it will be available in the repository. From there, you can deploy it to the Azure Container Instances service and run it.

Using the Azure CLI

We have created an Azure Container Registry instance via the Azure portal. It is also possible to use the Azure CLI and PowerShell to perform the same task. We will be following the Azure CLI steps and we encourage you to attempt this process using PowerShell on your own.

To start with, we need a Linux VM in which Docker and the Azure CLI are installed.

Let's start by creating a resource group, or you can use the same resource group that was used in the portal example. Just to recall the command we studied in the beginning, in the *Docker Installation* section; we will proceed with a new resource group:

```
az group create --name az-acr-cli --location eastus
```

Once you get the success message, proceed with the creation of the container registry using the following:

```
az acr create --resource-group az-acr-cli --name azacrcliregistry --sku
Basic --admin-enabled true
```

Here, we are creating the container registry with the Basic SKU. There are other SKUs available that offer more storage options and throughput. SKUs point to different pricing tiers of container registry. Visit the Microsoft Azure pricing page (https://azure. microsoft.com/en-in/pricing/details/container-registry/) to see the pricing of each SKU. Since this is a demonstration and to keep the cost minimal, we will go with Basic.

After the deployment of the Azure Container Registry instance, we will log in to the registry. But to sign in, we require the password. We already know the username, which is the name of the registry, so let's find the password of the registry:

```
az acr credential show --name azacrcliregistry --resource-group az-acr-cli
```

The output will show the username and password. Please make a note of them. You can use password 1 or password 2. Now that we are sure of the credentials, we'll log in to the Azure Container Registry instance by executing the following:

```
az acr login --name azacrcliregistry --username azacrcliregistry --password
<password>
```

If the login is successful, you should receive the output shown in the following screenshot:

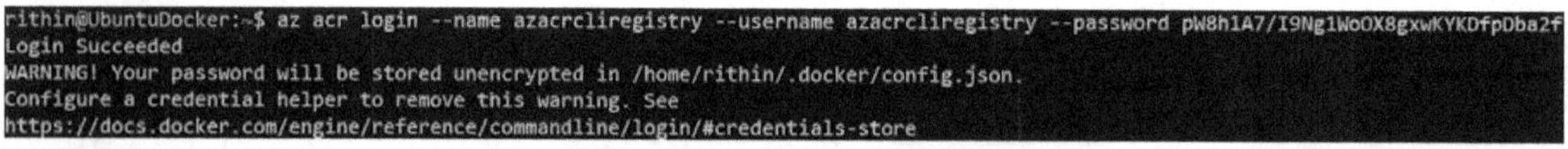

Figure 9.22: Azure Container Registry login successful

Let's go ahead and push an image to the registry. In order to push an image, first we need to have an image. If you are using the same VM that was used in the previous examples, you might have some images pulled in. If the images are not there, you can use **docker pull <image name>** to get the image. You can verify the list of available images using the **docker images** command. Since we already have an nginx image, we are not going to pull it from Docker Hub.

Now that we have the image, let's tag it. Tagging will help you know which image you are using. For example, if you have an image tagged as **v1** and you make some changes to it, you can tag it as **v2**. Tagging helps you to have a logical organization of your images based on release date, version number, or any other identifier. We need to tag in a **<AcrLoginName>/<image name>:<version tag>** format, where **acr-name** is the FQDN of the Azure Container Registry instance. To get the FQDN of the Azure Container Registry instance, execute the following:

```
az acr show -n azacrcliregistry -g az-acr-cli | grep loginServer
```

For the nginx image, we are going to tag it as **nginx:v1**:

```
docker tag nginx azacrcliregistry.azurecr.io/ngnix:v1
```

Let's push the tagged image to Azure Container Registry using the **docker push** command:

```
docker push azacrcliregistry.azurecr.io/ngnix:v1
```

All layers should be pushed, as shown in the screenshot:

Figure 9.23: Pushing the tagged image to the container registry

Suppose you have pushed multiple images to Azure Container Registry and would like to get a list of all images. Then you can make use of the **az acr repository list** command. To list all the images in the Azure Container Registry instance we created, use this command:

```
az acr repository list --name azacrcliregistry -o table
```

You can use the **docker run** command to run the container. But always make sure that the image name is in the format **<AcrLoginName>/<image>**. The era of Docker is going to end, and eventually it will be replaced with daemonless next-generation tools.

The next section is all about these tools and how you can create an analogy with Docker for a smooth transition.

Buildah, Podman, and Skopeo

In the previous section, we discussed how Docker works and how it can be used to deploy containers. As previously stated, Docker uses the Docker daemon, which helps us to achieve all this. What if we say people have started bidding goodbye to Docker? Yes, with the introduction of next-generation container management tools, Docker is fading away. We are not saying that Docker is completely out of the picture, but in time it will be replaced by rootless or daemonless Linux container tools. You read it right: there is no daemon running for these tools, and the approach of using the monolith daemon is coming to an end. No wonder people have started calling the containers deployed using these tools "Dockerless containers."

History

You might wonder when this all happened. Back in 2015, Docker Inc. and CoreOS, along with some other organizations, came up with the idea of the **Open Container Initiative (OCI)**. The intention behind this was to standardize the container runtime and image format specs. OCI image format is supported by most container image registries, such as Docker Hub and Azure Container Registry. Most container runtimes that are available now are either OCI-compatible or they have OCI in the pipeline. This was just the beginning.

Earlier, Docker was the only container runtime available for Kubernetes. Obviously, other vendors wanted to have support for their specific runtimes in Kubernetes. Due to this dilemma and the lack of support for other vendors, Kubernetes created CRI in 2017. CRI stands for Container Runtime Interface. You can use other runtimes, such as CRI-O, containerd, or frakti. Since Kubernetes was booming and due to their support for multiple runtimes, the monopoly of Docker started to topple. In no time, the monopoly status of Docker changed and it became one of the supported runtimes in Kubernetes. The ripples made by this change actually gave birth to the idea of daemonless tools and the idea to overthrow the approach of using the monolith daemon, which requires superuser access.

Instead of using generic terms, let's try to understand popular ones. Buildah is for building containers, Podman is for running containers, and Skopeo lets you perform various operations on images and repositories where images are stored. Let's take a closer look at each of these tools. Some people suggest removing Docker before using these tools, but we suggest keeping Docker so that you can constantly compare these tools to it. If you have followed the previous sections on Docker, you will be able to create an analogy.

Installation

Installing these tools is very straightforward. You can use apt in Ubuntu or yum in RHEL to install these tools. Since we are using the same VM, we will be following the Ubuntu installation of these packages. To install Buildah, execute the following:

```
sudo apt update

sudo apt install -y software-properties-common

sudo add-apt-repository -y ppa:projectatomic/ppa

sudo apt update

sudo apt install -y buildah
```

Since we already have the PPA repository added during the installation of Buildah, we can deploy Podman straight away using **apt install**. To install Podman, execute the following:

```
sudo apt -y install podman
```

In order to install Skopeo, we need **snap** to be installed on the Ubuntu VM. If you are on Ubuntu 16.04 LTS or later, snap will be installed by default. Otherwise, you have to manually install it using **apt install snapd**.

Let's install Skopeo using snap:

```
sudo snap install skopeo --edge
```

> **Note**
>
> If you are getting an error message stating that **revision is not meant production**, you can use the **-devmode** parameter to install; this will skip this error and complete the installation.

Now we are ready to explore these tools.

Buildah

In the previous section, we discussed Dockerfiles. Here is the interesting part: Buildah has full support for Dockerfiles. All you have to do is write the Dockerfile and use the **bud** command, which stands for build-using-docker. Let's take the same example we used in the Dockerfile section. Create a Dockerfile by executing **vi Dockerfile** (you can use any text editor) and add the following lines:

```
FROM nginx
RUN apt-get --yes update
RUN apt-get --yes install apache2
CMD /usr/sbin/apachectl -e info -DFOREGROUND
EXPOSE 80
```

Save the file.

Before we build, there is something else we need to take care of. Buildah looks for the list of registries in the **/etc/containers/registries.conf** file. If this file doesn't exist, we need to create one, add the following code, and save the file:

```
[registries.search]
registries = ['docker.io']
```

By doing so, we are instructing to search Docker Hub for the image. You can also add your Azure Container Registry instance to the list if required.

Let's go ahead and build the image; make sure you are in the directory where the Dockerfile is. Start the build process using this:

```
buildah bud -t ngnix-buildah .
```

We have created an image called **nginx-buildah**. To see the list of images, you can use the **buildah images** command. Yes, we know it looks very similar to how you list images in Docker. We need to keep this analogy in mind and it will help you learn.

The output will be similar to this:

```
rithin@UbuntuDocker:~$ buildah images
REPOSITORY                  TAG      IMAGE ID      CREATED         SIZE
localhost/ngnix-buildah     latest   98c5425ab01e  4 minutes ago   193 MB
docker.io/library/ubuntu    latest   775349758637  11 days ago     66.6 MB
```

Figure 9.24: Listing the images using the buildah command

You can see that Buildah lists the image we pulled from Docker Hub and also the image we created that is stored in the localhost repository.

To build a container from an image, we can use the following:

```
buildah from <image>
```

This will create a container called **<image>-working-container**. If you want to build an nginx container, execute this:

```
buildah from nginx
```

You will get a similar output to this:

```
rithin@UbuntuDocker:~$ buildah from nginx
Getting image source signatures
Copying blob abc291867bca done
Copying blob 5b07f4e08ad0 done
Copying blob 8d691f585fa8 done
Copying config 540a289bab done
Writing manifest to image destination
Storing signatures
nginx-working-container
```

Figure 9.25: Building an nginx container

Just like using **docker ps** to list all the containers, we will run **buildah ps** and we will be able to see the **nginx-working-container** we just created:

```
rithin@UbuntuDocker:~$ buildah ps
CONTAINER ID  BUILDER  IMAGE ID      IMAGE NAME                     CONTAINER NAME
439a82c747c2     *      540a289bab6c  docker.io/library/nginx:latest  nginx-working-container
```

Figure 9.26: Listing the containers using the buildah ps command

Also, we can execute commands directly in the container using the **buildah run** command. The syntax is as follows:

```
buildah run <container name> <command>
```

Let's try to print the content of the **/etc/os-release** file of the nginx container we created. The command will be as follows:

```
buildah run nginx-working-container cat /etc/os-release
```

The output will be similar to this:

```
rithin@UbuntuDocker:~$ buildah run nginx-working-container cat /etc/os-release
PRETTY_NAME="Debian GNU/Linux 10 (buster)"
NAME="Debian GNU/Linux"
VERSION_ID="10"
VERSION="10 (buster)"
VERSION_CODENAME=buster
ID=debian
HOME_URL="https://www.debian.org/"
SUPPORT_URL="https://www.debian.org/support"
BUG_REPORT_URL="https://bugs.debian.org/"
```

Figure 9.27: Printing the content of the nginx container

Like Docker, Buildah has support for commands such as **push**, **pull**, **tag**, and **inspect**.

Podman

The images we build via Buildah follow OCI compliance and can be used with Podman. In Podman, the analogy keeps on continuing; all we have to do is replace all Docker commands with Podman commands. One of the key things that we have to keep in mind is that in Podman, we cannot do port binding for a container as a non-root user. If your container needs a port mapping, then you have to run Podman as root. As we have already covered Docker and you are already familiar with Docker commands, we will just try to run a container and verify. Let's create an nginx container with the port mapped to **8080**. Since we need to map a port, we will run the command as **sudo**:

```
sudo podman run -d -p 8080:80 --name webserver nginx
```

Since we have created the container using the **sudo** command, it will be owned by the root user. If a container is created using **sudo**, make sure you chain sudo for all actions related to that container.

To list the containers, use **podman ps**, and we can see that the container is listening on **0.0.0.0:8080** of the host, which is mapped to the port of the container:

Figure 9.28: Listing the containers using the podman ps command

Let's do a **curl** call and confirm whether the web server is running on port **8080** or not:

```
curl localhost:8080
```

If everything is working, you will be able to see the nginx welcome page:

```
rithin@UbuntuDocker:~$ curl localhost:8080
<!DOCTYPE html>
<html>
<head>
<title>Welcome to nginx!</title>
<style>
    body {
        width: 35em;
        margin: 0 auto;
        font-family: Tahoma, Verdana, Arial, sans-serif;
    }
</style>
</head>
<body>
<h1>Welcome to nginx!</h1>
<p>If you see this page, the nginx web server is successfully installed and
working. Further configuration is required.</p>

<p>For online documentation and support please refer to
<a href="http://nginx.org/">nginx.org</a>.<br/>
Commercial support is available at
<a href="http://nginx.com/">nginx.com</a>.</p>

<p><em>Thank you for using nginx.</em></p>
</body>
</html>
```

Figure 9.29: Verifying the authentication to the port of the web server

Yes, the container is running daemonless!

We are not covering all Podman commands here, and once you are familiar with Docker, all you have to do is replace **docker** with **podman** in the command line.

Skopeo

If you recall, earlier we tried to get the tags of an image using Docker. Using Skopeo, you can inspect a repository, copy images, and delete images. To start with, we will use the **skopeo inspect** command to obtain the tags of an image in Docker Hub without pulling it:

```
skopeo inspect docker://nginx:latest
```

Running this command will trigger some warnings. You can ignore them. If you check the output, you can see that it is giving the tags, layers, OS type, and so on.

You can use the **skopeo copy** command to copy container images across multiple storage repositories. Also, you can use Skopeo with Azure Container Registry.

We will not be covering all these. However, you can visit the GitHub repositories of these tools:

- Buildah: https://github.com/containers/buildah
- Podman: https://github.com/containers/libpod
- Skopeo: https://github.com/containers/skopeo

Containers and Storage

This section aims to give you a basic idea of containers and storage. Every build tool that can create images provides the option to add data to your container.

You should use this feature only to provide configuration files. Data for applications should be hosted, as much as possible, outside the container. If you want to quickly update/remove/replace/scale your container, it's almost impossible if the data is within the container.

When we create a container, storage is attached to the container. However, the containers are ephemeral, which means that the storage is also destroyed when you destroy the container. Let's assume you created a Ubuntu container for testing and you saved some scripts that were tested on the container in the hope that you can use them later. Now, if you accidentally deleted this container, all the scripts that you tested and saved for later would be gone.

Your application data is important and you would like to retain it even after the container's life cycle is complete. So, we want to separate the data from the container life cycle. By doing so, your data is not destroyed and can be reused if needed. In Docker, this is achieved by using volumes.

Docker supports a wide range of options for persistent volumes, including Azure Files. In other words, you can tie your Azure file share to a Docker container as a persistent volume. To demonstrate this, we will go for the host volume, where a location will be mounted as a volume to the container. The purpose of these steps is to show how data can be saved even after the container is removed from the host.

Volume info is passed to the **docker run** command using the **-v** parameter while creating the container. The general syntax is as follows:

```
docker run -v /some-directory/on host:/some-directory/in container
```

Assume that you have an application that will create a file in a **/var/log** directory in the container and we need to make this persistent. In the next command, we are mapping a directory in the host to the **/var/log** directory of the container.

To complete this exercise, you need a Linux VM with Docker running on it. Let's create a **~/myfiles** directory on the host machine that will be mapped to the container:

```
mkdir ~/myfiles
```

Let's create an Ubuntu container with an interactive shell, where the **-v** parameter is passed to mount the volume:

```
docker run -it -v ~/myfile:/var/log ubuntu
```

If the container was created successfully, you will be logged in as a root user to the container:

```
root@vm-docker-host:/home/rithin# docker run -it -v ~/myfiles:/var/log ubuntu
root@05e166b89c11:/#
```

Figure 9.30: Creating the Ubuntu container

We will go to the **/var/log** directory of the container and create 10 empty files using this command:

```
touch file{1..10}
```

Listing the contents of the directory will show the 10 files we just created:

```
root@05e166b89c11:/var/log# touch file{1..10}
root@05e166b89c11:/var/log# ls -lah
total 8.0K
drwxr-xr-x 2 root root 4.0K Dec  3 15:45 .
drwxr-xr-x 1 root root 4.0K Oct 29 21:25 ..
-rw-r--r-- 1 root root    0 Dec  3 15:45 file1
-rw-r--r-- 1 root root    0 Dec  3 15:45 file10
-rw-r--r-- 1 root root    0 Dec  3 15:45 file2
-rw-r--r-- 1 root root    0 Dec  3 15:45 file3
-rw-r--r-- 1 root root    0 Dec  3 15:45 file4
-rw-r--r-- 1 root root    0 Dec  3 15:45 file5
-rw-r--r-- 1 root root    0 Dec  3 15:45 file6
-rw-r--r-- 1 root root    0 Dec  3 15:45 file7
-rw-r--r-- 1 root root    0 Dec  3 15:45 file8
-rw-r--r-- 1 root root    0 Dec  3 15:45 file9
```

Figure 9.31: Listing the contents of the /var/log directory

Exit from the interactive shell using *Ctrl* + D, and now we are back in the host machine. Now we will delete the container:

```
docker rm <id/name of the container>
```

The **id/name** can be obtained from the output of the **docker ps --all** command.

Now that the container has been deleted, we will go to the **~/myfiles** directory of the host machine to verify the contents.

In the following screenshot, you can see that the container has been successfully deleted; however, the **~/myfiles** directory still holds the files we created inside the container:

```
root@vm-docker-host:/home/rithin# docker rm 05e166b89c11
05e166b89c11
root@vm-docker-host:/home/rithin# cd ~/myfiles
root@vm-docker-host:~/myfiles# ls -lah
total 8.0K
drwxr-xr-x 2 root root 4.0K Dec  3 15:45 .
drwx------ 4 root root 4.0K Dec  3 15:41 ..
-rw-r--r-- 1 root root    0 Dec  3 15:45 file1
-rw-r--r-- 1 root root    0 Dec  3 15:45 file10
-rw-r--r-- 1 root root    0 Dec  3 15:45 file2
-rw-r--r-- 1 root root    0 Dec  3 15:45 file3
-rw-r--r-- 1 root root    0 Dec  3 15:45 file4
-rw-r--r-- 1 root root    0 Dec  3 15:45 file5
-rw-r--r-- 1 root root    0 Dec  3 15:45 file6
-rw-r--r-- 1 root root    0 Dec  3 15:45 file7
-rw-r--r-- 1 root root    0 Dec  3 15:45 file8
-rw-r--r-- 1 root root    0 Dec  3 15:45 file9
```

Figure 9.32: Listing the files in the ~/myfiles directory

Now we know how to make our volume persistent. For Docker, there are solutions such as https://github.com/ContainX/docker-volume-netshare.

If you are using Docker and want to use Azure Files, you can use Cloudstor, a plugin that is available at https://docs.docker.com/docker-for-azure/persistent-data-volumes.

Using Azure File Storage maybe not the cheapest solution, but this way you get all the availability and backup options you need.

If you're going to use Kubernetes, it's a whole other story. We'll cover that in the next chapter.

Summary

In this chapter, another way of deploying your workload in Azure was discussed. After an introduction to the history, ideas, and concepts of container virtualization, we went into some of the available options. Along with older implementations, such as LXC, we discussed other great and rock-solid implementations to host containers: systemd-nspawn and Docker.

We not only saw how to run existing images pulled from repositories but also how to create our own image. Perhaps the greatest news is that there is a tool called Buildah that is able to create an image using the OCI standard from the Open Container Initiative and can be used for Docker.

The majority of this chapter was about Docker. This is by far the most widely implemented container solution today. And, talking about implementations, there are many ways to implement/deploy Docker:

- Deploy it manually in a VM

- Deploy a ready-to-go VM from the marketplace

- Docker Machine

- Azure Container Instances

Working with Docker Hub and Azure Container Registry was also discussed.

Finally, we discussed new container technologies such as Buildah, Podman, and Skopeo.

We ended the chapter with a few words about containers and storage. You might be wondering what will happen to the storage attached to a container if the container is destroyed, or how to make the storage persistent. You will learn about persistence in the next chapter, *Chapter 10*, *Working with Azure Kubernetes Service*. Also, we will be discussing the famous container orchestration tool Kubernetes.

Questions

1. What are the reasons for using containers?

2. When are containers not the solution that you need?

3. If you need something like a virtual private server, do you want a VM, or is there a container virtualization solution available that may be a good idea?

4. Why shouldn't it be difficult to migrate from one solution, let's say Docker, to another, for example, Buildah?

5. What is a development machine used for?

6. Why is using Buildah such a good idea, even if it is under heavy development?

7. Why shouldn't you store application data in a container?

Further Reading

Carrying out further reading is not a very easy thing to do in the area of container virtualization. For `systemd-nspawn`, it's relatively easy: the man pages are an easy read. Let's make a suggestion that is relevant for `systemd-nspawn` and even Docker: Red Hat provides a document on their website called the Resource Management Guide (https:// access.redhat.com/documentation/en-us/red_hat_enterprise_linux/7/html/ resource_management_guide/) with good information about cgroups.

A couple of references on Docker are listed here:

*   *Orchestrating Docker*, by Shrikrishna Holla, where you can understand how to manage and deploy Docker services

*   *Mastering Docker Enterprise: A companion guide for agile container adoption*, by Mark Panthofer, where you can explore add-on services of Docker EE and how they can be used

10

Working with Azure Kubernetes Service

In the previous chapter, we explored the world of container virtualization, and in particular Docker containers. This chapter is all about managing containerized workloads using **Azure Kubernetes Service** (**AKS**).

This chapter is different from all the other chapters in this book. Until now, every chapter has been about infrastructure and providing a platform: the classic system administrator working in the cloud. Even *Chapter 9, Container Virtualization in Azure*, contained questions such as "How do we install Docker?" and "How do we get the container up and running?" The questions we'll answer in this chapter are the following:

- How do we deploy and manage our workload during the development phase and afterward?

- How can we scale up/down?

- What are the availability options?

Kubernetes provides an important answer to all of these questions. It is a solution that is used to automate important tasks such as the deployment, management, scaling, networking, and management of the availability of container-based applications.

Kubernetes was originally designed by Google and is now maintained by the Cloud Native Computing Foundation (https://www.cncf.io). Microsoft is a big partner of this foundation and is an important contributor to Kubernetes projects in terms of money and code. Actually, one of the co-founders of Kubernetes, Brendan Burns, works for Microsoft and leads the teams that work on container orchestration within Microsoft. On top of that, Microsoft has started several open source projects with additional tooling for Kubernetes.

Because Microsoft is so heavily involved in Kubernetes, it is able to implement a version of Kubernetes in Azure that is fully upstream-compatible. This is also important for developers so that they can use a local Kubernetes installation to develop software, and when the development is done, release it to the Azure cloud.

AKS provides a fully managed containers-as-a-service solution for Kubernetes. This means that you don't have to think about the configuration, management, and upgrading of the Kubernetes software. The control plane is managed by Azure.

AKS makes it easy to deploy and manage Kubernetes within Azure: it can handle the complete maintenance process, from provisioning to keeping your applications up to date and upscaling as per your needs.

Even the process of upgrading your Kubernetes cluster without any downtime can be done with AKS.

And last but not least, monitoring is available for every part of your Kubernetes cluster.

By the end of this chapter, you'll be able to:

- Explain what Kubernetes and AKS are.
- Use AKS to deploy and manage your clusters.
- Maintain the complete life cycle of your applications in AKS.

So, let's go ahead and first understand what the technical requirements are before we actually start using AKS.

Technical Requirements

As stated in the introduction of this chapter, this chapter is different from all the other chapters and this affects the technical requirements. Until now, the technical requirements were simple: you just needed a bunch of virtual machines.

This chapter needs a DevOps environment in which developers and operators are in the same team, working closely together, and where there is also someone who is doing both development- and operations-related tasks.

Another choice has to be made: where do we develop? Locally, or in the Azure cloud? Both are possible and it shouldn't make any difference! Cost-wise, it may be better to do it on a workstation. In this chapter, it's sort of assumed that you're doing it locally. So, you'll need a workstation (or virtual machine). We need the following:

- The Azure CLI.
- Docker and build tools.
- Kubernetes.
- Some essential developer tools, such as Git.
- Some other tools, such as Helm, covered later on.
- A good **integrated development environment** (**IDE**). We prefer Microsoft **Visual Studio** (**VS**) Code with the Microsoft extensions for Docker and Kubernetes (only if a graphical interface is available; otherwise, use the Nano editor).
- Optionally, an orchestration tool such as Ansible. Please have a look at the Ansible `azure_rm_aks` and `8ks_raw` modules.

Using WSL and VS Code

You can use **<u>Windows Subsystem for Linux</u>** (**<u>WSL</u>**) and VS Code along with the VS Code Remote WSL extension to get a Linux development environment on your Windows desktop or laptop without the overhead of having a virtual machine. This will enable you to access your Linux files from PowerShell or CMD and your Windows files from Bash. VS Code is a source code editor that can run on various platforms and supports many languages. You can develop, run, and debug Linux-based applications from your favorite Windows platform using WSL and VS Code. WSL features can be enabled using PowerShell and by installing Linux from the Microsoft Store. VS Code is available for Windows and Linux and can be downloaded from https://code.visualstudio.com/. Since the configuration settings of VS Code are maintained across both Windows and Linux platforms, you can easily switch back and forth from Windows to Linux and Linux to Windows.

You can find the step-by-step tutorial for WSL at https://docs.microsoft.com/en-us/learn/modules/get-started-with-windows-subsystem-for-linux/ and a detailed installation guide at https://docs.microsoft.com/en-us/windows/wsl/install-win10. You can configure default shells and choose between PowerShell and WSL when running on Windows, and you can choose Zsh or Bash on Linux.

Installing Dependencies

We are going to use Ubuntu 18.04 LTS Desktop edition. But you can use an Ubuntu 18.04 LTS server in an Azure virtual machine as well. With all the knowledge that you've gained in the other chapters, it's easy to transfer what we'll be doing to other Linux distributions, macOS, and even Windows:

1. First, upgrade Ubuntu:

   ```
   sudo apt update &&sudo apt upgrade
   ```

2. Install the developer tools, including some other dependencies and **openssh**:

   ```
   sudo apt install build-essential git curl openssh-server \
   ebtablesethtoolsocat
   ```

3. First, we are going to install the Azure CLI.

   You can install the Azure CLI by running a single command:

   ```
   curl -sL https://aka.ms/InstallAzureCLIDeb | sudo bash
   ```

   Alternatively, you can use the following instructions for manual installation.

   Get the required package:

   ```
   sudo apt-get install ca-certificates curl apt-transport-https lsb-release
   gnupg
   ```

   Get and install the signing key:

   ```
   curl -sL https://packages.microsoft.com/keys/microsoft.asc | gpg --dearmor
   |
   sudo tee /etc/apt/trusted.gpg.d/microsoft.asc.gpg> /dev/null

   sudo apt-add-repository \
     https://packages.microsoft.com/repos/azure-cli

   curl -L https://packages.microsoft.com/keys/microsoft.asc \
     | sudo apt-key add -

   sudo apt update

   sudo apt install azure-cli
   ```

4. To install PowerShell and VS Code, we are using snaps, universal software packages similar to portable apps for Windows:

   ```
   sudo snap install --classic powershell

   sudo snap install --classic vscode
   ```

Alternatively, you can use the following commands to install PowerShell Core:

```
curl https://packages.microsoft.com/keys/microsoft.asc | sudo apt-key add -

curl https://packages.microsoft.com/config/ubuntu/18.04/prod.list | sudo tee /etc/apt/sources.list.d/microsoft.list

sudo apt update

sudo apt install -y powershell
```

5. Type **pwsh** to start PowerShell Core:

```
admin123@kubes:~$ pwsh
```

If the PowerShell Core starts successfully, you will get the following output:

```
admin123@kubes:~$ pwsh
PowerShell 6.2.3
Copyright (c) Microsoft Corporation. All rights reserved.

https://aka.ms/pscore6-docs
Type 'help' to get help.

PS /home/admin123>
```

Figure 10.1: Starting PowerShell Core

6. Install the Azure cmdlet for Azure:

```
sudo pwsh -Command "Install-Module PowerShellGet -Force"

sudo pwsh -Command "Install-Module -Name AzureRM.Netcore \
 -AllowClobber"

sudo chown -R $USER ~/.local/
```

7. Install Docker:

```
curl -sSL https://get.docker.com/ | sudo sh
sudo usermod -aG docker $USER
```

You will get the Docker version details as follows:

```
+ sh -c docker version
Client: Docker Engine - Community
 Version:           19.03.4
 API version:       1.40
 Go version:        go1.12.10
 Git commit:        9013bf583a
 Built:             Fri Oct 18 15:54:09 2019
 OS/Arch:           linux/amd64
 Experimental:      false

Server: Docker Engine - Community
 Engine:
  Version:          19.03.4
  API version:      1.40 (minimum version 1.12)
  Go version:       go1.12.10
  Git commit:       9013bf583a
  Built:            Fri Oct 18 15:52:40 2019
  OS/Arch:          linux/amd64
  Experimental:     false
 containerd:
  Version:          1.2.10
  GitCommit:        b34a5c8af56e510852c35414db4c1f4fa6172339
 runc:
  Version:          1.0.0-rc8+dev
  GitCommit:        3e425f80a8c931f88e6d94a8c831b9d5aa481657
 docker-init:
  Version:          0.18.0
  GitCommit:        fec3683
```

Figure 10.2: Docker version details

8. Stop Docker for now:

```
Sudo systemctl stop docker.service
```

kubectl Installation

kubectl is a command-line interface that can be used to manage your Kubernetes clusters. It can be used for many operations. For example, use **kubectl create** to create one or more files and use **kubectl delete** to delete resources from a file. We are going to use the Azure CLI to install **kubectl** and execute the following commands as root to grant the required permissions:

```
sudo -i
```

```
az login
```

```
az aks install-cli
```

First, you need to download the latest release using the following command:

```
curl -LO https://storage.googleapis.com/kubernetes-release/release/v1.16.3/
bin/linux/amd64/kubectl
```

Next, make it executable:

```
chmod +x ./kubectl
```

Now, move it to your **PATH:**

```
Sudo mv ./kubectl /usr/local/bin/kubectl
```

Verify the installation by asking for the version information:

```
kubectl version
```

To enable autocompletion, which could save you from a lot of typing. For Bash and Zsh in **kubectl**, execute the following:

```
kubectl completion bash > ~/.kube/completion.bash.inc


printf"
 # Kubectl shell completion
 source '$HOME/.kube/completion.bash.inc'
">> $HOME/.bash_profile


source $HOME/.bash_profile
```

For Zsh, execute the following:

```
sudo -i


kubectl completion zsh>"${fpath[1]}/_kubectl"


exit


source <(kubectl completion zsh)
```

So far, we have installed the latest version of the kubectl binary with a **curl** command on Linux and enabled shell auto-completion for kubectl. We are now ready to use AKS.

> **Note**
>
> If you are using kubectl and you get error messages similar to **Error from server (NotAcceptable): unknown (get nodes)**, downgrade your client using **https:// dl.k8s.io/v1.10.6/kubernetes-client-linux-amd64.tar.gz**.

Though this is completely outside the scope of this book, we personally like to use the Zsh shell with a nice customization called Spaceship. The prompt gives you more insight into where you are and what you are doing while working with AKS.

Here is the quick installation:

```
sudo apt install zshnpm fonts-powerline

zsh # and create a .zshrc file with option 0

npm install spaceship-prompt

chsh -s /bin/zsh
```

Starting to Use AKS

Azure AKS makes it easy to deploy and manage your container applications. You can quickly define, deploy, and debug Kubernetes applications in addition to automatically containerizing your applications using Azure AKS. You can automate the monitoring, upgrading, repair, and scaling, which reduces the manual infrastructure maintenance. With kubectl installed, it's time to set up and explore the Kubernetes environment in Azure:

1. Create a cluster.

2. Find information about the cluster.

3. Deploy a simple workload.

Creating a Cluster with the Azure CLI

In Kubernetes, we're going to work with clusters. A cluster contains a master or control plane that is in control of everything and one or more worker nodes. In Azure, we don't have to care about the master, only about the nodes.

It's a good idea to make a new resource group for the purposes of this chapter:

```
az group create --location eastus--name MyKubernetes
```

In this resource group, we will deploy our cluster:

```
az aks create --resource-group MyKubernetes \
  --name Cluster01 \
  --node-count 1 --generate-ssh-keys
```

This command can take up to 10 minutes. As soon as you get your prompt back, verify it with the following:

```
az aks list
```

In the output, you'll find a lot of information, such as the fully qualified domain name, the name of the cluster, and so on:

```
        "id": "/subscriptions/21b59b21-18b2-4cd7-a680-274381b22d7e/resourceGro
ups/MC_MyKubernetes_Cluster01_eastus/providers/Microsoft.Network/publicIPAddress
es/f8262df1-a059-4de3-87ea-aeaa3d359542",
        "resourceGroup": "MC_MyKubernetes_Cluster01_eastus"
      }
    ],
    "managedOutboundIps": {
      "count": 1
    },
    "outboundIpPrefixes": null,
    "outboundIps": null
  },
  "loadBalancerSku": "Standard",
  "networkPlugin": "kubenet",
  "networkPolicy": null,
  "podCidr": "10.244.0.0/16",
  "serviceCidr": "10.0.0.0/16"
},
"nodeResourceGroup": "MC_MyKubernetes_Cluster01_eastus",
"provisioningState": "Succeeded",
"resourceGroup": "MyKubernetes",
"servicePrincipalProfile": {
  "clientId": "01dfa061-3e33-47fd-9caf-2c200002fe21",
  "secret": null
},
"tags": null,
"type": "Microsoft.ContainerService/ManagedClusters",
"windowsProfile": null
```

Figure 10.3: Details of the deployed cluster

There is a web interface available called Kubernetes Dashboard that you can use to access the cluster. To make it available, execute the following:

```
az aks browse --name Cluster01 --resource-group MyKubernetes
```

Point your browser to **http://127.0.0.1:8001**:

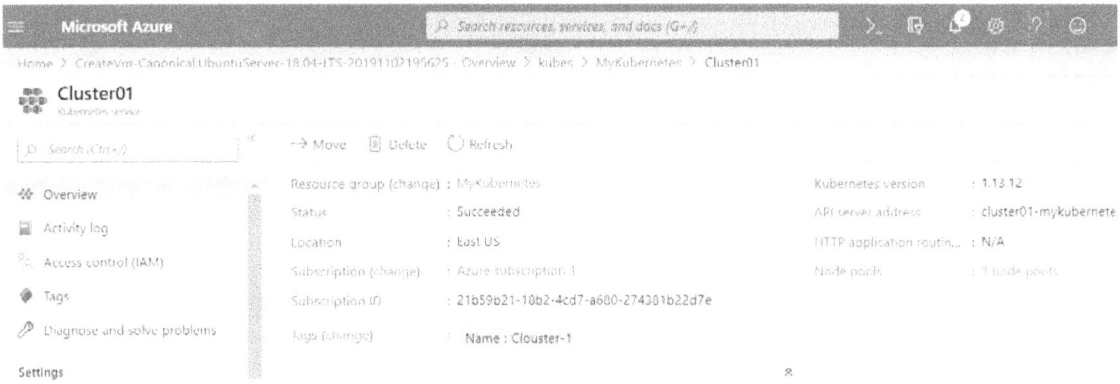

Figure 10.4: Kubernetes Dashboard

The **az** utility is tunneling the portal to your localhost. Press *Ctrl* + C to exit the tunnel.

To be able to use the **kubectl** utility, we need to merge the configuration into the local configuration file:

```
az aks get-credentials --resource-group MyKubernetes \
  --name Cluster01
```

The output of the preceding command is as follows:

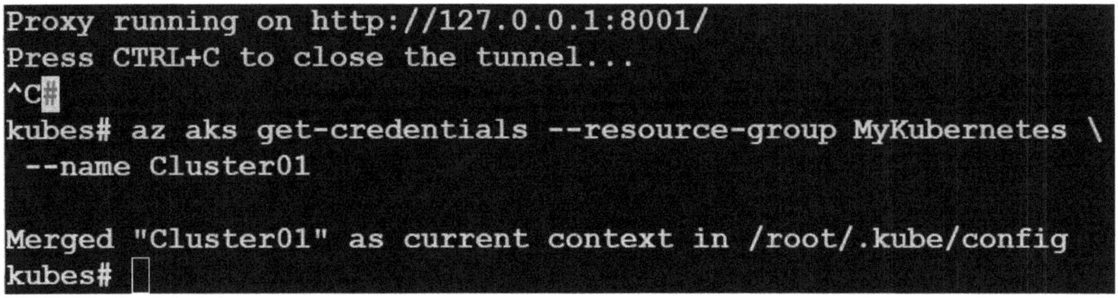

Figure 10.5: Merging the configuration into the local configuration file

Thanks to our fancy Command Prompt, you can see that we switched from our local Kubernetes cluster to the cluster in Azure. To see the available clusters, execute the following:

```
kubectl config get-contexts
```

The output of the preceding command is as follows:

```
kubes# kubectl config get-contexts
CURRENT    NAME       CLUSTER      AUTHINFO
*          Cluster01  Cluster01    clusterUser_MyKubernetes_Cluster01
           minikube   minikube     minikube
kubes#
```

Figure 10.6: Viewing the available clusters

You can switch to the other cluster using **kubectl config use-context <cluster>**.

You can also find information about your cluster using **kubectl**:

```
kubectl cluster-info
```

The output of the preceding command is as follows:

```
kubes# kubectl cluster-info
Kubernetes master is running at https://cluster01-mykubernetes-21b59b-00688edf.h
cp.eastus.azmk8s.io:443
CoreDNS is running at https://cluster01-mykubernetes-21b59b-00688edf.hcp.eastus.
azmk8s.io:443/api/v1/namespaces/kube-system/services/kube-dns:dns/proxy
kubernetes-dashboard is running at https://cluster01-mykubernetes-21b59b-00688ed
f.hcp.eastus.azmk8s.io:443/api/v1/namespaces/kube-system/services/kubernetes-das
hboard/proxy
Metrics-server is running at https://cluster01-mykubernetes-21b59b-00688edf.hcp.
eastus.azmk8s.io:443/api/v1/namespaces/kube-system/services/https:metrics-server
:/proxy

To further debug and diagnose cluster problems, use 'kubectl cluster-info dump'.
kubes#
```

Figure 10.7: Information about the cluster

We created a Kubernetes cluster here called **Cluster01** using the **az aks create** command. Now let's list the nodes, which are the worker machines of Kubernetes and are managed by a master node:

```
kubectl get nodes
```

The output of the preceding command is as follows:

```
kubes# kubectl get nodes
NAME                                STATUS    ROLES    AGE    VERSION
aks-nodepool1-16056130-vmss000000   Ready     agent    29m    v1.13.12
kubes#
```

Figure 10.8: Listing the nodes

First Deployment in AKS

AKS allows you to build and deploy applications into a managed Kubernetes cluster, which manages the connectivity and availability of your containerized application. You can use a simple **kubectl create** command to deploy a Docker container in AKS:

```
Kubectl createnginx --image=nginx --port=80
```

And within seconds, there is a message: **deployment.apps/nginx created**.

Verify the deployment using the following:

```
kubectl get deployment
```

The output of the preceding command is as follows:

```
PS /usr/local/bin> kubectl get deployment
NAME      READY    UP-TO-DATE    AVAILABLE    AGE
nginx     1/1      1             1            67s
PS /usr/local/bin>
```

Figure 10.9: Verifying the image deployment

When we executed the **run** command, the Docker container was deployed in the cluster. Or, more specifically, a pod was created with the container running in it. A pod is a group of containers with shared resources, such as storage and network resources and it also contains the specification for how to run the containers. To see the created pod, execute the following:

```
kubectl get pods
```

The output of the preceding command returns the list of pod names, pod statuses (running, pending, succeeded, failed, or unknown), the number of restarts, and the uptime, as follows:

```
PS /usr/local/bin> kubectl get pods
NAME                       READY   STATUS     RESTARTS   AGE
nginx-57867cc648-dkv28     1/1     Running    0          3m12s
PS /usr/local/bin>
```

Figure 10.10: Details of the pods

Pods come and go; they are created dynamically while scaling up/down, among other things. Using the **explain** command, you can find all kinds of information about the pod:

```
kubectl explain pods/nginx-57867cc648-dkv28
```

Let's delete the pod:

```
kubectl delete pod nginx-57867cc648-dkv28
```

Execute **kubectl get pods** again; you should see that a new pod is available.

Creating Services

But actually, you shouldn't care about the pod: the service is what's important. A service is an object that makes the application accessible to the outside world. Behind the service, there are one or more pods. The service keeps tracks of the pods and their IP addresses, and it is an abstraction of a logical set of pods and their policies. You can use the following command to list all the services in a namespace:

```
kubectl get services
```

The output of the preceding command is as follows:

```
PS /usr/local/bin> kubectl get services
NAME          TYPE        CLUSTER-IP   EXTERNAL-IP   PORT(S)    AGE
kubernetes    ClusterIP   10.0.0.1     <none>        443/TCP    3h47m
PS /usr/local/bin>
```

Figure 10.11: Listing all the services in a namespace

Only one service is found, **CLUSTER-IP**. More details can be found using the following command:

```
kubectl describe services/kubernetes
```

```
PS /usr/local/bin> kubectl describe services/kubernetes
Name:              kubernetes
Namespace:         default
Labels:            component=apiserver
                   provider=kubernetes
Annotations:       <none>
Selector:          <none>
Type:              ClusterIP
IP:                10.0.0.1
Port:              https   443/TCP
TargetPort:        443/TCP
Endpoints:         52.170.92.17:443
Session Affinity:  None
Events:            <none>
```

Figure 10.12: Getting the description of the Kubernetes services

Let's get rid of our first deployment:

```
kubectl delete deployment nginx
```

```
PS /usr/local/bin> kubectl delete deployment nginx
deployment.extensions "nginx" deleted
PS /usr/local/bin>
```

Figure 10.13: Deleting the first deployment

Let's create a new one:

```
kubectl run nginx --image=nginx
```

```
PS /usr/local/bin> kubectl run nginx --image=nginx
kubectl run --generator=deployment/apps.v1 is DEPRECATED and will be removed in
a future version. Use kubectl run --generator=run-pod/v1 or kubectl create inste
ad.
deployment.apps/nginx created
PS /usr/local/bin>
```

Figure 10.14: Creating a new nginx image

Please note that we didn't expose the ports. Let's list the pods using **kubectl get pods**. To make the resource accessible, we add a service of the **LoadBalancer** type:

```
kubectl expose pod <pod name> --port=80 --target-port=80 \
    --type=LoadBalancer
```

The output should be similar to the following:

```
PS /usr/local/bin> kubectl get services
NAME                    TYPE            CLUSTER-IP      EXTERNAL-IP     PORT(S)         AGE
kubernetes              ClusterIP       10.0.0.1        <none>          443/TCP         3h56m
nginx-7cdbd8cdc9-t2d4n  LoadBalancer    10.0.64.102     20.42.33.199    80:30372/TCP    67s
PS /usr/local/bin>
```

Figure 10.15: Listing the pods and adding a service of the LoadBalancer type

Use the **EXTERNAL-IP** address in your browser. It will show you the welcome page of **nginx**.

Multi-Container Pods

A pod is also an abstraction layer used by Kubernetes to maintain the container. There are many use cases and real-world scenarios to have multiple containers in a single pod to support microservices container applications to communicate with each other, as shown in the following diagram. The persistent storage in this diagram shows how each container communicates for read and write operations during the life of the pod and the shared persistent storage data is lost when you delete the pod:

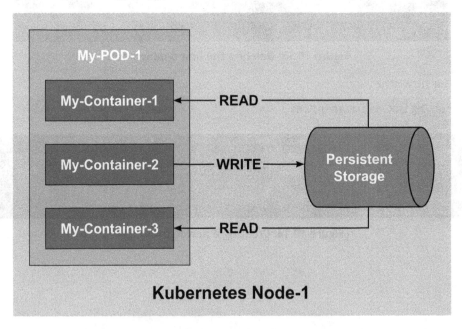

Figure 10.16: Architecture of multi-container pods

But there are use cases that are based on the fact that a pod provides shared resources for the containers within the pod, such as:

- Containers with helper applications such as logging and monitoring
- Reverse proxies

Until now, we used the **-image** parameter to create a simple pod. For a more complex pod, we need to make a specification in YAML format. Create a file called **myweb.yaml** with the following content:

```
apiVersion: v1
kind: Pod
metadata:
  name: myweb
spec:

restartPolicy: Never

  volumes:
  - name: logger
emptyDir: {}

  containers:
  - name: nginx
    image: nginx
volumeMounts:
    - name: logger
mountPath: /var/log/nginx
readOnly: false
  - name: logmachine
    image: ubuntu
volumeMounts:
    - name: logger
mountPath: /var/log/nginxmachine
```

In this file, a shared volume is created, called **journal**. The **emptydir** directive makes sure that the volume is created while creating the pod.

To verify, execute the following:

```
kubectl exec myweb -c nginxfindmnt | grep logger
```

This command executes in the **myweb** pod on the **nginx** container by using the **findmnt** command. We have created containers, pods, and shared storage. Now let's shift our focus to Helm, which is the package manager for Kubernetes.

> **Note**
>
> The preceding option cannot be used as a cluster solution and you should probably mount one of the containers' filesystems as read-only using the **mountOptions** flag.

Working with Helm

Helm (https://helm.sh and https://github.com/helm) is an application package manager for Kubernetes. You can compare it with **apt** and **yum** for Linux. It helps to manage Kubernetes using charts, which define, install, and upgrade the application you want to deploy on Kubernetes.

There are many charts available in Helm's GitHub repository and Microsoft, which is one of the biggest contributors to this project, also provides a repository with examples.

Installing Helm

If you are on an Ubuntu system, you have two choices—you can install Helm with a **snap** package or just download the binary from https://github.com/kubernetes/helm/releases. Using the binary works for every Linux distribution, and the **snap** repository doesn't always have the latest version of Helm. So, let's use https://github.com/helm/helm/releases to find the latest release of Helm and change **x** in the **helm-vx.x.x-linux-amd64.taz.gz** filename accordingly:

```
cd /tmp


wget https://storage.googleapis.com/kubernetes-helm/\
   helm-v2.9.1-linux-amd64.tar.gz


sudo tar xf helm-v2.9.1-linux-amd64.tar.gz --strip=1 -C \
   /usr/local/bin linux-amd64/helm
```

Always check for the latest release on the website and change the command accordingly.

macOS users can use Brew (https://brew.sh/):

```
brew install kubernetes-helm
```

The client is installed, and with this client, we can deploy the server part, Tiller, into our Kubernetes cluster:

```
helm init
```

```
kubes# helm init
Creating /root/.helm
Creating /root/.helm/repository
Creating /root/.helm/repository/cache
Creating /root/.helm/repository/local
Creating /root/.helm/plugins
Creating /root/.helm/starters
Creating /root/.helm/cache/archive
Creating /root/.helm/repository/repositories.yaml
Adding stable repo with URL: https://kubernetes-charts.storage.googleapis.com
Adding local repo with URL: http://127.0.0.1:8879/charts
$HELM_HOME has been configured at /root/.helm.

Tiller (the Helm server-side component) has been installed into your Kubernetes
Cluster.

Please note: by default, Tiller is deployed with an insecure 'allow unauthentica
ted users' policy.
For more information on securing your installation see: https://docs.helm.sh/usi
ng_helm/#securing-your-helm-installation
Happy Helming!
kubes#
```

Figure 10.17: Deploying Tiller into the Kubernetes Cluster

Verify the versions:

```
helm version
```

The output should be similar to the following:

```
➜ helm version
Client: &version.Version{SemVer:"v2.9.1", GitCommit:"20adb27c7c586846
64e7390ebe710", GitTreeState:"clean"}
Server: &version.Version{SemVer:"v2.9.1", GitCommit:"20adb27c7c586846
64e7390ebe710", GitTreeState:"clean"}
```

Figure 10.18: Verifying the Helm version

To allow Helm to get access to the Kubernetes cluster, a service account must be created with a corresponding role:

```
kubectl create serviceaccount \
   --namespace kube-system tiller
```

As shown in the following screenshot, we created Tiller service account in the **kube-system** namespace using the **kubectl create** command:

```
kubes# kubectl create serviceaccount --namespace kube-system tiller
serviceaccount/tiller created
kubes#
```

Figure 10.19: Creating Tiller service account in the kube-system namespace

Grant cluster-admin access to Kubernetes resources to perform administrative tasks:

```
kubectl create clusterrolebinding tiller-cluster-rule \
   --clusterrole=cluster-admin \
   --serviceaccount=kube-system:tiller
```

As shown in the following screenshot, you can create a custom role based on your requirements:

```
kubes# kubectl create clusterrolebinding tiller-cluster-rule --clusterrole=clust
er-admin --serviceaccount=kube-system:tiller
clusterrolebinding.rbac.authorization.k8s.io/tiller-cluster-rule created
kubes#
```

Figure 10.20: Creating a custom role

Helm is the client installed on your local machine and Tiller is the server that is installed on your Kubernetes. To reconfigure Helm—that is, to make sure the version of Tiller matches with your local Helm—execute:

```
helm init --service-account tiller --upgrade
```

Helm Repository Management

A Helm repository is an HTTP server that can serve YAML files and consists of packaged charts and **index.yml** hosted on the same server. There are two repositories that are added during installation:

- https://kubernetes-charts.storage.googleapis.com/
- http://127.0.0.1:8879/charts

Let's add the repository from Microsoft:

```
helm repo add azure \

  https://kubernetescharts.blob.core.windows.net/azure
```

```
kubes# helm repo add azure https://kubernetescharts.blob.core.windows.net/azure
"azure" has been added to your repositories
kubes#
```

Figure 10.21: Adding the repository from Microsoft

Check the available repositories:

```
helm repo list
```

The output should be similar to the following:

```
→helm repo list
NAME     URL
stable   https://kubernetes-charts.storage.googleapis.com
local    http://127.0.0.1:8879/charts
azure    https://kubernetescharts.blob.core.windows.net/azure
```

Figure 10.22: Checking the available repositories

To update the repository information, execute the following:

```
helm repo update
```

You can also remove repositories using the **remove** parameter.

Installing Applications with Helm

Let's see what is available in the repositories:

```
helm search wordpress
```

The output of the preceding command is as follows:

```
kubes# helm search wordpress
NAME                CHART VERSION    APP VERSION    DESCRIPTION
azure/wordpress     0.10.1           4.9.8          Web publishing platform
stable/wordpress    7.6.0            5.2.4          Web publishing platform
kubes#
```

Figure 10.23: Searching the wordpress repository

If you want information about the chart, how to use it, the available parameters, and so on, you can use the **helm inspect** command. For now, we're just going to deploy it:

```
helm install stable/wordpress
```

The installation output log from the preceding command contains the necessary details to access the **WordPress** instance.

Verify the status of the Helm charts in the cluster using the following command:

```
helm ls
```

The output of the preceding command returns the revision name, update timestamp, status, chart, and its namespace as follows:

```
kubes# helm ls
NAME                        REVISION    UPDATED                     STATUS      CHART           NAMESPACE
contrasting-chicken   1           Sun Nov   3 21:17:10 2019   DEPLOYED    wordpress-7.6.0 default
kubes#
```

Figure 10.24: Verifying the status of the Helm charts

Review the previous output of the installation process:

```
helm status contrasting-chicken
```

This command returns the deployment timestamp, namespace, and status, in addition to resource details such as **v1/PersistentVolumeClaim**, **v1/Service**, **extensions/Deployment**, **v1/Secret**, and the **connection** details of the database server:

```
kubes# helm status contrasting-chicken
LAST DEPLOYED: Sun Nov   3 21:17:10 2019
NAMESPACE: default
STATUS: DEPLOYED

RESOURCES:
==> v1/PersistentVolumeClaim
```

Figure 10.25: Reviewing the helm status

And, of course, **kubectl** will also show you the following results:

```
kubes# kubectl get deployment
NAME                                        READY    UP-TO-DATE    AVAILABLE    AGE
contrasting-chicken-wordpress   1/1      1             1            10m
nginx                                       1/1      1             1            10h
kubes#
```

Figure 10.26: Using kubectl to get the deployment details

The following screenshot shows the output of the **kubectl get service** command:

```
kubes# kubectl get service
NAME                             TYPE           CLUSTER-IP     EXTERNAL-IP      PORT(S)                       AGE
contrasting-chicken-mariadb      ClusterIP      10.0.73.195    <none>           3306/TCP                      12m
contrasting-chicken-wordpress    LoadBalancer   10.0.73.123    52.146.56.131    80:32212/TCP,443:31278/TCP    12m
kubernetes                       ClusterIP      10.0.0.1       <none>           443/TCP                       14h
nginx-7cdbd8cdc9-t2d4n           LoadBalancer   10.0.64.102    20.42.33.199     80:30372/TCP                  10h
kubes#
```

Figure 10.27: Output of the kubectl get service command

Let's remove our deployment (the name can be found using **helm ls**):

```
helm delete <NAME>
```

```
kubes# helm delete contrasting-chicken
release "contrasting-chicken" deleted
kubes#
```

Figure 10.28: Removing the deployment with the helm delete command

To customize the application, execute the following:

```
helm inspect stable/wordpress
```

Then, search for the WordPress settings:

```
podAnnotations: {}
## Prometheus Exporter / Metrics
##
metrics:
  enabled: false
  image:
    registry: docker.io
    repository: bitnami/apache-exporter
    tag: 0.7.0-debian-9-r86
    pullPolicy: IfNotPresent
    ## Optionally specify an array of imagePullSecrets.
    ## Secrets must be manually created in the namespace.
    ## ref: https://kubernetes.io/docs/tasks/configure-pod-container/pull-image-private-registry/
    ##
    # pullSecrets:
    #   - myRegistryKeySecretName
  ## Metrics exporter pod Annotation and Labels
  podAnnotations:
    prometheus.io/scrape: "true"
    prometheus.io/port: "9117"
  ## Metrics exporter resource requests and limits
  ## ref: http://kubernetes.io/docs/user-guide/compute-resources/
  ##
  # resources: {}
```

Figure 10.29: Searching for the WordPress settings

Create a YAML file, for instance, **custom.yaml**, with the following content:

```
image:
  registry: docker.io
  repository: bitnami/wordpress
  tag: 4-ol-7


wordpressUsername: linuxstar01
wordpressEmail: linuxstar01@example.com
wordpressFirstName: Kamesh
wordpressLastName: Ganesan
wordpressBlogName: Linux on Azure - 2nd Edition!
```

Then, deploy the WordPress application:

```
helm install stable/wordpress -f custom.yaml
```

You can verify the results using the **kubectl** command. First, get the Pod's name:

```
kubectl get pod
```

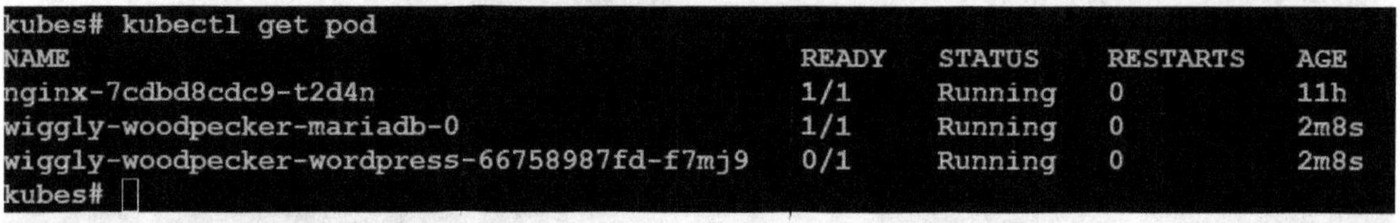

```
kubes# kubectl get pod
NAME                                            READY   STATUS     RESTARTS   AGE
nginx-7cdbd8cdc9-t2d4n                          1/1     Running    0          11h
wiggly-woodpecker-mariadb-0                     1/1     Running    0          2m8s
wiggly-woodpecker-wordpress-66758987fd-f7mj9    0/1     Running    0          2m8s
kubes# 
```

Figure 10.30: Verifying the deployment of the WordPress application

After that, execute the following:

```
kubectl describe pod <podname>
```

```
kubes# kubectl describe pod wiggly-woodpecker-wordpress-66758987fd-f7mj9
Name:            wiggly-woodpecker-wordpress-66758987fd-f7mj9
Namespace:       default
Priority:        0
Node:            aks-nodepool1-16056130-vmss000000/10.240.0.4
Start Time:      Sun, 03 Nov 2019 21:53:16 +0000
Labels:          app=wiggly-woodpecker-wordpress
                 chart=wordpress-7.6.0
                 pod-template-hash=66758987fd
                 release=wiggly-woodpecker
Annotations:     <none>
Status:          Running
IP:              10.244.0.15
IPs:             <none>
Controlled By:   ReplicaSet/wiggly-woodpecker-wordpress-66758987fd
Containers:
  wordpress:
    Container ID:   docker://29c3de6471803a91606ac1b75ba15f8017ef47d3876
    Image:          docker.io/bitnami/wordpress:4-ol-7
    Image ID:       docker-pullable://bitnami/wordpress@sha256:4f12df4cb
b37e1d5
    Ports:          80/TCP, 443/TCP
    Host Ports:     0/TCP, 0/TCP
    State:          Running
      Started:      Sun, 03 Nov 2019 21:54:19 +0000
    Ready:          True
```

Figure 10.31: Getting the pod description

For instance, in the **Events** section, you'll see that the **docker.io/bitnami/wordpress:4-ol-7** image is pulled.

Clean everything up:

```
helm delete stable/wordpress
```

```
kubectl scale sts --all --replicas=0
```

```
kubectl delete pod --all
```

```
kubectl delete sts --all --cascade=false
```

Don't bother about the stateful sets (**sts**); they were created by this application to have an ordered deployment and shared persistent storage.

Creating Helm Charts

Helm charts are similar to software packages used in Linux distributions and you can browse the package repository (chart) directory structure using the Helm client. There are many charts created for you, and it is also possible to create your own.

First, create a working directory and make it ready for use:

```
helm create myhelm
```

```
cd myhelm
```

The preceding command should give you a similar output:

```
kubes# cd myhelm
kubes# ls -al
total 28
drwxr-xr-x 4 root      root      4096 Nov  3 22:11 .
drwxr-xr-x 9 admin123  admin123  4096 Nov  3 22:11 ..
-rw-r--r-- 1 root      root       333 Nov  3 22:11 .helmignore
-rw-r--r-- 1 root      root       102 Nov  3 22:11 Chart.yaml
drwxr-xr-x 2 root      root      4096 Nov  3 22:11 charts
drwxr-xr-x 2 root      root      4096 Nov  3 22:11 templates
-rw-r--r-- 1 root      root      1021 Nov  3 22:11 values.yaml
kubes#
```

Figure 10.32: Creating a working directory

Some files and directories are created:

- The **Chart.yaml** file: This file contains basic information about the chart.

- The **values.yaml** file: The default configuration value.

- The **charts** directory: The dependency charts.

- The **templates** directory: This is used to create manifest files for Kubernetes

Additionally, you can add a **LICENSE** file, a **README.md** file, and a file with requirements, **requirements.yaml**.

Let's modify **Chart.yaml** a little bit:

```
apiVersion: v1

appVersion: 1.15.2

description: My First Nginx Helm

name: myhelm

version: 0.1.0

maintainers:

- name: Kamesh Ganesan

    email: kameshg@example.com

    url: http://packtpub.com
```

The file is more or less self-explanatory: the maintainers are optional. **appVersion** refers to the version of, in this example, nginx.

Verify the configuration with the following:

```
helm lint
```

Take some time to investigate the files in the **templates** directory and the **value.yaml** file. Of course, there is a reason why we used nginx as an example, because the files that are created by **helm create** also use nginx as an example.

First, execute a dry run:

```
helm install --dry-run --debug ../myhelm
```

This way, you can see the manifest that will be used to deploy the application. After that, you're ready to install it:

```
helm install ../myhelm
```

After the installation, we realized that looking at the dry run, there is something that is not OK: the version of nginx is **nginx: stable**, which is version 1.14.0. Open the **values.yaml** file and change **tag: stable** to **tag: 1.15.2**.

Use **helm ls** to find the name and update it:

```
helm upgrade <name> ../myhelm
```

A new pod will be created; the old one will be deleted:

Figure 10.33: Updating the pod version

There is even a **rollback** option if you want to revert back to your old version:

```
helm rollback <RELEASE> <REVISION>
```

You just need to specify the release and revision to which you want to revert.

Working with Draft

Helm is typically something you're going to use, as a developer, on applications that are more or less production-ready and should be maintained. It's also most likely that you hosted the code on a version control system such as GitHub.

This is where Draft (https://github.com/Azure/draft) comes in. It tries to streamline the process, starting with your code, in the Kubernetes cluster.

The tool is in heavy development. Draft is getting more popular and stable with new languages and features being added regularly.

If the development phase turns into something that seems to be usable, you can still use Draft, but it's more likely that you'll switch to Helm as well.

To find out what programming languages are supported by Draft, you can execute the following commands after the installation:

```
draft pack list
Available Packs:
  github.com/Azure/draft/clojure
  github.com/Azure/draft/csharp
  github.com/Azure/draft/erlang
  github.com/Azure/draft/go
  github.com/Azure/draft/gradle
  github.com/Azure/draft/java
  github.com/Azure/draft/javascript
  github.com/Azure/draft/php
  github.com/Azure/draft/python
  github.com/Azure/draft/ruby
  github.com/Azure/draft/rust
  github.com/Azure/draft/swift
```

Installing Draft

To be able to use Draft, Helm must be installed and configured.

Get your copy from https://github.com/Azure/draft/releases:

```
cd /tmp

wget https://azuredraft.blob.core.windows.net/draft/\
  draft-v0.15.0-linux-amd64.tar.gz

sudo tar xf draft-v0.15.0-linux-amd64.tar.gz --strip=1 \
  -C /usr/local/bin linux-amd64/draft
```

Always check for the latest release on the website and change the command accordingly.

macOS users can install it with Brew:

```
brew tap azure/draft && brew install draft
```

You can see that the developers who work on Helm are also involved with the development of Draft. In both cases, many of them are Microsoft developers. Similar to Helm, after installing the client, you have to initialize Draft:

```
draft init
```

This will install some default plugins and set up the repositories you can use within Draft.

Check the version with the following:

```
draft version
```

At the time of writing, its version is 0.16.0:

```
kubes% draft version
&version.Version{SemVer:"v0.16.0", GitCommit:"5433afea1421810ae9d8
kubes%
```

Figure 10.34: Checking the Draft version

The last step involves configuring a Docker repository, Docker Hub, or Azure. For the purposes of this book, we are using Azure.

Create an **Azure container registry (ACR)**:

```
az acr create --resource-group MyKubernetes --name LinuxStarACR --sku Basic
```

Log in to **LinuxStarACR**:

```
az acr login --name LinuxStarACR
```

```
kubes% az acr login --name LinuxStarACR
Login Succeeded
kubes%
```

Figure 10.35: Logging in to LinuxStarACR

Configure the repository:

```
draft config set registry LinuxStarACR
```

Log in to the registry:

```
az acr login --name LinuxStarACR
```

Create trust between Draft and the ACR:

```
export AKS_SP_ID=$(azaks show \
  --resource-group <resource group> \
  --name <Kubernetes Cluster>
  --query "servicePrincipalProfile.clientId" -o tsv)


export ACR_RESOURCE_ID=$(azacr show \
  --resource-group <resource group>\
  --name <ACR Name> --query "id" -o tsv)


az role assignment create --assignee $AKS_SP_ID --scope $ACR_RESOURCE_ID
--role contributor
```

We have successfully installed Draft v0.16.0 and created ACR. Finally, we created trust between Draft and ACR. It's time to go ahead and start using Draft.

Using Draft

Let's develop some simple Draft code. For this, we'll create a directory and name it **mynode**. In this directory, we'll create a file called **mynode.js** with the following code:

```
var http = require('http');


var server = http.createServer(function(req, res) {
res.writeHead(200);
res.end('Hello World!');
});
server.listen(8080);
```

This is a simple web server that serves a page saying **Hello World!**. We're in a very early stage of our development process. To create a **package.json** file, execute the following:

```
npminit
```

Fill in the information:

```
name: (mynode)
version: (1.0.0) 0.0.1
description: My first Node App
entry point: (mynode.js)
test command: node mynode.js
git repository:
keywords: webapp
author: Kamesh Ganesan
license: (ISC)
```

Now we are ready to execute Draft:

```
draft create
```

```
kubes% draft create
--> Draft detected JSON (60.687961%)
--> Could not find a pack for JSON. Trying to find the next likely language match
--> Draft detected JavaScript (39.312039%)
--> Ready to sail
kubes%
```

Figure 10.36: Creating a Dockerfile using the draft create command

This will create a Dockerfile and all the information for Helm.

The last line of the output, **Ready to sail**, actually means that you are ready to execute:

```
draft up
```

The preceding command generates the following output:

```
kubes% draft up
Draft Up Started: 'mynode': 01DRSZRPHEFQ7C50WR772KFH0R
mynode: Building Docker Image: SUCCESS ⚓  (108.0175s)
mynode: Pushing Docker Image \panic: send on closed channel

goroutine 61 [running]:
github.com/Azure/draft/pkg/builder/docker.(*Builder).Push.func1.1(0xc4203dbe20,
0xc4202ca090, 0x4, 0xc4200b0300, 0xc42024c310, 0xc420708000, 0x47)
        /go/src/github.com/Azure/draft/pkg/builder/docker/builder.go:134 +0x2af
created by github.com/Azure/draft/pkg/builder/docker.(*Builder).Push.func1
        /go/src/github.com/Azure/draft/pkg/builder/docker/builder.go:122 +0x149
kubes% 
```

Figure 10.37: Building and pushing the Docker image

This will build the image and release the application.

Executing **helm ls** will show the **mynode** application:

```
NAME     REVISION     UPDATED                  STATUS       CHART
mynode   1            Wed Aug  1 05:10:27 2018 DEPLOYED     javascript-v0.1.0
```

Figure 10.38: Getting the details of mynode application

Use **kubectl get services** to show the service:

```
✦ ➜ kubectl get services
NAME                 TYPE          CLUSTER-IP      EXTERNAL-IP     PORT(S)
kubernetes           ClusterIP     10.0.0.1        <none>          443/TCP
mynode-javascript    ClusterIP     10.0.156.106    <none>          8080/TCP
```

Figure 10.39: Using kubectl get services to display the service

Everything seems to be OK here, but **kubectl get pod** tells us otherwise:

```
✦ ➜ kubectl get pod
NAME                                      READY     STATUS
mynode-javascript-576bcfffbc-sd5dv        0/1       Error
```

Figure 10.40: Checking the status of the pod

The **draft logs** command doesn't show any errors. So, let's find out what Kubernetes thinks:

```
kubectl logs <Pod Name>
```

It states **npm ERR! missing script: start**. On purpose, we made a mistake in the **package.json** file. Change the content, modifying the values as per the following example:

```
{
"name": "mynode",
"version": "0.0.2",
"description": "My first Node App",
"main": "mynode.js",
"scripts": {
"start": "node mynode.js",
"test": "echo \"Error: no test specified\"& exit 1"
  },
"keywords": [
"webapp"
  ],
"author": "Kamesh Ganesan",
"license": "ISC"
}
```

Update the application by executing the following again:

```
draft update
```

Connect to the application:

```
draft connect
```

```
➡ draft connect
Connect to javascript:8080 on localhost:39053
[javascript]:
[javascript]: > mynode@0.0.2 start /usr/src/app
[javascript]: > node mynode.js
[javascript]:
```

Figure 10.41: Connecting to the application

Open another terminal:

```
curl localhost:39053
```

The output must be **Hello World!**.

Press *Ctrl* + C in the terminal, run **draft connect**, and remove the deployment:

```
draft delete
```

Check the cluster resources with **kubectl get all** and clean up, if needed.

Managing Kubernetes

We've created a Kubernetes cluster, and we've learned about the **kubectl** utility and about some of the tools that are available to develop and maintain your applications in a Kubernetes cluster.

So, if you look back at our three questions in the introduction of this chapter, we've answered the first question. In this section, we are going to answer the other two questions and also cover how to update the Kubernetes version.

Updating Applications

Earlier on, we used Helm and Draft to manage our application, which meant all the hard work was done for us. But you can also update the workload with the help of **kubectl**.

Normally, our cluster will be empty now, so let's quickly deploy our **nginx** pod again:

```
kubectl run nginx --image=nginx
```

Have a good look at the deployment:

```
kubes% kubectl get deployment
NAME       READY    UP-TO-DATE    AVAILABLE    AGE
nginx      1/1      1             1            22s
kubes% 
```

Figure 10.42: Deploying the nginx pod

This actually tells us that we wanted one instance, there is one running, it is up to date (the number of instances that were updated to match the desired capacity), and it is available. The version of nginx running is not the latest one, so we want to update it to version 1.17.5. Execute the following:

```
kubectl edit deployment/nginx
```

Change the image to **nginx:1.17.5**:

```
spec:
  containers:
  - image: nginx:1.17.5
    imagePullPolicy: Always
```

Figure 10.43: Changing the image to nginx:1.17.5

The **kubectl rollout** command can be used to manage your resource deployment. Some of the valid rollout options are status, history, pause, restart, resume and undo. **kubectl rollout status** displays the current status of a rollout whereas **kubectl rollout history** lists previous revisions and configurations.

```
kubectl rollout status deployment nginx
```

```
kubectl rollout history deployment nginx
```

Alternatively, even better, you can use the **describe** command, which provides you with a more detailed output than the preceding two commands combined:

```
kubectl describe deployment nginx
```

```
kubes% kubectl describe deployment nginx
Name:                   nginx
Namespace:              default
CreationTimestamp:      Mon, 04 Nov 2019 01:49:19 +0000
Labels:                 run=nginx
Annotations:            deployment.kubernetes.io/revision: 2
Selector:               run=nginx
Replicas:               1 desired | 1 updated | 1 total | 1 available | 0 unavailable
StrategyType:           RollingUpdate
MinReadySeconds:        0
RollingUpdateStrategy:  25% max unavailable, 25% max surge
Pod Template:
  Labels:   run=nginx
  Containers:
   nginx:
    Image:          nginx:1.17.5
```

Figure 10.44: Detailed information of the nginx deployment

Another way to update the deployment is by using the **set image** command to roll out the updated nginx containers with the new version, 1.17.5, of your deployment by updating the image as shown here:

```
kubectl set image deployment/nginxnginx=nginx:1.17.5 --record
```

As you can see from the preceding screenshot, the nginx container image has been upgraded to version 1.17.5 successfully.

Scaling Applications

At the moment, there is one pod running, but to handle all the load coming in, you may need more instances and to load balance the incoming traffic. To do so, you'll need replicas to define a specified number of pod replicas that are running at any given time.

Let's go back to **kubectl** and get the current deployment:

```
→ kubectl get deployment
NAME      DESIRED   CURRENT   UP-TO-DATE   AVAILABLE   AGE
nginx     1         1         1            1           19m
```

Figure 10.45: Getting the status of the current deployment

The desired (configured) state at this moment is 1. The current situation is 1 and there is 1 available.

To scale up to three instances, execute the following:

```
kubectl scale deployment nginx --replicas=3
```

Run **kubectl get deployments** again; after that, look at the available pods:

```
kubectl get pods -o wide
```

```
kubes% kubectl get pods -o wide
NAME                          READY   STATUS    RESTARTS   AGE     IP             NODE
  GATES
nginx-6b84c79449-k6r4t        1/1     Running   0          2m11s   10.244.0.25    aks-nodepool1-16056130-vmss000000
nginx-6b84c79449-nx488        1/1     Running   0          2m11s   10.244.0.26    aks-nodepool1-16056130-vmss000000
nginx-6b84c79449-qmk6c        1/1     Running   0          21m     10.244.0.24    aks-nodepool1-16056130-vmss000000
kubes% 
```

Figure 10.46: Checking the available pods after scaling up

Create a load balancer service:

```
kubectl expose deployment nginx --type=LoadBalancer \
  --name=nginx-lb --port 80
```

```
kubectl get services
```

```
kubes% kubectl get services
NAME          TYPE           CLUSTER-IP     EXTERNAL-IP   PORT(S)         AGE
kubernetes    ClusterIP      10.0.0.1       <none>        443/TCP         19h
nginx-lb      LoadBalancer   10.0.3.204     <pending>     80:31060/TCP    11s
kubes% 
```

Figure 10.47: Creating a load balancer service

Now every HTTP request is taken by the load balancer and traffic is spread over the instances.

You can also use autoscaling. First, install Metrics Server:

```
git clone https://github.com/kubernetes-incubator/metrics-server.git


kubectl create -f metrics-server/deploy/1.8+/
```

Configure autoscaling: if the load is above **50** percent, an extra instance is created, to a maximum of **10**:

```
kubectl autoscale deployment nginx --cpu-percent=50 --min=3 --max=10
```

Of course, in this scenario, it makes sense to have at least two nodes available in your cluster:

```
azaks scale --name Cluster01 \
  --resource-group MyKubernetes \
  --node-count 2


kubectl get nodes
```

Note that this process will take about 10 minutes. To view the status of the autoscaling, execute the following:

```
kubectl get hpa
```

```
kubes% kubectl get hpa
NAME     REFERENCE          TARGETS          MINPODS   MAXPODS   REPLICAS   AGE
nginx    Deployment/nginx   <unknown>/50%    3         10        3          4m5s
kubes% 
```

Figure 10.48: Listing the autoscalers

Upgrading Kubernetes

As with any software or application, you need to keep your Kubernetes clusters up to date by upgrading them regularly. Upgrading is very important to get the most recent bug fixes and all the critical security features along with the latest Kubernetes features. Having multiple nodes available is also necessary if you want to upgrade the Kubernetes control plane without downtime. The following steps will show you how to quickly upgrade your Kubernetes clusters.

First, view the current version:

```
az aks list --query "[].kubernetesVersion"
```

Figure 10.49: Viewing the current version of Kubernetes

Ask for the versions available in your location:

```
az aks get-versions --location eastus --output table | egrep "^1.13.12"
```

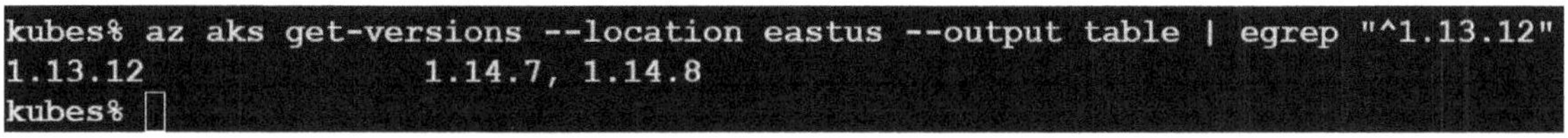

Figure 10.50: Available versions for East US location

We can upgrade to version 1.14.8:

```
az aks upgrade --resource-group MyKubernetes

  --name Cluster01 \

  --kubernetes-version 1.14.8 --yes --no-wait
```

Adding the **--no-wait** parameter has the effect that you'll get your prompt back almost directly.

This way, after about 3 minutes, you can start playing with **kubectl** to get the status of the nodes and pods (use the **-owide** parameter, for example, **kubectl get pods -o wide**) and find out that a new node has been created with the newest version. The workload is recreated on that node and the other node is updated. After that, the last one remaining is emptied and upgraded.

Persistent Storage

In the previous chapter, we stated that there are multiple ways to use persistent storage in our container, and we also referred to this in this chapter.

Kubernetes can configure persistent storage, but you have to provide it, for instance, via an NFS container or by implementing a StorSimple iSCSI Virtual Array (which is especially useful if you need read/write access from multiple containers). Even if you are using Azure Storage, there are many choices to make. Do you want to use disks or Azure Storage? Do you want to create them on the fly (dynamically) or use existing ones (statically)? Most of these questions are answered based on cost and the need for services such as replication, backup, and snapshots.

In this section, we want to cover the dynamic options; orchestration-wise, it's a better choice because you can do everything within Kubernetes (or using the tooling around it).

Whether you are using Azure Storage or disks, you'll need a storage account in the same resource group as Kubernetes:

```
az storage account create --resource-group MyKubernetes \
  --name mystorageest1 -sku Standard_LRS
```

Please revisit *Chapter 2, Getting Started with the Azure Cloud*, for the syntax of the preceding command. Remember that the name must be unique.

Azure Disk for Kubernetes

You can dynamically or statically provision persistent volume for use with one or many Kubernetes pods in an AKS cluster. There are two storage classes: standard Azure disk (the default) and premium Azure disk, which is a managed premium storage class:

1. First, create a YAML file to create the storage class. This makes it possible to automatically provision the storage:

   ```
   kind: StorageClass
   apiVersion: storage.k8s.io/v1
   metadata:
     name: storageforapp
   provisioner: kubernetes.io/azure-disk
   parameters:
   storageaccounttype: Standard_LRS
    location: eastus
    kind: shared
   ```

2. Apply it with the following:

```
kubectlapply -f storageclass.yaml
```

Replace the filename with the name of the file you just created.

3. Another YAML file is needed to claim the persistent volume, or in other words, create it:

```
kind: PersistentVolumeClaim
apiVersion: v1
metadata:
  name: claim-storage-for-app
  annotations:
volume.beta.kubernetes.io/storage-class: storageforapp
spec:
accessModes:
  - ReadWriteOnce
  resources:
    requests:
      storage: 5Gi
```

4. Please note that the match is made in the annotations. Apply this file as well:

```
kubectlapply -f persistentvolume.yaml
```

5. Verify the result with the following:

```
kubectl get sc
```

```
kubes% kubectl get sc
NAME                     PROVISIONER                 AGE
default (default)        kubernetes.io/azure-disk    20h
managed-premium          kubernetes.io/azure-disk    20h
storageforapp            kubernetes.io/azure-disk    11m
kubes%
```

Figure 10.51: Verifying the creation of the storage class

6. To use the storage in a pod, you can use it in a similar way to the following example:

```
kind: Pod
apiVersion: v1
metadata:
  name: my-web
spec:
  containers:
    - name: nginx
      image: nginx
volumeMounts:
    - mountPath: "/var/www/html"
      name: volume
  volumes:
    - name: volume
persistentVolumeClaim:
claimName: claim-storage-for-app
```

Azure Files for Kubernetes

When you mount your Azure disk with access mode type **ReadWriteOnce**, then it will be available to only a single pod in AKS. As such, you need to use Azure Files to share a persistent volume across multiple pods. The configuration for Azure Files is not that different than Azure Disk, as described in the preceding section. The YAML file to create the storage class is as follows:

```
kind: StorageClass

apiVersion: storage.k8s.io/v1

metadata:

  name: azurefile

provisioner: kubernetes.io/azure-file
```

```
mountOptions:
  - dir_mode=0888
  - file_mode=0888
  - uid=1000
  - gid=1000
  - mfsymlinks
  - nobrl
  - cache=none
parameters:
skuName: Standard_LRS
```

Use the persistent volume claim to provision the Azure file share by executing the following YAML file:

```
apiVersion: v1
kind: PersistentVolumeClaim
metadata:
  name: azurefile
spec:
accessModes:
    - ReadWriteMany
storageClassName: azurefile
  resources:
    requests:
      storage: 5Gi
```

Apply these two YAML files as follows:

```
kubes% vi azurefile.yaml
kubes% kubectl apply -f azurefile.yaml
storageclass.storage.k8s.io/azurefile created
kubes% vi azurefile.yaml
kubes% vi azurefile-claim.yaml
kubes% kubectl apply -f azurefile-claim.yaml
persistentvolumeclaim/azurefile created
```

Figure 10.52: Using the persistent volume claim to create Azure file

The result of executing the Azure file storage creation YAML and the storage volume claim YAML is as follows:

```
kubes% kubectl get sc
NAME                    PROVISIONER                     AGE
azurefile               kubernetes.io/azure-file        3m13s
default (default)       kubernetes.io/azure-disk        20h
managed-premium         kubernetes.io/azure-disk        20h
storageforapp           kubernetes.io/azure-disk        26m
kubes%
```

Figure 10.53: Verifying the creation of Azure files and Azure disks

As you can see, the specification in the pod remains the same. With these step-by-step implementations, we have successfully created Azure disks and Azure files for our persistent storage requirements.

Summary

This chapter was all about Kubernetes. We started this chapter by describing a possible work environment for a developer: a good workstation with tooling to start local development, even with Kubernetes locally installed. We used Ubuntu Desktop as an example, but in fact, it doesn't really matter as long as you are happy with your development environment.

With everything in place locally, we covered the configuration of Kubernetes clusters in Azure using the Azure CLI and PowerShell.

The deployment of workloads in Azure can be as simple as executing **kubectl run**, but more complex scenarios were also explored, such as multi-container applications.

As a developer, two tools are available to help streamline your development process: Draft and Helm. Draft is used for the initial development phase, and Helm is used afterward to install and maintain the application.

Kubernetes is a tool for managing your containers, making it easy to deploy, maintain, and update your workloads. Scalability is one of the advantages of using Kubernetes; it's even possible to automatically scale depending on the required CPU and memory resources.

The last section of this chapter covered the use of persistent storage in Kubernetes, actually providing you with a much better way than storing data in a container or attaching storage directly to a container.

In the next chapter, we're going back to the Ops part of DevOps – that is, troubleshooting and monitoring your workloads, and by workloads, we mean virtual machines with Linux installed, containers, and AKS.

Questions

1. What is a pod?

2. What would be a good reason to create a multiple-container pod?

3. What methods can you use to deploy your application in Kubernetes?

4. What methods can you use to update your application in Kubernetes?

5. Do you need to create extra nodes in Kubernetes if you want to upgrade the control plane?

6. Can you think of any reason why you would want an iSCSI solution?

7. As an exercise, recreate the multi-container pod using persistent storage.

Further Reading

The goal of this chapter was to provide a practical approach to get your workload running in the Azure cloud. We hope it's the beginning of a journey into the world of Kubernetes for you. There is so much more to discover!

Nigel Poulton, an author who has already written a great book about Docker, has also written a book about Kubernetes, *The Kubernetes Book*. It's a good starting point if you are really new to Kubernetes. Gigi Sayfan has written *Mastering Kubernetes*. Make sure you buy the second edition! Not only because the first edition was not that good, but just because it's a must-have and provides much more information than the first edition.

As a developer, you should give *Kubernetes for Developers* a try: Joseph Heck can tell you much more about the development life cycle using Kubernetes, using examples in Node.js and Python. In the last chapter of his book, he mentions emerging projects such as Helm and Brigade. We hope this will be explored in more detail in a later edition, or maybe even in another book.

Talking about Brigade, https://brigade.sh is described on its own website as "*a tool for running scriptable, automated tasks in the cloud — as part of your Kubernetes cluster.*" It's far beyond the scope of this book and it's more or less in the early stages of development. As a developer, you should invest some time in reading more about it and trying it.

Last but not least, another important source worth mentioning is the Open Service Broker for Azure (OSBA: https://osba.sh). It didn't make it into this chapter because it's not completely production-ready at the time of writing. OSBA is an open standard for communicating with external services such as databases and storage. It's another solution for providing data to and storing data from your container.

11

Troubleshooting and Monitoring Your Workloads

Troubleshooting and logging are very much related; you start analyzing the Event, Service and System logs when you experience problems.

Troubleshooting problems and fixing the problems found in a cloud environment can be different from troubleshooting in more classic deployments. This chapter explains the differences, the challenges, and the new possibilities of troubleshooting Linux workloads in the Azure environment.

By the end of this chapter, you'll be able to:

- Achieve performance analysis in a Linux system using different tools.
- Monitor metrics such as CPU, memory, storage, and network details.
- Use Azure tooling to identify and fix problems.
- Use Linux tooling to identify and fix problems.

Technical Requirements

For this chapter, you'll need one or two VMs running a Linux distribution. You can use the smallest size if you want. The **audit** daemon must be installed and, for the purpose of having audit system logs to analyze and understand, it's a good idea to install Apache and a MySQL/MariaDB server.

Here is an example in CentOS:

```
sudo yum groups install ''Basic Web Server''

sudo yum install mariadbmariadb-server

sudo yum install setroubleshoot

sudosystemctl enable --now apache2

sudosystemctl enable --now mariadb
```

auditd gives in-depth details about your server performance and activity by using audit rules that can be modified based on your needs. To install **audit** daemon, use the following:

```
sudo yum list audit audit-libs
```

On executing the preceding command, you'll get the following output:

```
[root@centos01 admin123]# sudo yum list audit audit-libs
Loaded plugins: fastestmirror, langpacks
Loading mirror speeds from cached hostfile
Installed Packages
audit.x86_64                        2.8.5-4.el7                        @os
audit-libs.x86_64                   2.8.5-4.el7                        @os
Available Packages
audit-libs.i686                     2.8.5-4.el7                        base
[root@centos01 admin123]# 
```

Figure 11.1: Installing the audit daemon

If you can see the list of installed audit packages as shown previously, then it's installed already; if not, then run the following command:

```
sudo yum install audit audit-libs
```

After installing **auditd** successfully, you need to start the **auditd** service to start collecting audit logs and then store the logs:

```
sudo systemctl start auditd
```

If you want to start **auditd** at boot time, then you have to use the following command:

```
sudo systemctl enable auditd
```

Now let's verify whether **auditd** is successfully installed and has started collecting logs using the following command:

```
tail -f /var/log/audit/audit.log
```

Figure 11.2: Verifying the successful installation of auditd and collection of logs

In this chapter, we will cover general Azure management and Azure Monitor. The Log Analytics agent for Linux, which is needed to collect information from the VM, is not supported in every Linux distribution; please visit https://docs.microsoft.com/en-us/azure/virtual-machines/extensions/oms-linux before making a decision about which distribution you want to use in this chapter.

> Note
>
> **Operations Management Suite** (**OMS**) in general was retired and transitioned to Azure and the name "OMS" is not used anywhere anymore, except in some variable names. It is now known as Azure Monitor. For more information on naming and terminology changes, please refer to https://docs.microsoft.com/en-gb/azure/azure-monitor/terminology, or you can also get detailed information about the transition at https://docs.microsoft.com/en-us/azure/azure-monitor/platform/oms-portal-transition.

Accessing Your System

Learning to troubleshoot your workloads will help you in your daily job. Troubleshooting in Azure is not different from doing so in other environments. In this section, we are going to see some tips and tricks that will help you in your daily job.

No Remote Access

When you don't have access to your Azure VM via SSH, you can run commands via the Azure portal.

To run a command on your Azure VM from the Azure portal, log in to your Azure portal, navigate to your VM and select **Run Command**:

Run Command uses the VM agent to let you run a script inside this virtual machine. This can be helpful for troubleshooting and recovery, and for general machine and application maintenance. Select a command below to see details.

NAME	DESCRIPTION
RunShellScript	Executes a Linux shell script
ifconfig	List network configuration

Figure 11.3: Navigating to the VM section within the Azure portal

Alternatively, you can use the command line, as follows:

```
az vm run-command invoke --name <vm name> \
  --command-id RunShellScript \
  --scripts hostnamectl \
  --resource-group <resource group>
```

The **az vm run** command can be used to run shell scripts in your VM for general machine or application management and to diagnose issues.

Whether you are doing it via the command line or via the Azure portal, the **az vm** command only works if the Microsoft Azure Linux agent is still running and reachable.

> **Note**
>
> You can get the latest Microsoft Azure PowerShell repository at https://github.com/Azure/azure-powershell, which has the installation steps and its usage. **az** is replacing AzureRM and all the new Azure PowerShell features will be available only in **az** going forward.

As per the security best practice, you need to change the password by logging in to your Azure account and using **az vm user** to reset the password as follows:

```
az vm user update \
   --resource-group myResourceGroup \
   --name myVM \
   --username linuxstar \
   --password myP@88w@rd
```

This only works if you have a user that is configured with a password. If you deployed your VM with SSH keys, then you are lucky: the **Reset password** option in the same section will do the job.

This option uses the VMAccess extension (https://github.com/Azure/azure-linux-extensions/tree/master/VMAccess). Like the **Run command** option discussed earlier, it needs the Azure VM Agent.

Working on the Port

The reason that you don't have remote access may be network-related. In *Chapter 5, Advanced Linux Administration*, the **ip** command was briefly introduced in the *Networking* section. You can use this command to verify the IP address and the route table.

On the Azure site, the network and the network security groups must be checked, as covered in *Chapter 3, Basic Linux Administration*. In the VM, you can use the **ss** command, such as **ip**, which is a part of the **iproute2** package to list the UPD (**-u**) and TCP (**p**) ports in a listening state, together with the process ID (**-p**) that opened the port:

```
[linuxstar@centos01 ~]$ ss -tulpn
Netid  State     Recv-Q Send-Q Local Address:Port              Peer Address:Port
udp    UNCONN    0      0          *:56260                      *:*
udp    UNCONN    0      0          *:42307                      *:*
udp    UNCONN    0      0          *:40604                      *:*
udp    UNCONN    0      0          *:57342                      *:*
udp    UNCONN    0      0          *:32801                      *:*
udp    UNCONN    0      0          *:68                         *:*
udp    UNCONN    0      0          *:43100                      *:*
udp    UNCONN    0      0          *:111                        *:*
udp    UNCONN    0      0      127.0.0.1:323                        *:*
udp    UNCONN    0      0      127.0.0.1:25229                      *:*
udp    UNCONN    0      0          *:58110                      *:*
udp    UNCONN    0      0          *:49919                      *:*
udp    UNCONN    0      0          *:842                        *:*
udp    UNCONN    0      0       [::]:111                     [::]:*
udp    UNCONN    0      0       [::1]:323                    [::]:*
udp    UNCONN    0      0       [::]:842                     [::]:*
tcp    LISTEN    0      100    127.0.0.1:25                         *:*
tcp    LISTEN    0      50         *:3306                       *:*
tcp    LISTEN    0      10     127.0.0.1:29130                      *:*
tcp    LISTEN    0      128        *:111                        *:*
```

Figure 11.4: Using the ss -tulpn command to check the ports

A quick check on the firewall rules can be done with `firewall-cmd --list-all --zone=public`; if you have multiple zones and interfaces, you need to execute this for every zone. To include the rules created by Azure Service Fabric, `iptables-save` can help:

```
[linuxstar@centos01 ~]$ sudo iptables-save
# Generated by iptables-save v1.4.21 on Wed Nov  6 07:04:50 2019
*security
:INPUT ACCEPT [8264:15594580]
:FORWARD ACCEPT [0:0]
:OUTPUT ACCEPT [7566:2599148]
-A OUTPUT -d 168.63.129.16/32 -p tcp -m owner --uid-owner 0 -j ACCEPT
-A OUTPUT -d 168.63.129.16/32 -p tcp -m conntrack --ctstate INVALID,NEW -j DROP
COMMIT
# Completed on Wed Nov  6 07:04:50 2019
[linuxstar@centos01 ~]$ []
```

Figure 11.5: Including the rules created by Azure Service Fabric

Unfortunately, there is no comment available to see all the access rules configured at the **systemd** unit level. Don't forget to verify them, as discussed in *Chapter 6, Managing Linux Security and Identities*.

Using nftables

nftables is easier to use than **iptables** and it combines the whole **iptables** framework with a simple syntax. **nftables** is built on a kernel **netfilter** subsystem that can be used to create grouped, complex filtering rules. nftables has many advantages over **iptables**. For instance, it allows you to perform multiple actions using a single rule. It uses the **nft** command-line tool, which can be used in interactive mode as well by using the **nft -i** command:

1. Install **nftables** using the following command:

    ```
    sudo apt install nftables
    ```

2. Then install **compat**, which loads the compatibility with the **nftables** kernel subsystem:

    ```
    apt install iptables-nftables-compat
    ```

3. Finally, enable the **nftables** service using the following command:

    ```
    sudo systemctl enable nftables.service
    ```

4. You can view the current **nft** configuration using this:

    ```
    nft list ruleset
    ```

5. Also, you can log into **nft** interactive mode using the following command:

    ```
    nft -i
    ```

6. Now you can list the existing ruleset by using the following **list** command:

    ```
    nft> list ruleset
    ```

7. Let's create a new table, **rule_table1**:

    ```
    nft>add table inet rule_table1
    ```

8. Now we will need to add the chain command to accept inbound/outbound traffic as follows:

    ```
    nft>add chain inet rule_table1 input { type filter hook input priority 0 ;
    policy accept; }
    ```

    ```
    nft>add chain inet rule_table1 output { type filter hook input priority 0 ;
    policy accept; }
    ```

9. You can use the following command to add rules to accept TCP (Transmission Control Protocol) ports:

```
nft>add rule inet rule_table1 input tcpdport { ssh, telnet, https, http }
accept
```

```
nft>add rule inet rule_table1 output tcpdport { https, http } accept
```

10. Here is the output of our new **nftables** configuration:

```
nft> list ruleset
```

```
table inet rule_table1 {
        chain input {
                type filter hook input priority 0; policy accept;
tcpdport { ssh, telnet, http, https } accept
        }

        chain output {
                type filter hook input priority 0; policy accept;
tcpdport { http, https } accept
        }
}
```

Boot Diagnostics

Let's say you've created your VM, probably orchestrated, and most likely it's your own VM, but it doesn't boot.

Before enabling the boot diagnostics on your VMs, you'll need a storage account to be able to store the data. You can list the storage accounts that are already available with the **az storage account list** and, if needed, you can create one with the **az storage account create** command.

Now let's enable the boot diagnostics by entering the following command in the Azure CLI:

```
az vm boot-diagnostics enable --name <vm name>\
  --resource-group <resource group> \
  --storage <url>
```

The difference is that you don't need the name of the storage account, but the name of the storage blob, which can be found with the **az storage account list** command as a property of the storage account.

Execute the following in the Azure CLI to receive the boot log:

```
az vm boot-diagnostics get-boot-log \
--name <virtual machine> \
  --resource-group <resource group>
```

The output is also automatically stored in a file; in the Azure CLI, it's a good idea to pipe it through **less** or redirect it to a file.

Logging in Linux

Many processes, services, and applications run on typical Linux systems, which produce different logs, such as application, event, service, and system logs, that can be used for auditing and troubleshooting. In earlier chapters, we encountered the **journalctl** command, which is used for querying and displaying logs. In this chapter, we'll discuss this command in much more detail and look at how you can slice and dice your logs using the **journalctl** utility.

In Linux distributions, such as the latest versions of RHEL/CentOS, Debian, Ubuntu, and SUSE, which use systemd as their **init** system, the **systemd-journald** daemon is used for logging. This daemon collects the standard output of a unit, a syslog message, and (if the application supports it) directs messages from the application to systemd.

The logs are collected in a database that can be queried with **journalctl**.

Working with journalctl

If you execute **systemctl status <unit>**, you can see the last entries of the log. To see the full log, **journalctl** is the tool that you need. There is a difference with **systemctl**: you can view the status on other hosts using the **-H** parameter. You can't use **journalctl** to connect to other hosts. Both utilities have the **-M** parameter to connect to the **systemd-nspawn** and **Rkt** containers.

To view the entries in the journal database, execute this:

```
Sudo journalctl --unit <unit>
```

```
[admin123@centos01 ~]$ sudo journalctl --unit atd.service
-- Logs begin at Wed 2019-11-06 05:53:21 UTC, end at Wed 2019-11-06 08:35:31 UTC
Nov 06 05:53:36 localhost.localdomain systemd[1]: Started Job spooling tools.
```

Figure 11.6: Viewing the entries in the journal database

By default, the log is paged with **less**. If you want another pager, such as **more**, then you can configure it via the **/etc/environment** file. Add the following line:

```
SYSTEMD_PAGER=/usr/bin/more
```

Here is an example of the output:

```
[root@centos01 admin123]# sudo journalctl -u sshd
-- Logs begin at Wed 2019-11-27 11:01:43 UTC, end at Wed 2019-11-27 11:28:06 UTC. --
Nov 27 11:01:57 centos01 systemd[1]: Starting OpenSSH server daemon...
Nov 27 11:01:57 centos01 sshd[924]: Server listening on 0.0.0.0 port 22.
Nov 27 11:01:57 centos01 sshd[924]: Server listening on :: port 22.
Nov 27 11:01:57 centos01 systemd[1]: Started OpenSSH server daemon.
Nov 27 11:15:16 centos01 sshd[5655]: reverse mapping checking getaddrinfo for 104-136-48-216.re
```

Figure 11.7: Using the journalctl command to get the log entries of the processes

Let's examine the output:

- The first column is the timestamp. In the database, it's defined in EPOCH time, so if you change your time zone, no problem: it will be translated.

- The second column is the hostname, as shown by the **hostnamectl** command.

- The third column contains an identifier and the process ID.

- The fourth column is the message.

You can add the following parameters to filter the logs:

- **--dmesg**: Kernel messages, a replacement for the old **dmesg** command

- **--identifier**: Identifier string

- **--boot**: Messages during the current boot process; you can also select previous boots if the database is persistent across reboots

Filters

Of course, you can **grep** on the standard output, but **journalctl** has some parameters that really help to filter out the information you want:

- **--priority**: Filter on **alert**, **crit**, **debug**, **emerg**, **err**, **info**, **notice**, and **warning**. The classification of these priorities is the same as in the syslog protocol specification.

- **--since** and **--until**: Filter on timestamp. Refer to **man systemd.time** to see all the possibilities.

- **--lines**: Number of lines, similar to **tail**.

- **--follow**: Similar behavior to **tail -f**.

- **--reverse**: Puts the last line first.

- **--output**: Changes the output format to formats such as JSON, or adds more verbosity to the output.

- **--catalog**: Adds an explanation of the message if one is available.

All the filters can be combined, as here:

```
sudo journalctl -u sshd --since yesterday --until 10:00 \
  --priority err
```

```
[admin123@centos01 ~]$ sudo journalctl -u sshd --since yesterday --until "1 minu
te ago"
-- Logs begin at Wed 2019-11-06 05:53:21 UTC, end at Wed 2019-11-06 08:45:05 UTC
Nov 06 05:53:40 localhost.localdomain systemd[1]: Starting OpenSSH server daemon
Nov 06 05:53:40 localhost.localdomain sshd[983]: Server listening on 0.0.0.0 por
Nov 06 05:53:40 localhost.localdomain sshd[983]: Server listening on :: port 22.
Nov 06 05:53:40 localhost.localdomain systemd[1]: Started OpenSSH server daemon.
Nov 06 05:53:49 centos01 systemd[1]: Stopping OpenSSH server daemon...
Nov 06 05:53:49 centos01 systemd[1]: Stopped OpenSSH server daemon.
Nov 06 05:53:49 centos01 systemd[1]: Starting OpenSSH server daemon...
Nov 06 05:53:49 centos01 sshd[1378]: Server listening on 0.0.0.0 port 22.
Nov 06 05:53:49 centos01 sshd[1378]: Server listening on :: port 22.
Nov 06 05:53:49 centos01 systemd[1]: Started OpenSSH server daemon.
```

Figure 11.8: Filtering the log entries by using multiple filters with journalctl

Filtering Based on Fields

We can also filter on fields. Type this:

```
sudojournactl _
```

Now press *Ctrl* + *I* twice; you'll see all the available fields. The same principle applies to these filters; that is, you can combine them:

```
sudo journalctl _UID=1000 _PID=1850
```

You can even combine them with normal filters:

```
sudo journalctl _KERNEL_DEVICE=+scsi:5:0:0:0 -o verbose
```

Database Persistence

Now you may need to store the logs for a certain period of time for compliance reasons or audit requirements. So, you can use an Azure Log Analytics agent to collect logs from different sources. By default, the logging database is not persistent. To make it persistent, for any audit- or compliance-related reason (though it is not a best practice to store the logs in localhost), you have to edit the configuration file, **/etc/systemd/journald.conf**.

Change the **#Storage=auto** line to this:

```
Storage=persistent
```

Restart the **systemd-journald** daemon with **force**:

```
sudo systemctl force-reload systemd-journald
```

Use this to view the recorded boots:

```
sudo journalctl --list-boots
```

```
[admin123@centos01 ~]$ sudo journalctl --list-boots
 0 c6c834bf52b64db1b27b5b17d55433d7 Wed 2019-11-06 05:53:21 UTC—Wed 2019-11-06 0
```

Figure 11.9: Viewing the recorded boots

You can add the boot ID as a filter using the **--boot** parameter:

```
journalctl --priority err --boot <boot id>
```

By this means, the output of **hostnamectl** shows the current boot ID.

The journal database is not dependent on the daemon. You can view it using the **--directory** and **--file** parameters.

Syslog Protocol

Logging in Linux and other members of the Unix family was enabled during the implementation of the syslog protocol. It is still used to send logging to remote services.

It is important to understand that this protocol uses facilities and severity. Both are standardized in RFC 5424 (https://tools.ietf.org/html/rfc5424). Here, a facility specifies the type of program that is logging the message; for instance, the kernel or cron. The severity label is there to describe the impact, such as informational or critical.

The programmers' man page for syslog (**man 3 syslog**) also gives a good insight into these facilities and severities and shows how a program can use this protocol. The bad news about syslog is that it only works if the application supports it and the application runs long enough to provide this functionality. **journald** is able to get everything regarding the output of a program.

Adding Log Entries

You can manually add entries to a log. For syslog, the **logger** command is available:

```
logger -p <facility.severity> "Message"
```

For **journald**, there is **systemd-cat**:

```
systemd-cat --identifier <identifier> --priority <severity><command>
```

Let's look at an example:

```
systemd-cat --identifier CHANGE --priority info \
   echo "Start Configuration Change"
```

As an identifier, you can use free strings or syslog facilities. Both **logger** and **systemd-cat** can be used to generate entries in your log. You can use this if the application doesn't have syslog support; for instance, in an Apache configuration, you can use this directive:

```
errorlog  "tee -a /var/log/www/error/log  | logger -p local6.info"
```

You can also use this as a part of change management.

Integrating journald with RSYSLOG

To collect your data for your own monitoring service, your monitoring service needs syslog support. Good examples of these monitoring services are available as a ready-to-go VM in Azure: **Splunk** and the **Elastic Stack**.

RSYSLOG is the most commonly used syslog protocol implementation nowadays. It's already installed by default in Ubuntu-, SUSE-, and Red Hat–based distributions.

RSYSLOG can work very well together with the journal database using the `imjournal` module. In SUSE- and Red Hat–based distributions, this is already configured; in Ubuntu, you have to make a modification to the **/etc/rsyslog.conf** file:

```
# module(load="imuxsock")


module(load="imjournal")
```

After the modification, restart RSYSLOG:

```
sudo systemctl restart rsyslog
```

Using the settings in **/etc/rsyslog.d/50-default.conf**, it logs to plain text files.

To send everything coming from the local syslog to a remote syslog server, you have to add the following to this file:

```
*. *   @<remote server>:514
```

> **Note**
>
> This is the name of the file in Ubuntu. In other distributions, use **/etc/rsyslog.conf**.

Use `@@` if you want TCP instead of the UDP protocol.

Other Log Files

You can find log files of applications that don't support syslog or `systemd-journald` in the **/var/log** directory structure. One important file to notice is the **/var/log/waagent.log** file, which contains the logging from the Azure Linux VM agent. There is also the **/var/log/azure** directory, which contains logging from other Azure agents (such as Azure Monitor) and VM extensions.

Azure Log Analytics

Azure Log Analytics is a part of Azure Monitor that collects and analyzes log data and takes the appropriate actions. It is a service in Azure that collects log data from multiple systems in a single data store in a central place. It consists of two important components:

- The Azure Log Analytics portal, with alerts, reports, and analysis features

- The Azure Monitor agent, which needs to be installed on a VM

There is also a mobile app available (in the iOS and Android store, you can find it under the name *Microsoft Azure*) if you want to view the state of your workloads while you are on the go.

Configuring the Log Analytics Service

In the Azure portal, select **All Services** from the left-hand bar and search for **Log Analytics**. Select **Add** and create a new Log Analytics workspace. At the time of writing, it is not available in all regions. Using the service is not limited to the region; if a VM is in another region, you can still monitor it.

> **Note**
>
> There is no upfront cost for this service and you pay for what you use! Read http:// aka.ms/PricingTierWarning for more details.

Another way to create the service is with the Azure CLI:

```
az extension add -n application-insights
```

After the creation of the service, there is a pop-up that allows you to navigate to the newly created resource. Alternatively, you can search again in **All Services**.

Please note, at the top-right of the resource pane, Azure Monitor and the workspace ID; you'll need this information later on. Navigate to **Advanced settings** to find the workspace key.

In the Azure CLI, you can collect this information using the following:

```
az monitor app-insights component create --app myapp
    --location westus1
    --resource-group my-resource-grp
```

To list all the workspaces of your Azure subscription, you can use the following Azure CLI command:

```
az ml workspace list
```

You can get detailed information about a workspace in JSON format using the following Azure CLI command:

```
az ml workspace show -w my-workspace -g my-resource-grp
```

Installing the Azure Log Analytics Agent

Before installing the Azure Monitor agent, make sure that the **audit** package (in **auditd**) is installed.

To install the Azure Monitor agent in a Linux VM, you have two possibilities: enable the VM extension **OMSAgentforLinux**, or download and install the Log Analytics Agent in Linux.

First, set some variables to make the scripting easier:

```
$rg = "<resource group>"
$loc = "<vm location>"
$omsName = "<OMS Name>"
$vm = "<vm name">
```

You need the workspace ID and key. The **Set-AzureVMExtension** cmdlet needs the keys in JSON format, so a conversion is needed:

```
$omsID = $(Get-AzOperationalInsightsWorkspace '
  -ResourceGroupName $rg -Name $omsName.CustomerId)


$omsKey = $(Get-AzOperationalInsightsWorkspaceSharedKeys '
  -ResourceGroupName $rg -Name $omsName).PrimarySharedKey
```

```
$PublicSettings = New-Object psobject | Add-Member '
  -PassThruNotePropertyworkspaceId $omsId | ConvertTo-Json


$PrivateSettings = New-Object psobject | Add-Member '
  -PassThruNotePropertyworkspaceKey $omsKey | ConvertTo-Json
```

Now you can add the extension to the VM:

```
Set-AzureVMExtension -ExtensionName "OMS" '
    -ResourceGroupName $rg -VMName $vm '
    -Publisher "Microsoft.EnterpriseCloud.Monitoring"
    -ExtensionType "OmsAgentForLinux" -TypeHandlerVersion 1.0 '
    -SettingString $PublicSettings
    -ProtectedSettingString $PrivateSettings -Location $loc
```

The previous procedure is pretty complex and takes a while. The download method is easier, but you have to log in to your VM via SSH as a guest. Of course, both methods can be automated/orchestrated:

```
cd /tmp


wget \
https://github.com/microsoft/OMS-Agent-for-Linux \
/blob/master/installer/scripts/onboard_agent.sh


sudo -s


sh onboard_agent.sh -w <OMS id> -s <OMS key> -d \
  opinsights.azure.com
```

If you have problems during the installation of the agent, look in the **/var/log/waagent. log** and **/var/log/azure/Microsoft.EnterpriseCloud.Monitoring.OmsAgentForLinux/*/ extension.log** configuration files.

The installation of the extensions also creates a configuration file for **rsyslog, /etc/rsyslogd.d/95-omsagent.conf**:

```
kern.warning @127.0.0.1:25224

user.warning @127.0.0.1:25224

daemon.warning @127.0.0.1:25224

auth.warning @127.0.0.1:25224

syslog.warning @127.0.0.1:25224

uucp.warning @127.0.0.1:25224

authpriv.warning @127.0.0.1:25224

ftp.warning @127.0.0.1:25224

cron.warning @127.0.0.1:25224

local0.warning @127.0.0.1:25224

local1.warning @127.0.0.1:25224

local2.warning @127.0.0.1:25224

local3.warning @127.0.0.1:25224

local4.warning @127.0.0.1:25224

local5.warning @127.0.0.1:25224

local6.warning @127.0.0.1:25224

local7.warning @127.0.0.1:25224
```

It basically means that the syslog messages (**facility.priority**) are sent to the Azure Monitor agent.

At the bottom pane of the new resource, there is a section entitled **Get started with Log Analytics**:

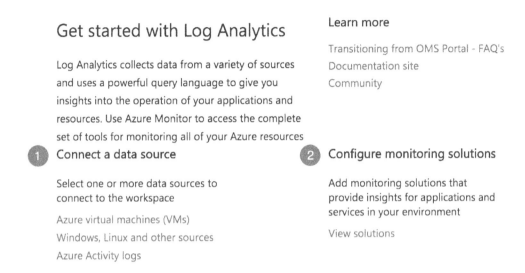

Figure 11.10: Get started with Log Analytics section in Azure Portal

Click on **Azure virtual machines (VMs)**. You'll see the VMs that are available in this workspace:

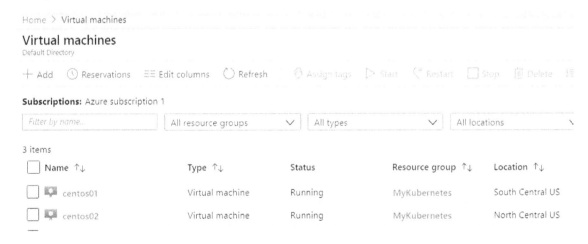

Figure 11.11: Available VMs in the workspace

The preceding screenshot represents the available VMs in the workspace. It also shows that we have connected to the data source.

Getting the Data

In the **Advanced settings** section of this resource, you can add performance and syslog data sources. You can access all the data via the log search using a special query language. If you are new to this language, you should visit https://docs.loganalytics.io/docs/Learn/Getting-Started/Getting-started-with-queries and https://docs.loganalytics.io/index.

For now, just execute this query:

```
search *
```

To see whether there is data available, limit the search to one VM:

```
search * | where Computer == "centos01"
```

Alternatively, to get all the syslog messages, as a test, you can reboot your VM, or play with this:

```
logger -t <facility>. <priority> "message"
```

Execute the following query in syslog to view the results:

```
Syslog | sort
```

There are also many examples available if you click on the **Saved searches** button.

Monitoring solutions provide a very interesting add-on to make this process even easier. In the **Resource** pane, click on **View solutions**:

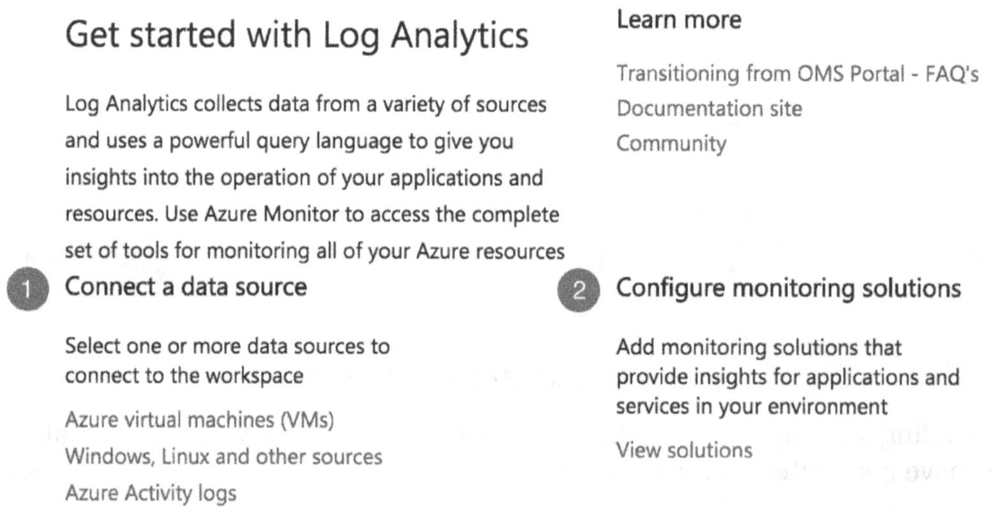

Get started with Log Analytics

Log Analytics collects data from a variety of sources and uses a powerful query language to give you insights into the operation of your applications and resources. Use Azure Monitor to access the complete set of tools for monitoring all of your Azure resources

Learn more

Transitioning from OMS Portal - FAQ's
Documentation site
Community

1 Connect a data source

Select one or more data sources to connect to the workspace

Azure virtual machines (VMs)
Windows, Linux and other sources
Azure Activity logs

2 Configure monitoring solutions

Add monitoring solutions that provide insights for applications and services in your environment

View solutions

Figure 11.12: Navigating to the monitoring solutions option

Select the desired option and click on **Add**:

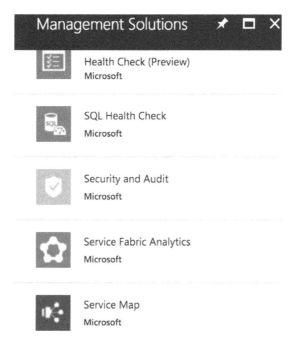

Figure 11.13: Management Solutions within Log Analytics

Service Map is an important service. It gives a great overview of your resources and provides an easy interface for logs, performance counters, and so on. After installing **Service Map**, you have to install an agent in the Linux machine, or you can log in to the portal and navigate to the VM, which will install the agent automatically for you:

```
cd /tmp


wget --content-disposition https://aka.ms/dependencyagentlinux \
-O InstallDependencyAgent-Linux64.bin


sudo sh InstallDependencyAgent-Linux64.bin -s
```

After the installation, select **Virtual Machines** > **Monitoring** > **Insights** > **Service Map**. Now, click on **Summary**:

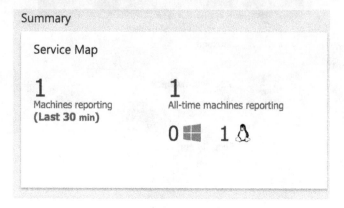

Figure 11.14: The Summary section of the Service Map

You can monitor your applications, view the log files, and so on:

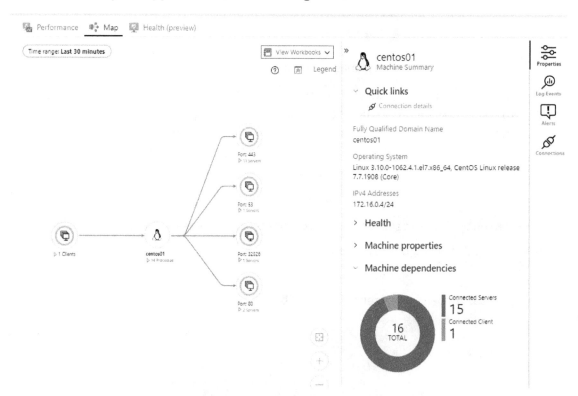

Figure 11.15: Service Map overview

Log Analytics and Kubernetes

In order to manage your containers, you need detailed insights into CPU, memory, storage, and network usage and performance information. Azure Monitor can be used to view Kubernetes logs, events, and metrics, allowing for container monitoring from a single location. You can enable Azure Monitor for containers for your new or existing AKS deployments using the Azure CLI, Azure PowerShell, the Azure portal, or Terraform.

To create a new **AKS** (**Azure Kubernetes Service**) cluster, use the `az aks create` command:

```
az aks create --resource-group MyKubernetes --name myAKS --node-count 1
--enable-addons monitoring --generate-ssh-keys
```

To enable Azure Monitor for your existing AKS cluster, use the `az aks` command with this modification:

```
az aks enable-addons -a monitoring -n myAKS -g MyKubernetes
```

You can enable monitoring for your AKS cluster from the Azure portal by selecting **Monitor** and then selecting **Containers**. Here, select the **Non-monitored clusters**, then choose the container and click **Enable**:

Figure 11.16: Monitoring AKS cluster from the Azure portal

Log Analytics for Your Network

Another solution in Azure Log Analytics is Traffic Analytics. It visualizes network traffic to and from your workloads, including open ports. It is able to generate alerts for security threats, for instance, if an application tries to reach a network that it's not allowed to access. Also, it provides detailed monitoring options with log export options.

If you want to use Traffic Analytics, first you have to create a network watcher for every region you want to analyze:

```
New-AzNetworkWatcher -Name <name> '

  -ResourceGroupName<resource group> -Location <location>
```

After that, you have to reregister the network provider and add Microsoft Insights so the network watcher can hook into it:

```
Register-AzResourceProvider -ProviderNamespace '

  "Microsoft.Network"


Register-AzResourceProvider -ProviderNamespaceMicrosoft.Insights
```

You can't use this solution with other providers, such as `Microsoft.ClassicNetwork`.

The next step involves using **network security group (NSG)**, which controls the flow of logging by allowing or denying the incoming traffic. At the time of writing, this is only possible using the Azure portal. In the left-hand bar of the Azure portal, select **Monitor>Network watcher** and then select **NSG flow logs**. Now you are able to select the NSG that you want to enable an **NSG flow log** for.

Enable it, select a storage account, and select your Log Analytics workspace.

It will take some time before the information comes in and is collected. After about 30 minutes, the first information should be visible. Select **Monitor** in the left-hand bar of the Azure portal, go to **Network watcher**, and then **Traffic Analytics**. Alternatively, start from your Log Analytics workspace:

Figure 11.17: Viewing the network traffic flow distribution with Traffic Analytics

Performance Monitoring

In Azure Monitor, there are many options available for monitoring. For instance, performance counters give you a lot of insight into your workload. There are also application-specific options.

Even if you don't use Azure Monitor, Azure can provide all kinds of metrics for each VM, but not in one central place. Just navigate to your VM. In the **Overview** pane, you can see performance data for CPU, memory, and storage. Detailed information is available in the **Metrics** section, under **Monitoring**. All kinds of data are available, such as CPU, storage, and networking data:

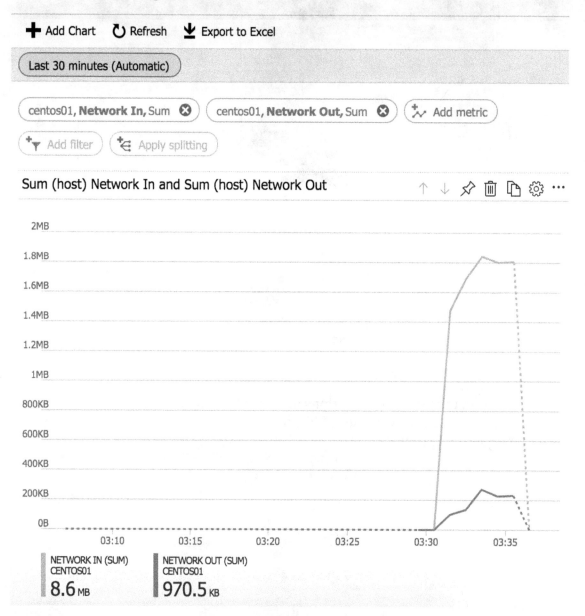

Figure 11.18: Viewing the performance data of the VM

The problem with many of these solutions is that they are application-specific, or you are looking at the end result without knowing what the cause is. If you need information about the general performance of the resources utilized by the virtual machine(s), use the information provided by Azure. If you need information on the web server or database you're running, look and see whether there is an Azure solution. But in many scenarios, it is very helpful if you can do performance troubleshooting in the VM as well. In a way, we're going to start where the *Process management* section in *Chapter 3, Basic Linux Administration*, left off.

Before we start, there are multiple methods and ways of doing performance troubleshooting. Can this book provide the only method you should use, or tell you the one tool you'll need? No, unfortunately not! But what it can do is make you aware of the tools that are available and cover at least their basic usage. For more specific needs, you can always dive into the man pages. In this section, we're especially looking into what the load is and what is causing it.

And one last thing: this section is called *Performance monitoring*, but that may not be the perfect title. It's balancing monitoring, troubleshooting, and analysis. However, isn't that often the case in the daily life of every system engineer?

Not all the tools mentioned are available by default in the Red Hat/CentOS repository. You'll need to configure the **epel** repository: `yum install epel-release`.

Displaying Linux processes with top

If you look into a topic such as performance monitoring and Linux, **top** is always mentioned. It is the number-one command to use to quickly get an idea of what is running on a system.

You can display many things with **top**, and it comes with a good man page explaining all the options. Let's focus on the most important ones, starting at the top of the screen:

```
top - 09:51:08 up  3:57,  2 users,  load average: 0.32, 0.15, 0.13
Tasks: 130 total,   2 running, 128 sleeping,   0 stopped,   0 zombie
%Cpu(s):  6.3 us,  3.0 sy,  0.0 ni, 89.8 id,  0.0 wa,  0.0 hi,  1.0 si,  0.0 st
KiB Mem :  3510240 total,  1006784 free,   577348 used,  1926108 buff/cache
KiB Swap:        0 total,        0 free,        0 used.  2629764 avail Mem

  PID USER      PR  NI    VIRT    RES    SHR S %CPU %MEM     TIME+ COMMAND
 1417 root      20   0  398280  26552   5660 S  4.3  0.8   8:06.19 python
 3246 root      20   0  984140  35508   8700 S  1.3  1.0   0:30.11 mdsd
52286 root      20   0  158804   5320   4012 S  0.7  0.2   0:00.02 sshd
  985 root      20   0  574204  17424   6120 S  0.3  0.5   0:02.17 tuned
 3299 root      20   0  505300   6408   5192 S  0.3  0.2   0:05.74 omiagent
45336 root      20   0   39432   6436   6064 S  0.3  0.2   0:01.16 systemd-jo+
52246 admin123  20   0  162008   2248   1584 R  0.3  0.1   0:00.13 top
```

Figure 11.19: Displaying resource usage using the top command

Let's take a look at the options mentioned in the preceding screenshot:

- **Wait IO (wa)**: If this value is continuously above 10%, this means that the underlying storage is slowing down the server. This parameter shows the CPU waiting time for I/O processes. Azure VMs use HDDs instead of SSDs, and using multiple HDDs in a RAID configuration can help, but it's better to migrate to SSDs. If that is not enough, there are premium SSD solutions available as well.

- **Userspace CPU (us)**: CPU utilization by applications; please note that the CPU utilization is totaled across all CPUs.

- **System CPU (sy)**: The amount of time the CPU spends on kernel tasks.

- **Swap**: Memory paged out caused by having not enough memory for your applications. It should be zero most of the time.

The bottom of the **top** screen also has some interesting columns:

PID	USER	PR	NI	VIRT	RES	SHR	S	%CPU	%MEM	TIME+	COMMAND
1417	root	20	0	398280	26552	5660	S	5.0	0.8	8:09.10	python
3299	root	20	0	505300	6408	5192	S	0.3	0.2	0:05.77	omiagent
52246	admin123	20	0	162008	2248	1584	R	0.3	0.1	0:00.35	top
1	root	20	0	128076	6804	4152	S	0.0	0.2	0:13.92	systemd
2	root	20	0	0	0	0	S	0.0	0.0	0:00.00	kthreadd
4	root	0	-20	0	0	0	S	0.0	0.0	0:00.00	kworker/0:+
6	root	20	0	0	0	0	S	0.0	0.0	0:01.62	ksoftirqd/0
7	root	rt	0	0	0	0	S	0.0	0.0	0:00.00	migration/0
8	root	20	0	0	0	0	S	0.0	0.0	0:00.00	rcu_bh
9	root	20	0	0	0	0	S	0.0	0.0	0:07.84	rcu_sched
10	root	0	-20	0	0	0	S	0.0	0.0	0:00.00	lru-add-dr+
11	root	rt	0	0	0	0	S	0.0	0.0	0:00.22	watchdog/0
13	root	20	0	0	0	0	S	0.0	0.0	0:00.00	kdevtmpfs
14	root	0	-20	0	0	0	S	0.0	0.0	0:00.00	netns
15	root	20	0	0	0	0	S	0.0	0.0	0:00.00	khungtaskd
16	root	0	-20	0	0	0	S	0.0	0.0	0:00.00	writeback
17	root	0	-20	0	0	0	S	0.0	0.0	0:00.00	kintegrityd

Figure 11.20: The bottom entries of the output obtained from the top command

Personally, we wouldn't advise worrying about the priority and nice values for now. The effect on the performance is minimal. The first interesting field is **VIRT** (virtual memory). This refers to the amount of memory the program can access at present. It includes memory shared with other applications, video memory, files that are read into memory by the application, and more. It also includes idle memory, swapped memory, and residential memory. Residential memory is memory that is physically in use by this process. **SHR** is the amount of memory that is shared between applications. This information can give you an idea of the amount of **swap** you should configure on your system: take the top five processes, add up **VIRT**, and subtract **RES** and **SHR**. It's not perfect, but it's a good indicator.

The **S** column in the preceding screenshot is the status of the machine:

- **D** is uninterruptible sleep, most of the time caused by waiting on storage or network I/O.

- **R** is running–consuming CPU.

- **S** is sleeping–waiting on I/O, no CPU usage. Waiting for a trigger by a user or another process.

- **T** is stopped by the job control signal, most of the time because the user pressed *Ctrl* + *Z*.

- **Z** is zombie–the parent process has died. It's labeled as a zombie by the kernel while the kernel is busy cleaning up. On physical machines, it can also be an indication of failing CPUs (caused by temperature or shoddy bios); in that scenario, you may see many zombies. In Azure, this won't happen. Zombies don't hurt, so don't kill them; the kernel takes care of them.

Top Alternatives

There are many utilities similar to **top**, such as **htop**, which looks fancier and is easier to configure.

Very similar but even more interesting is **atop**. It contains all the processes and their resource usage, even for processes that died between screen updates of **atop**. This comprehensive accounting is very helpful for understanding problems with individual short-lived processes. **atop** is also able to gather information about running containers, networking, and storage.

Another one is **nmon**, which is similar to **atop**, but is more focused on statistics and gives more detailed information, especially for memory and storage:

```
nmon─16g────────[H for help]────Hostname=centos01────────Refresh= 2secs ────14:32.19─
 CPU Utilisation Stats
ALL     3.5    0.0    0.0   96.0    0.0    0.0    0.0    0.0    0.0    0.0
CPU   User%  Nice%   Sys%  Idle%  Wait% HWirq% SWirq% Steal% Guest% GuestNice%
 1      3.5    0.0    0.0   96.0    0.0    0.0    0.0    0.0    0.0    0.0
 Memory and Swap
 PageSize:4KB    RAM-Memory  Swap-Space        High-Memory     Low-Memory
 Total (MB)          910.1         0.0        - not in use    - not in use
 Free  (MB)          154.5         0.0
 Free Percent         17.0%        0.0%
 Linux Kernel Internal Memory (MB)
                      Cached=     455.5     Active=        404.0
 Buffers=    2.0 Swapcached=        0.0  Inactive =       179.9
 Dirty  =    0.0 Writeback =        0.0  Mapped    =       24.7
 Slab   =   94.9 Commit_AS =      730.4 PageTables=        7.3
 Virtual Memory
nr_dirty    =       9 pgpgin    =        0            High Normal    DMA
nr_writeback=       0 pgpgout   =       60  alloc          0     0      0
nr_unstable =       0 pgpswpin  =        0  refill         0     0      0
nr_table_pgs=    1876 pgpswpout =        0  steal          0     0      0
nr_mapped   =    6325 pgfree    =       75  scan_kswapd    0     0      0
nr_slab     =      -1 pgactivate =       0  scan_direct    0     0      0
                        pgdeactivate=      0
allocstall  =       0 pgfault   =     1416  kswapd_steal   =       0
```

Figure 11.21: Performance details of memory, CPU and storage

nmon can also be used to collect data:

```
nmon -f -s 60 -c 30
```

The preceding command collects 30 rounds of information every minute in a comma-separated file format that is easy to parse in a spreadsheet. On the IBM's developers website, http://nmon.sourceforge.net/pmwiki.php?n=Site.Nmon-Analyser, you can find an Excel spreadsheet that makes this a very easy job. It even offers some extra data-analyzing options.

glances is also gaining a lot of popularity lately. It is Python-based and provides current information about the system, uptime, CPU, memory, swap, network, and storage (disk I/O and file):

```
centos01 (CentOS Linux 7.5.1804 64bit / Linux 3.10.0-862.3.3.el7.x86_64)        Uptime: 15:16:36

CPU  [  8.0%]    CPU        8.0%     MEM       60.9%    SWAP       0.0%      LOAD      1-core
MEM  [ 60.9%]    user:      5.2%     total:     910M    total:        0     1 min:     0.07
SWAP [  0.0%]    system:    2.3%     used:      555M    used:         0     5 min:     0.06
                 idle:     92.6%     free:      356M    free:         0     15 min:    0.05

NETWORK     Rx/s    Tx/s    TASKS 124 (215 thr), 2 run, 122 slp, 0 oth sorted automatically
eth0       442Kb   215Kb
lo            0b      0b    CPU%  MEM%    PID USER         NI S Command
                           3.8   1.6   2795 linvirt        0 R /usr/bin/python /usr/bin/glances
DISK I/O     R/s    W/s    2.6   2.7   3061 root           0 S python -u bin/WALinuxAgent-2.2.30
fd0            0      0    0.3   0.2    510 root           0 S /usr/lib/systemd/systemd-logind
sda1           0      0    0.3   0.4   1274 postfix        0 S cleanup -z -t unix -u
sda2           0     21K   0.3   0.6      1 root           0 S /usr/lib/systemd/systemd --switch
sdb1           0      0    0.3   0.4    350 root           0 S /usr/lib/systemd/systemd-journald
                           0.0   0.2    795 root           0 S /sbin/dhclient -q -lf /var/lib/dh
FILE SYS    Used   Total   0.0   0.2    372 root           0 S /usr/sbin/lvmetad -f
/ (sda2)    4.38G  29.5G   0.0   0.0     28 root           5 S ksmd
/boot        105M   497M   0.0   0.0  47876 root           0 S kworker/u256:1
_resource   16.0M  3.87G   0.0   0.0    277 root         -20 S xfs-cil/sda2
                           0.0   0.0    278 root         -20 S xfs-reclaim/sda
```

Figure 11.22: Using the glances utility to view the performance

glances is the most advanced alternative to **top**. It offers all the features of the alternatives, and, on top of that, you can use it remotely. You need to provide the username and password of your server to launch **glances**:

```
glances --username <username> --password <password> --server
```

Execute the following on the client too:

```
glances --client @<ip address>
```

By default, port **61209** is used. If you use the **-webserver** parameter instead of **--server**, you don't even need a client. A complete web interface is available on port **61208**!

glances is able to export logs in many formats and can be queried using an API. Experimental support for the **SNMP** (**Simple Network Management Protocol**) protocol is on the way as well.

Sysstat – a Collection of Performance-Monitoring Tools

The **sysstat** package contains utilities for performance monitoring. The most important ones in Azure are **sar**, **iostat**, and **pidstat**. If you are also using Azure Files, **cifsiostat** can be very handy as well.

sar is the main utility. The main syntax is this:

```
sar -<resource> interval count
```

For instance, use this command to report CPU statistics 5 times with an interval of 1 second:

```
sar -u 1 5
```

To monitor cores **1** and **2**, use this:

```
sar -P 1 2 1 5
```

(If you want to monitor all the cores individually, you can use the **ALL** keyword.)

Here are some other important resources:

- **-r**: Memory
- **-S**: Swap
- **-d**: Disk
- **-n <type>**: Network types, such as these:

    DEV: Displays network devices statistics

    EDEV: Displays network devices failure (error) statistics

    NFS: Displays **NFS** (**Network File System**) client activities

    SOCK: Displays sockets in use for IPv4

    IP: Displays IPv4 network traffic

    TCP: Displays TCPv4 network traffic

    UDP: Displays UDPv4 network traffic

    ALL: Displays all of the preceding information

pidstat can collect CPU data from a specific process by its process ID. In the next screenshot, you can see that 2 samples are shown every 5 seconds. **pidstat** can do the same for memory and disk:

```
[root@centos01 bin]# pidstat
Linux 3.10.0-1062.1.1.el7.x86_64 (centos01)        11/06/2019        _x86_64_

10:29:54 AM   UID       PID    %usr %system  %guest     %CPU  CPU  Command
10:29:54 AM     0         1    0.04    0.06    0.00     0.10    0  systemd
10:29:54 AM     0         6    0.00    0.01    0.00     0.01    0  ksoftirqd/0
10:29:54 AM     0         9    0.00    0.06    0.00     0.06    0  rcu_sched
10:29:54 AM     0        11    0.00    0.00    0.00     0.00    0  watchdog/0
10:29:54 AM     0        32    0.00    0.00    0.00     0.00    0  khugepaged
10:29:54 AM     0       112    0.00    0.00    0.00     0.00    0  kauditd
10:29:54 AM     0       253    0.00    0.00    0.00     0.00    0  scsi_eh_1
10:29:54 AM     0       305    0.00    0.01    0.00     0.01    0  kworker/0:1H
10:29:54 AM     0       348    0.00    0.03    0.00     0.03    0  xfsaild/sda2
10:29:54 AM     0       479    0.00    0.00    0.00     0.00    0  hv_balloon
10:29:54 AM     0       571    0.00    0.00    0.00     0.00    0  xfsaild/sda1
10:29:54 AM     0       640    0.00    0.00    0.00     0.00    0  auditd
10:29:54 AM   998       669    0.00    0.00    0.00     0.00    0  lsmd
10:29:54 AM   999       672    0.00    0.00    0.00     0.00    0  polkitd
10:29:54 AM     0       674    0.00    0.00    0.00     0.00    0  smartd
10:29:54 AM    32       678    0.00    0.00    0.00     0.00    0  rpcbind
10:29:54 AM    81       683    0.02    0.01    0.00     0.03    0  dbus-daemon
10:29:54 AM   997       691    0.00    0.00    0.00     0.00    0  chronyd
```

Figure 11.23: Displaying CPU statistics using pidstat

iostat is a utility, as the name suggests, that can measure I/O, but it also creates reports for CPU usage:

```
[root@centos01 bin]# iostat
Linux 3.10.0-1062.1.1.el7.x86_64 (centos01)        11/06/2019        _x86_64_

avg-cpu:   %user   %nice %system %iowait  %steal   %idle
            6.22    0.09    2.73    0.57    0.00   90.40

Device:            tps    kB_read/s    kB_wrtn/s    kB_read    kB_wrtn
fd0               0.00         0.00         0.00          4          0
scd0              0.00         0.01         0.00        124          0
sdb               0.05         0.56       453.23       9457    7588672
sda               8.54        20.23       171.25     338758    2867288
```

Figure 11.24: Getting the CPU and Device report and statistics using iostat

tps means the number of transfers per second issued to the device. **kb_read/s** and **kB_wrtn/s** are the numbers of kilobytes measured during 1 second; the **avg-cpu** column in the preceding screenshot is the total number of statistics since the time of your Linux system startup.

During the installation of the **sysstat** package, a cron job was installed in the **/etc/cron.d/sysstat** file.

> **Note**
>
> In modern Linux systems, both **systemd-timers** and the old method using **cron** are available. **sysstat** still uses **cron**. To check whether **cron** is available and running, go to **systemctl | grep cron**.

cron runs the **sa1** command every 10 minutes. It collects system activity and stores it in a binary database. Once a day, the **sa2** command is executed to generate a report. The data is stored in the **/var/log/sa** directory. You can query that database with **sadf**:

```
[root@centos01 bin]# sadf -s 09:00:00 -e 10:10:00
localhost.localdomain    600    2019-11-06 09:10:01 UTC all    %user     4.19
localhost.localdomain    600    2019-11-06 09:10:01 UTC all    %nice     0.00
localhost.localdomain    600    2019-11-06 09:10:01 UTC all    %system   1.85
localhost.localdomain    600    2019-11-06 09:10:01 UTC all    %iowait   0.00
localhost.localdomain    600    2019-11-06 09:10:01 UTC all    %steal    0.00
localhost.localdomain    600    2019-11-06 09:10:01 UTC all    %idle     93.95
localhost.localdomain    601    2019-11-06 09:20:01 UTC all    %user     4.10
localhost.localdomain    601    2019-11-06 09:20:01 UTC all    %nice     0.00
localhost.localdomain    601    2019-11-06 09:20:01 UTC all    %system   1.92
localhost.localdomain    601    2019-11-06 09:20:01 UTC all    %iowait   0.00
localhost.localdomain    601    2019-11-06 09:20:01 UTC all    %steal    0.00
localhost.localdomain    601    2019-11-06 09:20:01 UTC all    %idle     93.98
localhost.localdomain    601    2019-11-06 09:30:01 UTC all    %user     5.42
localhost.localdomain    601    2019-11-06 09:30:01 UTC all    %nice     0.00
localhost.localdomain    601    2019-11-06 09:30:01 UTC all    %system   2.26
localhost.localdomain    601    2019-11-06 09:30:01 UTC all    %iowait   0.61
localhost.localdomain    601    2019-11-06 09:30:01 UTC all    %steal    0.00
localhost.localdomain    601    2019-11-06 09:30:01 UTC all    %idle     91.72
localhost.localdomain    601    2019-11-06 09:40:01 UTC all    %user     4.30
localhost.localdomain    601    2019-11-06 09:40:01 UTC all    %nice     0.00
```

Figure 11.25: Querying the database with sadf for system activity

This screenshot shows the data from November 6, between **09:00:00** and **10:10:00**. By default, it's displaying CPU statistics, but you can customize it using the same parameters as **sar**:

```
sadf /var/log/sa/sa03 -- -n DEV
```

This displays the network stats of every network interface on November 6.

dstat

sysstat is available for historical reports, while **dstat** is for real-time reports. While **top** is the monitoring version of **ps**, it's **dstat** that is the monitoring version of **sar**:

```
[root@centos01 bin]# dstat
You did not select any stats, using -cdngy by default.
----total-cpu-usage---- -dsk/total- -net/total- ---paging-- ---system--
usr sys idl wai hiq siq| read  writ| recv  send|  in   out | int   csw
  6   2  90   1   0   1|  22k  647k|   0     0 |   0     0 |  36   271
 11   1  87   0   0   1|   0    60k|  82k   15k|   0     0 |  51   312
  0   0  98   0   0   2|   0     0 | 328B  514B|   0     0 |  27   179
  4   5  91   0   0   0|   0     0 |1055B 2475B|   0     0 |  46   226
 12   4  83   0   0   1|   0    60k|  82k   14k|   0     0 |  49   340
  0   0  99   0   0   1|   0     0 |  60B  508B|   0     0 |  30   191
  0   2  97   0   0   1|   0    22k| 310B  490B|   0     0 |  22   180
  6   1  92   0   0   1|   0    28k|  44k 4353B|   0     0 |  38   219
  7   1  91   0   0   1|   0    32k|  37k   10k|   0     0 |  41   264
  1   3  95   0   0   1|   0     0 |  60B  358B|   0     0 |  34   226
  1   0  98   0   0   1| 938k    0 |  60B  358B|   0     0 |  23   213
 11   2  86   0   0   1|   0    60k|  81k   14k|   0     0 |  50   336
  0   1  98   0   0   1|   0     0 |  60B  358B|   0     0 |  31   187
  1   2  96   0   0   1|   0     0 |  60B  358B|   0     0 |  23   163
 13   4  83   0   0   0|   0    60k|  83k   16k|   0     0 |  71   413
  2   2  95   0   0   1|   0     0 |1173B 2572B|   0     0 |  50   243
  2   3  94   0   0   1|   0     0 |1710B 2843B|   0     0 |  38   225
 11   3  86   0   0   0|   0    60k|  82k   15k|   0     0 |  45   338
  1   2  96   0   0   1|   0    32k| 126B  358B|   0     0 |  31   201
  1   0  98   0   0   1|   0     0 | 513B  694B|   0     0 |  20   163
```

Figure 11.26: Getting real-time reports with dstat

If you don't want to see it all at once, you can use the following parameters:

- **c**: CPU
- **d**: Disk
- **n**: Network
- **g**: Paging
- **s**: Swap
- **m**: Memory

Network stats with iproute2

Earlier in this chapter, we talked about **ip**. This command also provides an option to get statistics for the network interface:

```
ip -s link show dev eth0
```

```
[root@centos01 bin]# ip -s link show dev eth0
2: eth0: <BROADCAST,MULTICAST,UP,LOWER_UP> mtu 1500 qdisc mq state UP mode DEFAU
LT group default qlen 1000
    link/ether 00:0d:3a:5d:e5:83 brd ff:ff:ff:ff:ff:ff
    RX: bytes   packets   errors   dropped overrun mcast
    887256259   771415    0        0       0       0
    TX: bytes   packets   errors   dropped carrier collsns
    108470865   325039    0        0       0       0
[root@centos01 bin]#
```

Figure 11.27: Getting the statistics for the network interface

It parses information from the **/proc/net** directory. Another utility that can parse this information is **ss**. A simple summary can be requested with this:

```
ss -s
```

Using the **-t** parameter not only shows you the ports in a listening state but also the incoming and outgoing traffic on this specific interface.

If you need more details, the **iproute2** package provides another utility: **nstat**. Using the **-d** parameter, you can even run it in interval mode:

```
[root@centos01 bin]# nstat
#kernel
IpInReceives            252238              0.0
IpInDelivers            252235              0.0
IpOutRequests           335633              0.0
IpOutDiscards           15                  0.0
IpOutNoRoutes           4                   0.0
IcmpInMsgs              47                  0.0
IcmpInDestUnreachs      47                  0.0
IcmpOutMsgs             49                  0.0
IcmpOutDestUnreachs     49                  0.0
IcmpMsgInType3          47                  0.0
IcmpMsgOutType3         49                  0.0
TcpActiveOpens          40658               0.0
TcpPassiveOpens         543                 0.0
TcpAttemptFails         7                   0.0
TcpEstabResets          825                 0.0
TcpInSegs               203553              0.0
TcpOutSegs              317365              0.0
TcpRetransSegs          204                 0.0
TcpInErrs               99                  0.0
TcpOutRsts              851                 0.0
TcpInCsumErrors         99                  0.0
```

Figure 11.28: Getting a detailed report about the ports in a listening state

That's already much more than a simple summary of **ss**. But the **iproute2** package has more to offer: **lnstat**.

This is the command that provides network statistics such as routing cache statistics:

```
lnstat--d
```

```
[root@centos01 bin]# lnstat -d
/proc/net/stat/nf_conntrack:
         1:  entries
         2:  searched
         3:  found
         4:  new
         5:  invalid
         6:  ignore
         7:  delete
         8:  delete_list
         9:  insert
        10:  insert_failed
        11:  drop
        12:  early_drop
        13:  icmp_error
        14:  expect_new
        15:  expect_create
        16:  expect_delete
        17:  search_restart
```

Figure 11.29: Getting the network statistics with lnstat -d

This shows you everything it can display or monitor. It's pretty low-level, but we've solved some firewall performance-related issues using **lnstat -f/proc/net/stat/nf_ conntrack**, while monitoring the **drops** counter.

Network Monitoring with IPTraf-NG

You can get network details from tools such as **nmon**, but if you want more details, then IPTraf-NG is a very nice tool for a real-time console-based network monitoring solution. It is a console-based network-monitoring utility that collects all the network IP, TCP, UDP, and ICMP data and is able to break down the information according to the size of the TCP/UDP. A few basic filters are included as well.

Everything is in a menu-driven interface, so there are no parameters that you have to remember:

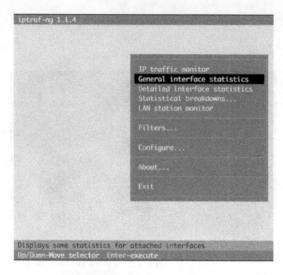

Figure 11.30: Menu window of IPTraf-NG

tcpdump

Of course, **tcpdump** is not a performance-monitoring solution. This utility is a great tool for monitoring, capturing, and analyzing network traffic.

To view network traffic on all the network interfaces, execute the following:

```
tcpdump -i any
```

For a specific interface, try this:

```
tcpdump -i eth0
```

In general, it's a good idea not to resolve the hostnames:

```
tcpdump -n -i eth0
```

You can add different levels of verbosity by repeating the **v** parameter up to a maximum verbosity level of three:

```
tcpdump -n -i eth0 -vvv
```

You can filter the traffic based on the host:

```
tcpdump host <ip address> -n -i eth0
```

Alternatively, you can filter based on the source or destination IP:

```
tcpdump src <source ip address> -n -i eth0
tcpdump dst <destination ip address> -n -i eth0
```

Filtering on a specific port is also possible:

```
tcpdump port 22
```

```
tcpdumpsrc port 22
```

```
tcpdump not port 22
```

All the parameters can be combined:

```
tcpdump -n dst net <subnet> and not port ssh -c 5
```

The **-c** parameter was added, so only five packets were captured. You can save the captured data to a file:

```
tcpdump -v -x -XX -w /tmp/capture.log
```

Two parameters were added to increase the compatibility with other analyzers that can read the format of **tcpdump**:

- **-XX**: Prints the data of each packet in hex and ASCII format

- **-x**: Adds headers to every packet

To read the data with a complete timestamp in human-readable format, use this command:

```
tcpdump -tttt -r /tmp/capture.log
```

> **Note**
>
> Another great network analyzer is Wireshark. It's a graphical tool that's available for many operating systems. This analyzer can import captured data from **tcpdump**. It comes with a great search filter and analyzing tools for many different network protocols and services.
>
> It makes sense to make the capture in your VM and download it to your workstation in order to analyze the data further in Wireshark.

We're sure that you will now be able to achieve good performance analysis in a Linux system using different tools to monitor metrics such as CPU, memory, storage, and network details.

Summary

In this chapter, we covered several topics regarding troubleshooting, logging, monitoring, and even analyzing. Starting with getting access to a VM, we investigated logging in Linux both locally and remotely.

There is a thin line between performance monitoring and performance troubleshooting. There are many, many different utilities available to find out the cause of your performance issues. Each has a different goal, but there is also a great deal of overlap. We have covered the most popular utilities in Linux and some of the options available.

In the first chapter, we saw that Azure is a very open source–friendly environment and that Microsoft has made a great effort to make Azure an open, standard cloud solution with interoperability in mind. In this chapter, we saw that Microsoft has not only put a lot of effort into supporting Linux while deploying your application but also into supporting it in Azure Monitor.

Questions

1. Why should you have at least one user with a password in a VM?

2. What is the purpose of the `systemd-journald` daemon?

3. What are syslog facilities?

4. What priorities are available in syslog?

5. How can you add entries to a log, and why should you do that?

6. What services are available to view metrics in Azure?

7. Why is **top** only useful to have a first look into performance-related problems, and what utility or utilities can fix that?

8. What is the difference between the `sysstat` and `dstat` utilities?

9. Why should you install Wireshark on your workstation?

Further Reading

A big source of information is the website of Brendan D Gregg (http://www. brendangregg.com), where he shares an unbelievably long list of Linux performance documentation, slides, videos, and more. On top of that, there are some nice utilities! He was the one who taught me, in 2015, that it is important to identify a problem correctly:

- What makes you think that there is a problem?
- Was there a time that there wasn't a problem?
- Has something changed recently?
- Try to find technical descriptions, such as latency, runtime errors, and so on.
- Is it only the application, or are other resources affected as well?
- Come up with an exact description of the environment.

You also have to consider the following:

- What is causing the load (which process, IP address, and so on)?
- Why was the load called?
- What resource(s) is/are used by the load?
- Does the load change? If so, how is it changing over time?

Last, but not least, there's *Red Hat Enterprise Linux Troubleshooting Guide* by Benjamin Cane. I know, some parts of the book are outdated, as it was printed in 2015. And, for sure, I definitely hope for a second edition, but, especially if you are new to Linux, buy this book.

3. It depends; do you develop your application on the same platform? If so, then PaaS is the service type for you; otherwise, use IaaS. SaaS provides an application; it's not a hosting platform.

4. It depends. Azure is compliant with and helps you to comply with legal rules and security/privacy policies. Plus, there is the concept of different regions if there are concerns about having data in other parts of the world. But there are always exceptions—most of the time, company policies or governmental rulings.

5. It is very important for scalability, performance, and redundancy.

6. It's a cloud-based identity management service for controlling access to your cloud and on-premises hybrid environment. It lets you sign in and access both cloud and on-premises environments instead of using your own AD servers and managing them.

Chapter 2: Getting Started with the Azure Cloud

1. It helps with automation. Besides that, the web-based portal changes frequently, and the command-line interface is much more stable. In our opinion, it also gives you a better understanding of the underlying technology, thanks to its more or less strict workflow.

2. It provides access for storing all your data objects. You'll need one for boot diagnostics and data for Azure Cloud Shell. More details can be found in *Chapter 4, Managing Azure*.

3. The storage account must be globally unique in Azure.

4. An offer is a group of related images offered by a publisher, such as Ubuntu Server. An image is a specific image.

5. A stopped Azure virtual machine keeps resources allocated, such as dynamic public IP addresses, and incurs costs, whereas a deallocated virtual machine frees all resources so it stops incurring resource costs. However, both incur storage costs.

6. Key-based authentication helps in automation as it can be used without exposing secrets/passwords in your scripts.

7. Both a public and a private key will be created (if they are still necessary) and stored in your home directory (`~/.ssh`); the public key will be added to the `authorized_keys` file in the virtual machine

Chapter 3: Basic Linux Administration

1. `for user in Lisa John Karel Carola; useradd $user; done`.

2. Execute `passwd <user>` and enter `welc0meITG` and it will ask you to enter the password again to confirm, so enter `welc0meITG` again.

3. `getent<user>`.

4. `groupadd finance; groupadd staff`.

5. `groupmems -g <group_name> -a <user_name>`; alternatively, `usermod -a -G <group_name> <user_name>`.

6. To create the directory and set group ownership, execute the following:

   ```
   mkdir /home/staff
   chown staff /home/staff
   chgrp staff /home/staff
   ```

   Similarly, for **finance**, execute these commands:

   ```
   mkdir /home/finance
   chown finance /home/finance
   chgrp finance /home/finance
   ```

7. `chmod -R g+r /home/finance`.

8. The default get access control list (`getfacl -d`) will list the ACL of a user.

Chapter 4: Managing Azure

1. You don't need anything when you create a virtual machine using the Azure portal. When you use the command line, you need virtual networks with the following:

   A resource group

   Azure **Virtual Network** (**VNet**)

   A configured subnet

   A network security group

   A public IP address

   A network interface

2. You need name services such as Diagnostics and Monitoring, which require a storage account.

3. Sometimes (for instance, for a storage account), the name must be unique. A prefix combined with a randomly generated number is a nice way to make the name recognizable and unique.

4. To define the IP range that can be used within a virtual network.

5. To create one or more subnets within the virtual network that can be isolated or routed to each other, without going outside the virtual network.

6. A network security group provides ACLs for the network and provides port-forwarding to the virtual machines or containers.

7. Traffic from the virtual machine to the internet is sent via **Source Network Address Translation** (**SNAT**). This means that the IP address of the originating packet is replaced with the public IP address, which is required for TCP/IP for outbound and inbound routing.

8. A dynamically allocated public IP address will be released when the virtual machine is deallocated. When the virtual machine starts again, it will get another IP address. You can create and assign static public IP address when it is mandatory to keep the same IP address even after the service IP address changes.

Chapter 5: Advanced Linux Administration

1. The Linux kernel.

2. `systemd-udevd`.

3. `ls /sys/class/net` and `ip link show`.

4. The Azure agent for Linux.

5. `ls /sys/class/net` and `lsblk`. The `lsscsi` command can be helpful as well.

6. It is a good idea to use `RAID0` to improve performance and allow improved throughput compared to using just a single disk.

7. At the filesystem level, using **B-Tree File System** (**BTRFS**) or the **Z File System** (**ZFS**), or at the block level using Linux Software RAID (`mdadm`) or **Logical Volume Manager** (**LVM**) (not covered in this chapter).

8. Create the RAID, format it, and make a mount point:

```
mdadm --create /dev/md127 --level 0 --raid-devices 3 \
    /dev/sd{c,d,e}
mkfs.xfs -L myraid /dev/md127

mkdir /mnt/myraid
```

Create a unit file, **/etc/systemd/system/mnt-myraid.mount**:

```
[Unit]
Description = myRaid volume

[Mount]
Where = /mnt/myraid
What = /dev/md127
Type = xfs

[Install]
WantedBy = local-fs.mount
```

Start and enable it at boot:

```
systemctl enable --now mnt-myraid.mount
```

Chapter 6: Managing Linux Security and Identities

1. Using the **firewall-cmd** file or by deploying **Extensible Markup Language** (**XML**) files in the **/etc/firewalld** directory.

2. The **--permanent** parameter makes it persistent across reboots and executes during start up configuration.

3. In Linux, you can restrict access using ACLs in systemd. Some applications also provide other host allow/deny options. In Azure, you have network security groups and the Azure Firewall service.

4. **Discretionary access control** (**DAC**) is used for restricting access based on users/ groups and permissions on files. **Mandatory access control** (**MAC**) further restricts access based on classification labels for each resource object.

5. If someone gained access illegally to an application or system, with DAC, there is no way to prevent further access, especially for files with the same user/group owner and files with permissions for others.

6. Every device will have a unique MAC address and you can find your virtual machine's MAC address using **ipconfig/ all** and then look for Physical Address.

   MAC frameworks that utilize Linux Security Modules are as follows:

   SELinux: Red Hat–based distributions and SUSE

   AppArmor: Ubuntu and SUSE

   The lesser-known TOMOYO (SUSE): Not covered in this book

7. Besides the fact that SELinux can protect more resource objects, AppArmor works directly with paths, while SELinux protects the whole system with fine-grained access control.

8. You need the following prerequisites before joining an AD domain:

   Kerberos client for authorization

   System Security Services Daemon (**SSSD**): A backend that is responsible for the configuration and utilization of features such as using and caching credentials

   Samba libraries to be compatible with Windows features/options

   Some utilities to join and manage the domain, such as `realm`, `adcli`, and the `net` command

Chapter 7: Deploying Your Virtual Machines

1. We use automated deployment to save time, to get a reproducible environment quickly up and running, and to avoid manual errors.

2. Besides the answer to the previous question, a standardized working environment makes team-based application development possible.

3. Scripting is very flexible. Scripts are easier to create and can be invoked manually anytime. The automation process can be triggered by events such as adding code to Git using `git push` or the stopping/starting of your virtual machines.

4. Azure Resource Manager is the most important one. In addition, you can use Terraform, Ansible, and PowerShell.

5. Vagrant deploys a workload in Azure; Packer creates a custom image that you can deploy.

6. For multiple reasons, the most important ones are the following:

   Security, to harden the image using CIS standards

   When customization is needed for a standard image

   Not dependent on the offerings of a third party

   Capture an existing virtual machine

   Convert a snapshot to an image

7. You can create your own image by building your own VHD file. The following are the options for doing so:

   Create a virtual machine in Hyper-V or VirtualBox, which is a free hypervisor available for Windows, Linux, and macOS.

   Create your virtual machine in VMware Workstation or KVM and use it in Linux qemu-img to convert the image.

Chapter 8: Exploring Continuous Configuration Automation

Example scripts are available on GitHub at https://github.com/PacktPublishing/Hands-On-Linux-Administration-on-Azure---Second-Edition/tree/master/chapter12/solutions_chapter08.

Chapter 9: Container Virtualization in Azure

1. You can use containers for packaging and distributing your applications, which can be platform-independent. Containers remove the need for virtual machine and operating system management and help you achieve high availability and scalability.

2. Containers are not suitable if you have a huge monolithic application that requires all the resources of the underlying virtual machines.

3. **Linux containers** (**LXCs**) are an optimal solution that can be provisioned in Azure.

4. Tools such as Buildah make it possible to create virtual machines that can be used in every solution. Rkt (pronounced "rocket") also supports the Docker format. The Open Container Initiative is working very hard to create standards to make the creation of virtual machines even easier.

5. You can develop everything in Azure or you can develop locally and then push to a remote environment.

6. It's container platform–agnostic, and the Buildah tool is easier to use than other tools. You can explore further at https://github.com/containers/buildah.

7. Containers can be built, replaced, stopped, and destroyed on demand without any impact upon the application or data, so it's not recommended to store any data in the container. Instead, store it in a volume.

Chapter 10: Working with Azure Kubernetes Service

1. A pod is a group of containers with shared resources, such as storage and network, as well as a specification for how to run the containers.

2. A good reason to create a multiple-container pod is to support co-located, co-managed helper processes for your primary application.

3. There are multiple methods available, including Draft and Helm, which were discussed in the chapter in addition to **Azure Kubernetes Service** (**AKS**).

4. You can use **kubectl** to update your application in AKS. In addition, you can also use Helm and Draft.

5. You don't need to do it yourself manually; it will be done automatically by AKS.

6. You will need an iSCSI solution and a clustered filesystem when you want to read/write simultaneously from multiple containers.

7. Example code is provided on GitHub at https://github.com/MicrosoftDocs/azure-docs/blob/master/articles/aks/azure-disks-dynamic-pv.md.

Chapter 11: Troubleshooting and Monitoring Your Workloads

1. You can access your virtual machine using Azure Serial Console as root without a password unless it's specifically blocked.

2. To collect all the standard output, syslog messages, and related messages from the kernel, systemd processes, and units.

3. syslog uses the following list of severities (per application):

   Alert: Action must be taken immediately.

   Critical: Critical conditions.

   Error: Error conditions.

   Warning: Warning conditions.

   Notice: Normal but significant conditions.

   Informational: Informational messages.

   Debug: Debug-level messages.

4. 0-Emergency, 1-Alert, 2-Critical, 3-Error, 4-Warning, 5-Notice, 6-Informational, 7-Debug.

5. Use **logger** or **systemd-cat**. You can use it if an application or script doesn't have syslog support. Another option is to add logging entries as a part of your change management.

6. The Azure Log Analytics service is used to view the metrics of a virtual machine.

7. There are several shortcomings of the **top** utility; for instance, you can't see short-lived processes. The **atop** and **dstat** utilities are solutions to this problem.

8. **sysstat** utilities provide historical data; **dstat** provides real-time monitoring.

9. It makes the collection of data coming from **tcpdump** of your Azure virtual machine (workstation) easier to read and it has great analysis potential.

Index

About

All major keywords used in this book are captured alphabetically in this section. Each one is accompanied by the page number of where they appear.

www.ingramcontent.com/pod-product-compliance
Lightning Source LLC
Chambersburg PA
CBHW060640060326
40690CB00020B/4464